NGOS:

LEGITIMATE SUBJECTS OF INTERNATIONAL LAW

Leiden University Press

Cover illustration: *Le 28 juillet 1830 : la Liberté guidant le people*
by Eugène Delacroix (1830); © RMN (Musée du Louvre)/
Hervé Lewandowski

Cover design: Maedium, Utrecht
Lay-out: The DocWorkers, Almere

ISBN   978 90 8728 149 6
e-ISBN   978 94 0060 067 6
NUR   828

NGOS: LEGITIMATE SUBJECTS OF INTERNATIONAL LAW

PROEFSCHRIFT

ter verkrijging van
de graad van Doctor aan de Universiteit Leiden,
op gezag van Rector Magnificus prof. mr. P.F. van der Heijden,
volgens besluit van het College voor Promoties
te verdedigen op donderdag 13 december 2012
klokke 11.15 uur

door

Eduardo Szazi

geboren te Sao Paulo, Brazilië

in 1965

Promotiecommissie:

Promotor: prof.dr. G.E. Lock

Overige leden: prof. dr. A.A.M. Kinneging
                dr. P. Overeem
                prof. dr. P.B. Cliteur
                prof. mr. H.R.van Gunsteren
                prof. dr. N.M. Blokker
                dr. F. Maiolo (Utrecht University)

To Andrea, André and Felipe

'When convictions have been accepted for a long time in a doctrine it is easy to lose sight of their derivation from certain assumptions: they therefore continue to be regarded as truths, even when these assumptions have been discarded.'

Robert Ago (1907 – 1995)

Acknowledgements

I am greatly indebted to several colleagues, friends and NGO leaders who have shared their ideas on new forms of democracy and participation in public affairs through non-governmental organizations, these new structures being so easy to see and so hard to understand. Jorge Laffitte, Rebecca Raposo, Judi Cavalcanti, Evelyn Ioschpe, Leo Voigt, Neylar Lins, Monica MacDowell, Francisco Tancredi, Silvio Sant'Anna and Eduardo Sabo Paes, you have all had a special place in my intellectual development.

In particular, I owe heartfelt thanks to my friend and partner Erika Bechara, for her relentless encouragement and support as well as for handling our law firm while I was in 'the cave', and to Fernando Fernandes da Silva, whose insightful comments were always essential to my research.

I am also especially grateful to some professors that I have had in my life: to Grahame Lock, for his guidance during this research; to Guido Silva Soares, who touched my heart with his lessons of international law; to Luiz Olavo Baptista, who taught me what being a lawyer is all about, and to Antonio Augusto Cançado Trindade, whose ideas have deeply influenced my understanding of the contemporary challenges in the international realm.

Finally, I owe a special thanks to Kimberly Paulin, who skillfully undertook the challenge of reviewing my typescript.

Table of contents

LIST OF ABBREVIATIONS

ACHR	American Convention of Human Rights
AICESIS	International Association of Economic and Social Council and Similar Institutions
AJIL	*American Journal of International Law*
AU	African Union
BINGO	Business related international non-governmental organizations
CBD	UN Convention on Biological Diversity
CCPR	International Covenant of Civil and Political Rights
CEC	NAEEC Commission on Environmental Cooperation
CFI	Court of First Instance
CILJ	*Cornell International Law Journal*
CITES	Convention on International Trade of Endangered Species of Wild Fauna and Flora
CoE	Council of Europe
CoR	EU Committee of the Regions
CONGO	The Conference of NGOs in Consultative Relationship with the UN
DESA	UN Department of Economic and Social Affairs
DPI	UN Department of Public Information
EA	European Association
EC	European Community
EComHR	European Commission of Human Rights
ECHR	European Court of Human Rights
ECJ	Court of Justice of the European Union
ECOSOC	UN Economic and Social Council
ECOSOCC	AU Economic, Social and Cultural Council
EEC	European Economic Community
EJIL	*European Journal of International Law*
EPIL	*Encyclopedia of Public International Law*
ESC	EU Economic and Social Committee
EU	European Union
FFWA	*the Fletcher Forum of World Affairs*
GEF	Global Environmental Facility
GLJ	*German Law Journal*

GRINGO   Government-related international non-governmental
            organizations
HPDJ   *Health Policy Development Journal*
HRQ   *Human Rights Quarterly*
IACHR   Inter-American Court of Human Rights
IAComHR   Inter-American Commission of Human Rights
ICC   International Criminal Court
ICJ   International Court of Justice
ICLQ   *International Comparative Law Quarterly*
ICRC   International Committee of the Red Cross
ICTR   International Criminal Tribunal for Rwanda
ICTY   International Criminal Tribunal for the Former Yugoslavia
IDI   Institut de Droit International
IGO   Intergovernmental Organization
ILA   International Law Association
ILC   International Law Commission
IMO   International Maritime Organization
INGO   International non-governmental organizations
IRRC   *International Review of the Red Cross*
ITO   International Telecommunication Organization
IUCN   International Union for Conservation of Nature
JIEL   *Journal of International Economic Law*
LJIL   *Leiden Journal of International Law*
LQR   *Law Quarterly Review*
M JIL   *Michigan Journal of International Law*
NAAEC   North-American Agreement on Environmental
            Cooperation
NAFTA   North-American Free Trade Agreement
NGO   Non-governmental organization
NGO Section UN DESA NGO Section
NGO Branch   UN DESA NGO Branch
NJIHR   *Northwestern Journal of International Human Rights*
NJIL   *Nordic Journal of International Law*
NPO   Nonprofit organization
OAS   Organization of American States
OECD   Organization for Economic Cooperation and Development
PCIJ   Permanent Court of International Justice
POPs   Stockholm Convention on Persistent Organic Pollutants
PVO   Private voluntary organization
RINGO   Religious international non-governmental organization
TEAEC   Treaty establishing the European Atomic Energy
            Community
TEC   Treaty establishing the European Community
TEU   Treaty on European Union

TRIPS	Agreement on Trade-related Aspects of Intellectual Property Rights
UIA	Union of International Associations
UN	United Nations
UN-NGO-IRENE	UN NGO Informal Regional Networks
UNCCD	UN Convention on Combat Desertification
UNCHR	UN Council on Human Rights
UNCTAD	UN Conference on Trade and Development
UNESCO	UN Educational, Scientific and Cultural Organization
UNFCC	UN Framework Convention on Climate Change
UNFPA	UN Population Fund
UNGA	UN General Assembly
UNHCHR	UN High Commissioner for Human Rights
UNHCR	UN High Commissioner for Refugees
UNHRC	UN Human Rights Commission
UNICEF	UN International Children's Emergency Fund
UNIDO	UN Industrial Development Organization
UNODC	UN Office on Drugs and Crime
UNSC	UN Security Council
UNTS	UN Treaty Series
WHO	World Health Organization
WMO	World Meteorological Organization
WUGSLR	*Washington University Global Studies Law Review*
YJWPO	*Yale Journal of World Public Order*

INTRODUCTION

In November 1989, when I obtained my Bachelor's Degree in law, the world in general and my country, in particular, were undergoing unexpected changes. If the Cold War was coming to an end with the reunification of Germany, in Brazil, we were witnessing the first general presidential elections after a period of forty years, under the auspices of a new, democratic Constitution. Both situations would have been inconceivable in the mind of even the most enlightened citizen, just five years earlier, when I attended my first class at Law School, which consisted of an inaugural lecture on the role of the State according to Hegel's *Philosophy of Right*. Twenty years later, even greater changes have taken place. Some NATO and Iron Curtain countries are now joint members in a Union and the US has its first Afro-American president, who has close ties to his Muslim origin. In Brazil, a man, who was considered a 'dangerous' proletarian candidate in 1989, has just ended his second presidential term in an ever wealthier country, approved by 80% of the nation's population. So, what happened?

I would say that the strong democratic winds that have been sweeping the world since 1989 have ushered in an unprecedented situation, in which electoral democracies now constitute the predominant form of government in the world. They have also given birth to a steady increase in the people's participation in public affairs, either at the national or international levels, through private bodies, the so-called non-governmental organizations (NGOs), the object of our study. As we will see, NGOs are new forms of people's participation in public affairs, based on the international legal personality of individuals and the right of people to self-determination, which has expanded way beyond the de-colonization process of the last century to encompass the right to democracy.

We are aware that the title of our essay – *NGOs: Legitimate Subjects of International Law* – may be regarded by some scholars as rather open to debate. After all, there is no conclusive definition of an NGO; legitimacy can be appraised from several different perspectives; some authors suggest that the subject/object dichotomy must be abandoned, and; finally, that international law is not a legal system at all. However, needless to say, criticism is not only necessary for the development of knowledge but also a key element in scientific inquiries. In the field of Law, many theories or theoretical approaches have been striving to explain international law and almost all of them 'seem to be better and more productive in criticizing rival approaches than contributing to the explanation of the reality of international law'.[1]

But, after all, what is reality?

One could say that reality is a singular historical fact. Given that men are not omnipresent, one may have the chance of observing it or not. Here, however, the first problem arises: Does reality exist only when we see it? We would be inclined to answer no, for if we thought so, no 'explanation of the reality of international law' could be given, because a lot of 'facts' would not be taken into account in our answer (for example, a rebellion in a distant land). Hence, it appears that answering that question necessarily implies in performing the task taking into consideration what we have observed. At this point, a second problem emerges: depending on our standpoint, one sees different characteristics of a given fact, which is exactly what happens when one observes, say, a man: from the front, one sees his beard and does not know that he is hurt; from the back, other sees some wounds but does not know that he is bearded. One person saw a bearded man, the other saw a wounded one. So, one's perception of the facts is highly influenced by the place one occupies at the moment of observation. But reality is not only affected by the 'objective' features of a standpoint, but also by its 'subjective' features. For the authorities dealing with the rebels, the bearded man was a criminal; for his followers, he was the leader that they had been expecting. The observation of reality is also affected by the 'context' (a people oppressed by a foreign ruler saw the bearded man as a leader capable of freeing them) and the 'values': for the authorities, he was an ordinary man; for his followers, he was the son of God. If we had been living in that distant year, as a Roman consul, we would have recorded an ordinary trial, as a disciple, we would have written a gospel; however, none of us would have been able to foresee that the teachings of that man would change the foundation of the legal system of the world forever.

So, if we endeavor to conduct research on the role of NGOs in international law aiming to contribute to the development of this field of legal science, we must necessarily assume that our study and, consequently, our findings, will be influenced by the facts that we have seen - from a given 'objective' and 'subjective' standpoint - in a given context, interpreted according to our values. In our quest, we will be neither a consul nor a disciple; however, we will interpret the facts and the context with the eyes of someone who values pluralistic democracy.

Legitimacy is the subjacent idea that has permeated our research. It is a question that has been discussed intensively by scholars with several standpoints and values, in different contexts. International law's legitimacy, for example, can be appraised from different standpoints: some scholars support that international law lacks legitimacy because one should see it from the perspective of national law and national interests, while others, diametrically opposed, support that legitimacy must be enhanced through the reshaping of international structures to allow the exercise of parliamentary and executive functions capable of coping with the global challenges. In intermediate positions, supporting less polarized stances, a third school advocates strengthening the presence of national parliamentarians in the international sphere, currently concentrated in the hands of the Executive, while a fourth supports qualified norm-making.[2] NGOs' legitimacy, in turn, can be studied from a political science standpoint, appraising its representativeness of civil society *vis-à-vis* the State; adopting an international relations perspective, one can appraise its power as an actor of the international sphere and; from a legal perspective, the one that we have chosen, its accommodation in a rational-legal model that recognizes rights and duties under international law. Finally, the legitimacy of individuals in international law can be appraised based on the theories of creation of States and the emergence of human rights, moreover after World War II and the massacres perpetrated by totalitarian States against their own people.

One can acknowledge two senses for legitimacy: au sens large, c'est la qualité de conformité au critère normatif qui fixe les paramètres de valorisation de l'object qu'il règle et par rapport auquel on prédit ou non la legitimité; au sens strict, cést la qualité qui, attribuée à un ordre juridico-politique suppose sa 'reconnaisance' comme domination, el la reconnaissance de sa capacité à dicter des ordres auxquels on doit obéir.'[3]

From a strictly legal perspective, the core idea of legitimacy has been historically centered in the figure of the State and in justification of *authority*, the capacity to establish binding rules that will be obeyed or make decisions bind. A given authority may be deemed legitimated if it has been empowered according to the consent of those who will be bound by its acts; its acts will be legitimated if taken according to determined fair procedures and both will have legitimacy if the outcome is deemed acceptable by those who will obey, compared to what they regard as right and just. It follows that 'without the clarification of what is to be understood by the rightness and justice of law, legitimacy cannot be comprehended either'.[4]

The basis for the *ex-ante* analysis of legitimacy is the principle of consent, the idea that more powerfully represents the source of value for individuals.[5] In the contemporary world, for example, the principle of self-determination has changed from its original pro-independence core into a specific kind of dependence – the dependence of governments on the will of the population,[6] following that the consent of people has been raised to a strengthened level in international law. The basis for the *ex-vi* procedural analysis must necessarily appraise its conformity with fair procedure, following that the decision-making process *indeed* matters, and, finally, the *ex-post* analysis will depend on whether the constituencies are capable of maintaining the authority accountable for its acts and decisions according to previously known needs and aspirations, a task that necessarily implies in transparency.

If the justification of the authority of intergovernmental organizations requires such three-step analysis and one assume that the States' representatives before those bodies were not elected by their people, a situation also observed in the international bureaucracy, the apparent obvious conclusion is that intergovernmental organization lack legitimacy in regard to the 'peoples of the United Nations'. We have found, however, that pluralism is admitted by the UN Charter not only *between* States, but also *beyond* States, because the Charter acknowledged that individuals could interact with the United Nations not only through governmental organizations but also through *non*-governmental organizations. Hence, the participation of individuals is critical to enhance the legitimacy of intergovernmental organizations, a network of bureaucratic bodies that has been growing incessantly since 1945, which, according to D'Amato, 'the more that international institutions prosper and grow, the closer we may be getting to a coalition of those institutions that proclaims itself the government of the world [hence, being necessary] to keep a vigilant eye upon the practice of "lawful" international institutions [because] if they turn out to stifle individual freedoms and abolish human rights, there will be no counterforce to overturn the government and reclaim those rights and freedoms'.[7]

NGOs, widespread democracy, and closely knit economic interdependency have been affecting the traditional concept of the sovereignty of States, moreover the legitimacy of undemocratic ones, and, consequently, international law. While NGOs' power is not absolute, it has become significant and is still growing[8] and this fact definitively cannot go unnoticed. However, such actors have never been legally defined nor has legal doctrine reached any conclusive concept regarding them. For that reason, we have decided to begin our appraisal by showing the importance of these entities in the contemporary world and, after addressing their main characteristics, by proposing a comprehensive, though focused, definition, a task carried out in the Preliminary Chapter.

NGOs, being a phenomenon of the 20th century, could not be considered in the formulation of the traditional theories of international law that regarded the States as the only legitimate channel of expression of the collective will of people in the international realm. Nevertheless, States and NGOs have several things in common. If they share similar ancient roots deeply embedded in contractarianism, they also have the common goal of ensuring the well-being of the people and, for that reason, they are constantly bombarded with criticism regarding a lack of transparency as well as questions as to their accountability. In order to determine the role of NGOs in the international sphere, we began our quest analyzing, in Chapter 1, the sources of legitimacy in international law, with a particular emphasis on Natural Law and the rights of individuals in their relations with the sovereign States.

Some authors suggest that since 1945, the world has been living a neo-Grotian era in so far as the principles of solidarity have been invigorated.[9] Not coincidently, this is the same period in which we observed the appearance of NGOs, which experienced a particularly explosive growth after the adoption of the International Covenant of Civil and Political Rights (1966) and the end of the Cold War (1991), both pivotal moments for civil society at large. A proper appraisal of the role of NGOs in the recent so-called era of solidarity in international relations must necessarily pass through the sources of international law and, for that purpose, the forthcoming chapters dealt with NGOs under each of them, which, according to authoritative legal doctrine, were listed in article 38 of the Statute of the International Court of Justice.

In Chapter 2 we will observe that the expression 'non-governmental organizations' was coined by the UN Charter, which, by establishing consultative procedures with NGOs, assumed that the public sphere was larger than the governmental one and that not only States had legitimacy to be heard in matters affecting the needs and aspirations of citizens. This *hard law* recognition of the importance of NGOs was followed by several similar provisions in the constitutive acts of intergovernmental organizations, both at the universal or regional levels, UN programmes and funds, as well as in other innumerous *soft law* instruments of interaction between governmental bodies and NGOs. It is quite relevant to observe that the relationship between traditional subjects of international law and NGOs has gone beyond consultations to encompass close working relationships, especially in the fields of human rights, humanitarian law and environmental protection. The International Committee of the Red Cross (ICRC), for example, has rights under the Geneva Conventions and is widely recognized as possessing international legal personality, having even entered into a Headquarter agreement with Switzerland, despite being an association with no more than twenty-five members, all of whom are individuals. Another organization, the International Union for the Conservation of Nature (IUCN), acts as substantive secretariat of a relevant environmental convention and has materially drafted some others. Of course, all this evidence shows that NGOs are legitimate players in the international sphere.

In the following chapter, we will appraise the place of NGOs in judicial and quasi-judicial bodies' decisions. The capacity to bring claims before international courts is traditionally recognized as one of the characteristics of international legal personality. Our research has shown a peculiar and non-uniform situation for NGOs that either fulfils or not the criteria. NGOs do not have *locus standi* before the ICJ, even though they managed to convince the UN General Assembly to request a historic advisory opinion on the use or threat of use of nuclear weapons, which ended in an unexpected *non liquet*, subverting the so-called completeness of the sources of international law enshrined in article 38 of the Court's Statute. At the European level, we will see that they cannot stand as parties before the Court of Justice of the European Union to defend shared and common rights – inasmuch performing the expected role of NGOs – but only their own personal rights. However, this awkward situation has not hindered, for instance, the judicial suspension of the application of an EC Council regulation supported in a UN Security Council resolution, in a marked victory of people's fundamental rights over State's covenants. From the Human Rights perspective, NGOs can stand as victims in the European specialized court but cannot represent a third party; in America, differently, they can represent a victim, but only at the Commission, having no access to the Court. If the situation is non-uniform when NGOs act in their own cases, it is far more complex when they try to act in third parties' cases, presenting *amicus* briefs, either in judicial or quasi-judicial bodies, a practice which is widely accepted in some bodies and rejected in others, being either acclaimed or contested by parties to the cases concerned.

But, if treaties and judicial decisions provide material evidence that allows for a greater understanding of the roles assigned to NGOs in international law, customary law has not provided such clarity. In our research, we have not found any former systematic study of customary state practice in regard to NGOs. For that reason, in Chapter 4, the appraisal of the fundamental elements (*consuetudo* and *opinion juris vel necessitatis*) required to create an international customary law called for a comprehensive analysis of the criteria adopted by the ICJ to recognize a state practice accepted as law according to a reputed methodology, a task that we have endeavored to accomplish with the help of Herman Meijers' concept of 'stages of growth'. The outcome was capable of evidencing that NGOs have achieved certain rights under international customary law, supported in constant, extensive and virtually uniform settled practice accepted as law by those parties whose interests are specially affected, without persistent objection.

The study of NGOs under the general principles of law required a broader approach, in which we addressed the germination of our legal thought from the seeds of Natural Law, the juridical conscience of humankind reflected in the principles common to the major contemporary legal systems that would further legitimize the existence of *jus cogens*. Given the physical and language restrictions imposed on conducting a direct survey in each of the systems, we decided, relying on article 9 of the Statute of the ICJ, to start Chapter 5 appraising the jurisprudence of the Court that, as a whole, represents the main forms of civilizations and of the principal legal systems of the world. The study has shown that the Court has progressively expanded the recognition of humanitarian principles and peoples' rights under international law. In a second approach, we focused on general principles of law related to society at large that have flourished more recently, such as those concerning environmental protection and civil and political participation, specifically the principle of self-determination, which has particularly experienced a broadening that has gone far beyond the narrow limits of de-colonization to become a truly continuous process of participation in public affairs that currently can be interpreted as the right to democracy. Decision-making process, hence, indeed matters.

The appraisal of the legal status of NGOs in the teachings of the most qualified publicists of the various nations presented an even greater difficulty, for, as we have pointed out, NGOs are a recent phenomenon, therefore they did not receive the attention of founding fathers of international legal theory nor even that of those who lived more recently, such as Anzilotti, Brierly, Brownlie, De Visscher, Lauterpacht, Scelle and Schwarzenberger, just to mention a few. Notwithstanding, given that our study possessed a focus on the status of NGOs in international law, we deemed it appropriate to concentrate in Chapter 6 on the analysis of the concept of subject of law or international legal personality, putting particular emphasis on the situation of the individual, who often operates internationally through NGOs, which, hence, would have a legitimated derived, functional and relative legal capacity stemming from the international legal personality of the individual, similarly to the one observed in the intergovernmental organizations in regard to their member-states. This chapter ends with an evaluation of the role of the individual and non-state actors in the work of organized law doctrine bodies, such as the International Law Commission, the International Law Association and the *Institut de Droit International*, the latter two, themselves, NGOs.

In Chapter 7, we resumed the ideas of the origins of the State, discussed in the beginning of our study, to evaluate to what extent the social contract metaphor is still valid in an era that has witnessed the debacle of strong states and the creation of new ones out of the decolonization perspective and from an overwhelmingly democratic context. Our study has shown that the relationship between international legal personality of individuals and the principle of self-determination, together with the right to participate in public affairs, directly or not, ensured by treaty law, have provided people with the necessary democratic entitlement to act in the international realm through NGOs. However, if democracy provides the contractual arrangement framework for the participation of people in public affairs through periodic elections, it is currently not capable of ensuring the same participation in the operator of the social contract, the Weberian bureaucracy that controls the State and the intergovernmental organizations and has replaced parliament as the main norm-creator. For that reason, having in mind Thomas Franck's ideas on Democratic Governance, we proposed adding a fourth building block to his model, through mechanisms of civil participation to hold bureaucracy accountable for its acts and decisions.

Chapter 8 expands on the topic discussed in the previous chapter, shifting the focus to the broad range of existing intergovernmental organizations (IGOs), which play a twofold role, both providing bureaucratic staff to accomplish their goals as well as acting as a *locus* for dialogue between the relevant actors in international law. Given that IGO officials are not elected nor do IGOs possess a parliament-like body composed of people elected by their own nations, they greatly lack democratic legitimacy, a handicap that must be compensated for by higher levels of compliance to objectives, transparency, ends-oriented accountability and democratic governance with different forms of interaction with civil society. The similarities between IGOs and NGOs (both instituted by agreements to pursue a specific aim without territorial boundaries with the help of a skilled staff) provide the needed conditions for adding the fourth building block to Franck's model, though be it at the international level.

In the Conclusion, we support that the Charter, aligned with the respect of human rights of individuals and the right to self-determination of collectivities of individuals (the nations) recognized that that right could be exercised at the UN, but making concessions to rationality and effectiveness, established that this would be done through a new kind of organization established by the individuals, coining, for the first time in a legal document, the expression 'non-governmental organization'. When individuals were to act in a broader collective perspective, i.e., as a nation, they would do so through governmental organizations (the States); when they were to act in another form, they would do so through *non*-governmental organizations. Pluralism may also be acknowledged from a universal perspective: since nations (and States) are deeply enrooted in their own cultural background, therefore lacking (*inter*)nationality, the United Nations, having universal aims, had to welcome a different perspective of interaction with individuals from several countries, for which the *inter*national NGOs appeared to be a reasonable and legitimate solution.

Notes

1   R Müllerson, *Ordering Anarchy* (Nijhoff, The Hague 2000) 18.
2   R Wolfrum, 'Legitimacy of International Law from a Legal Perspective' in R Wolfrum and V Röben (eds) *Legitimacy in International Law* (Springer, Berlin 2008) 5.
3   Dictionaire Encyclopédique de Théorie et de Sociologie du Droit (10th edn LGDJ, Paris 1993) 343.
4   CJ Friedrich, *The Philosophy of Law in Historic Perspective* (UCP, Chicago 1958) 202.
5   GP Fletcher, *Basic Concepts of Legal Thought* (OUP, Oxford 1996) 109.
6   R Müllerson, *Ordering Anarchy* (Nijhoff, The Hague 2000) 166.
7   A D'Amato, 'On the Legitimacy of International Institutions' in R Wolfrum and V Röben (eds) *Legitimacy in International Law* (Springer, Berlin 2008) 92.

8   PJ Shapiro, 'New Players on the International Stage', in WM Reisman and others, *International Law in Contemporary Perspective* (Foundation Press, New York 2004) 297.
9   R Jackson, *The Global Covenant: Human Conduct in a World of States* (OUP, Oxford, 2000) 385.

PRELIMINARY CHAPTER

1   The increasing role of NGOs in the contemporary world

After the fall of the Berlin Wall and the end of the bipolar political structure shaped by the Cold War, the States' concerns shifted from deterrence to cooperation. This move is noticeable not only in the rise of collective actions addressing a converging agenda, such as free trade and environmental protection, but also at the UN, with the 1990s decade of multilateral conferences and the unprecedented search for consensus at the General Assembly.[1]

From a citizen's perspective, the facility to move throughout the world and the real time interactions with other people provided by technology, together with the apparent reduction in the risk of another World War, have reduced the appeal of nationalism, which has become old-fashioned, if compared to other forms of group identification.[2] Massive individual migration as well as the integration of the States in blocks has also contributed to the decline of nationalism. If it is a truism that the traditional conception of nation is slowly vanishing, it is also true that it is giving space to a different kind of relationship between individuals; another form of citizenship shaped by shared issues of a global range, facilitated by the immediate contact provided by small devices carried in our pockets: global agendas.

The globalization of economic activity, together with the transnational information flow has led to the establishment of a so-called global civil society, which has been defined as the 'sphere of ideas, values, institutions, organizations, networks, and individuals located *between* the family, the State, and the market and operating *beyond* the confines of national societies, policies and economies.'[3] One could say that this conception reproduces at the international level, the same model of social space observed within the confines of States.

If there is a certain general agreement that the expression 'global civil society' refers to a response to rising concerns about the need for a new social, economic, and political deal at the global level - a new governance model – there is no further consensus as to how this response should be.[4] In a certain way, the emergence of international intergovernmental organizations (IGOs) has tried to respond to this challenge. But these institutions and their founding members, the States, incurred in the same mistake observed in national level, when they tried to monopolize the public sphere.[5] If social movements and similar organizations are recognized as legitimate voices of plural civil society and relevant players in democratic regimes at the national level, effectively helping to guide the country along a new path, they can perform accordingly at the international level, where transnational networks play an important role in transforming certain issues in politics and, subsequently, in international law, through the adoption of multilateral conventions on the subject.

We are not postulating that it is an easy task, nor are we assuming that States have a true willingness to accept newcomers to their post-Westphalian territory. But we do affirm that the 'states-only' club has eroded, and that we cannot regard an international system effective if it has divided the world as if into a puzzle, where each State is one piece and the only thing that matters. Individuals must have their natural right to an active voice in the decision-making process recognized in issues that go far beyond the national (own) interests of their representatives, the States, and that will shape global governance.

It is a truism that the international sphere is a fragmented and contentious arena, where States and IGOs, albeit aiming to cooperate, struggle to defend their own interests, often supported in claims of the needs of civil society, which, in turn, is trying to emerge and to be legitimized by those same institutions that purportedly represent it.[6] During the 20th century, we have witnessed the consolidation of a new form of expression of the voice of civil society at large that wants to join the arena. These self-proclaimed spokesmen or, sometimes, attorneys-at-law, have placed themselves together with traditional institutions that represent the interests of citizens, such as the election of the heads of government and parliament in democratic regimes, and brought to light a new model in the organization of individuals bound together by common goals in public interest themes, usually of a universal nature: They are the non-governmental organizations (NGOs).

NGOs cannot be regarded as being equal to civil society,[7] yet they are relevant non-state actors in the contemporary world that have demonstrated a great capacity in gathering collaborators[8] and financial supporters, being actively involved in the shaping of public policies, whether at a local, national or international level, addressing a broad range of issues, sometimes as supporters but also - and more often - as critics.[9] The examples are outstanding: from the long-serving International Committee of the Red Cross (ICRC) to the young and provocative Greenpeace and Oxfam, they are continuously extending their range of action. Currently, no longer operating solely towards famine and disaster relief, but also in social and economic development, advocacy, agenda setting and monitoring international agreements, NGOs perform a significant role in various sectors of international relations and, most relevantly, they are key players whilst dealing with the international public opinion in matters such as human rights, environment, peace and disarmament. They undoubtedly influence State decisions. The importance of some of their contributions for the creation of new international law has been compared with that of the teachings of the most highly qualified publicists in the sense of Art 38(1) (d) of the Statute of the International Court of Justice (ICJ).[10] NGO activities, in some cases, have reached global proportions and extraordinary persuasive power and, in some instances, even regulatory power.[11]

At the international level, we have witnessed an increasing participation of NGOs in global issues which led, for example, to awarding five Nobel Peace Prizes to such entities in the last 25 years, three of which just in the last 15 years.[12]

The Union of International Associations (UIA) database informs that the number of international NGOs (INGOs) has been growing steadily, rising from 832 entities of all types in 1951, to 952 in 1978, 20,635 in 1985 and 51,509 in 2006.[13] The same phenomenon can be observed in the United Nations Economic and Social Council (ECOSOC) database of INGOs with consultative status in the Council, where the number of accredited organizations has risen from 40 in 1948 to 180 in 1968, 724 in 1992 and 3,536 in 2012.[14] These figures represent only those organizations that have submitted their database to the UIA or applied for ECOSOC consultative status and, hence, despite being the best sources available, surely do not comprise all NGOs operating at an international level.

The role and presence of non-state actors in the UN system have also risen considerably over the last thirty years, with a spectacular participation in the cycle of major conferences. 2,400 NGOs participated in the UN Conference on Environment and Development held in Rio de Janeiro in 1992 (The Earth Summit), a number that reached 4,993 civil society representatives accredited to the UN Conference on Climate Change, in Bali (2007). It is estimated that 30,000 people participated in the NGOs forums that occurred together with the Fourth World Conference on Women (Beijing 1995)[15] and that 35,000 attended the 2002 Johannesburg World Summit on Sustainable Development side events, surpassing by far the diplomatic corps at those events. The presence of NGOs is perceived not only in the surroundings of the conference venues but also inside the meeting rooms, seeing as they were responsible for presenting fifty-two statements at the 1995 Beijing Conference,[16] had a remarkable influence in the agenda and the declaration of the 2002 Johannesburg Summit, and are often speaking at the UN Human Rights Council, the General Assembly (UNGA) and its committees and even at the Security Council (UNSC).

Their presence is relevant at the UN program level too, where they perform valuable work that the agencies are not able to undertake or, at least, to undertake directly.[17] One-third of the UNFPA and UNICEF funds are disbursed through NGOs, which also amass 21% of UNHCR's budget and are present in 72% of the projects financed by the World Bank.[18] According to a 1988 UN Secretary General report, NGOs collectively constitute the second largest source of development assistance in terms of net transfer.[19]

At a first glance, the NGO phenomenon may appear to be a new trend because, as we have seen, the number of NGOs has increased significantly in recent years, outnumbering tenfold the number of intergovernmental organizations, often having similar or identical goals.[20] From one perspective, this is not true, seeing as nonprofit and charitable organizations have existed and operated throughout the world since immemorial times, being based upon religious beliefs, solidarity, mutuality or altruism. The first known NGO-like international private organization was the Anti-Slavery and Aborigines Protection Society, established in 1837 in England, whose activity contributed positively to the enactment of the World Anti-Slavery convention of 1840.[21] Up until World War I, most of the organizations had pursued idealistic or scientific purposes and while several of the organizations created in the 19th century are still alive today,[22] the most famous one is the International Committee of the Red Cross (ICRC), a legal entity created in 1863 as a Swiss association with no room for more than twenty-five members, all Swiss citizens.[23] Its tiny membership, however, does not detract from its international importance, confirmed by its status in the Geneva Convention relative to the Treatment of Prisoners of War (1949),[24] its three Nobel Peace Prizes (1917, 1944 and 1963) and, quite relevantly, its budget (provided mainly by governments), which totaled € 664.7 million (CHF 1,049.2 million) in 2006 destined towards providing food to more than 2.5 million people and emergency supplies to more than 4 million people, among other activities.

The last three decades have shown an accelerated growth rate, whether in scope or scale, to such an extent that some authors have affirmed that we are in the midst of a 'global association revolution' that may permanently alter the relationship between States and citizens, impacting far beyond the limits of the material services provided.[25]

Taking Amnesty International - another Nobel Peace Prize laureate - as an example, we can see that its roots in civil society run deep, represented by more than 2.2 million voluntary members and subscribers in more than 150 countries who donated € 46.2 million in 2009/2010 to support the organization's activities.[26] A similar situation can be observed in another global organization, Greenpeace International, which has approximately 2.9 million supporters around the world who donated € 196 million to the organization in 2009.[27]

Both entities have more than 5 million supporters in local branches, most of whom are volunteers and participants in the organization's daily life, and have obtained resources equivalent to their counterparts in the UN system

(The OHCHR[28] gathered voluntary contributions of USD 95.7 million in 2007 and UNEP[29] obtained USD 89 million in 2008).

Unequivocally, another relevant aspect of the operation of NGOs in recent years has been the outstanding volume of financial resources that they have invested internationally in public interest efforts, several times greater than the sums provided by governmental and intergovernmental international aid. In the fiscal year 2009/2010, the American National Red Cross had operational revenues of USD 3.60 billion and expenditures of USD 3.37 billion with program services.[30] In the same period, another US-based humanitarian relief organization, Americares, obtained USD 801 million in support and revenues, which enabled an expenditure of USD 850 million that same year to assist people in need of relief in 97 countries.[31] Sound financial standing is not only to be seen in humanitarian organizations, as can be observed in the Nature Conservancy 2010 annual report, which shows USD 990 million in revenues, an expenditure of USD 719 million in programs and USD 4.9 billion in net assets'.[32]

2   The (lack of) definition of NGOs in international documents

Global activities, political influence at national, regional and international levels, worldwide networks of supporters and financial soundness have granted NGOs a striking presence in the contemporary world. But, what are they?

The UN Charter was the first international instrument to adopt the expression "non-governmental organization". Its article 71 prescribes that

> 'The Economic and Social Council may make suitable arrangements for consultation with non-governmental organizations which are concerned with matters within its competence. Such arrangements may be made with international organizations and, where appropriate, with national organizations after consultation with the Member of the United Nations concerned'.

Before the creation of the UN, during the existence of the League of Nations, legal reference was made solely to national Red Cross organizations and NGOs were referred to as "private institutions", while many of the entities gathered under the auspices of the UIA called themselves international institutes, international unions or simply international organizations.[33]

According to Willetts, 'the first draft of the UN Charter did not make any mention of maintaining cooperation with private bodies. A variety of groups, mainly but not solely from the USA, lobbied to rectify it at the

San Francisco Conference, which established the UN in 1945.'[34] The drafting was, thus, the subject of considerable dispute.[35]

Despite being successful in achieving a certain level of participation in
the major association of nation-states, NGOs remained technically undefined. Consultative status has provided NGOs with a recognized standing
and entitled them to certain limited rights and privileges within the UN
system. Nevertheless, this situation, from our point of view, has retarded
the evolution of their legal status, especially if we bear in mind that the
discussions about the crucial character of the definition of NGOs began
with the UN Charter and that the several attempts made throughout the
20th century to clarify their legal status have proven unsuccessful, as we
shall see hereinafter.

The lack of definition does not comprise only NGOs, these peaceful
non-state actors, but also extends to their disturbed counterparts, the terrorist groups, similarly composed of individuals aiming a 'new' world order.
Under the perspective of the latter, as Becker pointed out, if such non-state
(terrorist) actors can operate as subjects of international law in the international plane, then they should be viewed as capable of operating together
with States[36] with severe implications to the notion of State responsibility
and also in the conception of international legal personality.

NGOs share relevant common features that have justified positioning
them as an identifiable third "social sector" that merges the public purposes
of the State (the first sector) with the private identity of institutions of the
market (the second).[37] Notwithstanding having such an ostensive presence
in life nowadays, NGOs do not have a commonly agreed upon definition,
whether among scholars or common citizens.[38]

The reasons for this lack of consensus are, from our point of view, the
non-existence of a precise definition in international conventions and the
different formal requirements, duties and benefits governing them in each
national legal system, which have led to different approaches and perspectives in the international arena.

An aspect noticed is that NGOs have commonly been referred to as the
denial of the organizational models already in existence: they operate in
the public sphere, but are not government, and they are private entities but
do not aim profits. NGOs, also by their name, differ from the intergovernmental organizations created by the nation-states. These fundamental features must be explored in more detail.

3.   Conceptual framework of NGOs

3.1   Independence from States

Unequivocally, an NGO must be an organization independent from the direct or indirect control of any government or intergovernmental body in

order to ensure its private character. The four ECOSOC regulations on the consultative status of INGOs (1946, 1950, 1968 and 1996) shed an evolutionary light on the subject, attempting to reach an ideal concept which unfortunately remains unachieved.

The first initiative was the report of the Committee on Arrangements for Consultation with Non-Governmental Organizations adopted by ECOSOC Res. 2/3 (21 June 1946).[39] This report established the Council NGO Committee, making it responsible for reviewing the applications for consultative status submitted by NGOs, for making recommendations to the ECOSOC, and for setting certain rules for the accreditation and consultative procedure.

The rules were revised by ECOSOC Res. 288 B (X) (27 February 1950), which considered that 'any international organization which is not established by inter-governmental agreement shall be considered as a non-governmental organization.'[40] The third regulation was brought to light by ECOSOC Res. 1296 (XLIV) (23 May 1968).[41] It kept the main concept of private incorporation but, probably making concessions to the Cold War *realpolitik*, accepted that those 'organizations could accept members designated by governmental authorities, provided that such membership did not interfere with the free expression of views of the organization.'[42] We consider this to have been a bad move, since history has shown it to be quite difficult for civil society leaders and organizations to hold out against strong government pressure. Most of all, such a concession brought a certain legitimacy to the creation of government-related non-governmental organizations (GRINGOS in UN parlance) which currently, together with the business-oriented NGOs (the BINGOS) or religious organizations (RINGOS), epitomizing an important and growing global trend that threatens civil society's representative system and warrants greater scrutiny.

The current regulation introduced by ECOSOC Res. 1996/31 (25 July 1996) refined the concept again, adding that no organization that has been 'established by a governmental entity or intergovernmental agreement' should be considered an NGO, maintaining recognition to those organizations that accept members designated by governmental authorities provided, it must be stressed, that 'such membership does not interfere with the free expression of views of the organization'. The municipal law of some countries has adopted equivalent criteria to grant public interest status to NGOs.[43]

Private status and independence from governmental bodies have not only been stressed in political expression but also from a financial perspective.[44] The 1946 and 1950 regulations made no reference to the financial support of the accredited INGOs, which first appeared in the 1968 regulation, which has remained unaltered in its current rules. Res. 1996/31 prescribes that 'the basic resource of the organization shall be derived in the main part from contributions of the national affiliates or other components or from individual members.' However, assuming that some organizations obtain funding from governmental and international agencies, the rule establishes (para. 13) that 'any financial contribution or other support, direct or indirect, from a Government to the organization shall be openly declared to the ECOSOC Committee on Non-Governmental Organizations through the Secretary-General and fully recorded in the financial and other records of the organization and shall be devoted to purposes in accordance with the aims of the United Nations.'

3.2   Legal personality

It is important to debate to what extent the concept set forth in article 71 of the UN Charter refers only to formal, legal entities incorporated under the municipal law of any member-state or if it provides an opportunity for NGOs to be created under international law.

As we may note, the aforementioned article 71 addresses *arrangements for consultation with non-governmental organizations which may be made with international organizations and, where appropriate, with national organizations after consultation with the Member of the United Nations concerned.*

The adoption of the term 'organization' instead of, for example, 'movement', 'civil society' or 'non-state actor', in our point of view, undeniably leads to the understanding that it makes reference to a legal entity formally created.[45] The legal incorporation can also be inferred throughout the several subsequent regulations of the accreditation of consultative status when references are made to the existence of established headquarters with an executive officer, the representativeness of members, voting rights, a democratically adopted constitution, and the formation of joint committees among national organizations.

Another key aspect to be regarded is the law regulating the incorporation of the organization. If the UN Charter assumed that all non-governmental organizations *had to be* incorporated according to the municipal law of any member-state, then the *international organizations* mentioned in article 71 would not exist, hence making any differentiation between international and national organizations in the article irrelevant. Furthermore, if the referred consultation with a UN member-state concerned the territorial range of activities of the INGO, then, assuming that international organizations must operate in several countries to be 'international', all arrangements for consultation with INGOs should be previously submitted to any and all member-states involved, which, in some issues such as global warming or poverty relief, should lead to consultation with all member-states.

Therefore, despite being clear that INGOs have to be legal entities and that they cannot be established by a governmental entity or intergovernmental agreement, it still remains possible for them, in the future, to be incorporated under the guidance of general rules set forth in an international convention.[46]

To reinforce this perspective, we should point out that the Res. 1996/31 adopts the term 'organization' to make reference to non-governmental organizations at national, sub-regional, regional or international levels and does not expressly require, for granting consultative status, that the concerned entities be incorporated under the municipal law of any member-state.[47] However, in the absence of any consensus on the matter, presently INGOs granted consultative status under the auspices of article 71 of the UN Charter have been incorporated as legal private entities under the law of the member-state where they are headquartered.

The first remarkable regulation of international organizations was a national law enacted in Belgium on 25 October 1919 that granted civil personality to international associations that pursued scientific ends without profitable aims, provided that the entity was open to the participation of Belgian and foreign citizens and had a governing body headquartered in Belgium with at least one Belgian citizen. The law also authorized foreign-based associations to operate in the country without the participation of Belgian citizens in its management, provided it did not harm public order. According to Normandin, the law did not produce the expected effect, since just five institutions had applied for the legal recognition by 1926.[48] However, it is worthy of note that the 9th article of the law, which took into consideration the goal of international organizations obtaining a supernational status, authorized the Belgian government to 'negotiate with other States the needed treaties to establish an international status for the international associations with scientific ends based on the principles set forth in the same law'.[49]

At the international level, the first convention clearly addressing the issue that INGOs had to be incorporated under municipal laws is the European Convention on the Recognition of the Legal Personality of International Non-Governmental Organizations drawn up in Strasbourg in 1986 (Strasbourg Convention),[50] which defined INGOs as 'the associations, foundations and other private institutions that have been established by an instrument governed by the internal law of a member-state of the Council of Europe and that have their statutory office and their central management and control in the territory of one member-state'.[51]

3.3 International scope

Another material aspect is the international representativeness of INGOs. As we have seen in the 1919 Belgian Law formerly mentioned, the international character would be ensured by a multi-national governing body and membership and, most of all, by its range of activities. The Strasbourg Convention, assuming that national organizations perform their activities only in one country, usually where they are headquartered, adopted a similar conception, conditioning the international character to the performance of activities also in a foreign country and, therefore, required that the candidate INGOs 'carry on their activities with effect in at least two States'. This qualitative approach on representativeness has not been reproduced in the UN model, which adopted a quantitative approach. The 1950 ECOSOC regulation, for example, conditioned the consultative accreditation to the 'recognized standing and representation of a substantial proportion of the organized persons within the particular fields in which the organization operated and also to the existence of an international structure'.[52]

Going much further and virtually deeming the accreditation impossible due to the burden set down by the demand for a required quantity for legitimacy, the 1968 ECOSOC regulation considered eligible for receiving consultative status only those organizations with 'recognized international standing, representing a substantial proportion, and expressing the views of major sections, of the population or of the organized persons within the particular fields of its competence, covering, where possible, a substantial number of countries in different regions of the world'.[53]

Not surprisingly, this regulation did not prove satisfactory and, bearing in mind an attempt to express the opinion of the major part of the world population, the 1996 regulation maintained the required 'recognized (but no longer 'international') standing within the particular fields of its competence' but introduced the concept that the organizations could be divided up not only into national or international levels, but also into sub-regional and regional levels, hence portraying the distinct influence of the existing economic blocs and regional intergovernmental organizations established during the previous decades.

Another apposite aspect is the participation ensured, to the extent possible, of NGOs from all regions, and particularly from developing countries, based on the proclaimed goal to 'achieve a just, balanced, effective and genuine involvement of NGOs from all regions and areas of the world', also pursued by the encouraged participation of NGOs from developing countries in international conferences and a greater involvement of organizations from countries with economies in transition.[54] An aim of establishing a balance between the Northern and Southern hemispheres becomes clear, especially upon examining the evidence that the major part of accredited organizations is headquartered in Europe and the US.[55]

3.4   Public interest purposes

Another relevant aspect to be considered while trying to define an NGO is the purpose of its activities, which, on one hand, must keep a clear convergence with the goals, purposes and principles of the public administration without, on the other hand, being – or seeking to be – part of the government apparatus. Thus, for example, concerns with human rights must be general rather than restricted to a particular group, nationality or country. This convergence is the main factor that has led to the shaping of the expression 'non-governmental' since, from an ends perspective, such organizations have the same focus as governments – the reason for the similarity – but, from a means perspective, operate in a privately driven manner – this being the reason for the discrepancy.

The Strasbourg Convention recognizes those NGOs with 'an aim of international utility'. Such vagueness makes important to recall the preamble of the convention, where member-states recognized as worthy to the international community the work carried out by NGOs in the 'scientific, cultural, charitable, philanthropic, health and education fields', since they 'contribute to the achievement of the aims and principles of the UN Charter and the Statute of the Council of Europe'.

Similar general criteria have been adopted by the UN Resolutions on the ECOSOC accreditation that grants the consultative status to NGOs that 'can demonstrate that their programme of work is of direct relevance to the aims and purposes of the United Nations'. [56]

Furthermore, the ECOSOC Res. 1996/31, if compared with the Strasbourg Convention, proposed a formula of division of the NGOs into groups, in order to provide proper balance to nonequivalent capabilities and backgrounds, defining the following three categories with regards to the 'nature and scope of their activities and to the assistance they may be expected to give to the ECOSOC or its subsidiary bodies in carrying out the functions set out in Chapters IX and X of the Charter of the United Nations':

a. Organizations with general consultative status: 'those whose primary purpose is to promote the aims, objectives and purposes of the United Nations and a furtherance of the understanding of its work, or that are concerned with most of the activities of the ECOSOC and its subsidiary bodies and can demonstrate to the satisfaction of the Council that they have substantive and sustained contributions to make to the achievement of the objectives of the United Nations concerned with matters falling within the competence of the Council and its subsidiary bodies, and are closely involved with the economic and social life of the peoples of the areas they represent and whose membership, which should be considerable, is broadly representative of major segments of society in a large number of countries in different regions of the world';

b. Organizations with special consultative status: 'those that have a special competence in, and are concerned specifically with, only a few of the fields of activities covered by the ECOSOC and its subsidiary bodies, and that are known within the fields for which they have or seek consultative status. If the concerned organization operates in the field of human rights, it must pursue the goal of promotion and protection of

human rights in accordance with the spirit of the Charter of the United
Nations, the Universal Declaration of Human Rights and the Vienna
Declaration and Programme of Action*;*

c. Organizations included in the roster: 'those that do not have general or
special consultative status but the ECOSOC, or the Secretary General
of the United Nations in consultation with the council or its Committee
on non-Governmental Organizations, considers, can make occasional
and useful contributions to the work of the ECOSOC or its subsidiary
bodies or other United Nations bodies within their competence'.

These conceptual differences, while grading the consultative status, have
led to different rights for NGOs within the Council. Since those with general
consultative status have a substantive capability to contribute with the
UN and relevant support in the communities, both for close involvement in
local affairs and considerable membership, the ECOSOC Res. 1996/31
granted them some rights that are very similar to those ensured to the
member-states, excluding voting power and the right to participate in collective
bodies composed of representatives of member-states. Their rights
include (a) the proposition of placement of items of special interest in the
provisional agenda of the Council, commissions and subsidiary bodies; (b)
the designation of representatives to sit as observers at public meetings of
the Council, its commissions and its subsidiary bodies; (c) the presentation
of 2000-word written statements relevant to the work of the Council, its
commissions or other subsidiary organs, which shall be circulated by the
UN Secretary General to its members; and (d) the opportunity to make oral
statements to the Council, subject to approval.

Those with special consultative status were not granted the rights to propose
items for the agenda or to make oral presentations to the Council,
being the submission of written statements reduced to 500 words if addressed
to the Council or to 1500 words if aimed for consideration by its
commissions or other subsidiary organs. With more restrictive rights, the
organizations included in the roster are only allowed to send representatives
to meetings concerned with matters within their fields of competence
and may only make oral presentations or submit written statements, which
are not expected to exceed 500 words, if invited to do so by the Secretary
General.

Adopting another perspective, Daillier and Pellet have proposed a classification
of NGOs based on their purposes, dividing them into seven categories:
(a) humanitarian and religious; (b) political; (c) scientific; (d) social-economical;
(e) sports; (f) environmentalists; and (g) documentary.[57]
This formula has also been adopted by Salomon in his comparative research
of civil society organizations in the world. [58]

We believe that the nomination of specific areas of knowledge or activities
is an inappropriate approach for the subject, seeing as public interest

is a complex matter and it is common practice to identify NGOs operating in two or more categories.[59] Therefore, we support the UN and the Council of Europe's definitions that consider international NGOs as those entities whose aims and purposes have international utility and are in conformity with the spirit, purposes and principles of the UN Charter.

Furthermore, we must obviously consider excluded those entities constituted as political parties or that are related to political groups that seek direct political power (since they are or aim to be part of the government bodies), making it relevant to quote that para 57 (a) of the ECOSOC Res. 1996/31 determines the suspension or withdrawal of the consultative status of any NGO that 'either directly or through its affiliates or representatives acting on its behalf, clearly abuses its status by engaging in a pattern of acts contrary to the purposes and principles of the Charter of the United Nations, including unsubstantiated or politically motivated acts against member-states incompatible with those purposes and principles.'

3.5   Nonprofit aims

Resuming the denial by NGOs of the organizational models already in existence, and taking in account the conditions set down by the Strasbourg Convention and the ECOSOC Res. 1996/31, which address the funding of concerned NGOs, it is important to point out that NGOs are institutions that do not aim profits even when they have their income partially generated from commercial activities, notably consultancy contracts, courses or sale of publications or data, which are not expressly or indirectly prohibited in either of the aforementioned international norms.[60]

The ordinary idea of profit is reduced to a single positive arithmetic result [10 (revenues) - 7 (expenditures) = 3 (the profit)]. However, this dimension is not enough to comprise other relevant aspects of the definition, because profit is mainly a purpose, not just a result, and, as such, the profitable aim of a given initiative is set at its start not at its end, when the figures are obtained. Even in the case that an entity should set its strategy to make a surplus in a certain activity and it is very successful in accumulating an endowment or increasing its activities or facilities over the years, it will remain a nonprofit institution if it is previously made known that the result will not be distributed to managers, associates or other interested parties but reinvested in its own purposes.[61]

This continuous reinvestment of the surplus is not a matter of board decision, since sometimes businessmen decide to invest the companies' profits in their activities for a couple of years and the enterprises do not become NGOs due to these decisions. The continuous investment is, in fact, supported by a different legal concept: the property, or - more precisely put - the lack of property. Companies always have owners, even if pulverized on stock exchanges; NGOs do not. A group of people can create both a company and a nonprofit institution and they can also manage both, but they will only be the owners of the former, not the latter.

This specific characteristic of NGOs approximates them to the State, since the latter neither belongs to the statesmen or political party on duty nor to the citizens, because its purpose is to serve the entire nation, present and future. It also reinforces our point of view that it is not convenient to define NGOs based on the cause they address, since nowadays any cause, aim or issue can be the purpose of a private profit-oriented entity.[62] Needless to say, criminal organizations cannot be considered NGOs since they are profit-oriented and practice illegal activities, being either of these circumstances enough to warrant the suspension or withdrawal of the consultative status of any NGO under the ECOSOC Res. 1996/31.[63]

3.6   Voluntary and associative organization

Another germane concern while defining NGOs for the purpose of the study of their international role is the voluntary and associative character of those entities. This particular aspect, while presenting no discordance with respect to their voluntary organization, i.e., not determined by law or government orientation, presents a different situation when the needed existence of membership is addressed.

Recalling the conditions set down for granting consultative status to NGOs under the auspices of the ECOSOC Res. 1996/31, we can identify several references to an associative organization, as summarized below:

a. Para. 10 makes reference to a democratically adopted constitution;
b. Para. 11 determines that the organization shall have authority to speak for its members;
c. Para. 12 states that the organization must have a representative structure and possess appropriate mechanisms of accountability to its members, who shall exercise effective control over its policies and actions through the exercise of voting rights or other appropriate democratic and transparent decision making processes;
d. Para. 13 establishes that the resources of the organization shall be derived in the main part from contributions of the national affiliates or other components or from individual members; and
e. Para. 22, while defining the conditions for granting the general consultative status, makes reference to considerable membership of the candidate.

At a first glance, these references clearly make foundations ineligible for the international non-governmental organizations' consultative status with the ECOSOC, since this kind of legal entity does not have membership, despite having all of the other characteristics (independence from government, legal personality, international scope, public interest purposes, nonprofit aims and voluntary establishment). However, this ineligibility is not the current situation, as we can observe that several foundations have been granted general and special consultative status.

The member-states of the Council of Europe, in turn, expressly agreed that foundations should be considered as international non-governmental organizations under the auspices of the Strasbourg Convention.[64]

The UN system regulation for INGOs is coherent with the United Nations design itself, which adopts an associative model, in which major decisions are made in general assemblies, councils or committees of members, disregarding, at least in the formal voting process, the relevance of the financial stature of the member-states.

3.7 Peaceful Operations

Maintenance of peace is the main purpose of the UN and its structure has been conceived to deal with threats to peace originated by acts of States. Current times have shown that another kind of actor plays an important role in destabilizing peace in the world, the so-called terrorist groups, another form of non-state actor originated in civil society. Of course, the strengthening of the relationship between the UN and civil society organizations does not comprise terrorist groups that, based on their methods, could never be considered a kind of NGO - albeit their independence from States, international scope of activities, nonprofit aims and voluntary associative character - because they adopt violence, mainly against civil targets, as a means to achieve their goals. Thus, peaceful operations have become a relevant characteristic to distinguish NGOs from terrorist groups.

4 Conclusion: A NGO concept

In this Preliminary Chapter, we have addressed some aspects and facts that can contribute towards clearly establishing the definition of an international non-governmental organization since, as formerly stated in this present work, none of the treaties or conventions currently in force has been able to do so.

A 1994 Secretary General report of a task force established to undertake a general review of arrangements for consultations with NGOs, although having in mind that there is no universally accepted definition, tried to define that 'an NGO is a non-profit entity whose members are citizens or associations of citizens of one or more countries and whose activities are determined by the collective will of its members in response to the needs of the members or of one countries and whose activities are determined by the collective will of its members in response to the needs of the members or of one or more communities with which the NGO cooperates'.[65] This, however, is an incomplete definition, for a terrorist group fits it.

A document was produced in 2002 by the OECD Financial Action Task Force on Money Laundering, which analyzes international best practices in combating the abuse of non-profit organizations, in which the task force realized that non-governmental organizations can take on a variety of forms, depending on the jurisdiction and legal system, having recognized within the definition entities incorporated as associations, foundations, committees, community service organizations, corporations of public interest, limited companies and public benevolent institutions.[66] Bearing in mind a risk-based approach to the problem of abuse of NGOs, the organ decided to adopt a functional rather than legalistic definition of NGOs, considering them the 'non-profit organizations that engage in raising or disbursing funds for charitable, religious, cultural, educational, social or fraternal purposes, or for the carrying out of other types of good works'. This is a better definition, which excludes terrorist groups, but that does not suffice to define an INGO, because it does not address independence from State, voluntary incorporation and international scope.

This functional approach has also been adopted by the US Department of State, which released in 2006 ten Guiding Principles on Non-governmental Organizations regarding the treatment to be dispensed by governments to NGOs.[67] Instead of defining an NGO based on its own characteristics, the document decided to use the term as an 'umbrella name' for several legal forms of incorporation of legal entities, comprising 'independent public policy advocacy organizations, non-profit organizations that defend human rights and promote democracy, humanitarian organizations, private foundations and funds, charitable trusts, societies, associations and non-profit corporations, except political parties'. That's an even better concept, but that doesn't fit our needs because it does not highlight the international scope of activities and the voluntary incorporation.

The discrepancies among scholars on the characteristics of NGOs - these well-known but still undefined contemporary actors – are, on average, less glaring because most of them based their definition on a mix of the factors addressed in this chapter instead of their legal form.

However, the absence of a widely accepted definition represents an effective harm to the participation of civil society organizations in the UN bodies or events since there is material disagreement between UN member-states on whether participatory rights should be understood, especially among those with less democratic tradition that are often the subjects of criticism from the same NGOs that are applying for participation, a situation perceived in the ECOSOC practice in granting consultative status.[68]

Therefore, the challenge is to find a definition that comprises the commonly agreed upon characteristics of non-governmental organizations in a way that ensures their proper participation in the international arena, while avoiding their masquerade use for business or government-oriented practices or, much worse, criminal initiatives.

Under this perspective, we could define that international non-governmental organizations are those non-profit legal entities, voluntarily established by citizens or associations of citizens with residence in at least five countries, that are independent from government and political groups that seek political power, whose transnational aims and peaceful operations have international utility and are in conformity with the spirit, purposes and principles of the Charter of the United Nations.

We have left, deliberately, one aspect aside: legitimacy.

Who is to say that NGOs have legitimacy to interact in the international realm?

This is a task that we will endeavor to answer throughout the essay.

Notes

1   This convergence towards mutual goals however has proven to be harmful, since the UN General Assembly 'lost its nerve' to address international issues at depth and began adopting rather general and vague declarations or recommendations. See UNGA Secretary General Report 'In Larger Freedom' (2005) para 159.

2   Thomas Franck, for instance, argues that individuals, nowadays, may have more than one affiliation, exemplifying it with the dual or even multiple nationality, something unthinkable in the past. Moreover, he argues that such affiliative choices increasingly can be made by individuals acting autonomously. See T Franck, 'Is Personal Freedom a Western Value?' (1997) AJIL v 91, 593.

3   H Anheier, M Glasius and M Kaldor (eds), *Global Civil Society 2001* (OUP, Oxford 2001) 17.

4   J Keane, *Global Civil Society?* (CUP, Cambridge 2003) 2.

5   If, by the end of the 1960s, the states had become the main focus of protest movements, the 1990s showed that intergovernmental organizations, such as the IMF and WTO, had become the principal focus of criticism, demonstrating their inadequacy to respond to the issues of civil society. See, in this aspect, C Chandhoke, 'The Limits of Global Civil Society', in M Glasius, M Kaldor and H Anheier (eds), *Global Civil Society 2002* (OUP, Oxford 2002) 40.

6   ME Keck and K Sikkink, *Activist beyond Borders* (Cornell University Press, Ithaca 1998) 32-33.

7   For a critical commentary of the belief that international NGOs constitute a kind of international civil society, see K Anderson, 'The Ottawa Convention Banning Landmines, the Role of International Non-governmental Organizations and the Idea of International Civil Society' (2000) EJIL v 11 n 1, 91.

8   A remarkable aspect is the nonprofit sector employment as a percent of total nonagricultural employment. A research study released in 1998 identified that 12.4% of Dutch employees were working for nonprofit organizations, this being the highest rate among the 22 countries under study. See L Salomon and HK Anheiner, *The Emerging Sector Revisited: A Summary* (John Hopkins Institute for Policy Studies, Baltimore 1998).

9   The implications of an often usual situation - where NGOs start working as 'watch dogs' to become 'working dogs' under financial agreements - regarding the capacity

of NGOs to remain independent from the state, has been addressed, at the UK national level. See, D Morris, *Charities and the Contract Culture: Partners or
Contractors? Law and Practice in Conflict* (Charity Law Unit, Liverpool 1999).

10   EPIL, v III (1992) 617.

11   The regulatory power can be found, for example, in the International Association of
     Air Transportation (IATA) and the International Chamber of Commerce. The latter is
     an NGO incorporated under the French law with associates all over the world that
     has defined the INCOTERMS, bearing worldwide application in the trade of goods. It
     is also worthy of note that it applied for consultative status in the ECOSOC on 7
     January 1946 and obtained it on 1 October 1946. See, UN doc. E/189/Rev.2.

12   The award was granted in 1977 to Amnesty International, in 1985 to the
     International Physicians for the Prevention of Nuclear War, in 1997 to the
     International Campaign to Ban Landmines, in 1999 to Médecins Sans Frontières
     and in 2006 to Muhammad Yunus and the Grameen Bank.

13   Union of International Associations < http://www.uia.be/en/stats> accessed 13 April
     2008.

14   ECOSOC, Dept. of Economic and Social Affairs, NGO Sector
     <http://www.csonet.org/> accessed 20 July 2012.

15   A large number of non-governmental organizations were accredited to the
     Conference by the Commission on the Status of Women in decision 39/2 and the
     Economic and Social Council in decision 1995/229.

16   'Report of the Fourth Conference on Women' (Beijing 4-15 September 1995) UN
     Doc A/CONF.177/20/Rev.1.

17   S Rosenne, *The perplexities of modern international law* (Nijhoff, Leiden 2004) 269.

18   World Bank < http://web.worldbank.org/WBSITE/EXTERNAL/TOPICS/CSO/0,,
     contentMDK:20093224~menuPK:220429~pagePK:220503~piPK:220476~theSiteP-
     K:228717,00.html> accessed 13 April 2008.

19   UNGA 'Report of the Secretary General on Arrangements and practices for the inter-
     action of non-governmental organizations in all activities of the United Nations sys-
     tem' (10 July 1998) UN Doc A/53/170, para 2

20   EPIL v III (1992) 614.

21   A. Normandin, *Du Statut Juridique des Association Internationales* (Librairie Générale
     de Droit & de Jurisprudence, Paris 1926).

22   We can quote, for example, the YMCA (1855), The Salvation Army (1863), The
     Institut de Droit International (1873) and the International Law Association (1873).

23   ICRC statute at < http://www.icrc.org/web/eng/siteengo.nsf/html/icrc-statutes-
     080503> accessed 13 April 2008.

24   *The Geneva Convention relative to the Treatment of Prisoners of War* (adopted 12
     August 1949, entered into force 21 October 1950) UNTS 75 determines in article 10,
     that 'if protection cannot be arranged accordingly, the Detaining Power shall request
     or shall accept, subject to the provisions of this Article, the offer of the services of a
     humanitarian organization, such as the International Committee of the Red Cross, to
     assume the humanitarian functions performed by Protecting Powers under the pre-
     sent Convention'.

25   L Salomon, SW Sokolowski and R List, *Global Civil Society: an overview.* (Center for
     Social Studies, Baltimore 2003). The authors also quote the following reasons for
     such growth: (i) democracy, more specifically, parliamentary democracy; (ii) industrial
     maturity; (iii) affluence; (iv) a global communication revolution through the internet
     and air transportation; (v) retreat of the State in multiple forms, such as government
     failure, reinvigorated private market after privatizations and delegated welfare to cha-
     rities; and (vi) new citizen attitudes, mostly toward a better quality of life.

26 Amnesty International, *2009/2010* Annual Report (London, 2010), available at http://www.amnesty.org.

27 Greenpeace, Annual Report 2009 (Amsterdam, 2010), available at http://www.greenpeace.org.

28 OHCHR, *2007 Annual Report* (Geneva, 2008). <http://www.ohchr.org/Documents/Press/OHCHR_Report_07_Full.pdf> accessed 03 March 2009.

29 UNEP, *2008 Annual Report* (Nairobi, 2009). <http://www.unep.org/PDF/AnnualReport/2008/AnnualReport2008_en_web.pdf> accessed 03 March 2009.

30 American National Red Cross, *2010 Audited Financial Statements* (Washington, 2010), available at http://www.redcross.org/governance.

31 Americares, *Annual Report 2010* (Stamford, 2010), available at http://www.americares.org.

32 Nature Conservancy, *2010 Annual Report* (Arlington, 2010) available at http://www.nature.org

33 See the *Répertoires des organisations internationales* published by the League of Nations in Geneva, in 1921, 1923 and 1926. The existence of the Directory, however, did not mean that such organizations had a similar consultative status as the one observed in article 71 of the UN Charter. In 1921, studies were made to extend to all organizations the status granted to the national Red Cross organizations by the article 25 of the League's covenant, but the Council, on 2 July 1923, prohibited such organizations to directly address the League of Nations.

34 UNESCO Encyclopedia of Life Support System, Article 1.44.3.7 Non-Governmental Organizations. <www.eolss.net> accessed 24 March 2009.

35 EPIL, Vol. III (1992) 614.

36 T Becker, *Terrorism and the State: Rethinking the rules of state responsibility* (Hart Publishing, Portland 2006) 279.

37 L Salomon, *Global Civil Society: an overview* (n 25) 1.

38 Discrepant definitions can be seen, *e.g.*, at EPIL v III (1992) 612; LS Wisenberg 'Protecting Human Rights Activists and NGOs: What Can Be Done? 13 HRQ n 4 (1991) 529; P Daillier and A Pellet, *Droit international public* (7th ed LGDJ, Paris 2002) 643; G Breton-Le Goff, *L'Influence des Organisations non Gouvernamentales (ONG) sur la negotiation de quelques instruments internationaux* (Bruylant, Brussels 2001) 14; AK Lindbom. *Non-Governmental Organizations in International Law* (CUP, Cambridge, 2005) 46; C Chinkin, 'The Role of Non-Governmental Organisations in Standard Setting, Monitoring and Implementation of Human Rights', in J Norton, M Andenas and M Focter, *The Changing World of International Law in the Twenty-First Century: a tribute to the late Kenneth R. Simmonds*, (Kluwer Law, The Hague 1998) 47.

39 UN Doc E/43Rev.2 (1946).

40 UN Docs E/1661 and E/1619, Corr.1, Corr.2 and Add.1 (1950).

41 UN Doc E/4548 (1968).

42 This aspect is particularly problematic and it is at the root of the Southern countries' skepticism about the good faith and 'global' reasons of Northern countries NGOs. See, in this aspect, K Sellars, *The Rise and Rise of Human Rights* (Sutton Publishing, London 2002).

43 In Brazil, Law 9.790/1999 introduced the concept of a Public Interest Civil Society Organization as a title to be granted to private, nonprofit organizations operating in the public sphere, provided that such organizations have neither been created by any governmental body or political party nor have government appointed board members. For an appraisal of the origins of the law, see E Szazi, 'Creating a Favorable Environment for Philanthropy and Civil Society: the case of Brazil' in C Sanborn and

F Portocarrero, *Philanthropy and Social Change in Latin America* (Harvard University Press, Cambridge 2005) 307.

44 In this aspect, it is interesting that some scholars mentions the creation of a variant acronym for NGOs supported by governments, i.e. GONGOS, or government-or-iented/organized non-governmental organizations, which achieved notoriety during the Cold War because many so-called NGOs owed their very existence and entire fi-nancial support to communist governments in the Soviet bloc or authoritarian ones in the Third World. Such NGOs also existed in the West (particularly in the US, where we can quote the NED - National Endowment for Democracy), these often being a front for administration activities. See, in this regard, TG Weiss and L Gordenker (eds) *NGOs, the UN, and Global Governance* (Lynne Rienner, Boulder 1996) 18.

45 This, however, is not an undisputed understanding, since some authors support that it can comprise groups not established as legal entities.

46 In this aspect, we believe that is worth to anticipate that the first initiative in this field was made by the *Institut de Droit International*, which adopted a draft convention regarding the legal condition of international associations in 1912. We shall resume this issue on Chapter 6.

47 The conditions for admission have been defined in ECOSOC Res. 1996/31 (25 July 1996) paras. 1 to 4, 8 to 13 and 61 (h).

48 A. Normandin, *Du Statut Juridique des Association Internationales* (n 21) 122.

49 Art 9 – Le Gouvernement belge est autorisé à conclure avec les Etats étrangers des traités pour l'établissement d'un statut international des associations scentifiques in-ternationales sur les bases de la présente loi.

50 (adopted 24 April 1986, entered into force 1 January 1991) ETS 124.

51 Associations and foundations constituted in foreign countries, even without interna-tional activities, can be recognized under the *Convention on the Recognition of Legal Personality of Foreign Companies* (adopted 1 June 1956, not entered into force yet due to ratification by only three States).

52 ECOSOC Res. 288 B (X) 27 February 1950) paras 5 and 8.

53 ECOSOC Res. 1296/68 (23 May 1968) para 4.

54 ECOSOC Res. 1296/98 (23 May 1968) paras 5, 6 and 7.

55 According to the UN DESA/NGO Branch, in 1996, 79% of the NGOs were head-quartered in North America and Europe. In 2007, the participation of those Northern continents had been reduced to 66% < http://esango.un.org/paperless/Web?page=static&content=intro > accessed 20 March 2009.

56 Res 288 B (X) (27 February 1950) paras 3 and 15 to 18; Res 1296 (XLIV) (23 May 1968) paras 2 and 15 to 19; Res 1996/31 (25 July 1996) paras 8 and 21 to 26.

57 P Daillier and A Pellet, *Droit international public*, (n 38) 644.

58 L Salomon, *Global Civil Society: an overview.* (n 25)

59 Just to cite one entity, the IUCN - International Union for Conservation of Nature and Natural Resources, is a Switzerland based NGO that maintains the Environmental Law Centre, in Bonn, Germany, an important center of legal studies in comparative and international law, supporting the Environmental Law Information System, the most relevant data center on national environmental law and political documents on the subject. Additionally, it was appointed to perform the duties of Secretariat in the 1971 Ramsar Convention. Hence, in the case of the IUCN, should it be categorized as an environmentalist, documentary, scientific or po-litical NGO?

60 On the subject we can mention that article 1 of the Strasbourg Convention sets a con-dition that the candidate NGO must have a *non-profit-making aim of international uti-lity*, lacking any other reference to its funding structure, and that paragraph 13 of the

ECOSOC RES 1996/31 just defines that the *basic resources of the organization shall be derived in the main part from contributions of national affiliates or other components or from individual members.*

61 This aspect is relevant and often leads to conceptual confusion between revenue and profit. See, *e.g.* EPIL that divides NGOs into two kinds, those with non-profit and those with economic aims, such as multinational corporations. EPIL v III (1992) 612.

62 Under this perspective, we can name the several private hospitals, schools, environmental consultancies, human rights law firms, security companies and, more recently, as the Iraq war has shown, the private armies euphemistically called "Private Military Contractors". On the latter, see N Roseman, 'The Privatization of Human Rights Violations – Business Impunity or Corporate Responsibility? The case of Human Rights Abuses and Torture in Iraq' (2007) Non-State Actors and International Law v 7 77.

63 Para 57 (b) determines that the existence of substantiated evidence of influence from proceeds resulting from internationally recognized criminal activities such as illicit drug trade, money-laundering or the illegal arms trade may lead to the suspension or withdraw.

64 Article 1, This Convention shall apply to associations, *foundations* and other private institutions which satisfy the following conditions: (...)

65 UN Doc. E/AC.70/1994/5 (26 May 1994) para 9.

66 OECD Financial Action Task Force on Money Laundering, 'Combating the abuse of non-profit organizations, international best practices' (Report) (11 October 2002) < http://www.fatf-gafi.org/dataoecd/39/19/34033761.pdf> accessed 03 March 2009.

67 US Department of State, 'Guiding Principles on Non-governmental Organizations' (Report) (14 December 2006) < HTTP://www.state.gov/g/drl/rls/77771.htm> accessed 03 March 2009.

68 See, also, G Breton-Le Goff, *L'Influence des Organisations non Gouvernamentales* (n 38) 203.

CHAPTER 1

Legitimacy, Foundations and Sources in International Law

1.1   Overview

This essay addresses the participation and role of people in international law, through the non-governmental organizations, those private born, public oriented bodies that we have endeavored to define in the previous chapter. NGOs regard themselves as legitimate voices of the people in the international arena. A noticeable trend in State behavior, which will be observed throughout this essay, granting NGOs greater participation in international fora and organizations, provides apparent evidence of the recognition of that legitimacy.

The forthcoming chapters will appraise the NGOs under each of the sources of international law to verify to what extent they support our claim that international NGOs are legitimate expressions of the natural right of individuals to participate in the public affairs conducted in the international realm, which, due to this circumstance, cannot be regarded as a State-only sphere.

NGOs are recognized as legal entities under the major legal systems of the world and are notably present in the conduct of public affairs in democratic countries. Their recognition under international law is not as clear. Of course, one can argue that, when observed through the prism of national legal systems, even international law is not that clear. But, if we endeavor to regard international law as a separate legal system aimed at preserving *peace*,[1] then we will be able to observe that it is composed of mandatory and permissive rules and principles that regulate international rights and duties of States, organizations and individuals, built on fundaments and sources above and beyond any specific national legal system.[2]

International law, in contrast to municipal law, is not restricted to a certain national territory. It is composed of rules that, at one end, regulate enterprises located in small portions of land in border countries, *e.g.* the Asuncion Treaty adopted by Brazil and Paraguay to regulate the Itaipu Hydroelectric Dam,[3] and also, at the other end, by rules that regulate situations outside of our planet Earth, such as the Outer Space Treaty.[4] The existence of rules at the international level does also not imply in the

identification of any State structure similar to those observed in national legal models, usually regarded as fundamental features for the legitimacy of
any such rules. After all, there is no legislative body to pass 'ordinary international laws' systematically arranged, and international law has neither
established an executive branch for governing nor a judiciary body with
comprehensive power for solving conflicts and enforcing obedience to
those rules.

This apparently chaotic or under-developed picture of international law
hasn't hindered its emergence as a legal discipline, especially since the
nineteenth century, when Europe engaged in its 'civilizing mission' of the
world and needed a rational-legal support for its efforts.[5] It also fostered
the birth of hundreds of intergovernmental organizations with an extensive
public bureaucracy for operating and serving shared interests of each and
all constituencies, a structure that would certainly have pleased Hegel and
Weber.[6]

The absence of legislative, executive and judiciary bodies; rules issued
by different sources, with a different scope, nature and territorial application; institutions that are objects and also subjects of law; actors that are
not subjects; all of these discrepancies but still a system. This is international law and, in this chapter, we will explore to what extent it is capable
of dealing with the legitimacy of its own rules, actors and subjects.

1.2   Legitimacy: a permanent quest

In an effort to conceptualize legitimacy, Thomas Franck defined it as 'a
property of a rule or rule-making institution which itself exerts a pull toward compliance on those addressed normatively because those addressed
believe that the rule or institution has come into being and operates in accordance with generally accepted principles of right process'.[7] In the same
tone, Boyle and Chinkin, concisely defined it as being the 'normative belief that a rule or institution ought to be obeyed'.[8]

Historically, the core idea of legitimacy has been centered on the figure
of the State, and in the recognition, by the governed, of its authority, expressed by its capacity to enact and enforce binding rules. Individuals, as
Kelsen[9] wrote, 'are not actually subordinated to the individual from
whom the norm emanates, but to the order that delegates the authority to
this man; not to the lawmaker; but to the law; to the law on account of
which the lawmaker is a lawmaker; to the constitution which has granted
him competence to issue laws'. The legitimacy of the acts of State has
been a preeminent issue at national level, and a central problem of modern political and social philosophy, addressed distinctly by two main tra-
ditions: the Continental-European Enlightenment and the Anglo-American
Liberalism.

The Continental Enlightenment philosophy is embodied in the concept of *Rechtstaat,* a State administered by a rational bureaucracy that has no other political objective but to implement the laws enacted by the representatives of the people, aimed at the promotion of social and economic progress. While expressing the prevalence of the sovereignty of the people over that of the State, the Enlightenment philosophy circumscribed the legitimacy of the acts of State to the boundaries established by democratically enacted written laws, in an attempt to eliminate, or minimize, the risk of the State's abuse of power.

Taking a different angle, Anglo-American Liberalism, advocated the primacy of the fundamental rights of the people over governmental authority, in an attempt to define a legal system in which any act of government, even if supported by laws enacted by the parliament, would be deemed illegitimate if it should threaten the life, liberty or private property of the individuals. The power was in the hands of the individuals. It was quintessentially represented by the Declaration of Independence of the United States, which prescribes in its famous preamble that 'governments are instituted among men, deriving their just powers from the consent of the governed', a marked contractarianism.[10]

Consequently, while the Enlightenment philosophers sought to establish popular sovereignty over state sovereignty through a civilizing effort to implement a sustainable democracy, American Liberalism sought to establish the concept of rule of law over governmental authority to guarantee fundamental individual rights and freedoms. In America, the Hegelian mighty *State* has been reduced to *government.*

Yet, as argued by Heiskanen, 'while Enlightenment is more concerned with social progress and the welfare of the people than with the property rights of individuals, and while Liberalism is more interested in the happiness and prosperity of its citizens than in the promotion of a welfare state, the fact remains that both operate within the same conceptual framework – the relationship between the state/government and civil society (people/citizens)'.[11]

If the State is the 'who' and the law is the 'what', legitimacy certainly addresses the 'why'. Franck endeavored to answer the question affirming that it was the 'belief' of the addressees that the rule or institution was operating according to generally accepted principles of *right process.* If individuals, the ultimate addressees of any law, have to believe that the lawmaking process and/or the exercise of authority are legitimate, then, a 'how' question, related to the process, necessarily arises.

At a national level, the relationship between the state/government and civil society (people/citizens) is nowadays supported in the internationally recognized principle of self-determination of the peoples, by which citizens have a legitimate 'originary' power to *create* a State, to *reorganize* it, or even to *extinguish* it.[12] It is also supported by the rise of human rights and the consolidation of liberal democracy as the generally pursued form of government. These pillars form the foundations of a re-emerging understanding that the contractarian metaphor is still valid, a theme that we will address more extensively in Chapter 7.

However, if individuals have broad power to define the States in which they live, these same States resist in giving them more room to participate in the shaping of the legal order under which the States they have defined operate, despite increasing evidence toward enhanced participation.[13]

Apparently, the circumscription of the debate regarding legitimacy to national boundaries hindered academic research in the subject and its expansion in the international realm. Franck pointed out that international law was a 'no go' area for philosophers of law.[14] Charlesworth and Coicaud noted that 'questions of international legitimacy have received secondary attention' over time.[15] Similarly, Clark argued that 'in the discussions of international relations, the idea of legitimacy has not always proved a popular term of reference, and has more often been self-consciously eschewed'.[16]

Several reasons may be raised for such a lack of interest on behalf of scholars in addressing the question of legitimacy in international law. Perhaps one of the most straightforward reasons was raised by Brunée and Toope: 'in popular parlance, the world is a jungle, and the law of the jungle is simple: the strongest win'.[17] The 'legitimacy' of any rule, act or claim, hence, would be supported by the strength of the ruler, actor or claimant, as evidenced, for example, in the civilizing mission[18] of the European countries while partitioning Africa amongst themselves in the Berlin Conference of 1885, or in the heavy penalties imposed to Germany by the Versailles Treaty of 1919.

Such a claim is clearly influenced by the realist school of international relations theory, which, in brief, supports that State conduct is determined by its relative power and interests, and that international law is the expression of reciprocal deeds built upon those interests and relative power. It has also found an echo in the understanding of some legal scholars, such as De Visscher, who argued that some States have heavier footprints than others while shaping international custom,[19] and, more recently, Rosalyn Higgins, who wrote that reciprocity is a 'central element' for the basis of obligation.[20] It was also evidenced in the NATO bombing of Yugoslavia in 1999 and the US-led invasion of Iraq in 2003, both conducted by heavy foot printer States without previous UN Security Council authorization.

If, arguably, the legitimacy of law at the international level depends on the 'adhesion' of the States, whether by consent or consensus, at the national level the core idea of legitimacy has been historically centered on the figure of the State and on the justification of its capacity to establish rules that ought to be obeyed by the people it governs. Several features must be present to make an authority and its acts and rules legitimate.

These features gravitate around the understanding of what is right and just. It is also construed based on the idea of legality which, in either the Enlightenment's *Rechtstaat* or the Liberalism's primacy of fundamental rights, aims at constraining abuse of authority.

A given authority may be deemed legitimated if it has been previously empowered according to the consent of those who will be bound by its acts; its acts will be legitimated if taken according to determined fair pre-established rules of procedure, and both will have legitimacy if the outcome is deemed acceptable by those who will obey, compared to what they regard as right and just.

Fuller, for example, sustained that respect for law ('fidelity') relies on a perception of legitimacy arisen out of the fulfillment of eight internal criteria of legality (the 'internal morality of law'), which, according to his own words, is a 'procedural version of natural law'.[21] Such criteria are: legal norms must be general, prohibiting, requiring or permitting certain conduct; they must also be promulgated, and therefore accessible to the public; they should not be retroactive, but prospective; they must be clear; they should avoid contradictions, not requiring or permitting or prohibiting at the same time; law must be realistic and not demand the impossible; its requirements of citizens must be relatively constant; and there should be congruence between the norms and the action of officials operating under the law.

According to Brunée and Toope, Fuller's eighth criterion is a fundamental element for understanding the failures in international law, for it expresses that the enforceability of law does not rely on the power of sanction, but on congruence between the law and State behavior.[22] When, for instance, the US rejects the jurisdiction of the International Criminal Court and its military disregards international law in its war on terror, being upheld by its federal courts,[23] or NATO intervenes in Kosovo without UN Security Council Authorization, it is a 'signal that international law is becoming even less relevant than it has been to the solution of major international problems'[24] and the entire legitimacy of the international system of rules of war is put at risk by heavy foot printer States.

If such congruence may harm the system, it can also strengthen it. With respect to NGOs, there has been increasing awareness of their importance toward enhancing the legitimacy of international law-making in general, and intergovernmental organizations (IGOs) authority, in particular. This awareness is embodied in several hard law provisions granting NGOs the right to take part in debates within the UN System and in several soft law arrangements for joint work, congruently confirmed by State and IGO behavior in conferences, programmes and activities in several fields, to an extent that, as we will see in Chapter 4, was capable of creating Customary International Law.

Brunée and Toope, relying on the theories that Fuller had conceived for the domestic level, have construed their own theory for international law, which they called interactional theory of law. According to these authors, when shared understandings and rules met the criteria of legality, the actors will be able to pursue their purposes and organize their interactions through law, generating 'fidelity' to the legal system. For them, the increasing participation of actors other than States – including NGOs - in the international realm is 'indicative of the potential for major shifts in the breadth of international legal interaction', *indeed requiring it*, because of the need for reciprocity in the construction of the law, a task that 'demands an extension of society at the international level beyond the sphere of states'. Furthermore, they argue that 'influential norms will not emerge in the absence of processes that allow for the active participation of relevant social actors'; only when law is produced through an interactional framework with broad participation can it be said that the law is legitimate, and limited participation in norm building results in a legitimacy deficit, because 'citizens in domestic systems, and states and other actors at the international level are not consumers (of law): they are active agents in the continuing enterprise of law-making, through the elaboration of custom, treaty and soft law'.[25]

Their answer to the 'how' question possesses a strong argument, indeed a very strong one. It is unequivocal that broader participation intuitively enhances the legitimacy of international law-making yet other authors did not go that far.

Thomas Franck, acknowledging that international law lacks the coercive power observed in national legal systems, posed a stellar question: *Why do powerful nations obey powerless rules?* According to him, they behave so 'because they perceive the rule and its institutional penumbra to have a high degree of legitimacy.'[26] And, considering that there are thousands of rules, we can intuitively assume that some have higher (or lower) degrees of legitimacy than others. Why should a purported rule have more 'compliance pull' than others? According to Franck, it depends on four factors: *determinacy, symbolic validation, coherence* and *adherence*. Only when all features are present in a rule or rule process will it exert a strong pull on states to comply.[27]

At first sight, *determinacy* can be taken as synonymous of clarity, or the capacity of a rule to pass a clear and transparent message to its addressees. But determinacy is not just a matter of textual clarity or transparency, because it encompasses the whole range of plausible meanings of the rule. Let's take, for example, the 'nongovernmental organizations' which were granted consultative status with the ECOSOC by the UN Charter: one can say that the text makes reference to an organization that is not part of a government – this is the clarity dimension. However, several types of organizations fall within such a scope, whether they are profit-oriented or not. Considering that it was a newly coined expression, the UN Charter provision introduced an element of uncertainty, an issue that we have dealt with in the preliminary chapter. Fortunately, 'a rule with low textual determinacy may overcome that deficit if it is open to a process of clarification by an authority recognized as legitimate by those to whom the rule is addressed'.[28] The ECOSOC endeavored to carry out such a task when it worked to remedy such a deficit through the regulations on the consultative status of international NGOs (1946, 1950, 1968 and 1996), which were openly discussed (although not voted upon) with NGOs.

If determinacy is the linguistic element of legitimacy, *symbolic validation* provides its cultural and anthropological dimension. According to Franck, it can be observed in the several specialized agencies of the UN that, while ensuring equality of participation, provide a symbol of the equality of States in international law, counterbalancing the empirical evidence of inequality of power.[29] Similarly, it is arguable that when the UN Charter provided that the peoples of the world could interact with the UN through governmental organizations – the States – but also through *non*governmental organizations, it symbolically recognized their right to self-determination and, also, their democratic entitlement to act in the international realm.

Coherence is also essential to legitimacy. Franck asserted that 'the legitimacy of a rule is determined in part by the degree to which that rule is practiced coherently; conversely, the degree to which a rule is applied coherently in practice will depend in part on the degree to which it is perceived as legitimate for those applying it'.[30] As we will observe in Chapter 4, there is a consistent practice of major worldwide multilateral international organizations regarding the participation of NGOs in their decision-making proceedings, supported either by treaty or customary provisions, as well as an established state practice to allow their participation in major conferences. These practices are not only consistent – repeated through time; they are also coherent with the democratic (equality of states, one vote each) principle and with the right of self-determination enshrined in the UN Charter.

Lastly, let us examine *adherence*. It is meant as 'the vertical nexus between a primary rule of obligation and an hierarchy of secondary rules identifying the sources of rules and establishing normative standards that define how rules are to be made, interpreted, and applied.'[31] But, what makes a treaty (the primary rule) binding if apparently there is no secondary rule in international law capable of exerting a pull toward its compliance?

For the positivists, such as John Austin (1790-1859), no such pull existed because all laws were enacted by a sovereign person or a sovereign body of persons to members of a given independent political society wherein that person or body was sovereign.[32] Thus, from his perspective, the will of the sovereign was the will of the State, and international law could not be properly regarded as 'law", inasmuch as there was no sovereign at the international level. By the same token, George Jellinek (1851 – 1911) postulated that States were moral persons whose wills were subject to no external limitation but that could be reversibly self-limited to achieve certain needs.[33] Such theories lack coherence: if States have the free will to engage, then they could not remain bound if they withdrew their consent, as observed, for instance, in the *jus cogens* provision in article 43 of the Vienna Convention on the Law of Treaties[34], because, in that circumstance, their will would be submitted to an 'independent will' above their own; contradicting the original free will. Furthermore, actual international practice has continuously shown, for instance, that new States are bound by international customs, even if they did not participate in their definition or do not like them. The pull, therefore, exists.

States are bound because they are members of a community that believes so. Franck noted that 'the belief of states, governments, judges, and the public that such a rule hierarchy exists, and their tendency to act on that belief, is a sufficient, if contingent, proof of the thing believed', being 'the will of the sovereign states subordinated to obligations that derive from their status as members of a community'.[35]

The theory championed by Franck prescribes that the legitimacy of a rule depends on its capacity to exert compliance pull upon the States. But, as we have seen, such a capacity does not rely solely on the 'independent will' of the States, but rather on their membership to the community of nations, following that a primary rule (a treaty or custom) must be validated by adherence to a secondary rule (about rule-making) and to an ultimate rule of recognition of the binding character of the treaty/custom to achieve its pursued legitimacy.

In another work on Democratic Governance, Franck added a new indicator, *pedigree*, referring to the depth of the rule's roots in a historical process.[36] According to him, self-determination provided the pedigree of a democratic entitlement comprehending three different generations or 'building blocks': self-determination as the first; freedom of expression as the second; and finally, the right to free and open elections as the third. But it appears to be unquestionable in current days that the right to participate, directly or not, in public affairs ensured by the International Covenant of Civil and Political Rights (CCPR),[37] has gone beyond the participation in free elections.

A fourth building block, enhancing the participation of individuals in public affairs, must be added to effectively and properly answer the 'how' question embedded in Franck's definition of legitimacy. Throughout this essay, we will share Brunée and Toope's convictions that a broader participation of relevant actors in norm-building in international law is a fundamental feature for its legitimacy. We will endeavor to demonstrate that NGOs are actors capable of enhancing the process of international law-making and the authority of intergovernmental organizations, contributing to the reduction of their perceived legitimacy deficit.

In order to understand why individuals have the right to act in the international realm, and what the material sources of the legal legitimacy of the subjects of international law are, in the forthcoming sections of this chapter we will briefly appraise the foundations of international law and its sources, understanding by sources of international law the methods of creating international law.

1.3   Foundations: a brief appraisal on its historic development

Legal doctrine register the flourishing of international law in the treaties that ended the Thirty Years' War, signed in Münster and Osnabruck in 1648 – called the Peace of Westphalia – and consecrated the rule *cujus regio, ejus religio* (literally, 'in his region, his religion') previously agreed upon by the Religious Peace of Augsburg (1555), giving birth to the concept of a modern nation-state based on a Western (European) notion of sovereignty. We know that this notion is not crystal-clear, but, borrowing the words of Kelsen, 'whatever may be understood by this word of many meanings, and however much the definitions of this concept may differ from one another, most of them agree on one point: the thing characterized as "sovereign", whether it be an order, a community, an organ, or a power, must be regarded as the highest, above which there can be no higher, authority limiting the function of the sovereign entity, binding the sovereign'.[38]

The first systematic study on sovereignty was written in 1576 by Jean Bodin (1530 – 1596) and defined the State as *'un government juste de plusieur Familles et des choses qui leur étoient communes sus le puvoir absolut'*.[39] His approach was highly influenced by the political facts he observed in the 16th century, particularly in France, a unified kingdom which had nonetheless been deeply weakened by religious distensions and eight civil wars.[40] He understood that the remedy for such a situation was the concentration of power in the hands of the sovereign and, to support his idea, conceived his brainchild of associating the family to the State, and the father to the sovereign. Since the father was ultimately responsible for maintaining the order in his home – a territory – and for guaranteeing the well-being and happiness of his family members – the people of the nation – he was entitled to superior power (*summa potestas*) to rule his home – the sovereignty. This superior power consisted in his being granted permission to lay down the rules but did not imply that the sovereign was bound by them.[41] According to Bodin, the sovereign was only bound by the Laws of God and Nature (Reason), the laws common to all nations, and the customary fundamental laws of the kingdom. His approach, supported in the sacrosanct institution of the family in a Catholic nation, tired of conflicts, produced an outstanding impact on France and contributed to the birth of the absolutist monarchy with the House of Bourbon, established at the accession of Henry IV to the Throne of France, in 1590.

Although an apparent creation of the Modern Era, international law has deeper roots, laid down in far ancient grounds. Law was paramount among the cultural achievements of ancient Rome and the rules of Roman Law, together with their references to the conception of Natural Law, were compiled by order of the Byzantine emperor Justinian I to form the *Corpus Juris Civilis* (527 – 565). This magnificent work was written in Latin and certainly reached the fragments of the former Western Roman Empire, where it was considered the Holy Roman Empire's secular law, nevertheless being abandoned during the Dark Ages. Notwithstanding, it definitely influenced Canon Law.[42] Feudalism, despite being regarded as the antithesis of the centralized State ruled by a secular power, contributed to the further development of the conception of sovereignty through the creation of the suzerain–vassal linkage, which established a territorial connection of ruling power and loyalty, the embryo of the later idea of nationality.[43] Mostly, it also kept alive the notion of a unique human genre, submitted to one superior law that no one could revoke: the Natural Law, that would flourish after the Middle Ages.

The greatest theologian to address the idea of Natural Law was St. Thomas Aquinas (1225 – 1274), in his great unfinished work *Summa Theologica* (1265 – 1274), considered the epitome of the perennial jurisprudence of the Natural Law.[44] According to him, in the scholastic tradition, all laws come from the Divine Reason that rules the universe, and 'the natural law is nothing else than the rational creature's participation in the eternal law'.[45] Once the Natural Law is codified, it becomes human law (positive law). However, human laws can be unreasonable or unjust if they are contrary to the Natural Law. In these circumstances, they 'are no longer a law but a perversion of law'[46] and, thus, 'should not be obeyed'.[47] Most relevantly, he supported the concept that a lawful authority could be legitimately removed if he behaved or acted contrary to the Natural Law.[48]

The Natural Law and human (positive) laws are, thus, complementary elements, where the Natural Law, constituting the base of the juridical conscience of humankind, supports positive law, providing its binding character, and positive law, in turn, gives a more ordinate form to the principles of Natural Law.[49]

St. Thomas Aquinas' work is regarded as the definitive Catholic doctrine and has remained authoritative within the orbit of Catholic thought, while also notably influencing non-Catholic authors.[50] Furthermore, his *Summa Theologica* influenced the work of another Dominican priest, who is regarded as one of the founders of modern international law: Francisco de Vitoria.

Francisco de Vitoria (1480 – 1546) left no published work, but his lectures were compiled by his alumni and published after his death under distinctive titles, collectively known as *Relectiones*. In *De Potestate Civili* (1528) he argued that people had the immanent power to rule themselves, arisen out of Natural Law and God. Per contra, since it would not be naturally possible to exercise such power individually, it was placed in the hands of the sovereign, who could make laws, but only in the benefit of the Republic ('Si la ley no es util a la republica ya no es ley'). It is worthy to quote also that, according to Vitoria, the sovereign was bound by the laws that he issued ('las leyes dadas a la república obligan a todos. Luego, aunque estén dadas por el rey, obligan al mismo rey').[51]

We can attribute to Vitoria a vision far ahead of his times, not only because, as we have seen, he supported the idea that the King was bound by the Law (an idea that would later be rejected by Bodin) but also because in another compiled lecture, *De Indis et De Jure Belli* (1532), he affirmed that the '(Holy Roman) Emperor was not the lord of the whole world' neither was the Pope 'the civil or temporal lord of the whole world, in the proper sense of civil lordship and power'[52] and that the native people of the Americas had princes with legal positions similar to those of Christian princes and were 'not to be warred into subjection or despoiled of their property if they had given to the Spaniards unhindered freedom to preach the gospel, and this whether they accepted the faith or not'.[53] Christendom was no longer the whole world, which was composed of sovereign nations with different faiths and political arrangements, living together in a *societas naturalis,* a political community ('totus orbis, qui aliquo modo est una republica') with duties of solidarity and the power to establish fair laws for the common good (*jus gentium)* that not only had the strength of an agreement but the strength of Law.[54] We cannot assume, however, that Vitoria was a liberal thinker in contemporary terms since he lived in the 15th century and advocated ecclesiastical and papal authority. Additionally, one can observe in his writings that he considered resistance to missionaries a cause for just war and supported the replacement of the pagan princes by Catholic rulers, which did not properly indicate rigorous equality of Christian and pagan princes and much less equality of States. Notwithstanding, his ideas were ahead of their time and he could be regarded as a forefather of the concept of self-determination of the peoples, which, as we will study in chapter 5 of this essay, gave birth to the right of the individuals to participate in world governance, as observed, *e.g.,* in the Aarhus Convention.[55] The ideas of Francisco de Vitoria and the scholastics had a great influence on the work of another founding father of international law and student of the University of Leiden: Hugo Grotius (1583 – 1645).

Grotius' first relevant work is *Mare Liberum* (1609), in which he argued that the sea was international territory and that all nations had the right to use it for trade and navigation. This work is a part of his first known legal assignment, a treatise defending the seizure of a Portuguese ship in the Strait of Singapore by a flotilla of the Dutch East India Company (VOC) in 1601, when the Netherlands were at war with Spain and Portugal, then being under Spanish ruling.[56] One can identify its roots in the ideas of Francisco de Vitoria, since Grotius asserted that the Portuguese could claim no right of possession to the East Indies because those lands had already been inhabited by the natives before the arrival of its first ships and that the Pope could not transfer its *dominium* because he was not the civil or temporal lord of the whole world. Therefore, again recalling the ideas of Vitoria, the Dutch had the right to travel to those lands and carry on trade with its inhabitants.

In our point of view, a remarkable contribution made by Grotius to the 21st century is the idea that people have rights over common things, whose use is subject to two natural laws: 'that all surely might use common things without the damage of all and, for the rest, every man contented with his portion shall abstain from another's'.[57] One could see here the remote offspring of the contemporary idea of sustainable development.

Also noteworthy is a passage of his *Defense of Chapter V of Mare Liberum,* where he made a distinction between things that can become private and things that remain in common, quoting an affirmation made by Cicero that nothing was private by nature to conclude that 'it is evident that community is prior to property' and that necessity authorized to 'make common again things formerly owned'.[58] Grotius resumed this idea in his most important work, *De Jure Belli ac Pacis* (1625), where he asserted in Book II, Chapter 2, § 6 that:

> 'Let us now see whether men may not have a right to enjoy in common those things that are already become the properties of other persons; which question will at first seem strange, since the establishment of property seems to have extinguished all the right that arose from the state of community. But it is not so; for we are to consider the intention of those who first introduced the property of goods. There is all the reason in the world to suppose that they designated to deviate as little as possible from the rules of natural equity; and so it is with this restriction, that the right of proprietors have been established; for if even written laws ought to be thus explained, as far as possible; much more ought we to put that favorable construction on things introduced by a custom not written, and whose extent therefore is not determined by the signification of terms.
>
> From whence it follows, first, that in a case of absolute necessity, that ancient right of using things, as if they remained common, must revive, and be in full force: for in all laws of human institutions and

> consequently, in that of property too, such cases seem to be excepted.[59]

It is important to notice that Grotius didn't mean that the 'privileges of necessity' could be invoked freely, since he conditioned them to the previous adoption of any and all other means to avoid the necessity; to the non-existence of equal necessity by the owners, a situation in which they would have an advantage, and finally, to the obligation to restitute it.[60] We have addressed this aspect of his work with the purpose of raising another important contribution made by Grotius to the development of international law, i.e., the idea that humankind had a 'right' over some 'things' that could not be appropriated by someone in clear disadvantage to the rest of the society based on human laws that were, thus, enacted against the law of the nature. In the 17th century, Grotius regarded the high seas. In the 21st century, could one regard the right to development?

In *De Jure Belli ac Pacis* (1625), Grotius, within the tradition of Natural Law, sustained that 'amongst Things peculiar to Man is his Desire of Society, that is, a certain Inclination to live with those of his own kind, not in any Manner whatever, but peaceably, and in a Community regulated according to the best of his Understanding'.[61]

Therefore, Grotius, following Aristotle, supports the notion that men have an innate inclination to live in society in a peaceful manner according to certain rules regarding what is right and due, which have arisen from of the rational nature of man. He, thus, removes natural law from theology by his famous statement that law of nature would be valid even if 'which cannot be admitted without utmost wickedness, that there is no God and that human affairs do not concern to Him'.[62] This sociable instinct, which differs from the one observed in animals because it is based on Reason, is the 'Fountain of Right'.[63] Human nature, thus, is the mother of Natural Law, and positive law arises from the latter, aiming at living peaceably in a society. Grotius was neither a pure naturalist nor a pure positivist, rather, he proposed a 'workable synthesis of Natural Law and State practice'.[64] As Nussbaum notes, 'Grotius' Natural Law may be called the rule of reasonableness with little left for a truly divine law'.[65]

De Jure Belli ac Pacis is a treatise about private rights, and wars to defend violated rights with the aim of reaching peace.[66] It has unequivocally contributed to the definition of the fundaments of international law. From Grotius' perspective, one can understand peace as the absence of war or peace as the respect for rights. That is the idea that arises from the aforementioned work. Peace is the main purpose of the United Nations, and, as we have seen at the beginning of this chapter, it is at the core of the understanding of international law as a legal body aimed at preserving peace, composed of mandatory and permissive rules and principles that regulate international rights and duties of States, organizations and individuals.

However, peace is far more than the absence of war. If we take, for example, the Nobel Peace Prize, it is awarded 'to the person who shall have done the most or the best work for fraternity between nations, for the abolition or reduction of standing armies and for the holding and promotion of peace congresses'.[67] The list of laureates includes several individuals and even organizations that were not properly or directly involved in situations of wars or armed conflicts, which, at least from the Norwegian Nobel Committee's perspective, leads to a more comprehensive understanding of Peace.[68] Based on the more recent laureates, it also embraces environmental protection (2007), advancing economic and social opportunities for the poor (2006), sustainable development and democracy (2005) and human rights, including the struggle for the rights of women and children (2004, 2010 and 2011).

Peace, then, can be regarded as respect for immanent human rights. Resuming Grotius and bearing in mind the struggle for peace in the 21st century, we cannot neglect that he considers the violation of what belonged to everyone by right a justified cause for war.[69] In his epoch, he could only regard the sea, the air and the banks of sand as things common to humankind.[70] Today, one can see other things, such as human rights, 'the rights that everyone is said to have by virtue of his or her very humanity'.[71] Health, for example, is regarded by the World Health Organization as 'one of the fundamental rights of every human being' which is 'fundamental to the attainment of peace and security and is dependent upon the fullest cooperation of individuals and States.'[72]

Grotius also supported that men have a right to use those things which are another's property, if thereby there arises no detriment to the proprietor. To justify his argument, he exemplified the right to drink water from a river that was within someone else's property or a free passage through third parties' land.[73] This idea is particularly of interest in the contemporary world if we have in mind, for example, the demands of breach of patents in cases of endemic diseases such as HIV/AIDS.[74] Of course, one could not say that Grotius was exposing his particular concerns about basic human rights, since he personally supported a *Jus rectorium* where, in societies, some individuals were unequal, as that of masters and servants.[75] But the centrality that 'Common Rights' has in his work can't go unnoticed. And that is, in our opinion, his main contribution to our study of international law and to the justification that individuals can indeed interfere in the international realm to pursue a broad conception of peace.

His conception may be currently observed, for example, in article 31 of the Agreement on Trade Related Aspects of Intellectual Property Rights (TRIPS), which addresses the issue of use of protected rights without authorization from the holder.[76] This provision is considered the legitimate legal permission to the compulsory licensing in situations of 'national emergency or other circumstances of extreme urgency or in cases of public non-commercial use'. It has been invoked several times, mostly concerning patent-protected medicine for the treatment of HIV/AIDS, aiming to expand public access to essential drugs at an affordable cost.[77] This interpretation of the TRIPS has raised several concerns as to whether article 31 could be regarded as a supportive element for pro-public-health initiatives, which, as is to be expected, was challenged by developed countries and the pharmaceutical industry.[78] However, it was confirmed by the 2001 Doha Declaration on the TRIPS Agreement and Public Health, which acknowledged the importance of public health and the rights of WTO member- states, under emergency conditions, to adopt all the necessary flexibilities of TRIPS in order to protect public health.[79]

The compulsory licensing does not represent damage to the economic rights of the patent holder, considering royalties will be paid (TRIPS, article 31 'h'). It represents, however, the supremacy of the interests of the Society over exclusive economic rights, reaffirming the Grotian conception of international relations, although he 'does not explicitly distinguish a category of *human* rights from those of States or citizens or princes'.[80] We shall resume the analysis of Grotius' contribution to the 21st century debate about the limits of international law in the Conclusion, since, now, we think it is appropriate to address one of his contemporaries that also influenced international law: Pufendorf.

Samuel von Pufendorf (1632 - 1694) is considered the founder of the naturalist school of jurisprudence, which strived to identify international law completely through the law of nature, abandoning the idea of the joint existence of a positive law agreed upon by Nations, supported by Grotius.[81] In his work *De officio hominis et civis* ("On the Duties of Men and Citizens") of 1673, Pufendorf broke with the ancient tradition of legitimacy of the States, arguing that men established the States not because they needed satisfaction of their primary needs, which 'could have been abundantly satisfied through the first communities'.[82] Rather, men accepted a certain loss of natural liberty and subjection to an authority with rights of life and death to 'fortify themselves against the evils which threaten man from man'.[83] In an individualistic, voluntarist and rationalist perception, he saw the State as a humane construction aimed to protect one man from another, in spite of peaceful living in the state of nature.[84] Fear, for instance, was the amalgamating factor of citizens into the State, a moral person 'whose will, intertwined and united by virtue of the compacts of the many, is regarded as the will of all'[85] individuals that gathered into a joint agreement to form it.[86] According to Stephen Hall:

> 'The 'natural' element in the Enlightenment's conception of the natural law was not a moral, ethical and rational standard as it is in the natural law itself. Rather, it was an essentially empirical or

descriptive standard resting upon the state of nature in which people had supposedly existed before entering into their social contract.'[87]

The influence Hobbes had on Pufendorf is remarkable. Although Thomas Hobbes (1588 – 1679) was not concerned with war between nations such as were Grotius and Pufendorf, all of them worried about peace. In his *Leviathan* (1651), Hobbes, adopting a purely interest-based perspective, postulated that men were by nature equal in abilities and entitled to everything in the world. That circumstance inevitably led to conflict among men based on competition, diffidence and glory. Since men could not live securely in this state of permanent war of everyone against all, they all lived in continuous fear and danger of violent death, in a solitary, poor, nasty and brutish short life.[88] According to Hobbes, this situation was against the fundamental law of nature, *i.e*, 'to seek Peace, and follow it by all means we can, to defend ourselves'; in order to obtain peace, men – the Authors - should 'lay down the right to all things and be contented with so much liberty against other men, as he would allow other men against himself', doing it by a Contract where such rights were delegated to another person – The Actor.[89] This person was the sovereign that, therefore, had no divine right, inasmuch as his power had been received through a covenant made by all individuals that, as we've seen, lived in nature in equal conditions. Democracy, hence, is at the genesis (and *only* at the genesis) of the theory of Social Contract proposed by Hobbes, where the State has no mission other than that of preserving peace, requiring indivisible power to achieve this objective on behalf of its constituencies, who, we reinforce, have delegated their power to regulate their lives to the sovereign.

For Hobbes, men are no longer the 'political animal' conceived by Aristotle.[90] They do not have a natural inclination to live in society for the common good; rather, they 'agree' to do so for mutual advantage in a social contract metaphor. However, if Hobbes supported that such arrangement was done because individuals were rational and individualistic and were moved by fear, hence purely interest-based, the later Enlightenment authors, Locke, Rousseau and Kant, supported that the it was done on the assumption of existing prior moral and natural rights. This latter approach has been resumed in the 20th century by John Rawls, whose ideas we will discuss on chapter 7.

Once a covenant is made, it must be performed. This principle *(pacta sunt servanda)* constitutes, for Hobbes, the Fountain of Justice, seeing as before the Social Contract, no right had been delegated and every man had the right to everything; consequently, no action could be called unjust nor could anyone be called owner of something. Injustice, for him, is nothing other than 'the not Performance of Covenant' and propriety only begins to exist after the creation of a coercive power, strong enough to make men respect their covenants.[91]

Man's sociable instinct is no longer the fountain of 'Right', as Grotius had determined; the Social Contract is the fountain of 'Justice'; Society is no longer the result of an innate sociability pointed out by the jusnaturalists; instead, it is created by contract, moved by fear; Propriety, a bourgeois core value, is no longer intrinsically guaranteed, since it depends on the will of an omnipotent sovereign, whose power does not arise out of patriarchy, theocracy, divine right or strength, but rather from a covenant, a concatenated consent of all men.

The Hobbesian treatise of power and the theory of Social Contract can be clearly perceived in Pufendorf's conception that positive law could not exist in international relations, because agreements entered into by sovereigns were based on their will and, therefore, could not be regarded as true positive law, which relied on the existence of a sovereign power ruling other subjects. Hence, if there were only natural law and positive law, international law would be nothing but the 'natural law of the States'.[92]

Also influenced by Hobbes was Spinoza (1632 – 1677), whose ideas, strongly reinforcing individual liberty and freedom of expression, introduced a 'distinctively urban, egalitarian and commercial type of republicanism' that considered the democratic form as 'always the most natural, freest and best kind of state'.[93]

Spinoza considered that the power of nature was the very power of God, who had supreme power to do all things. However, he said, 'since the universal power of the whole of nature is nothing but the power of all individual things together, it flows that each individual thing has the sovereign right to do everything that it can do' or, to put it more straightforwardly, 'the right, and the order of nature, under which all human beings are born and for the most part live, prohibits nothing but what no one desires or no one can do'.[94] This entitlement to do everything in the world could be pursued according to the laws of appetite, as any intemperate person might do, or according to the laws of reason, as the wise men should do. Accordingly, to ensure that men 'would collectively have the right to all things that each individual had from nature', they would have to rely in the power and will of all of them together, instead of in the force and appetite of each individual. Thus, argued Spinoza, men 'had to make a firm decision, and reach agreement, to decide everything by the sole dictate of reason', curbing their appetites if their desires suggested things that could hurt someone else and refraining from doing 'anything to anyone they did not want done to themselves'. To achieve this and preserve the contract in its entirety with complete fidelity, he continued, men had to surrender all the power they possessed to the society, in order to make society, alone, the supreme power, with supreme natural right over all things, that had to be obeyed by everyone, either willingly or through fear of punishment. The right of such society, Spinoza called democracy, defining it as 'a united gathering of people which collectively has the sovereign right to do all that it has the power to do'.[95]

Curiously, Spinoza hasn't shared his thoughts about how this democracy should be exercised, vaguely arguing that, when constituting a state, it was indispensable that 'the entire power of decision-making should be lodged in all the people, or else in some, or else just in one'. Also curious and rather conflicting with his advocacy of democracy, are his claims that people had to defend the government with all their strength, being also obliged to carry out absolutely all the commands of the sovereign power, 'however absurd they might be', although attenuating his assertion by claiming that sovereigns, wishing to protect their position and retain power, had to direct all things by the dictate of reason, working for the common good and for the security of the whole people of the state, therefore being unlikely that they would issue absurd commands.[96]

Despite this, it is a fact that Spinoza's Theological-Political Treatise (1670) was a sound effort to strengthen individual freedoms of expression and thought and to weaken the power of the Pope and the importance of theology in the Netherlands after the end of the Thirty Year's War. By arguing that 'a state can never succeed very far in attempting to force people to speak as the sovereign power commands' and that the 'ultimate purpose of the state is to free everyone from fear so that they may live in security so far as possible' he reached the remarkable conclusions, back in the 17th century, that the 'true purpose of the state is in fact freedom' and that 'trying to control everything by law will encourage vices rather than correcting them'.[97]

It was Hegel,[98] at the beginning of the 19th century, who proposed a different perspective, in which the State was no longer a collection of individuals who gathered to form an abstract entity with anthropocentric origin; rather the State was an anthropomorphic organism with a mind of its own, fruit of the participation of every human mind. For him, individuals had to sacrifice their lives for the State, and could possess objectivity only as a member of the State, who was sovereign and could resort to war against other State if the co-existence was deemed unsatisfactory. His doctrine, followed by the positivists, supported that the State possessed unlimited rights over the individuals. The emergence of the positivist doctrine in international law is regarded as a reaction against the naturalist school of jurisprudence and also as a fruit of the termination of the Napoleonic wars, which gave birth to a homogeneous, interstate, nationalist and Eurocentric society, affected by the shift of many countries from absolutism to parliamentary governments, which would experiment an exceptional evolution in science and technology, making rational thinking prevail.[99] The prominence of positivist theories in international law relied on the notion that 'laws were basically commands issuing from a sovereign person or body' and that 'any question of ethics and morality was irrelevant to discussion of the validity of man-made laws'.[100]

This conception of international law as a *co-existence* voluntary system based on contractual arrangements made by fully sovereign States that were, hence, self-limited only according to their interests, allowed the strengthening of nationalism and absolutist theories and remained the major understanding until the end of World War I when, taking into account the two previous Peace Conferences held at The Hague in 1899 and 1907 and the creation of the League of Nations after the end of the hostilities, it gave place to a new perception of international law as a normative system aiming at *cooperation* among the States to achieve *pax perpetua*.[101]

The League was conceived to pursue cooperation among States to reach peace, in an epoch in which international society had far fewer States and was far more homogeneous than today. In 1919, the Treaty of Versailles was signed by a handful of States, mostly European. In 1920, the list of signatories to the Covenant of the League of Nations comprised only 30 States.[102] In 1945, the creation of the United Nations was approved by only 51 States. Today, the UN has 193 member-states, most of them located in Africa, the Middle East and Asia. The heterogeneity of the international society in the 21st century is a fact that will lead to a different, less 'western-like', approach to international relations, which is admitted even by the United States.[103]

Judt postulates that World War I and World War II together could be regarded as a thirty-year war, since the causes of the first conflict remained at the beginning of the second.[104] Most important, however, is the fact that the second conflict had a tremendous impact on the *civil* population, contributing to a death toll of 19 million people, more than half the total 37 million casualties in the period 1939-1945, in Europe alone. This tremendous massacre due to massive bombing and ethnical cleansing, together with the appearance of mass destruction weapons, challenged the classical rules of war and raised several humanitarian issues. Not without reason, the UN was conceived to pursue World Peace, laid down by the Universal Declaration of Human Rights; the rights that, once achieved, would lead to obtaining peace, since no war would be deemed necessary.

On the European concert, Judt asserts that the pacific and cooperative Europe that is observed today, wasn't born from the optimistic, ambitious and progressist project conceived by the idealists that defend the European Union and the euro; on the contrary, Europe was the insecure child born from anxiety, and this situation was experienced on both sides of the continent.[105] Nonetheless, the aggregation of long-standing rivaling European nations around a common and cooperative project that struggles to reduce the differences within the bloc and works to ensure to all citizens access to similar living standards, together with the participation of *individuals* in some relevant decision-making, looks, despite the tremendous difficulties experienced, like an interesting paradigm for a heterogeneous world.

Although the bipolar political world ended with the fall of the Berlin Wall in 1989 and the subsequent dismantling of the Soviet Union in 1990, currently the heterogeneity relies not only on the countries' cultural background, but also on their social and economical ones. It would be hard to affirm that the 193 UN member-states share the same interests. But cooperation is still pursued, because humankind's needs disregards boundaries. From an economic perspective, the sovereignty of the majority of these States is a myth, since they all compete for investments from transnational corporations or international financial aid and, once economical sovereignty becomes weak, political sovereignty goes the same way. The impact of the 2008 financial crisis in Iceland, Latvia and Ukraine is a remarkable example.

Therefore, a cooperative approach in international law, centered on the respect for universal human rights (particularly through the reduction of wealth inequality) and the protection of the common good (such as the environment) is a contemporary goal, which is witnessing the renaissance of the social contract theories and the recurrent invocation of Natural Law, due to the economic problems left unsolved by international positive (written or customary) law.

As we'll explore in more detail in this essay, it is necessary to definitively abandon the positivist idea that individuals, and as a consequence, NGOs, are just objects of international law, not only due to the increasing number of rules concerning international protection of human rights and access to international tribunals, whether at a global or regional level, but, mostly, because the human being has always been the ultimate concern of international law, which, as we have seen, has been constructed upon the ancient, deep and solid roots of Natural Law.[106]

In Chapter 8, we will see that the States gave birth to international organizations, entities that despite being created (thus, being objects), became subjects of international law, even without having their own nation and territory to rule, both classical – and essential - attributes for the recognition of a State. Recalling the Contractarians and adopting the Hobbesian terminology, the States, as Authors, by covenant created Actors to represent them and gave to these Actors the authority to act on their behalf. Could individuals, as Authors, in another form of democracy or expression of Natural Law, create NGOs as Actors that, thus, have authority to represent their constituencies in the international realm? Could these Actors have recognized their legitimacy to participate in the defense and regulation of the common wealth that, in ultimate analysis, does not belong to the States, but to human beings? We believe that, yes, they can. That is what we will explore in the conclusion of our essay. But firstly, it seems appropriate to appraise in what extent individuals and NGOs can be regarded as subjects of international law according to its formal sources.

1.4   Sources: article 38 of the statute of the ICJ

In 1920, the Permanent Court of International Justice (PCIJ) was established under the auspices of the League of Nations. Article 38 of its
Statute, materially reproduced in the statutes of the future International
Court of Justice (ICJ), provided that while appreciating the cases brought
to its ruling, it would apply treaties, international customs and the general
principles of law recognized by civilized nations, together with judicial decisions and the teachings of the most qualified publicists of the various nations as subsidiary means for the determination of the rule of law.

Despite aiming to guide the works of the mentioned tribunals – and,
thus, having a functional purpose - article 38 has always been regarded as
a typology of formal sources of international law.[107] The origin of the theory of formal sources of international law is attributed to positivism, which
separated Law (formal source) from its ethical or moral background (material source), and, thus, isolated law from politics, enabling its systematic
analysis of the juridical phenomena.[108]

Article 38 was not the first attempt to establish the formal sources of international law. The Hague Convention of 1907 included a section (XII)
aimed at the creation of an International Prize Court, the only section that
did not enter into force. In its article 7, it established that:

> 'If a question of law to be decided is covered by a treaty in force
> between the belligerent captor and a Power which is itself or whose
> subject or citizen is a party to the proceedings, the Court is gov-
> erned by the provisions in the said treaty. In the absence of such
> provisions, the Court shall apply the rules of international law. If no
> generally recognized rule exists, the Court shall give judgment in
> accordance with the general principles of justice and equity.'[109]

As one can observe, it tried to establish a hierarchy in the formal sources,
commencing with written consented rules, followed by non-written consented rules and closing with the general principles of law and equity,
where the tribunal could only apply the posterior source in the case of absence of the anterior one. Thirteen years later, when the statute of the
Permanent Court of International Justice was established, this hierarchy was
no longer mentioned. This circumstance caused some controversy regarding
the legal doctrine.

Some scholars supported that the tribunal should follow the order prescribed in article 38, because it represented a modulation of the consent of
the States.[110] Other authors supported that this hierarchy did not exist and
the tribunal was free to use the sources to the best of its understanding,
although, in practice, priority would be given to the treaties since they
represented a formal consent on a certain object, and, in sequence, the

custom, because the existence of these rules created no need to appeal to the general principles of law.[111] Another group, relying on the analysis of the jurisprudence of the tribunal,[112] argued that all sources could be used together without preclusion in the case of application of one of them, and that treaties could not be regarded as the most important source, due to the *jus cogens* established in article 43 of the Vienna Convention on the Law of Treaties[113] that prescribed that the invalidity, termination or denunciation of a treaty, should not in any way impair the duty of any State to fulfill any obligation embodied in the treaty to which it would be subject under international law independently of the treaty.[114]

Another aspect that deserves attention is the fact that the text of article 38 cannot be regarded as the ultimate definition of the formal sources of international law, because it was conceived almost a century ago, when the international society had far fewer States, was more homogeneous and could not imagine the existence of intergovernmental organizations regulating virtually all aspects of life. Some authors have pointed out that it disregarded the existence of other formal sources of international law, such as the unilateral declarations of the States and the resolutions of intergovernmental organizations.[115] There are elements of truth in these remarks, as we will study in Chapter 4.

Notwithstanding any criticism on the comprehensiveness of article 38, we have decided to adopt it as guidance for the appraisal of the situation of NGOs in international law in the forthcoming chapters, with only one discreet difference: we have decided to re-ordinate them, starting our appraisal with treaties and judicial decisions, due to their greater empirical support, following with custom, general principles of law and international legal doctrine, which we regarded as more analytical.

Notes

1   The idea of international law as a system of mandatory and permissive rules established to preserve peace can be observed in the writings of Hersch Lauterpacht. See H Lauterpacht, *The Functions of Law in the International Community* (Oxford 1933).
2   See the *Serbian Loans* case PCIJ Rep Series A No 14.
3   Treaty concerning the hydroelectric utilization of the water resources of the Parana River owned in condominium by the two countries, from and including the Salto Grande de Sete Quedas or Salto del Guaira, to the mouth of the Iguassu River (adopted 26 April 1973, entered into force 13 August 1973) UNTS 923.
4   Treaty on principles governing the activities of States in the exploration and use of outer space, including the Moon and other celestial bodies (adopted 27 January 1967, entered into force 10 October 1967) UNTS 188. In the case of this specific treaty, it is worthy of note that an NGO, the International Astronautical Federation, carried out important work concerning legal and practical problems of outer space, providing valuable support towards defining the terms of the treaty.

5   M Koskenniemi, *The Gentle Civilizer of Nations: The Rise and Fall of International Law 1870-1960* (CUP, 2001) 71.

6   Union of International Organizations, *Yearbook of International Organizations* (Report) (Brussels 2002).

7   T Franck, *The Power of Legitimacy among Nations* (OUP, 1990) 24.

8   A Boyle and C Chinkin, *The Making of International Law* (OUP, New York 2007) 24.

9   H Kelsen, *Principles of International Law* (Lawbook Exchange, Clark, 2003) 104

10 U.S. Declaration of Independence, preamble.

11 JM Coicaud and V Heiskanen, *The Legitimacy of International Organizations* (UN University Press, Tokyo, 2001) 4.

12 The creation is observed in several declarations of independence and their reorganization, in the also often common approval of new constitutions. The extinction, quite rare, may be observed in the case in the German Democratic Republic, an independent state since 1949 that disappeared in 1990, when its provinces were incorporated in the Federal Republic of Germany.

13 We have been observing an increasingly direct participation of citizens in the establishment of transnational rules, being relevant to quote, in this regard, the experience of the European Union with the national referenda to the EU Constitution, where French and Dutch citizens could act to blockade an international agreement made by their governments. It is, in our opinion, an outstanding example of the submission of the State and of international agreements not to the States' will but to that of the citizens.

14 T Franck, *The Power of Legitimacy* (n 7) 5.

15 H Charlesworth and JM Coicaud, *Fault Lines of International Legitimacy* (CUP, Cambridge, 2010) 1.

16 I Clark, *Legitimacy in International Society* (OUP, Oxford, 2007) 11.

17 J Bruneé and SJ Toope, *Legitimacy and Legality in International Law* (CUP, 2010) 3.

18 A Boyle and C Chinkin, *The Making of International Law* (n 8) 29.

19 PE Corbett (tr) C de Visscher, *Theory and Reality in Public International Law* (2nd edn, PUP Princeton 1957) 147.

20 R Higgins, *Problems and Process: International Law and How We Use It*, (OUP, Oxford 1994) 16.

21 L Fuller, *The Morality of Law* (YUP, 1969) 96-7 ('What I have called the internal morality of law is ... a procedural version of natural law,,, [it is] concerned, not with substantive aims of legal rules, but with the ways in which a system of rules for governing human conduct must be constructed and administered if it is to be efficacious and at the same time remain what it purports to be'). Quoted in J Bruneé and SJ Toope, *Legitimacy and Legality* (n 17) 29.

22 J Bruneé and SJ Toope, *Legitimacy and Legality* (n 17) 35.

23 See, for example, *Al-Bihani v. Obama*, in 49 ILM 265 (2010) in which the DC Court of Appeal disregarded international laws of war as a limit on the presidential authority under the 2001 Congressional Authorization of Use of Force in a petition presented by a cook – a material supporter of Taliban - detained in Guantanamo.

24 A Buchanan, *Justice, Legitimacy and self-Determination* (OUP, Oxford, 2004) 473.

25 J Bruneé and SJ Toope, *Legitimacy and Legality* (n 17) 36, 45, 52-55.

26 T Franck, *The Power of Legitimacy* (n 7) 3, 25.

27 T Franck, *The Power of Legitimacy* (n 7) 49.

28 T Franck, *The Power of Legitimacy* (n 7) 61.

29 T Franck, *The Power of Legitimacy* (n 7) 101.

30 T Franck, *The Power of Legitimacy* (n 7) 142.

31 T Franck, *The Power of Legitimacy* (n 7) 184.

32 J Austin, *The province of jurisprudence determined* (1832).

33   G Jellinek, *Teoria General del Estado* (Continental, Mexico 1958).
34   (Adopted 23 May 1969, entered into force 27 January 1980) UNTS 1155.
35   T Franck, *The Power of Legitimacy* (n 7) 188.
36   T Franck, *The Emerging Right to Democratic Governance* (1992) AJIL v 86, 50.
37   (adopted 16 December 1966, entered into force 23 March 1976) UNTS 999.
38   H Kelsen, *Principles of International Law* (n 9) 108
39   J Bodin, *De la République* (Elibron, Paris 2005) 17. See, also, JH Franklin (ed) *On Sovereignty: four chapters from six books of the Commonwealth / Jean Bodin* (Cambridge Texts in the History of Political Thought, CUP, Cambridge 1992), D Carreau, *Droit International* (7th edn Pedone, Paris 2001) 15, MN Shaw, *International Law* (5th edn CUP, Cambridge 2003) 21.
40   D Carreau, *Droit International* (n 39) 15.
41   J Bodin (n 39) 282. See, also, Thomas Aquinas, *Summa Theologica*, I-II, q.96 a. 5: "Hence, in the judgment of God, the sovereign is not exempt from the law, as to its directive force; but he should fulfill it to his own free-will and not of constraint. Again the sovereign is above the law, in so far as, when it is expedient, he can change the law, and dispense in it according to time and place."
42   Lex Ripuaria, tit. 58, c. 1: 'Episcopus archidiaconum jubeat, ut ei tabulas secundum legem romanam, qua ecclesia vivit, scribere faciat'.
43   D Carreau, *Droit International* (n 39) 14.
44   S Hall, 'The Persistent Spectre: Natural Law, International Order and the Limits of Legal Positivism' (2001) EJIL, v 12 n 12, 269-307.
45   *Summa Theologica*, I-II, q. 91 a. 2.
46   *Summa Theologica*, I-II, q. 95 a. 2.
47   *Summa Theologica*, I-II, q. 96 a. 4.
48   *Summa Theologica*, I-II, q. 96 a. 4.
49   S Hall, *The Persistent Spectre* (n 44).
50   Aquinas ideas are observed, for instance, on Grotius works.
51   *De Postestate Civili* Spanish edn <**http://metalibri.incubadora.fapesp.br/portal/ authors/DePotestateCivili**> accessed 01 November 2008.
52   A remarkable statement coming from a Spanish Catholic priest, if we consider that Pope Alexander VI had assumed the theory that the Pope was the lord paramount of the world in order to divide the New World between Portugal and Spain in 1493 in the bull *Inter Caetera*, giving legitimacy to the Treaty of Tordesillas between those countries in 1494.
53   *De Indis et de Jure Belli* english edn <http://en.wikisource.org/wiki/ De_Indis_De_Jure_Belli> accessed 1 November 2008.
54   'Asi, pues, habiendo sido constiutidas las sociedades humanas para este fin, a saber, para ayudarmos los unos a los otros y al ser entre todas las sociedades la sociedad civil aquella em la que más cómodamente atienden los hombres a suas necesidades, siguese que la comunidad es uma naturalísima comunicación conformísma a la naturaleza...' *De Potestate Civili* item 4.
55   *Convention on access to information, public participation in decision-making and access to justice in environmental matters* (adopted 25 June 1998, entered into force 30 October 2001) UNTS 2161.
56   This work was provisionally entitled *De Indis (On the Indies)* and was first published in the late 19th century under the title *De Jure Praedae (On the Law of Spoils* or *On the Right of Capture)*.
57   H Grotius, *The Free Sea* (Natural Law and Enlightenment Classics, Liberty Fund, Indianapolis 2004) 6.
58   H Grotius, *The Free Sea* (n 57) 85-86.

59 H Grotius, *The Rights of War and Peace* (Natural Law and Enlightenment Classics, Liberty Fund, Indianapolis 2005) 433-434.

60 H Grotius, *The Rights of War and Peace*, Chapter 2, § 7, 435-437.

61 H Grotius, *The Rights of War and Peace*, Prolegomena VI, 79-81.

62 H Grotius, *The Rights of War and Peace*, Prolegomena XI, 89.

63 H Grotius, *The Rights of War and Peace*, Prolegomena VIII, 85-86.

64 H Lauterpacht, 'The Grotian Tradition of International Law', in *International Law: Collected Papers* (CUP, Cambridge 1975) v 2, 307.

65 A Nussbaum, *A concise history of the Law of the Nations* (Macmillan, New York 1962) 109.

66 H Grotius, *The Rights of War and Peace*, Book 3, Chapter XXV § 2.

67 Excerpt from the Will of Alfred Nobel < http://nobelprize.org/alfred_nobel/will/ short_testamente.html> accessed on 03 November 2008.

68 P Cohen, 'Nobel committee expands definition of "peace"' *International Herald Tribune* (New York 14 October 2007) < http://www.iht.com/articles/2007/10/14/europe/nobel.php> accessed 05 November 2008.

69 H Grotius, *The Rights of War and Peace*, Chapter 2, § 1, 420.

70 H Grotius, *The Rights of War and Peace*, Chapter 2, § 3, 428.

71 RJ Vincent, 'Grotius, Human Rights and Intervention' in H Bull, B Kingsbury and A Roberts, *Hugo Grotius and International Relations* (OUP, Oxford 2002) 241.

72 Constitution of the World Health Organization (adopted 22 July 1946, entered into force 7 April 1948) UNTS 14.

73 H Grotius, *The Rights of War and Peace*, Chapter 2, § 11, 438.

74 Brief information regarding this issue can be seen at a recent UN Chronicle Online < http://www.un.org/Pubs/chronicle/2003/issue2/0203p13.html> accessed on 5 November 2008.

75 H Grotius, *The Rights of War and Peace*, Chapter 1 § 3, 136-137.

76 Annex to the Marrakesh Agreement establishing the World Trade Organization (adopted 15 April 1994, entered into force 1 January 1995) UNTS 1867.

77 L Ciccio, 'Patenting drugs from 1st January 2005: implications and problems' in HPDJ 2 (2) 136, 137 < https://tspace.library.utoronto.ca/bitstream/1807/6054/1/hp04028.pdf> accessed on 7 November 2008.

78 See, *e.g.*, World Trade Organization, *TRIPS and pharmaceutical patents: fact sheet* < http://www.wto.org/english/tratop_e/trips_e/factsheet_pharm00_e.htm> accessed on 7 November 2008.

79 See also World Health Organization. *Globalization, TRIPS and Access to Pharmaceuticals*, Geneva: WHO, 2001 (WHO Policy Perspectives on Medicines n°3) (WHO/EDM/2001.2)

80 RJ Vincent, *Grotius, Human Rights and Intervention* (n 71) 242.

81 H Grotius, *The Rights of War and Peace*, Prolegomena XVIII, 94. See also MN Shaw, *International Law* (n 39) 24; A Nussbaum, *A concise history of the Law of the Nations* (n 65) 148; CD Albuquerque Mello, *Curso de Direito Internacional Publico* (8th edn, Freitas Bastos, Rio de Janeiro 1986).

82 S Pufendorf, *On the Duty of Man and Citizen* (1675) Book II, Chapter V, 2, English edn < http://www.constitution.org/puf/puf-dut.htm> accessed on 7 November 2008.

83 S Pufendorf, *On the Duty of Man and Citizen*, Book II, Chapter V, 7.

84 S Pufendorf, *On the Duty of Man and Citizen*, Book II, Chapter I, 11.

85 S Pufendorf, *On the Duty of Man and Citizen*, Book II, Chapter VI, 10.

86 S Pufendorf, *On the Duty of Man and Citizen*, Book II, Chapter VI, 7.

87 S Hall, *The Persistent Spectre* (n 44).

88 T Hobbes, *Leviathan*, (1651) Chapter XIII.

89 T Hobbes, *Leviathan*, Chapter XIV.

90 Aristotle, *The Politics*, I, ii.
91 T Hobbes, *Leviathan*, Chapter XV.
92 S Pufendorf, *De Jure naturae et gentium libri octo*. Also Hall, *The Persistent Spectre* (n 42).
93 J Israel, *Introduction* to B Spinoza, *Theological-Political Treatise* (CUP, Cambridge, 2007) ix, xxviii.
94 B Spinoza, *Theological-Political Treatise* (CUP, Cambridge, 2007) Chapter 16 [2] and [4].
95 B Spinoza, *Theological-Political Treatise* Chapter 16 [5].
96 B Spinoza, *Theological-Political Treatise* Chapter 16 [8].
97 GFW Hegel, *Elements of the Philosophy of Right* (CUP, Cambridge 1991).
98 S Hall, *The Persistent Spectre* (n 44) 273; D Carreau, *Droit International* (n 39) 19; MN Shaw, *International Law* (n 39) 26; A Nussbaum, *A concise history of the Law of the Nations* (n 65) 199.
99 MN Shaw, *International Law* (n 39) 28.
100 The idea of cooperation among the States is observed in Vitoria and was later resumed by Abee Saint Pierre in his work *Projet pour rendre le paix perpetuelle en Europe* (1713), which tried to eternalize the Treaty of Utrecht to avoid war, and also by Kant in his book *Toward Perpetual Peace* (1795).
101 14 states were from Europe, 12 from the Americas, 3 from Asia and just 1 from Africa.
102 According to the US National Intelligence Council, by 2025, nation-states will no longer be the only—and often not the most important—actors on the world stage and the "international system" will have morphed to accommodate the new reality, due to the growth of the relative power of various non-state actors. Additionally, there will be multi-polarity without multilateralism and the US will no longer be hegemonic, although it will remain the strongest player. See in this regard, US National Intelligence Council, 'Global Trends 2025 – A Transformed World' (Report) <http://www.dni.gov/nic/PDF_2025/2025_Global_Trends_Final_Report.pdf> accessed 21 November 2008.
103 JR O'Shea (tr), T Judt, *Postwar: A History of Europe since 1945* (Objetiva, Rio de Janeiro 2008) 18
104 JR O'Shea (tr), T Judt, *Postwar: A History of Europe since 1945*, (n 103) 20. In a certain way, a Hobbesian-like social contract, in which European citizens transfer their power to the sovereign, located in Brussels.
105 MN Shaw *International Law* (n 39) 232; P Daillier and A Pellet, *Droit International Public* (7th edn LGDJ, Paris 2002) 650.
106 PM Dupuy, *Droit International Publique* (6th edn, Paris, Dalloz) 251; MN Shaw, *International Law*, (n 39) 67; CD Albuquerque Mello, *Curso de Direito Internacional Publico* (n 81) 157; GFS Soares, *Curso de Direito Internacional Publico* (Atlas, São Paulo, 2002) 55.
107 PM Dupuy, *Droit International Publique* (n 106), 251; P Daillier and A Pellett, *Droit International Public*, (n 105) 111-112.
108 Available at <http://humanrights.law.monash.edu.au/instree/1907k.htm> accessed on November 21, 2008.
109 PM Dupuy, *Droit International Publique* (n 106) 252.
110 CD Albuquerque Mello, *Curso de Direito Internacional Publico*, (n 81) 157.
111 *Military and Paramilitary Activities in and against Nicaragua (Nicaragua v United States of America)* (Judge Ni separate opinion) [1996] ICJ Rep 207.
112 (Adopted 23 May 1969, entered into force 27 January 1980) UNTS 1155.
113 GFS Soares, *Curso de Direito Internacional Publico* (n 106) 55.

114 GFS Soares, *Curso de Direito Internacional Publico,* (n 106) 56; D Carreau, *Droit International,* (n 39) 108; A Boyle and C Chinkin, *The Making of International Law* (n 8) VI.

CHAPTER 2

NGOs in International Treaties and other Documents

Despite playing an important role in international relations, several relevant international documents are not treaties, and, thus, are not covered by the Vienna Convention on the Law of the Treaties nor are widely considered sources of law in the sense of article 38(1) of the Statute of the ICJ. Such documents are often referred to as *soft law* because they are not subject to the fundamental principle of *pacta sunt servanda* that regulates international treaty law and, therefore, they do not impose international legal obligations – compensations and reprisals - to the signatories, especially if the parties expressly excluded their registration in accordance with article 102 of the UN Charter.[1]

Some reasons have been invoked to justify this apparently incoherent practice of engaging diplomats in extensive negotiations to reach non-binding agreements, but we would like to stress a few of those mentioned by Hillgenberg that, for the sake of our study, are closely related to the actual situation of NGOs in international law. These reasons are:

- A general need for mutual confidence-building;
- The need to stimulate development still in progress;
- The creation of a preliminary, flexible regime, possibly providing for its development in stages; and
- The possibility of agreements being made with parties which do not have the power to conclude treaties under international law.

The first reason is a marked aspect of the relationship between States and NGOs, particularly in democracies, where governments have maintained a long-standing cooperation with NGOs at a national level, comprising, together with the joint execution of programs, the service of several former NGO board members or executives as government officials and the customary participation of NGO representatives in official delegations to UN Conferences and even to the General Assembly.[2] This close relationship, however, is often turbulent, because both sides of the relationship invoke the legitimate representation of the same constituencies – the civil society – but with different plans, approaches or objectives regarding the same issue. Therefore, confidence building is continuously at stake at the national level, where the existence of a government, on one side, and multiple un-coordinated NGOs, on the other, can be observed, a situation which poses severe difficulties for reaching a successful outcome. This situation is far more complex at the international level, because INGOs often invoke the representation of 'global civil society' and, hence, one can notice multiple players on both sides of the negotiation table, coordinating their efforts in a matrical scheme, sometimes leading certain kinds of coalitions of States and NGOs to oppose the proposals of other States, such as in the debate regarding global warming.

While the interaction of NGOs with States is experiencing steady growth, it is also true that they are even more active in other spheres. Currently, we can observe that the relationship between NGOs and Intergovernmental Organizations (IGOs) has been improving continuously, with NGOs providing reliable information, technical expertise and logistic support to implement the goals of IGOs and evaluate the actual performance of States in several fields, particularly human rights and the protection of the environment.[3] We could assume that this willingness to cooperate is based on the converging characteristics of both types of entities that differentiate them from the States: They are newcomers to the international arena, without specific territories to rule or a defined nation to represent, and they are also 'issue focused' entities created by agreements of some constituencies to achieve specific goals. These similar characteristics make it easier for IGOs and NGOs to work together. The innumerable contractual arrangements concluded to regulate international cooperation in all fields of their activities, according to a UN agency report, have made UN-NGO relations evolve into a 'symbiotic relationship'.[4]

The second reason for implementing non-binding agreements is frequently the case of 'a text which has been laid down at a conference as a non-treaty-binding standard (that) gradually becomes, as awareness grows, a binding and possibly a "hard" obligation'.[5] An outstanding example is the Universal Declaration of Human Rights (1948), which acquired the force of customary international law and gave birth to a set of legally binding international instruments, still in evolution.[6]

The creation of a preliminary, flexible regime to enable its further development in stages deserves more attention. As we shall see in this chapter, diverse treaties, starting with the UN Charter itself, ensure NGOs a consultative status. Other documents go further, granting them the capacity of observers at meetings of the UN General Assembly, a treatment equivalent to the one assured to the Holy See, the Sovereign Military Order of Malta and Palestine. NGOs have already been admitted as members in international organizations, together with States and IGOs.[7] Evidence shows that an evolutionary customary practice is in course and a lengthy but rising debate ensues as to whether NGOs can be parties in treaties and whether they can bear responsibility under international law. This situation is not exactly new, since similar debates occurred half a century ago, a few years after the creation of the UN, which ended with the understanding that IGOs were subjects of international law, together with States, although they had no nation to represent nor a territory to rule – or, to the contrary – they represented all nations and operated in all territories.[8]

The fourth and last reason – the possibility of making agreements with parties that cannot conclude treaties – is customary practice for a State, often engaged in written agreements with non-state actors, such as companies, some of which are even economically stronger than the State itself. The situation has been appreciated in the *Texaco (TOPCO) v. Libyan Arab Republic* case where the arbitrators ruled that such agreements could not be regarded as treaties because only sovereign States could conclude treaties.[9] In another judgment, the *Gabdcikovo-Nagymaros* case, in 1997, the ICJ considered a wider view of the relations between the parties, instead of a mechanical application of the rules of treaty breach, showing 'that international law can endow obligations with greater or lesser possibilities for enforcement'.[10] Thus, a 'self-contained regime' could be created by a specific set of rules that does not violate *jus cogens* in which 'the parties exclude the application of rules that follow from *pacta sunt servanda* but not, for instance, from *inadimplenti non est adimplendum*',[11] making it possible to envisage this kind of 'self-contained regime' in agreements drawn up in the usual treaty language and concluded between States and non-state actors, such as INGOs, on a bilateral or multilateral basis, even open to accession by other States or INGOs, whose occasional disputes could be submitted to settlement procedures, with recourse to the principle of good faith.

The emergence of *soft law* and the steady growth of multilateral negotiations under the auspices of the UN and other major intergovernmental organizations are being regarded as favorable elements for the enhancement of the participation of NGOs in the international sphere.[12] This participation is also perceived through some *soft law* instruments of persuasion of States, such as the Human Rights Council (The Human Rights Commission up to 2006), whose reports may constrain States before the public opinion.[13] Hillgenberg emphasized that non-treaty agreements cannot directly produce customary international law, but can contribute to its creation as an emerging *opinio juris* if taken as 'subsequent practice' for the sake of Article 31(3)(b) of the Vienna Convention on the Law of Treaties, while interpreting a treaty.[14]

In the fields of human rights and environmental protection there is a tendency for *soft law* provisions to develop into *hard law* rules. It can be observed, for instance, by Principle 21 of the 1972 Stockholm Declaration, reaffirmed as Principle 2 of the 1992 Rio Declaration, further enshrined in a binding agreement, as article 3 of the Biological Diversity Convention,[15] which ended up considered by the International Court of Justice as part of the 'corpus of the international law relating to the environment'.[16] This idea demonstrates its relevancy if we analyze the evolution of the treatment of INGOs in international documents within the institutional framework of the UN and other international organizations, as we will see hereinafter.

2.1   The UN System

Some authors affirm that the UN Charter was not conceived as one of many multilateral treaties that operates within international law, but as the constitution of the international community, therefore occupying the highest level in the hierarchy of norms, providing the framework within which international law would operate.[17] Accordingly, they argue that its principles cannot be modified, restricted or revoked by further customary law or treaties. Considering the development of humanitarian law and environmental law since 1945, it is beyond any doubt that contemporary society is challenging the UN to become more 'responsive to the demands and needs of peoples rather than exclusively those of States'.[18] After all, the opening phrase of the Preamble to the UN Charter begins with the expression 'We, the *peoples* of the United Nations'. Hence, increasing people's participation in the UN system is necessary to enhance the practice of the principles enshrined in the Charter, such as self-determination and respect for human rights, and also to reduce the democratic deficit of the organization.

In general terms, the UN Charter allows for a formal channel of participation of NGOs at the UN: the application for consultative status with the ECOSOC (art 71).[19] Based on this ('international constitutional') *right* of participation, the subsequent practice of UN subsidiary organs and agencies demonstrates that INGOs can be invited to participate in the sessions of work of the General Assembly in the capacity of Observer or ask for accreditation for special UN Conferences, both without voting rights. They can also associate themselves with the UN Department of Public Information (DPI) or establish working relations with other UN special bodies. As we will see, the bureaucratic structure of the UN provides various channels of communication and interaction with NGOs, despite some overlapping of scope.

The so-called 'focal point' for NGOs seeking consultative status with the ECOSOC is the UN Dept. of Economic and Social Affairs NGO Branch (DESA NGO Branch) in New York, which acts as the substantive secretariat of the ECOSOC Committee on NGOs. The DESA NGO Branch is responsible for screening applications, processing reports, facilitating consultative arrangements between the ECOSOC and qualified NGOs and also providing advice and assistance to secretariats of other UN-sponsored events in all aspects related to NGO participation or contributions.

Once the consultative status is obtained, the NGO is referred to another 'focal point' within the UN system, represented by the NGO Liaison Office in Geneva, which liaises NGOs holding consultative status with the ECOSOC, facilitating their participation in UN activities. The office also assists Permanent Missions based in Geneva in all aspects related to the relationship between the UN and the NGOs.

A third structure offered by the UN to support the mentioned relationship is the NGO Section of the UN Dept. of Public Information (DPI NGO Section), which acts as the liaison between the UN and NGOs and civil society organizations, whether with consultative status or not, in order to develop and promote effective information programs for NGOs to disseminate information about issues on the UN's agenda and its work. We will address the association with the DPI in more detail below.

Finally, a fourth formal channel is represented by the UN Non-Governmental Liaison Service (NGLS), which occupies a self-called 'unique place and role in the interface between the UN system and NGOs'[20] due to its mission to 'promote dynamic partnerships between the UN and NGOs by providing information advice, expertise and support services to strengthen dialogue and win public support for economical and social development'.[21]

The UN system also interacts with NGOs through three other 'private' collective structures, which are: (i) the UN NGO Informal Regional Networks (UN-NGO-IRENE), created in response to the UN Secretary General's Report of 1999 to the General Assembly,[22] which underlined the need to establish regional networks of NGOs to promote partnerships, share information and contribute to the work of the ECOSOC; (ii) The International Association of Economic and Social Councils and Similar Institutions (AICESIS), composed of consultative assemblies fostered by public authorities to promote dialogue with civil society in key social and economic issues, which has been granted a permanent observer status at the ECOSOC by Council decision 2001/318; and (iii) The Conference of NGOs in Consultative Relationship with the UN (CONGO), a network of national, regional and international NGOs possessing consultative status with the UN that aims to assist its members to facilitate and enhance their participation in UN decision-making, strengthening their voices and promoting a consensus-building approach among the associated members, which is particularly relevant considering the more than 3,000 organizations with consultative status.

The existence of these seven structures to support the interaction of NGOs and the UN, together with several other NGO liaison offices in the various UN funds, agencies and programmes, undoubtedly demonstrates that NGOs are non-state actors with legitimacy to express the views of their constituencies, yet the bureaucratic division of access between diverse structures shows that these opinions may be heard but not necessarily always taken into account in a UN structure where States call to themselves the sole representativeness of the nations of the world in the international arena. Notwithstanding, it is a fact that the UN system is paying more attention to NGOs even at its main structure, the General Assembly.

2.1.1 General Assembly

NGOs were particularly active during the first years of the UN. The first reference of a UN General Assembly (UNGA) document to NGOs is Res. 4(I) of 14 February 1946, which recommended that the ECOSOC adopt suitable arrangements to put into practice the consultative status set forth in article 71 of the UN Charter, acceding to the request of the World Federation of Trade Unions, the American Federation of Labor and the International Cooperative Alliance, all very active during the San Francisco Conference. This recommendation led to a report from the committee on arrangements for consultation with NGOs, setting the principles to be applied for such consultation, adopted on 21 June 1946, which finally granted consultative status to the mentioned entities.[23] Since Res. 2/3 only allowed the considered NGOs to submit written statements and sit as observers at all public meetings of the ECOSOC (para 2), the NGOs put more pressure on the UNGA and achieved a further step in participation, when the UNGA approved Res. 49(I) of 15 December 1946, recommending the ECOSOC to give the World Federation of Trade Unions the *right* to submit questions to the ECOSOC for insertion in the provisional agenda, in accordance to procedures then applicable to specialized agencies. This right was further expanded to all NGOs with general consultative status.

Once consultative status with the UN had become effective, some NGOs deemed it necessary to establish a closer relationship with the States themselves while maintaining a certain level of immunity in their operations. Acceding to the request of the Red Cross and Red Crescent, the UNGA passed Res. 55(I) of 19 November 1946, encouraging the member-states to cooperate with recognized national Red Cross and Red Crescent societies, recalling that 'at all times' the independent voluntary nature of those entities should be respected in 'all circumstances', in order to allow them to carry out their humanitarian task according to the principles of the Geneva and The Hague Conventions.

However, NGOs pursued more extensive rights. During its 2nd Session, in 1947, the UNGA invited the Secretary General to prepare, in consultation with the ECOSOC, draft rules for the calling of international conferences.[24] It gave NGOs with consultative status a remarkable opportunity to improve their participation in the UN system. The draft rules were presented at the UNGA's 4th session in 1949 and proposed that NGOs with consultative status would have the same rights and privileges ensured to them at the ECOSOC, while participating at conferences called according to those rules.[25] This extension of rights was fiercely challenged at the General Assembly, where some member-states supported that the draft rules could lead to a misinterpretation of their legal status, which, based on article 71, should not be taken as the same ensured to States.[26] The proposed draft rules were never actually adopted, though the participation of NGOs with consultative status in international conferences is currently regulated by ECOSOC Res. 1996/31 (25 July 1996).

In a new *tour de force,* NGOs got the General Assembly to approve the first structured model of collective consultation with NGOs, when it adopted Res. 479(V) of 12 December 1950, setting down the rules for the calling of non-governmental conferences by the ECOSOC on any matters of its competence, allowing the participation of NGOs with consultative status but also national NGOs without it, provided that the invitation of the latter should be preceded by a consultation of the member-state concerned.

Another expressive movement of NGOs can be observed at the UNGA's 6th Session, in 1951, where, after obtaining a preliminary achievement on the ECOSOC, the NGOs succeeded in getting a UNGA authorization for the Secretary General to make, upon request of the ECOSOC, the due arrangements to enable NGO representatives to attend public meetings of the General Assembly whenever economic and social matters within the Council and the concerned organization's competence were discussed.[27] Since the sessions were public and the custom allowed the presence of observers without invitation, at first sight, this did not seem to represent any advancement. However, the main purpose behind the NGOs' convincing the member-states to pass this resolution was that of extending the application of the UN Headquarters Agreement to NGO representatives, since the US government had been interfering in their participation in the works of the ECOSOC by not admitting representatives of certain Eastern European NGOs into the country, which represented an arbitrary McCarthyist interference in an intergovernmental organization.[28]

Improvement in the working relationship with the UN was also an NGO goal. The first references of UN-NGOs cooperation are observed in UNGA Res. 280(III) of 13 May 1949, which invited the ECOSOC to consider, after consultation with NGOs concerned, the possibility of drafting a general report on the world's social and cultural situation, in UNGA Res. 833 (IX) of 4 December 1954, which invited NGOs to stimulate public interest in the draft covenant on human rights and in UNGA Res. 926(X) of 14 December 1955, which called NGOs to supplement the UN advisory services to member-states in the field of human rights with similar programs designed for further research and studies, exchange of information and assistance. The partnership of NGOs with the UN has shown signs of continuous improvement since these first years and is mentioned in dozens of other UNGA resolutions.[29]

The very first years of the UN were extremely fruitful for NGOs, marked by significant achievements in their lobbying activities, setting a pattern of participation that could lead to further rights under international law if the pace of achievements had remained the same. However, this proved not to be the case, seeing as NGOs made few strides in their rights during the following decades, certainly due to the tense relationship between NGOs - seeking more power - and States, providing resistance to them.

The next remarkable improvement in the status of INGOs at the General Assembly was provided by UNGA Res. 45/6 of 16 October 1990, which invited the International Committee of the Red Cross to participate in the sessions of the General Assembly in the capacity of Observer, a status further extended to the International Federation of Red Cross and Red Crescent Societies in 1994[30] and to the International Union for the Conservation of Nature (IUCN) in 1999.[31] It is relevant to quote that the Sovereign Military Order of Malta achieved similar status in 1994[32] and Palestine in 1998.[33] Since then, an evolutionary practice has allowed a certain degree of informal participation of NGOs at the General Assembly, mainly in subsidiary bodies (such as the 4th Committee) but also addressing its plenary meetings during special sessions.[34]

Although there is no doubt that the UN has neither received a mandate from the member-states to engage them in treaties nor constitutes a super-State,[35] it is unquestionable that the General Assembly represents a qualified forum for the development of the understanding of international law. Given that it works to obtain consensus on its resolutions,[36] it may contribute to the formation of customary international law,[37] a theme that will be explored in the Chapter 4.

2.1.2   ECOSOC Consultative Status

In the Preliminary Chapter, we analyzed the evolution of the rules concerning the application of INGOs for the consultative status with the ECOSOC and the difficulties encountered in clearly defining the kind of organizations that were meant by article 71 of the UN Charter. Evidence shows that the UN adopts different criteria for recognizing an INGO, since accreditation to a UN conference does not require the previous granting of consultative status with the ECOSOC,[38] nor does the association with the DPI provide a 'fast track' for the consultative status or ensure the establishment of working relationships with other UN bodies. All these channels of participation are in fact independent from each other and, albeit having some similarities, cannot be regarded as having a single criterion. This situation reinforces the need for a substantive definition of an INGO and a coordinated set of rules regulating their participation within the UN system, moreover if we take into consideration some practices upheld by the ECOSOC.

The ECOSOC is composed of 54 States elected for three-year terms by the General Assembly. According to article 62 of the UN Charter, the ECOSOC may make or initiate studies and reports with respect to international economic, social, cultural, educational, health, and related matters and may make recommendations with respect to any such matters, and also for the purpose of promoting the observance of human rights and fundamental freedoms, to the General Assembly and to the specialized agencies concerned. Since the INGOs holding consultative status with the Council can attend its meetings and address its members orally or in writing, it is important, especially for those countries with a past record of violation of human rights, to control who is admitted and remains on the ECOSOC. Taking a look at the 2009 composition of the Council,[39] it is certainly surprising to realize that the UN body in charge of promoting respect for human rights was composed – together with longstanding democracies – of several countries under dictatorship or in civil war and, most astonishingly, that it had, as a member of the Council and at the Chair of the Committee on NGOs, a country (Sudan) governed by the only head of State ever to have received an ICJ warrant of arrest for crimes against humanity and war crimes, *while in office*. How is this possible? For several reasons, the first being the division of seats among the continents in order to ensure equitable geographical representation, and the consequent regional agreement to nominate the candidates to the General Assembly, but, most of all, because it is important to be at the 'door' to control the entrance and permanence of 'troublemakers' on the 'party's' premises.[40]

Consultative status is granted by the ECOSOC upon recommendation of the ECOSOC Committee on NGOs, which is comprised of nineteen member-states: five from Africa; four from Asia; two from Eastern Europe; four from Latin America and the Caribbean; and four from Western Europe and other regions. The Committee on NGOs is the 'only intergovernmental body mandated to monitor the evolving relationship between those organizations and the UN'.[41]

At the 2009 Regular Session, held from 19 to 28 January and on 2 February 2009, the Committee on NGOs had before it one hundred and fifty-seven applications for consultative status, including applications deferred from its past sessions. Of those applications, the Committee recommended sixty-seven for consultative status, did not recommend one, deferred eighty-six for further consideration, took note that two applications had been withdrawn, and closed without prejudice consideration of four applications. The Committee also had before it four requests for reclassification of consultative status, and recommended all of them. In addition, it had before it ninety-five quadrennial reports, of which it took note of ninety-four and deferred one. The Committee heard fourteen representatives of NGOs.[42]

An analysis of the outcome of the 2009 Committee on NGOs' regular
session reveals some similarities with the 2000 regular session addressed
by Aston in his article.[43] In the 2009 session, a lengthy debate was raised
by the Egyptian representative as to whether it was possible or not to appreciate the application of national organizations whose host State had not
offered its opinion on the candidate, as set forth in ECOSOC Res. 1996/
31.[44] The claim was supported by States with low democratic records
(such as Cuba, China, India and Pakistan) but was challenged by open liberal democracies (the US, the UK, Switzerland, Chile, and Mexico), which
stated that the resolution had been in force for more than ten years and that
the question had never arisen in the past. Evaluating the session from an
outsider's point of view and having at hand only the detailed press releases
made public by the Committee, reporting a never-ending request for additional information from the NGOs that led to a continuously deferred procedure, it seems evident that the 'gatekeepers' were controlling access to
the 'party' in a strategy to reduce (or, better put, avoid) criticism to their
own governmental practices, especially if we notice that ECOSOC Res.
1996/31 allows the possibility of the non-existence of such a view from
the host country ('The views expressed by the member-state, *if any...*) and
that the considered NGOs were active in sensitive human rights issues.[45]
Furthermore, if the new interpretation were to become effective, then, any
country could impose an insurmountable obstacle for the accession of
NGOs to consultative status just by its silence. This issue remains open to
debate. It is also crystal clear that the procedure of the member-states at
the Committee shows a relevant concern about the works of any NGO that
might impact their domestic policies and practices, hence demonstrating
the increasing importance of NGOs in the international arena and especially their role in forming public opinion on the concerned issues in an
era of 'audience democracy' and media sympathy for NGOs.[46]

The proceedings of the Committee on NGOs provide evidence that, recalling Aston's words, the UN is a 'politically divided house' in which the
current mechanisms of NGO participation at the UN reveal certain weak-
nesses and a variety of discrepant views, when considering whether and to
what extent the current participatory rights of NGOs in the UN decision-
making process should be kept or expanded.[47] In a certain way, the
Committee debate can be regarded as a reproduction, on a smaller scale, of
the current debate at the UN General Assembly and conferences on the
role of NGOs. While there appears to be a consensus that the UN should
remain, in principle, an inter-state body and that NGOs can make important
contributions towards the pursuit of UN goals,[48] it remains unclear what
kind of arrangements should be made to efficiently run joint efforts or,
what proves to be more complicated, to make collective decisions, with
thousands of NGOs proud of their independence located all over the globe
and without permanent missions in New York or Geneva. Nevertheless, we

strongly disagree with the argument presented by the Conference of NGOs with Consultative Relationship with the UN (CONGO) that the expanded granting of consultative status might backfire, since it would make substantive collaboration between NGOs and the UN less feasible,[49] because, in essence, it relies on the same argument presented by States to deny increasing participation of NGOs in the decision-making process: the existence of several other representatives of the civil society. Furthermore, if the 'people' in the 'ark' assume that no one else can be admitted, then the question as to whether they are the 'chosen people' necessarily arises, providing more arguments for the NGO's detractors, usually from countries with a lesser tradition for recognizing civil society and human rights, as formerly mentioned in the discussion of the 2009 Committee's regular session. What surely represents backfiring is closing the gates, not keeping them open. Of course, there is need and room for improvement in the relationship, as we will propose in the conclusion of this study, but, for the sake of our analysis, we must address beforehand the other channels of interaction of NGOs with the UN system established by international documents other than the UN Charter.

2.1.3 Secretariat DPI Association

In 1947, the Secretariat Department of Public Information (DPI) was established with the purpose of providing information about the work and aims of the UN to the civil society. Since its enactment, close contacts have been maintained with NGOs, culminating in an official relationship in 1968.[50] Currently, the DPI/NGO Section acts as a liaison between the UN and the NGOs that can become associates to the DPI. In 2009, there were 1664 NGOs with strong information programmes associated with the DPI, 668 of which were also associated with ECOSOC.[51]

This association differs substantially from the consultative status with the ECOSOC that is focused on providing information *to* the UN and offering subsidies to the decision-making process, including influencing the agenda. Rather, it establishes a working relationship between the UN and the NGOs that have the duty to effectively disseminate information *about* the UN principles, issues on its agenda and its activities to the general public. If the NGOs' evaluation reports do not provide satisfactory evidence about its collaboration with the UN system, the NGO in concern can be disassociated.[52]

Observing the themes of the last fifteen years' Annual DPI/NGO Conferences, one can notice a useful dialogue about relevant world issues such as globalization challenges, post-conflict rebuilding, security, the Millennium Development Goals, human rights and climate change, which are certainly at stake at the UN and in the international community. Regarding this last theme, the 2007 conference, for the first time in sixty years of regular meetings, produced a Conference Declaration committing the 500 participating NGOs to reach a concerted set of proposals comprising both individual and collective action plans to combat issues of climate change. The NGOs also reiterated their pledge to be active partners of the UN, States and civil society to act on the matter.

Although association with the DPI does not induce a further change in the legal status of NGOs in international law, since the DPI regards them as private 'service provider' institutions, the fact of maintaining a continuous dialogue through working partnerships, weekly briefings, communication workshops, orientation programs and the mentioned annual DPI/NGO conferences, is extremely positive for fostering an increased awareness of civil society issues and, more importantly, for the establishment of a different UN channel of concerted interaction that does not pass through the States' permanent missions, enhancing mutual confidence building between the UN and NGOs.

2.1.4 Security Council

Under the UN Charter, the functions and powers of the Security Council (UNSC) include, among others, the maintenance of international peace and security and the investigation of any dispute or situations which might lead to international friction, recommending methods of adjusting such disputes or the terms of the settlement. The Council is authorized to make binding decisions, particularly under Chapter VII of the UN Charter. Based on its state-only composition and its sensitive role, there is no room for formal interaction with NGOs in the decision-making process, moreover if we bear in mind the individual veto power assured to its five permanent members. This does not mean, however, that the UNSC does not interact with NGOs in some circumstances, notably when humanitarian issues are at stake, through a protocol trick, the so-called Arria Formula.[53] To exemplify such interaction, we can quote UNSC Resolution 666 (1990), which acknowledged a privileged role to the ICRC in executing humanitarian measures in Iraq during the first Gulf War, and UNSC Resolution 771 (1992), which, in dealing with the Bosnia and Herzegovina war, demanded – imposing a binding obligation – that the conflicting parties grant unimpeded and continued access of relevant international humanitarian organizations and, in particular, the ICRC, to camps, prisons and detention centers within the territory of the former Yugoslavia, also calling upon those organizations to provide the Council with any substantive information in their possession relating to the violations of humanitarian law or grave breaches of the Geneva Conventions.

Though the Council has little contact with NGOs, it does not mean that it has little concern about non-state actors in the international arena. Since the 11 September 2001 terrorist attacks in the US, another kind of civil society group has drawn the attention of its members: terrorist organizations.

It is out of the scope of this study to address at length the situation of such non-state actors in international law, but it is a fact that they are subverting some important legal categories of a system conceived to govern the relations between sovereign States which, thus, cannot deal with such actors simply because they fall outside of the model.[54] The attacks surely highlighted the limitations of the Westphalian state-centric system.[55]

As Cassese remarks, the UN Charter ensures to all nations the right of self-defense if attacked by another State, provided that such reaction is a timely response to repel the attack, targeting the attacking State with proportional force and with respect to humanitarian law.[56] Obviously, the 9/11 events didn't fit this model, because the US was not under attack by a State. How could it respond to the attacks?

When the UNSC passed Resolution 1368 (12 September 2001), smoke was still in the air in New York and its members had no legal option but to define the attacks as 'a threat to peace' and to call all States to work together to bring to justice the perpetrators, organizers and sponsors, stressing that those who *harbored* them would be *held accountable*. Of course, the terrorists had to have a base in some State. Could this State become accountable for acts of individuals or groups of individuals that lived in its territory? If the answer is affirmative, that is a remarkable shift (perhaps irreconcilable with the UN Charter rules on self-defense) in the customary law on state responsibility that supported that a State had to be considered responsible for the conduct of a person or group of persons only if the person or group of persons was in fact acting on the 'instructions' of, or under the 'direction' or 'control' of, that state in carrying out the conduct.[57]

However, *realpolitik*[58] has shown that, yes, States could be held accountable for acts of non-states actors.[59] On 7 October 2001, the US-led coalition launched air strikes against Taliban targets in Afghanistan (an act of self-defense? reprisal?) based on the claim that the Afghan government allowed the Al'Qaeda to establish training camps in the country, which entitled the US government to pre-emptive use of force against its potential enemies, a decision that would later give birth to the so-called Bush doctrine.[60] Once the use of military force was a reality, without previous Council authorization, and the Taliban had been removed from power in Afghanistan, the UNSC authorized the deployment of an international security force to the country to assist the new government in the maintenance of security in the region of Kabul.[61]

The future development of the UNSC's understanding on the legal status of terrorist non-state actors, their responsibilities to the international community and their relationship with any lodging or financing State, will certainly influence the understanding of the legal status of NGOs inasmuch as one could regard both non-state actors as the opposite sides of the same coin, minted by the inadequate response of international law to contemporary challenges.[62]

2.1.5 Specialized Agencies

a. General overview

The ECOSOC's consultative status model has been adopted by all the funds, programmes and specialized agencies of the UN system as guidance for their dialogue with NGOs. Some of them had the procedure established in their constitutive acts, as is the case of FAO, ICAO, IMO, ITU, UNESCO, UNICEF, WHO, WIPO and WMO. Other bodies had it established by decision of their governing structures, such as the IFAD, UNDP, UNIFEM, UNODC, UPU, WFP and World Bank. Finally, some other subsidiary organs go further, establishing NGO bodies that meet regularly, such as the UN Populations Fund (UNFPA) NGO Advisory Committee, composed of twenty-five to thirty representatives of NGOs, and the 'WFP-NGO Consultation', an annual policy dialogue, jointly managed and organized.[63] Given the similarities, we will appraise in this chapter just some of them, that we have regarded as interesting paradigms for study.

b. ILO

The International Labor Organization (ILO) is the only UN 'family member' that has adopted a tripartite scheme of governance, integrating sectors of civil society representing workers and employers into its structure together with governments. Employers' and workers' national representative organizations are not members of the ILO, whose membership is open only to States, but they can participate in the decision-making because the constitution of this international organization imposed to the member-states the obligation to select their delegates to the governing bodies with the participation of national civil society organizations. Adopting this model, the ILO Constitution by-passed the debate regarding the international legal personality of civil society organizations, nonetheless ensuring the right of participation of those entities.[64]

According to the ILO Constitution,[65] employers' and workers' delegates are chosen by member-states in agreement with the industrial organizations which are the most representative of employers and work people in their respective countries and join the government representatives of all member-states at the organization' supreme organ, the International Labor Conference. Every three years, the individual employers' and workers' delegates of all member-states organize themselves into electoral colleges to elect their representatives to the ILO Governing Body, also a tripartite body, where its members enjoy equal status, including voting rights, whatever the segment they represent.

In addition to this unique integration of governments and non-state actors in the high level decision-making process of an intergovernmental organization, the Constitution of the ILO also established another channel of dialogue with organizations of employers, workers, agriculturists and cooperatives, provided by the consultative status with recognized international NGOs with convergent purposes that can be granted at either general or regional levels, depending on the territorial scope of the activities of the NGO concerned (article 12(3)). The dialogue with civil society is not restricted to the employer/worker binomial as the ILO set down, back in 1956, a special list of INGOs that share the same principles and objectives as the ILO Constitution and the Declaration of Philadelphia,[66] which currently comprises more than one hundred and fifty NGOs focused on human rights, poverty relief, social security, etc. In a further movement in the dialogue with civil society, the ILO also invites qualified NGOs to attend, in the condition of observers, some of its meetings, those for which they have demonstrated particular interest.

The exceptional participation of civil society in the decision-making process of an intergovernmental organization in charge of such an important matter as employment, demonstrates that there is plenty of room for the structured enlargement of non-state actors' participation in IGOs and, in particular, in the UN system. This affirmation is even stronger if we recall that the ILO was established almost a century ago, together with the League of Nations, at a time when public concerns about global governance and democracy, just to mention two contemporary issues, seemed far less relevant.

We understand that the ILO model has been extremely facilitated by the preexistence of matching structured representative bodies of either employers or workers in most of the countries, which generally adopt a pyramidal shape with local, regional and national layers of representativeness. Surely, several other contemporary issues do not have similar structures to support them. Nevertheless, some 'classic' issues, such as Health and Education, have worldwide structures and could definitely adopt an ILO-like governance. Probably, workers and employers were granted a golden opportunity to take part in the organization due to the remarkable prominence of the labor union movement at the beginning of the 20th century. We believe that some other windows of opportunity are open now.

c. UNESCO

The Constitution of 1945 of the United Nations Educational, Scientific and Cultural Organization (UNESCO)[67] laid down the initial provisions for the interaction between the organization and NGOs, establishing two channels of participation: consultative status (Art XI(4)) and the possibility of summoning international non-governmental conferences on education, the sciences and humanities or the dissemination of knowledge (art IV(3)).

Those initial provisions were first detailed in the General Conference in 1960, later replaced in 1995, and amended in 2001. The current Directives authorize UNESCO to establish 'operational relations' with NGOs at international, regional, sub-regional, national, local and grass-roots levels before establishing 'official relations'. The former relationship comprises those dynamic partnerships in the implementation of UNESCO programs at all the mentioned levels, and the latter, the sustained cooperation with UNESCO in its fields of competence, being granted to INGOs with recognized international structure and membership, either consultative or associate, depending on their role and structure.[68]

Once the official relation has been established, INGOs can be invited to send observers to sessions of the General Conference and its commissions, where they may make statements to the audience, with the consent of the presiding officer, or submit written statements to the Director-General for further communication to the Executive Board or to the General Conference.[69]

Compared with the ILO and the ECOSOC, the participation of NGOs in policy decision-making at UNESCO is far less relevant, even if one considers that their partnerships have been conceived to be of an essentially intellectual nature, promoting the exchange of ideas, technical cooperation and advising.

d. WHO

The World Health Organization (WHO) upholds the purpose, among other issues, of acting as the directing and coordinating authority on international health issues. To support this function, its Constitution stipulates that the organization may 'on matters within its competence make suitable arrangements for consultation and cooperation with non-governmental international organizations and, with the consent of the Government concerned, with national organizations, governmental or non-governmental'.[70]

According to the 'Principles Governing Relations with Nongovernmental Organizations', the WHO should act in conformity to any relevant resolutions of the UNGA and the ECOSCOC and its relationship with NGOs is an process evolving in separate stages which does not comprise different categories, as do the relationships maintained by the ECOSOC, the ILO or UNESCO, rather just one – known as official relations – being all other contacts, including working relations, considered of an informal character. The evolutionary approach demands a previous working relationship between the parties, supported by letters exchanged agreeing on the basis for the collaboration, the outcome of which will be further jointly assessed.[71]

NGOs in official relations have the right to participate in WHO meetings or in those of the committees and conferences convened under its auspices with the possibility of speaking before those bodies, but without voting rights. They can request access to non-confidential documentation and can also submit written statements to the Director General, who has the authority to define their circulation as well as access to the data requested.

The tighter restrictions in participation, if compared to the ILO and the ECOSOC, haven't prevented NGOs from reaching a striking achievement of convincing the 54th World Health Assembly in 1993, and later, the 1994 UN General Assembly, to ask the ICJ for an urgent advisory opinion, formulating the following question: 'Is the threat of or use of nuclear weapons in any circumstance permitted under international law?' More noticeable, however, was the outcome: Albeit the apparent impossibility of getting an affirmative answer and the completeness – an *a priori* assumption of every legal system – of international law ensured by article 38 of the ICJ Statutes, the Court pronounced a *non liquet,* i.e., decided that it 'cannot conclude definitively whether the threat or use of nuclear weapons would be lawful or unlawful'.[72]

Although probably not the expected result, beyond any doubt NGOs definitively influenced the agenda and the decision-making process of both the WHO and the UNGA and, what's more, gave birth to a fierce debate by the ICJ and, afterwards, among scholars, as to the limits and openness of international law, an issue that we will further appraise in the next chapter.

e. World Bank

There is no provision for any kind of formal relationship between NGOs and the World Bank in its formation acts, but in 1982 an NGO-WB Committee was formed to provide a forum for formal discussion among senior bank managers and twenty-six international NGO leaders on new policies, programs, studies or the design of specific projects, aiming to improve development effectiveness and sustainability and hold governments and policymakers publicly accountable.[73] Additionally, the bank has established one hundred and twenty Civil Society Focal Points, experienced social scientists and communication officers working in over eighty country offices that act as liaison officers with civil society.

The interaction with NGOs is also supported by the World Bank Inspection Panel, established in 1993, a body that accepts complaints from any affected parties regarding the bank's projects and any failure of the bank to follow its own rules. It is the sole check on the bank's activities and the implementation of its supported projects.[74] We shall return to the Inspection Panels and their role as tools for an enhanced accountability on Chapter 8.

f. Other specialized agencies

Among other UN specialized agencies that have formal consultative relationships with NGOs established in their Constitutions, we mention the Food and Agriculture Organization (FAO),[75] the International Monetary

Fund (IMF),[76] the International Civil Aviation Organization (ICAO),[77] the International Maritime Organization (IMO),[78] the World Meteorological Organization (WMO),[79] the World Intellectual Property Organization (WIPO),[80] the International Fund for Agricultural Development (IFAD)[81] and the UN Industrial Development Organization (UNIDO).[82]

2.2   The OECD

The Organization for Economic Co-operation and Development (OECD) has maintained a continuous dialogue with civil society organizations, including NGOs, businesses and trade unions since its inception in 1961. The relationship does not rely on treaty obligations, but rather relies on a 1962 OECD Council decision, still in force, that set down two consultative bodies, the Business and Industry Advisory Committee and the Trade Union Advisory Committee. Those formal bodies have annual meetings with the OECD Council and pre-ministerial consultations, together with informal contacts, consultations, seminars and workshops throughout the year, and participation in several OECD activities through the Labor/Management Programme.[83]

OECD's goal of introducing high standards of governance in public institutions, through increased citizen awareness and understanding of public policies, legitimizes information sharing, consultation and active engagement of citizens in policy-making as guiding approaches, although such partnership is still rare in the member-states.[84]

Active engagement of civil society is pursued in areas such as trade and the environment, where the OECD Trade Committee holds regular consultation with civil society organizations, and also on global and corporate governance, fighting corruption and environmental policy, development co-operation, biotechnology, food and agriculture, information and communications technologies, territorial development and nuclear energy, where consultation has been established on a variable basis, either in formal or informal meetings.[85] Worthy to quote, too, is the initiative of the OECD Forum, an international public conference that offers civil society organizations the opportunity to discuss key global issues with government ministers and leaders of international organizations, together with the possibility of contributing to the OECD annual ministerial summit.

But OECD contact with civil society has not always been smooth going. One impact derived from the 9/11 attacks was that certain malfeasance practices came to light, in which charitable fundraising and institutions had been used as coverage for financing of terrorism, which included shelter to terrorists, logistical support and illicit arms. Those circumstances led the OECD Financial Action Task Force on Money Laundering (FATF-GAFI) to study and propose international best practices to combat the abuse of non-profit organizations, focusing on their financial transparency, programmatic verification, administration, oversight bodies and sanctions.[86]

As aforementioned, while discussing the interaction of NGOs with the UNSC, either NGOs or terrorist groups have roots in civil society and, also, in their supporters' dissatisfaction with the world's current state of affairs and/or government strategies to deal with them. Therefore, it is important to implement a set of rules and procedures capable of enhancing civil participation in global policy decision-making processes in order to address the manifold issues at stake and counterbalance the appealing 'The end justifies the means!' call of certain groups before the deafness of States' representatives.

2.3   The Council of Europe

The ideas and ideals enshrined in the UN Charter have roots in European thought, as well as the conception of the welfare state, which offers a high standard of State's respect toward its citizens. Therefore, it is not without reason that the relationship of the European institutions with NGOs had its onset more than a half century ago, in 1951, when the Council of Europe (CoE) authorized the Committee of Ministers to make suitable arrangements for consultation with INGOs with activities and purposes within the competence of the Council.[87]

Similar to the situation observed on the ECOSOC, there have been continuous improvements in the rules on consultative status, with new rules being enacted in 1976 and 1993, when consultative status was extended to national NGOs. The current rules were adopted in 2003 and have incorporated a sensitive advance in the relationship because they have 'underlined the participatory character' of the interaction of NGOs with the CoE.[88]

In practical terms, the Council has remained a state-only organization and the NGOs' participation can neither be regarded as membership to the Council nor represent the acquisition of voting rights in any of its bodies. Notwithstanding it, the new regime provided an 'upgrade' to NGOs, that, then, leave the status of consultants, who answer whatever and whenever they are asked, to become true participants in the debates, with more opportunities to share their point of view, submitting memoranda without size limitations and providing expertise advice on a more regular basis, although not voting in the decision-making process.[89] The enhanced status was welcomed in a CoE Parliamentary Assembly that supported 'the principle of changing the consultative status to a participatory one' and manifested its intention 'to consider in the future the possibility of creating a specific status based upon appropriate criteria for the NGOs with the Parliamentary Assembly in order to enhance direct contact and co-operation with them'.[90]

To obtain participatory status, the candidate NGO must submit an application to the CoE Secretary General, according to the aforementioned Res. 2003(8). Once the documentary conditions have been met, the Secretary General submits the list of candidates to the Liaison Committee, a democratically elected body representing all NGOs with participatory status within the Council, for any remarks, which must be given within two months. Once the period has expired, the Secretary General submits the list to the Committee of Ministers, Parliamentary Assembly and the Congress of Local and Regional Authorities, whose members can raise objections to any candidate within a three-month period. If the period should expire without any remarks being made, the Secretary General concludes the procedure by appointing the NGO to the list of those entities with participatory status. In a manner different from that of the ECOSOC, where the member-states must actively vote to approve granting the status, at the CoE their silence is enough to approve the candidacy.

Together with the new rules concerning participatory status, a new resolution has been adopted that addresses the status of partnership between the CoE and NGOs, providing directives about modalities of co-operation (program implementation, public awareness-raising events, expert advice) and procedures for partnership agreements.[91] To foster participation of individuals through civil society organizations in CoE activities, the 'Conference of INGOs in the Council of Europe' has been established, which is a network of NGOs with participatory status, that, similarly to the CONGO in the UN system, aims to concatenate efforts of their members to make them more effective in the CoE and enhance their political role. Member NGOs are organized in committees aligned to the structure of CoE bodies, with the clear intention of bolstering their influence in CoE steering committees and groups of experts.[92]

The relationship of the CoE with NGOs has gone beyond simply regulating their consultative (participatory) status or even working relations in international documents other than treaties, since, back in 1986, the member-states adopted the Strasbourg Convention, recognizing NGOs as those associations, foundations or other non-profit making private institutions with aims of international utility, carrying on their activities with effect in at least two States with statutory offices and central management.

Despite silencing in recognizing the international legal personality of NGOs, a necessary outcome of the rights ensured to them in other international instruments, the Strasbourg Convention is a relevant 'entrance door' of NGOs in international law, not only because it demonstrates that they are subjects that deserves regulation in multi-lateral treaties, but, most importantly, that their condition can undergo further improvement, especially if we take into account the cited Opinion 246 of the CoE Parliamentary Assembly, which, while addressing the low adhesion of member-states to the Convention, assumed the possibility of adapting it through an amending protocol (para 4 (iii)).

2.4 The European Union

In 1991, the European Commission proposed a draft regulation of the European Parliament and of the Council on the statute for a European Association (EA), the first governmental attempt to regulate a supernational legal personality for NGOS.[93] The project proposed an extensive regulation for the EA that had to be established by a grouping of natural and/or legal persons to pursue non-profit aims in accordance to the objectives of the European Community (EC), and public interest. The draft ensured its legal personality in its registration of the member-state in which it established its registered office and also full legal capacity. The supernationality was guaranteed not only by the operation in all of the European Community but also by the existence of founding members from at least two different member-states and the possibility of transfer of the registered office to any other member-state without resulting in the winding up of the EA or in the creation of a new legal person. Unfortunately, the proposal was withdrawn by the Commission on 17 March 2006. [94]

Currently, the European Union (EU), together with the institutions (governing bodies), has two advisory bodies, the Economic and Social Committee (ESC),[95] composed of representatives of various categories of economic and social activity, in particular, representatives of producers, farmers, carriers, workers, dealers, craftsmen, professional occupations and representatives of the general public, and the Committee of the Regions (CoR), consisting of representatives of regional and local bodies. The CoR represents an interaction channel with regional and local authorities and the ESC, with civil society. Both bodies have a defined, although not equal, number of seats available to member-states. According to the treaty, the ESC must be consulted by the Council or by the Commission wherever the treaty so provides and in all cases in which these institutions consider it appropriate. The ESC may take the initiative of issuing an opinion in cases in which it considers such action appropriate. Despite the advisory status, it can be noticed that the structure of the EU contemplates a regular body for interaction between civil society organizations capable of balancing the social and economic forces *within* the States and *between* the States.

Governance is also a relevant focus at the European level, and the participation of civil society is deemed necessary, especially if we bear in mind the content of the Commission's White Paper on European Governance, laid down on the principles of participation, openness, accountability, effectiveness and coherence.[96] Further to the 2001 Commission discussion paper on partnership with NGOs,[97] and Declaration 17 of the Final Act of the Treaty on European Union[98] on the right of access to information, the Council and Commission adopted a joint code of conduct ensuring that the public will have the widest possible access to documents held by both bodies.[99] We shall resume this issue in Chapter 8.

2.5   The OAS, MERCOSUR and NAFTA

2.5.1   The Organization of American States

The Organization of American States (OAS) Charter recognized the importance of 'the contribution of organizations such as labor unions, cooperatives, and cultural, professional, business, neighborhood, and community associations to the life of the society and to the development process' (Art 45 (g)) and assigned to the Permanent Council the possibility of entering into special agreements or arrangements between the Organization 'and other American agencies of recognized international standing' (art 91 (d)) which, as OAS practice has shown, comprises NGOs either at the national or international level.[100] The first General Assembly regulation of such partnership was established in 1971.[101] On several occasions, the member-states emphasized the importance of NGOs in fostering democracy.[102]

In 1997, a comprehensive study on the legal status of NGOs in the OAS was released by the Committee on Juridical and Political Affairs,[103] which supported the establishment, within the Permanent Council, of the Committee on Civil Society Participation in the OAS in 1998, followed by the adoption of Guidelines for participation of NGOs in OAS activities.[104] According to these Guidelines, NGOs 'may attend the activities of the OAS, make presentations, provide information, and, at the request of the organs, agencies, and entities of the OAS, provide expert advice. They may also participate in operational activities relating to the design, financing, and execution of cooperation programs, in accordance with applicable regulations and specific agreements negotiated for this purpose' (art 3 (a)). The participation includes the right to apply for participation in OAS Conferences (art 12) and, after registration with the OAS, the right to attend, as observers, public meetings of the Permanent Council, Inter-American Council for Integral Development and subsidiary bodies, being allowed to present written documents not exceeding 2000 words (art 13). Despite the open access to the Organization, the participation of NGOs does not imply in recognizing to them any negotiating functions neither membership to the OAS, functions exclusively preserved to the States (art 4 (d)).

In order to improve and increase participation of NGOs in the organization's activities, the OAS Summits of Americas Department has prepared and released a manual covering the role, principles and means of that participation, a practical and comprehensive tool that is still not available within the UN system.[105]

2.5.2   The MERCOSUR

The Southern Common Market (MERCOSUR) was established by the Treaty of Asuncion in 26 March 1991 with the purpose of economically integrating the countries of the South America southern cone, Argentina, Brazil, Uruguay and Paraguay, in a customs union. On December 1994, the Protocol of Ouro Preto established the institutional structure of MERCOSUR, providing its international legal personality and creating the Social Economic Consultative Forum. The Forum is composed of an equal number of representatives (nine) from each member-state, which ordinarily meet twice a year with the purpose of integrating the social and economic sectors, represented by civil society organizations of several scopes, such as NGOs, Academia, workers' and business' associations, and scientific societies. The Forum does not have decision-making powers, but can make recommendations or submit draft new rules or policies to the MERCOSUR governing bodies.[106]

The huge discrepancies in economic strength, territory and population of the member-states pose a severe difficulty in the integration, a fact that can be observed by the tiny achievements reached in economic integration since its establishment. Despite this situation, it is noticeable that the structure of this intergovernmental organization contemplates a regular body for interaction between civil society organizations capable of balancing the social and economic forces *within* the States and *between* the States.

2.5.3   The NAFTA

The North-American Free Trade Agreement (NAFTA) aims to integrate economically the US, Canada and Mexico into a free commercial zone that, in addition to the main treaty, is regulated by several other 'side agreements', including the North-American Agreement on Environmental Cooperation (NAAEC).[107] This is the first world experience in integrating commercial and environmental issues in a commercial agreement, due to the intense pressure of NGOs and civil society, including through congressmen during the negotiation process.

One relevant aspect of the NAAEC is the obligation imposed to the Commission for Environmental Cooperation (CEC), steward of the implementation of the NAAEC with a quasi-judicial role, of considering written submissions from any non-governmental organization or person asserting that a Party to the treaty is failing to effectively enforce its environmental law. The CEC also supports arbitral panel processes involving disputes between the state-parties on certain trade-related issues associated with failure to comply with environmental law enforcement. The CEC consists of a Council of Ministers, comprised of Environmental Ministers from each of the state-parties, a Secretariat headed by an Executive Director and a Joint Public Advisory Committee, comprised of fifteen citizens, five from each country, representing a broad range of interests.

If the submission satisfies the legal criteria, a response will be requested from the party named in the submission. In light of that response, the CEC Secretariat will prepare a factual record on the matter, objectively outlining the history of the issue, the obligations of the party under the law in question, the actions of the party in fulfilling those obligations, and the facts relevant to the assertions made in the submission of a failure to enforce environmental law effectively. Once completed, the CEC Council of Ministers may, by a two-thirds vote, make the final factual record publicly available. Publicity on the failure to enforce environmental law produces considerable political impact and may lead to legal obligations at the national level, if brought to the local courts.[108]

2.6   The African Union

The African Union (AU) Constitutive Act[109] adopted the participation of African peoples in the activities of the Union as one of its founding principles (art 4 (d)) and created the Economic, Social and Cultural Council (ECOSOCC), an advisory organ composed of different social and professional groups of the member-states of the Union (art 22). This structure gives a distinctive character to the ECOSOCC, if compared to the UN ECOSOC, because it allows African civil society to play an active role in charting the future of Africa. Again, as observed in the EU and MERCOSUR, a regional international convention created a specific body *within* an intergovernmental organization to interact with civil society.

The Statutes of the ECOSOCC, approved in the 2004 General Assembly, establish that the Council has the purpose of strengthening partnerships between governments and all segments of civil society, promoting the participation of civil society in the implementation of programs and policies of the Union together with strengthening the institutional, human and operational capacities of the African civil society. The Council is composed of one hundred and fifty civil society organizations, such as NGOs, professional associations and social groups, either at a national, regional or continental level, and, quite interestingly, of African Diaspora, provided that those organizations are managed by at least fifty per cent of Africans, a marked position against any threat of neo-colonialism by Western NGOs.[110]

It is also interesting to note that the ECOSOCC's agenda has been divided into themes to be addressed by one of its subsidiary bodies, the

Sectoral Cluster Communities, instituted to formulate opinions and provide inputs on the policies and rams of the AU in the following fields: Peace and Security, Political Affairs, Infrastructure and Energy, Social Affairs and Health, Human Resources, Science and Technology, Trade and Industry, Rural Economy and Agriculture and Economic Affairs.

2.7   Human Rights Treaties

One could deem human rights as one 'entrance door' of individuals and civil society organizations into the realm of international law. Since the Battle of Solferino, in 1859, the improvement in the conditions of the human being in all kinds of struggles between States has been continuously feeding the enhancement of what is now called humanitarian international law.

The first known NGOs, established in the 19th century, worked to ensure the now non-derogable human right of freedom from slavery (the Anti-Slavery Society) and the right to life (The ICRC). Currently, human rights are protected by either international or regional conventions, being enshrined in the UN Charter and in the constitutions of most States.

The ICRC, a Swiss association, gained relevant status in the Geneva Convention relative to the Treatment of Prisoners of War (1949) and its additional Protocols (1977), which determined that the conflicting parties should accept the services of a humanitarian organization, such as the ICRC, to assume the humanitarian functions to be performed during the conflict. Its access to prisoner camps, as we observed above while addressing the role of NGOs before the UNSC, is often confirmed by Council resolutions.

Relevant to the purpose of our analysis is the 'executive' humanitarian function embedded in the mandate granted to the ICRC by the Geneva Convention and Protocols, because it granted an NGO certain international rights that could be opposed to any recalcitrant State, which, as mentioned, includes the right to enter the territory of a sovereign State. This is a unique feature in international law, since none of the classical subjects of international law – i.e., the States and intergovernmental organizations – have the right to do so.[111] Again, as pointed out while addressing the ILO Constitution, civil society organizations can achieve certain rights in an international treaty even not being one of its signatories.

Since World War II, when civil losses surpassed for the first time military casualties, armed conflicts have been imposing severe death tolls on civil society. Likewise, NGOs (and their personnel) that are active in the field of human rights have been suffering the same threats as those posed to the people they aim to protect. This conflictuous situation reached such an unacceptable level that the World Conference on Human Rights, held in

Vienna in 1993, introduced a paragraph in its final declaration to affirm that NGOs and their members genuinely involved in the field of human rights should enjoy the rights and freedoms recognized in the Universal Declaration of Human Rights, and the protection of national law.[112]

Excluding the specific situation of the ICRC, none of the more relevant human rights treaties explicitly makes reference to NGOs. Some authors support that NGOs should be considered included in the expression 'other competent bodies' of article 45 (b) of the Convention on the Rights of the Child,[113] since NGOs customarily provide technical advice or assistance, but this remains a question open to debate.[114]

At the operational level, NGOs are extremely active within the Human Rights agencies because those bodies operate under enormous restraints of time and resources, with an expressive backlog of reports due to the rising number of State ratifications. NGOs have been a reliable source of information, suggestions and support for the High Commissioner for Human Rights (UNHCHR) since the creation of the post in 1993.[115] They provide relevant support to the monitoring of human rights due to their capillarity and grass-root activities, which enable them to contribute, mostly by raising questions on targeted or omitted issues, to better access to a country's reports.[116]

Another relevant feature of the role of NGOs in human rights treaties is their *locus standi,* i.e., their right to petitioning. The American Convention on Human Rights[117] establishes (art 44) that any NGO legally recognized in one or more member-states of the OAS may lodge petitions with the Inter-American Commission on Human Rights containing denunciations or complaints of violation of the Convention by a State party. Direct access to the Inter-American Court of Human Rights is not allowed. A similar right is ensured by the European Convention on Human Rights[118] (art 25), which establishes that individual applications may be submitted by individuals or NGOs claiming to be victims of a violation. At the African level, the African Charter on Human and People's Rights[119] authorizes the African Commission on Human and People's Rights to consider communications received by parties other than the member-states concerning violations or threats on the protected rights (art 55-56), and the African Charter on the Rights and Welfare of the Child[120] authorizes the Committee of Experts on the Rights and Welfare of the Child to consider communication, from any person, group or nongovernmental organization recognized by the Organization of African Unity, by a member-state, or the United Nations relating to any matter covered by the Charter (art 44). We shall address the situation of NGOs before judicial or quasi-judicial bodies at greater depth in the next chapter.

2.8   Environmental Treaties

A second - and more active - entrance door of NGOs to international law is, definitively, environmental law. The oldest environmental treaty with a worthy reference to NGOs is the Ramsar Convention.[121] In order to review and promote the implementation of the convention, it established a Conference of the contracting parties whose representatives should include persons who are experts on wetlands or waterfowl by reason of knowledge and experience gained in scientific, administrative or other appropriate capacities (Art 7 (1)). Since that expertise is quite rare in diplomatic corps, the convention demanded the participation of people customarily found in civil society organizations, such as the Academia or NGOs.

However, the participation of civil society has gone much further ahead than the condition of simply having individuals among the State representatives, because the Convention has nominated an NGO, the International Union for Conservation of Nature and Natural Resources (IUCN), to act as the substantive Secretariat of the Convention, performing 'the continuing bureau duties under the Convention until such time another organization or government is appointed by a majority of two-thirds of all contracting parties', a replacement that has not yet occurred. The activities to be performed by the IUCN include: (i) to assist in the convening and organizing of Conferences; (ii) to maintain the List of Wetlands of International Importance and to be informed by any of the contracting parties of any additions, extensions, deletions or restrictions concerning wetlands included in the List; (iii) to be informed by any contracting party of any changes in the ecological character of wetlands included in the List; (iv) to forward notification of any alterations to the List, or changes in character of wetlands included therein, to all contracting parties and to arrange for these matters to be discussed at the next Conference; (v) to make known to the contracting party concerned, the recommendations of the Conferences with respect to such alterations to the List or to changes in the character of wetlands included therein.[122] The Ramsar Secretariat has also signed several Memoranda of Understanding and Cooperation with NGOs, including five international organization partners and ten other NGOs.[123]

The substantial activities of the IUCN in the protection of the wetlands differ from those performed by the ICRC with regards to the protection of human rights. Nevertheless, despite this material and procedural discrepancy, these activities maintain a common situation within international law, since both have received a mandate from the States to act on their behalf in the fulfillment of an agreed convention.

The IUCN is also an active member of the Intergovernmental Committee for the Protection of the Cultural and Natural Heritage of Outstanding Universal Value (the World Heritage Committee) established within the UNESCO by the Convention concerning the Protection of the

World Cultural and Natural Heritage where, together with a representative of the International Center for the Study of the Preservation and Restoration of Cultural Property (Rome Center), a representative of the International Council of Monuments and Sites (ICOMOS), and other NGO representatives, invited at the request of States parties, it participates in the meetings in an advisory capacity (art 8 (3)).[124]

Another important environmental convention supporting the legitimacy of NGOs in the international real is the CITES,[125] drafted as a result of a resolution adopted in 1963 at a meeting of members of the IUCN. The convention ensures that any international NGO technically qualified in protection, conservation, or management of wild fauna and flora which has informed the Secretariat of its desire to be represented at meetings of the conference, *shall be admitted* as observer, without voting rights, unless at least one-third of the parties object (art 11 (7)). This provision represents a substantive step forward in terms of civil society participation, because, differently from the UN conferences, in which the participation depends on the acceptance of the Secretariat, at CITES Conferences the participation is guaranteed, unless a qualified group of member-states reject it. The participatory right is also extended to national NGOs, provided that their participation is approved by the State where they are located (art. 17 (2)).

A fourth international environmental structure with relevant participation of NGOs is the Global Environment Facility (GEF), a global partnership among one hundred and seventy-eight countries, international institutions, NGOs, and the private sector established to address global environmental issues while supporting national sustainable development initiatives. The GEF started as a World Bank program in 1991 but due to the outcome of the 1992 Rio Earth Summit, it became an independent organization in 1994,[126] designated to be the financial mechanism for the UN Convention on Biological Diversity (CBD), the UN Framework Convention on Climate Change (UNFCC), the Stockholm Convention on Persistent Organic Pollutants (POPs) and the United Nations Convention to Combat Desertification (UNCCD). It also provides funding to projects in partnership with the Montreal Protocol of the Vienna Convention on Ozone Layer Depleting Substances.[127] The GEF is open to participation of any State member of the UN or its specialized agencies and is structured into a General Assembly, a Council and a Secretariat. Participation with the right to vote at the General Assembly is given only to State representatives. Partnerships with NGOs are not created at the Assembly or Council levels, being focused on the Secretariat and the Implementing Agencies, either for consultation or assisting in the design, execution, and monitoring of projects. The GEF maintains regular structured consultations with NGOs through the 'GEF-NGO Network'.

The Earth Summit approved Agenda 21, introducing a global partnership for sustainable development. According to this extensive document, partnerships with civil society, through its major groups, are recognized, valued and pursued. According to its paragraph 27.1, 'NGOs play a vital role in the shaping and implementation of participatory democracy' and 'should be recognized as partners in the implementation of Agenda 21'.[128]

Given these few examples, it becomes evident that the development of international environmental law does not conform to the classic doctrinal division of States/subjects – Non-state/objects not only because it allows for the participation of individuals and civil society organizations, some with executive roles such as the IUCN in the Ramsar convention, but mostly because 'international law imposes direct environmental responsibilities on individuals and companies through the polluter pays principle, transboundary civil liability for environmental damage and extra-territorial criminal jurisdiction over certain environmental offences'.[129]

What becomes clear after quoting these few agreements, among the dozens of environmental treaties, either at the international or regional levels, legitimizing the role of civil society, is that environmental law is not simply a system of rules and obligations, but rather a complex decision-making process in the realm of goals, values, methods and priorities that operate both at the municipal and international levels, through the notions of 'common concern' (Agenda 21), 'property of humankind' and 'sustainable development', which cannot be legitimate if relying only on the hands of States. It demands the participation of other actors, including individuals, through procedures of transparency and public participation, such as those prescribed in the Aarhus Convention and the NAAEC.

Challenging this understanding, some authors argue that these so-called 'environmental human rights' suffer from cultural relativism and lack the universal value normally thought to be inherent to human rights and may prove potentially meaningless and ineffective - such as the right to development - and undermine the very notion of human rights.[130] Others support that international conventions that define the civil responsibility of individuals and companies for damages caused to the international environment actually have defined internationally a legal regimen to be applicable within the countries concerned. Thus, they have not created an international responsibility to individuals and companies, but rather created a uniform municipal responsibility to those internal subjects.[131]

With all due respect to the quality of the arguments, we understand that people's rights to the environment are not only 'material rights' but mostly 'procedural rights' (Aarhus, NAAEC, etc), because international treaties have legitimized their access to environmental justice and their participation in environmental decision-making. These rights require and benefit from notions of civil participation in public affairs already reflected in existing civil and political rights (1966 International Covenant on Civil and Political Rights, arts 19, 25) and environmental documents (1992 Rio Declaration, principle 10), which achieved an universal character by their adoption in several other treaties and international documents such as the World Charter for Nature,[132] the 1985 Vienna Convention,[133] the 1987 Montreal Protocol,[134] the 1992 Framework Convention on Climate Change,[135] the 1991 UN/ECE Espoo Convention on Environmental Impact Assessment,[136] the 1991 UN/ECE Helsinki Convention on the Transboundary Effect of Industrial Accidents,[137] the 1992 Biological Diversity Convention,[138] and the 2003 CoE Lugano Convention on Civil Liability for Damage Resulting from Activities Dangerous to the Environment, [139] just to quote a few.

Regarding the second argument, that environmental law defines internationally a uniform municipal law for individual responsibility, we understand that, even considering that it may be true in certain aspects of environmental protection, it is not general at all, because the purpose of the international environmental law is protecting the human being in general, focusing on the effects of human behavior that transcends the States boundaries. The fact that a given individual will be prosecuted or penalized under a certain municipal regimen does not imply that the challenged conduct is irrelevant for other individuals living in other States. This international impact evidences that environmental law is not just a coordinated set of municipal legal standards, rather a truly international concern that require international regulation.

As concluding remarks to this chapter, we can summarize that the practice of States in international treaties and other documents concerning the role and status of NGOs is not uniform, albeit recognizing their importance in one way or another. Additionally, one can observe that the more recent the document, the greater the participation of civil society, evidence that undoubtedly attests a evolutionary relevance in the international arena. Recalling protests against the WTO Conference in Seattle, in 1999, Charles-Albert Morand wrote that

> 'por reprendre la distinction de Montesquieu, elles (les ONG) n'on pas directement la faculté de statuer, mas parfois la faculté d'empêcher. (...) Pour le juriste positiviste, cela ne représente rien, puisque formellement les Etats ne perdent pas leur monopole dans la formation du droit international. Mais sociologiquement et politiquement cela représent l'irruption de la societé civile dans la vie internationale. (...) Par leur action, les ONG peuvent infléchir l'application et l'interpretation des normes internationales, dans la mesure où elles dépendent du contexte, de l'opinion publique internationale.'[140]

As we will observe in the forthcoming chapters, NGOs are promoting changes in international custom and definitively affecting the decisions of judicial and quasi-judicial bodies.

Notes

1   H Hillgenberg, 'A Fresh Look at Soft Law' (1999) EJIL, v 10 n 3, 504.

2   The author of this study had this experience, when accredited as a member of the Brazilian delegation to the 2002 World Summit on Sustainable Development, in Johannesburg.

3   PH Baher, 'Mobilization of the Conscience of Mankind: Conditions of Effectiveness of Human Rights NGOs' in E. Denters, N. Schrijver (eds), *Reflections of International Law from the Low Countries* (Nijhoff, The Hague 1998) 135-155.

4   UN ECOSOC NGO Committee, *The NGO Committee: a ten year review* (New York 2008) 5.

5   H Hillgenberg, *A Fresh Look at Soft Law* (n 1) 501.

6   NGOs were instrumental in the drafting of the Declaration, as we can observe in UNGA Res. 217A (III) (10 December 1948).

7   This is the case of the World Tourism Organization, a specialized UN Agency, and the International Institute for Democracy and Electoral Assistance, an international organization headquartered in Sweden, which has, as members, States and intergovernmental organizations and, as associate members, international non-governmental organizations, all with seats and voting rights at the Council.

8   *Reparation for Injuries Suffered in the Service of the United Nations* (Advisory Opinion) [1949] ICJ Rep 174.

9   *Texaco Overseas Petroleum Company and California Asiatic Oil Company v Government of Libyan Republic* (Merits) (1979) 53 ILR 389.

10   H Hillgenberg, *A Fresh Look at Soft Law* (n 1) 508.

11   H Hillgenberg, *A Fresh Look at Soft Law* (n 1) 509.

12   MR Sanches, 'Atores não estatais e sua relação com a Organização Mundial do Comércio', in A Amaral Junior, *Direito do Comércio Internacional* (Juarez Oliveira, São Paulo 2002) 154.

13   CA Morand, 'La Souveraineté, un concept dépassé', in LB de Chazournes and V Gowland-Debbas, *The International Legal System in Quest of Equity and Universality* (Martinus Nijhoff, The Hague 2001) 174.

14   H Hillgenberg, *A Fresh Look at Soft Law* (n 1) 514.

15   *Convention on Biological Diversity* (adopted 5 June 1992, entered into force 29 December 1993) UNTS 1760.

16   *Legality on the Threat or Use of Nuclear Weapons* (Advisory Opinion) [1996] ICJ Rep 226 para 29.

17   G Tunkin, 'Is General International Law Customary Law Only?' (1993) EJIL n 4, 541; B Fassbender, 'The Better Peoples of the United Nations? Europe's Practice and the United Nations', (2004) EJIL, v 15 n 5, 879.

18   C Chinkin, 'The Role of Non-Governmental Organisations in Standard Setting, Monitoring and Implementation of Human Rights', in J Norton, M Andenas and M Focter, *The Changing World of International Law in the Twenty-First Century: a tribute to the late Kenneth R. Simmonds*, (Kluwer Law, The Hague 1998) 46.

19   Some authors consider that the ECOSOC 'consultative' status should be regarded as equal to 'observer'. See, GFS Soares, 'As ONGs e o direito internacional do meio ambiente' Revista de Direito Ambiental, v 17, 21.

20   UN ECOSOC NGO Committee, *The NGO Committee: a ten year review* (New York 2008) 51.

21   UN NGLS mission statement available at http://www.un-ngls.org/ accessed on 15 March 2009

22 UNGA Report of the Secretary General on 'Arrangements and practices for the inter-
    action of non-governmental organizations in all activities of the United Nations sys-
    tem' (10 July 1998) UN Doc A/53/170.
23 ECOSOC Res 2/3 (21 June 1946) UN Doc E/43Rev.2.
24 UNGA Res 173 (III) (17 November 1947).
25 Doc A/943. *Projet de réglementation pour la convocation des conférences internacio-
    nales: raport du Secrétaire General.* Article 7: 'Aux conférences d'Etats convoquées
    conformément au present règlement, les institutions spécialisées reliées à
    l'Organisation des Nations Unies et les organisations non gouvernementales aux-
    quelles le Conseil a accordé le statut consultatif jouiront des memes droits and privi-
    leges qu'aux sessions do Conseil sous reserve des dispositions de l'article 2'.
26 AC Kiss, *Repertóire de la pratique française em matiére de droit international public*
    (Centre National de la Recherche Scientifique, Paris 1962) v 5, 363.
27 UNGA Res 606 (VI) (1 February 1952).
28 AC Kiss, *Repertóire de la pratique française* (n 26) 366.
29 Just to summarize a few, we quote Resolutions 2435 (XXIII) (19 Dec 1968), 2717
    (XXV) (15 Dec 1970), 3271 (XXIX) (10 Dec 1974), 31/149 (20 Dec 1976), 32/90 (13
    Dec 1977), 34/56 (29 Nov 1979), 34/114 (14 Dec 1979), 35/34 (14 Nov 1980), 35/64 (5
    Dec 1980), 57/299 (20 Dec 2002), 59/171, 59/193, 59/201 and 59/204 (all from 20
    Dec 2004), and 60/161 (16 Dec 2005).
30 UNGA Res. 49/2 (19 October 1994).
31 UNGA Res. 54/195 (17 December 1999).
32 UNGA Res. 48/265 (24 August 1994).
33 UNGA Res. 52/250 (7 July 1998).
34 UNGA Report of the Secretary General on 'Arrangements and practices for the inter-
    action of non-governmental organizations in all activities of the United Nations sys-
    tem' (10 July 1998) UN Doc A/53/170 para 10.
35 *Reparation for Injuries* (n 8).
36 Although authorized to make relevant decisions by a two-thirds majority of the mem-
    bers present and voting (Article 18 para. 2, UN Charter).
37 H Hillgenberg, *A Fresh Look at Soft Law* (n 1) 514.
38 Although NGOs with consultative status, as a rule, should be accredited (ECOSOC
    Res. 1996/31 para. 42).
39 In 2009, the Council was composed of the following countries: Algeria, Barbados,
    Belarus, Bolivia, Brazil, Cameroon, Canada, Cape Verde, China, Congo, Côte d'Ivoire,
    El Salvador, Estonia, France, Germany, Greece, Guatemala, Guinea-Bissau, India,
    Indonesia, Iraq, Japan, Kazakhstan, Liechtenstein, Luxembourg, Malawi, Malaysia,
    Mauritius, Morocco, Mozambique, Namibia, Netherlands, New Zealand, Niger,
    Norway, Pakistan, Peru, Philippines, Poland, Portugal, Republic of Korea, Republic
    of Moldova, Romania, Russian Federation, Saint Kitts and Nevis, Saint Lucia, Saudi
    Arabia, Somalia, Sudan, Sweden, the United Kingdom, the United States, Uruguay
    and Venezuela.
40 JD Aston, 'The United Nations Committee on Non-governmental Organizations:
    Guarding the Entrance of a Politically Divided House', (2001) EJIL v 12 n 5, 943-962.
41 Albeit the existence of other 'focal points' and 'unique' interfaces of the UN with
    NGOs, as explained in the beginning of this chapter, the cited role of the Committee
    on NGOs was mentioned in a report available at <http://www.un.org/News/Press/
    docs/2009/ecosoc6375.doc.htm> accessed 18 March 2009.
42 According to the Committee on NGO press reports available at http://esango.un.org/
    paperless/Web?page=static&content=committee accessed 18 March 2009.
43 JD Aston, *The United Nations Committee* (n 40) 950.

44 ECOSOC Res. 1996/31 para 8 prescribes that 'national organizations (...) may be admitted (...) after consultation with the Member State concerned. The views expressed by the Member State, *if any*, shall be communicated to the non-governmental organization concerned, which shall have the opportunity to respond to those views through the Committee on Non-Governmental Organizations.

45 Dalits (untouchables) in India, women and gays in Muslim countries, Palestinians in Gaza and civil liberties in Cuba and China, just to quote a few.

46 B. Manin, in his work *Principles of Representative Government*, supports the centrality of mass communication in the current system of political representation, in which the media has replaced the parliament as the *locus* of public debate.

47 JD Aston, *The United Nations Committee* (n 40).

48 UNGA Secretary General Report on 'Views of Member States, Members of the Specialized Agencies, Observers, Intergovernmental and Non-Governmental Organizations From All Regions on the Report of the Secretary General on Arrangements and Practices for the Interaction of Non-Governmental Organizations in All Activities of the United Nations System' (8 September 1999) Doc A/54/329.

49 JD Aston, *The United Nations Committee* (n 40) 951.

50 ECOSOC Res. 1297 (XLIV) (27 May 1968).

51 According to < http://www.un.org/dpi/ngosection/about-ngo-assoc.asp> accessed 20 March 2009.

52 See, in this regard and for association requirements < http://www.un.org/dpi/ngosection/ngo-partnership.asp> accessed 20 March 2009.

53 The Arria Formula enables off-the-record consultation with people not admitted to Council meetings, such as NGOs, off of the Security Council's premises. It was implemented in March 2002. See, J Paul, *The Arria Formula* (New York, 2003) < www.globalpolicy.org/security/mtgsetc/arria.htm> accessed 24 April 2009.

54 See, for example, A Cassese, 'Terrorism is Also Disrupting Some Crucial Legal Categories of International Law', (2001) EJIL, vI2 n 5, 993; and F Hoffman, 'Watershed or Phoenix from the Ashes? Speculations on the Future of International Law After the September 11 Attacks', (2001) GLJ n 16, both written in the heat of the attacks. For a more comprehensive study, see RP Barnidge Jr, *Non-State Actors and Terrorism* (TMC Asser, The Hague, 2008).

55 Even before the attacks, several authors had supported the inadequacy of the Westphalian system of juxtaposed states for the 21st century international community and its failure in incorporating non-state actors. Some offered a provocative so-called 'plausible' conception of contemporary international law, arguing that the whole notion of 'subjects' or 'objects' has no credible reality and functional purpose, demanding the adoption of the concept of 'participants' in the international legal system, comprising not only states and IGOs, but also individuals, multinational corporations, and international NGOs. See, in this particular approach, R. Higgins, *Problems and Process: International Law and How We Use It*, (OUP, Oxford 1994) 49.

56 A Cassese, *Terrorism is Also Disrupting*, (n 54) 995.

57 ILC Articles on State Responsibility, article 8.

58 Some authors attribute the silence of European countries on the US' problematic reinterpretation of the right of self-defense to the fact that a couple of years before, the European members of NATO themselves had bombed Yugoslavia on grounds of 'humanitarian intervention' in Kosovo, which was also a reinterpretation of the limited scope of use of force enshrined in the UN Charter, carried out without the previous consent of the UN Security Council. See B Fassbender, *The Better Peoples* (n 17) 865.

59 In this particular aspect, it is noteworthy to mention the understanding of the ICJ in the *Corfu Channel* case. The case addressed Albania's responsibility for damages caused to two British ships by a minefield in Albanian territorial waters, which had

not been notified for the benefit of shipping in general. In the judgment, the Court stated that the notification of the existence of the minefield was obligatory, based on certain 'general and well-recognized principles', *inter alia*, every State's obligation not to knowingly allow its territory to be used for acts contrary to the rights of other States. *Corfu Channel (UK v Albania)* (Judgment) [1949] ICJ Rep 4.

60 The National Security Strategy of the United States of America (September 2002) <http://www.monde-diplomatique.fr/cahier/irak/a9687> accessed 22 March 2009.

61 UNSC Res. 1386 (23 December 2001).

62 For an appraisal of the role of non-state actors in self-defense law, see J Kammerhofer, 'The Armed Activities casa and Non-State Actors in Self-Defense Law' (2007) LJIL 20, 89

63 UNGA Report of the Secretary General on 'Arrangements and practices for the interaction of non-governmental organizations in all activities of the United Nations system' (10 July 1998) UN Doc A/53/170. paras 16-20.

64 Although this model can be regarded as corporativist, in the style of the defunct 'Second World'. See CA Morand, *La Souveraineté, un concept dépassé* (n 13) 172.

65 Constitution of the International Labor Organization (adopted 19 November 1946, entered into force 14 December 1946) UNTS 1, Article 3(5).

66 Declaration of Philadelphia <http://www.ilo.org/ilolex/english/iloconst.htm#annex> accessed 21 March 2009.

67 Constitution of the United Nations Educational, Scientific and Cultural Organization (adopted 16 November 1945, entered into force 4 November 1946) UNTS 4.

68 UNESCO, 'Directives concerning UNESCO's relations with non-governmental organizations'   <http://portal.unesco.org/en/ev.php-URL_ID=33137&URL_DO=DO_TOPIC&URL_SECTION=201.html> accessed 21 March 2009.

69 UNESCO *Directives* (n 68) para 8.

70 Constitution of the World Health Organization (adopted 22 July 1946, entered into force 7 April 1948) UNTS 14.

71 World Health Organization, 'Principles Governing Relations with Nongovernmental Organizations' <http://www.who.int/civilsociety/relations/principles/en/> accessed 21 March 2009.

72 *Legality on the Threat or Use of Nuclear Weapons* (Advisory Opinion) [1996] ICJ Rep 226

73 UNGA Report of the Secretary General on 'Arrangements and practices for the interaction of non-governmental organizations in all activities of the United Nations system' (10 July 1998) UN Doc A/53/170 (n 11) para 27.

74 Res IBRD 93-10 (23 September 1993).

75 *Constitution of the Food and Agriculture Organization*, Article XIII(4).

76 *Articles of Agreement of the International Monetary Fund* (adopted 27 December 1945, entered into force 27 December 1945) UNTS 2. Articles X.

77 *Convention on International Civil Aviation* (adopted 7 December 1944, entered into force 4 April 1947) UNTS 15. Articles 65.

78 *Convention on the International Maritime Organization* (adopted 6 March 1948, entered into force 17 March 1958) UNTS 289. Articles 59-63.

79 *Convention on the World Meteorological Organization* (adopted 11 October 1947, entered into force 23 March 1950) UNTS 77. Article 26(b).

80 *Convention establishing the World Intellectual Property Organization* (adopted 14 July 1967, entered into force 26 April 1970) UNTS 828. Article 13(2).

81 *Agreement establishing the International Fund for Agricultural Development* (adopted 13 June 1976, entered into force 30 November 1977) UNTS 1059. Article J (section 2).

82 *Constitution of the United Nations Industrial Development Organization* (adopted 8 April 1979, entered into force 21 June 1985) UNTS 1401. Article 19.

83 OECD Police Brief, *Civil Society and the OECD – November 2002 update* (Paris 2002) < www.oecd.org/publications/Pol_brief> accessed 20 March 2009.

84 OECD, *Citizens as Partners: Information, Consultation and Public Participation in Policy-making* (OECD, Paris 2001).

85 See, in this regard, the two reports, 'OECD Guidelines for Multinational Enterprises', available at < www.oecd.ord/daf/investment/guidelines> and the 'OECD Principles on Corporate Governance', available at < www.oecd.org/daf/corporate-affairs/> both accessed 21 March 009.

86 FATF-GAFI, *Combating the Abuse of Non-Profit Organizations: International Best Practices* (report) (11 October 2002) < http://www.fatf-gafi.org/dataoecd/39/19/34033761.pdf> accessed 21 March 2009.

87 CoE Res. (51) 30F (3 May 1951) para 4.

88 CoE Res. (2003)8 (19 November 2003).

89 The role of NGOs in the Council of Europe member-states has been extensively addressed in the document *Fundamental Principles on the Status of Non-Governmental Organizations in Europe and explanatory memorandum.* CoE Doc RAP-ONG(2003)4 (24 March 2003).

90 Opinion 246 (2003). *Relations between the Council of Europe and non-governmental organizations,* Assembly debate on 29 September 2003.

91 CoE Res. (2003)9 (19 November 2003).

92 Memorandum on Reorganization of the Conference of INGOs of the Council of Europe (2007) < www.coe/int/t/e/ngo/public/memo_reorganization_Conference_January_session_2008> accessed 21 March 2009.

93 Proposal for a Regulation of the European Parliament and of the Council on the statute for a European Association. EC Doc 1991/0386/COD. The proposal was submitted together with a draft directive supplementing the statute with regards to the involvement of employees (EC Doc 1991/0387/COD).

94 Despite the failure of establishing a regulation at the European level for associations, the Commission issued, on 4 June 1997, a document entitled 'Communication on the Promotion of the role of associations and Foundations in Europe' proposing a series of measures to strengthen their participation in the European institutions. EC Doc EC COM/97/0241 Final.

95 The ESC was introduced by the Treaty of Nice (adopted 26 February 2001, entered into force 1February 2003).

96 Commission (EC) 'European governance' (White Paper) COM(2001) 428 final, 25 July 2001.

97 Commission (EC) 'The Commission and non-governmental organizations: building a stronger partnership' (discussion paper) CES 811/2000, 18 January 2000.

98 Declaration 17 establishes that 'The Conference considers that transparency of the decision-making process strengthens the democratic nature of the institutions and the public's confidence in the administration. The Conference accordingly recommends that the Commission submit to the Council no later than 1993 a report on measures designed to improve public access to the information available to the institutions.' Treaty on the European Union (adopted 7 February 1992, entered into force 1 November 1993).

99 Council and Commission joint Code of Conduct (OJ 1993 L 340/ 41); Council Decision of 20 December 1993 on public access to Council documents (OJ 1993 L 340/43); Commission Decision of 8 February 1994 on public access to Commission documents (OJ 1994 L 46/58).

100 *Charter of the Organization of American States* (adopted 30 April 1948, entered into force date 13 December 1951) UNTS 119. Further amended by the Protocol of Buenos

Aires in 1967, by the Protocol of Cartagena de Indias in 1985, by the Protocol of Washington in 1992, and by the Protocol of Managua in 1993.

101 OAS Doc OEA/Ser.P AG/doc.109.rev.1 (22 April 1971)

102 See, in this regard, the 1994 Summit of the Americas, the 1996 Summit of the Americas on Sustainable Development and the 1998 Second Summit of the Americas.

103 OASPC 'Report by the Committee on Juridical and Political Affairs on the Status of Non-governmental Organizations (NGOs) in the OAS' (23 May 1997) OAS Doc OEA/Ser.G CP/Doc.2946/97.

104 OASPC Res. 'Guidelines for the Participation of Civil Society Organizations in OAS Activities' (15 December 1999) OAS Doc OEA/Ser.G CP/RES.759 (1217/99).

105 OAS Summit of the Americas Secretariat, *Manual for Civil Society Participation in the OAS and its Summits of the Americas Process* (OAS, Washington 2008) <www.civil-society.oas.org> accessed 21 March 2009.

106 MERCOSUR founding documents are available only in the member-states' official languages, Portuguese and Spanish at <www.mercosur.int> accessed 21 March 2009.

107 *North American Agreement on Environmental Cooperation* (adopted August 1993, entered into force 1 January 1994)

108 Commission for Environmental Cooperation, *Bringing the Facts to Light: a guide to articles 14 and 15 of the North-American Agreement on Environmental Cooperation* (CEC, Montreal 2007) <http://www.cec.org/files/PDF/SEM/Bringing%20the%20Facts_en.pdf> accessed 21 March 2009.

109 (adopted 11 July 2000, entered into force 26.05.2001) <http://www.africa-union.org/root/au/AboutAu/Constitutive_Act_en.htm> accessed 21 March 2009.

110 AUGA Dec 48 (III) (6-8 July 2004). AU Doc Assembly/AU/Dec 48 (III).

111 In this aspect, it is noteworthy mention that the ICJ, on the *Wall* advisory opinion, acknowledged the relevance of the ICRC by stating that its 'special position with respect to execution of the Fourth Geneva Convention must be "recognized and respected at all times" by the parties pursuant to Article 142 of the Convention'. The Court also gave weight to the ICRC opinion on humanitarian matters when affirmed that it "has always affirmed the *de jure* applicability of the Fourth Geneva Convention to the territories occupied since 1967 by the State of Israel, including East Jerusalem". *Legal Consequences of the Construction of a Wall in the Occupied Palestinian Territory* (Advisory Opinion) [2004] ICJ Rep 136.

112 World Conference on Human Rights (14-25 June 1993), 'Vienna Declaration and Program of Action', UN Doc A/CONF 157/23 (12 July 1993) para 38.

113 *Convention on the Rights of the Child* (adopted 20 November 1989, entered into force 02 September 1990) UNTS 1577 3. Article 45 (b).

114 C Chinkin, *The Role of Non-Governmental Organisations in Standard Setting*, (n 18) 60.

115 For an appraisal of the role of NGOs, see A Clapham, 'Creating the High Commissioner for Human Rights. The Untold History' (1994) EJIL v 5, 556; and T van Boven, 'The UN High Commissioner for Human Rights: the Story of a Contended Project' (2007) LJIL v 20, 767.

116 For an appraisal of the protection of human rights in the international sphere, see AA Cançado Trindade, *O Esgotamento de Recursos Internos no Direito Internacional* (Editora UnB, Brasilia 1997); For an appraisal of the protection of human rights in Brazil, see AA Cançado Trindade, *A Proteção Internacional dos Direitos Humanos e o Brasil* (2nd edn Editora UnB, Brasilia 2000).

117 *American Convention on Human Rights "Pact of San José, Costa Rica"* (adopted 22 November 1969, entered into force 18 July 1978) UNTS 1144.

118 *Convention for the Protection of Human Rights and Fundamental Freedoms* (adopted 4 November 1950, entered into force 3 September 1953) UNTS 213.

119 (adopted 27 June 1981, entered into force 21 October 1986). OAU Doc. CAB/LEG/ 67/3 rev. 5, 21.

120 (adopted July 1990, entered into force 29 November 1990). OAU Doc. CAB/LEG/ 24.9/49 (1990).

121 *Convention on Wetlands of International Importance especially as Waterfowl Habitat* (adopted 2 February 1971, entered into force 21 December 1975) UNTS 14583. Further amended by the Paris Protocol, 3 December 1982, and Regina Amendments, 28 May 1987.

122 *Convention on Wetlands of International Importance especially as Waterfowl Habitat*, article 8.

123 To reach the full content of the memoranda, see < http://www.ramsar.org/index_- mou.htm> accessed 21 March 2009.

124 *Convention concerning the Protection of the World Cultural and Natural Heritage* (adopted 16 November 1972, entered into force 17 December 1975) UNTS 15511.

125 *Convention on International Trade in Endangered Species of Wild Fauna and Flora* (Adopted 3 March 1973, entered into force 1 July 1975) UNTS 993. Further amended at Bonn, on 22 June 1979.

126 *Instrument for the Establishment of the Restructured Global Environment Facility* (adopted March 1994). < http://www.gefweb.org/uploadedFiles/GEF_Instrument_ March08.pdf> accessed 21 March 2009.

127 *Vienna Convention for the Protection of the Ozone Layer* (adopted 22 March 1985, entered into force 22 September 1988) UNTS 1513.

128 Agenda 21, < http://www.un.org/esa/sustdev/documents/agenda21/english/agen- da21toc.htm> accessed 21 March 2009.

129 A Boyle, remarks on the panel 'The participation of non-state actors in the promotion of sustainable environment', in ASIL/NVIR, *Contemporary International Law Issues: Conflicts and Convergence, Proceedings of the 3RD Joint Conference.* (TMC Asser, The Hague 1996) 80.

130 AA Cançado Trindade (ed), *Human Rights, Sustainable Development and the Environment* (San Jose, 1992) 17.

131 J Combacau and S Sur, *Droit International Public* (7th edn Montchristien, Paris 2006) 321.

132 UN Doc A/RES/37/7 (28 October 1982).

133 *Vienna Convention for the Protection of the Ozone Layer* (adopted 22 March 1985, entered into force 22 September 1988) UNTS 1513.

134 *Montreal Protocol on Substances that Deplete the Ozone Layer* (adopted 16 September 1987, entered into force 1 January 1989) UNTS 1522.

135 *UN Framework Convention on Climate Change* (adopted 9 May 1992, entered into force 21 March 1994) UNTS 1771.

136 *Convention on Environmental Impact Assessment in a Transboundary Context* (adopted 25 February 1991, entered into force 10 September 1997) UNTS 1989.

137 *Convention on the Transboundary Effect of Industrial Accidents* (adopted 17 March 1992, entered into force 19 April 2000) UNTS 2105.

138 *Convention on Biological Diversity* (adopted 5 June 1992, entered into force 29 December 1993) UNTS 1760.

139 (adopted 21 June 1993, not entered into force yet) ETS 150.

140 CA Morand, *La Souveraineté, un concept dépassé* (n 13) 171.

CHAPTER 3

NGOs in Judicial and quasi-judicial bodies' decisions

In 1946, the UN Charter established consultative status with NGOs, assuming, for the first time in an international treaty, that the public sphere was larger than the governmental one and that other kinds of organizations had legitimacy to be heard on matters affecting the needs and aspirations of citizens. This treaty provision, in conferring upon NGOs consultative rights, implicitly recognized that other actors should be recognized, as subjects of law, in the then exclusively inter-state Westphalian system.

A few years later, in 1949, the ICJ issued its memorable advisory opinion on the *Reparation for injuries* case, holding in an *obiter dictum* that 'the subjects of law in any legal system are not necessarily identical in their nature or in the extent of their rights and their nature depends upon the needs of the community'.[1] This opinion was rendered in response to a UN consultation as to whether the organization held the legal capacity to bring an international claim against a State if the government of that State caused injuries to the organization's activities or personnel. By releasing this opinion, the ICJ understood that if the organization possessed rights and obligations conferred by a multilateral treaty, it had, at the same time, a large measure of international personality and the capacity to operate on the international plane, making it clear that the international sphere was no longer a 'state-only club' and that entities other than States could be subjects of law. In just three years, a major treaty and an international court decision delivered a deadly blow to the States' exclusive international legal personality supported by the positivist doctrine that had engulfed international law since the 19th century, blazing a secure path for the evolution of an international legal theory capable of recognizing that individuals and private organizations with public aims possessed international legal personality, a status more coherent with the needs of a global civil society.

It is beyond any doubt that the decisions of judicial and quasi-judicial international bodies affect the lives of real people, not only those legal-political structures named 'States'.[2] It is also beyond any doubt that international affairs have become far more complex than they used to be in the past, when the state-centric model was conceived, and that several new rights and public concerns have been recognized as relevant by a contemporary society with an unprecedented capacity of mobility and communication, the impacts of which extend way beyond the boundaries of the territorial divisions of the world. In national legal systems, the emergence of collective rights, i.e., those belonging to a large group of identifiable individuals, led to the introduction of new forms of defense of such rights before the Courts, with unions and associations playing a relevant role. A couple of decades later, when the common and shared rights, i.e., those owned by the society at large, became recognized by national legal systems, new advocates, the NGOs, took the bench to defend these newly acknowledged rights against the acts or omissions of individuals, companies and even the State. While this evolution may be clearly observable in the national sphere, it is not so in the international realm, where the States have tried to maintain their position as the sole players, anchored in the classic positivist subject/object dichotomy, by which they consider that they fall into the first category, while everything else falls into the second.

It is desirable that judicial proceedings be conducted in order to deliver in due time appropriate protection to any threatened or jeopardized right, hence making it necessary to establish a legal proceeding that balances the collection of evidence and arguments with the defense of the accused, within the physical and budgetary limits imposed to the parties and to the Tribunal. If opening the floodgates may lead to inundations, keeping them closed may lead to drought.[3]

As we will explore in more detail in this chapter, the situation of individuals and NGOs has been experiencing an evolution in judicial and quasi-judicial bodies' decisions. In general terms, NGOs cannot stand as parties before international tribunals to defend shared and common rights – inasmuch acting as an NGO – but only their personal rights – inasmuch acting as a private legal entity. Nonetheless, having international *locus standi* necessarily implies in acknowledging that they have international legal personality. Depending on the rules of the Court concerned, NGOs, acting as such, can be victims, witnesses or expert witnesses, and can also perform certain assignments for the Court, such as carrying out inquiries, or voluntarily presenting *amici curiae*[4] and documentary evidence of facts relevant to the case, either on their own initiative or through the parties' memorials to the case. NGOs experience an improvement in their situation before quasi-judicial bodies, mostly within the human rights protection systems, where they are entitled to an enhanced intervention, which also includes the right, along general lines, to submit petitions and, in particular, to file complaints concerning alleged violations of human rights, although they lose such standing rights if the case is forwarded to the Courts.

Evidence shows that quasi-judicial bodies are keener to accept the participation of NGOs than Courts and that regional bodies are more sympathetic to their initiatives than world bodies. Additionally, it should be noted that, as acknowledged by Lauterpacht, 'there is nothing inherent to the structure of international law which prevent individuals from being parties to procedures before international courts.'[5] Hence, the participation of NGOs as third-parties in Court proceedings is not objectively hindered by the statutes of the Courts, which can strengthen the participation of INGOs and NGOs in their proceedings even without reforms in their own rules of procedure, by expressing a broader willingness in obtaining a more comprehensive evaluation of the question under consideration and a better judicial remedy. If the tribunals are not keen to 'open the floodgates', would not common sense lead the courts to conclude that it might be best to let some water pass through?

In this chapter we will appraise the situation of NGOs before the active international tribunals and before the more relevant quasi-judicial bodies.

3.1   The Courts

3.1.1   The Permanent Court of International Justice

The PCIJ was established in the aftermath of World War I, through, and by, the League of Nations, although it was never a part of the League nor did its Statute form a part of its Covenant. According to its Statute, the Court was open to the members of the League and to those States mentioned in the Annex of the Covenant (art 35), but other States could be parties in cases before the Court (art 34). The fact that NGOs had not been granted *locus standi* did not prevent the Court from entrusting any bodies or organizations to carry out inquiries or give expert opinions (art 50). The Statute also allowed any 'international organizations' considered by the Court as likely to be able to furnish information on the question for which the advisory opinion of the Court had been requested, to submit written statements, or be heard at a public sitting to be held for that purpose (art 66). The PCIJ understood that the concept of international organizations embraced private institutions such as unions, which were openly admitted to be heard on the very first Advisory Opinion of the Court, which addressed the participation of workers' delegates in the newly created ILO.[6] This important precedent in listening to civil society organizations, unfortunately, is not being kept by the ICJ.

The PCIJ had a short operational existence – between 1922 and 1940 – and dealt with twenty-nine contentious cases between States and delivered twenty-seven advisory opinions. This does not mean that it did not address situations where human rights – a key civil society concern - were at stake, even before the Universal Declaration of Human Rights, as we can observe in the *Polish Upper Silesia*[7] and *Minority Schools*[8] cases. These cases are particularly interesting because in a contentious situation involving Germany and Poland before the beginning of World War II, the Court ruled that national minorities living in a foreign country had the right to keep their own institutions in order to maintain the very essence of their condition of minority and that they deserved protection under the principle of non-discrimination, the imposition of restrictions to those rights by the host country being hence prohibited. The Court decision ensured such rights to German speaking minorities living in Poland. However, it could not prevent the events that started a couple of years later, on 1 September 1939.

3.1.2. The International Court of Justice

The ICJ Statute (art 34) defines that only States may be parties before the Court, but admits that it may give an advisory opinion at the request of States or whatever bodies are authorized by or in accordance to the UN Charter (Art 65). The Court may entrust any bodies or organizations to carry out inquiries or give expert opinions (art 50), which, in principle, does not hinder the Court to assign such tasks to NGOs. The Statute provides a twofold rule to deal with information provided by third parties: if the Court is appreciating a case, it may request to *public* international organizations any information relevant to the question, which can also be presented by those organizations on their own initiative (Art 34 (2)); if it is appreciating a demand for advisory opinion, then, the Statute (art 66 (2)) authorizes the Court Registrar to notify 'any international organization considered by the Court as likely to be able to furnish information on the question submitted for the advisory opinion, that the Court will be prepared to receive written statements or to hear, at a public seating to be held for that purpose, oral statements related to the question'. Hence, at least theoretically, IGOs could provide information for both contentious and advisory proceedings and INGOs only for the latter.

Although the statutory commands of the PCIJ and the ICJ on the participation of international organizations in the advisory proceedings are identical, the ICJ did not follow the practice of its predecessor, because it has extensively worked to limit the capability to give expert opinions, *proprio motu* or under the Court request, to 'public international organizations', considering as such only international organizations of States.[9] Hence, private institutions, such as INGOs, have neither *locus standi* before the Court nor can freely submit information, via *amicus* briefs, to the ICJ, as can be observed by the very scant evidence of NGOs trying to do so. However, since the restriction on the participation in advisory proceedings does not rely on ICJ Statute, there is some room for improvement in the participation of INGOs in ICJ proceedings if such restrictions are overridden by new rules, more sensitive to the contemporary status of non-state actors in the international sphere. A timid movement toward this direction can be observed, for example, in Practice Direction XII,[10] which accepted written statements or documents submitted by INGOs in an advisory opinion case on its own initiative, but defined that they would not be considered as part of the case file. Since those papers will be made public, any parties to the case can incorporate them to their own submissions to the Court, a situation that is not particularly new.[11]

If water cannot pass through the floodgate, it finds its course along another path. The restrictions to act before the Court do not imply that NGOs are not entitled to persuade States to act on their behalf. This was exactly the situation of the emblematic ICJ *Nuclear Weapons* Advisory Opinion[12] released after a consultation of the UN General Assembly, on whether 'the threat of or use of nuclear weapons is in any circumstance permitted under international law?'

The initiative was the main goal of the World Court Project, a coalition of some NGOs that sought to convince member-states at those fora to submit the request for the advisory opinion to the ICJ, formulating it in such a way that nothing but a negative answer could be expected. Lindblom observed that 'the issue of the strong involvement of civil society in the issue brought to the ICJ was regarded as a relevant issue by some States as well as by some of the judges'.[13] Judge Oda, for example, when addressing the historic background of the case, wrote that he had 'the impression that the request for an advisory opinion which was made by the General Assembly in 1994 originated in ideas developed by some NGOs'.[14]

A remarkable aspect of those considerations was the very nature of the participation of NGOs in the case: Should it be regarded as 'political' or considered 'legal'? Definitively, NGOs had not submitted the request for the advisory opinion. Nonetheless, also unequivocally, they had succeeded in convincing the majority of the member-states – which do not have nuclear weapons and are threatened by them – to assume the request as theirs and forward it to the ICJ. They also convinced 3.5 million people around the globe to declare in writing their personal opposition toward nuclear weapons, documentary evidence that was brought to the Court.

In practical terms, any criticism to the role of NGOs in the issue became technically irrelevant because the request had been presented by a legitimate international body and demanded a formal answer from the Court. Additionally, the Court could not disregard the question based on the process that had been used to reach the decision to submit the request because it had been formally approved by the member-states in a legitimate meeting of an international body, it being beyond the scope of the Court to evaluate the reasoning of the request, which, at least in the case of the UNGA, was within the scope of the organization: the promotion of peace.[15] Furthermore, since a representative part of the UN member-states are governed by democratically elected representatives, acceding to civil society pressure is an expected attitude, within the 'rules of the game'.

Nevertheless, the outcome of the case was both disappointing and astonishing, because the Court pronounced a *non liquet*, i.e., refused to formulate a definitive answer to the legal question, understanding that 'law is

silent or applicable rules are insufficient or obscure'.[16] As a result, the
Court decided by seven votes to seven, by the President's casting vote, that

> 'it follows from the above-mentioned requirements that the threat or
> use of nuclear weapons would generally be contrary to the law ap-
> plicable in armed conflicts, and in particular the principles and rules
> of humanitarian law. However, in view of the current state of inter-
> national law, and of the elements of fact at its disposal, the Court
> cannot conclude definitively whether the threat or use of nuclear
> weapons would be lawful or unlawful in an extreme circumstance
> of self-defense, in which the very survival of a State would be at
> stake'.

The outcome was disappointing because the lobbying effort and the cap-
tious wording of the question had not achieved the ultimate objective of
the World Court Project, i.e., the declaration of the unlawfulness of the
threat or use of nuclear weapons, and represented an astonishing end for
an orchestrated initiative that seemed to be invincible.[17] It was also astonishing because it spurred an unprecedented clash of opinions within the
Court and had to be decided by the casting vote of the President.
Moreover, it eroded the understanding of the completeness of international
law supposedly ensured by the proclaimed comprehensive sources of international law defined in article 38 of the ICJ Statutes, and, thus, the idea of
the illegality and illegitimacy of a *non liquet*.[18] It was a disappointing end
for a so-considered *a priori* assumption of every legal system.

Another aspect of the activities of the ICJ which deserves our attention
is the increasing presence of human rights law in its cases. As pointed out
by Rosalyn Higgins, until recent times, the Court was a 'Court of sovereign States', but it has become a Court concerned with human rights because those rights have found their proper place within international law,
and moved from the margins toward the center of the Court jurisdictional
activities.[19] If we compare the works of the PCIJ with those of the ICJ and
these works through time, the deepening and broadening of human rights
can be seen. Higgins, for example, pointed that out when the Court addressed the concept of self-determination in the *South West Africa,
Namibia* and *Western Sahara* cases,[20] 'there were still many within the UN
who insisted that self-determination was nothing more than a political aspiration. The Court was the forerunner in recognizing self-determination as
a legal right.'[21] We can also notice the increasing awareness and participation of NGOs in the problem-defining processes[22] and enforcement of the
Court's decisions,[23] both working towards an improved participation of
NGOs in the activities of the ICJ in a world cast by the challenges of a
global civil society.

3.1.3. The International Criminal Courts (ICC, ICTY, ICTR)

A natural outcome of the rising centrality of human rights and the increasing participation of individuals in international law was the creation of international criminal courts, a kind of judiciary body that would have been unthinkable in positivist pure inter-state international law. The forerunner of these tribunals is the International Military Tribunal at Nuremberg, established in 1945 to appraise crimes perpetrated by the Nazis during World War II. In holding that 'crimes are committed by men, not by abstract entities,' the tribunal acknowledged that individuals, not only States, were subjects of international law, therefore possessing duties, as well as rights.[24] Pragmatically, in order to avoid the risks of application of the legal principle of *nullo crime sine lege* to its activities, the constitutive acts avoided the words 'law' or 'code', nevertheless laying down the conceptual basis for the further establishment of international criminal tribunals.[25]

In this aspect, it is worth observing that NGOs played a relevant role in the establishment of the International Criminal Court (ICC)[26] and likewise provide valuable and reliable information about the atrocities appraised by the ICC, the International Criminal Tribunal for the Former Yugoslavia (ICTY)[27] and the International Criminal Tribunal for Rwanda (ICTR). The UN Security Council, for instance, requested to NGOs the submission of information concerning violations of international humanitarian law in Yugoslavia.[28]

The Statutes of the three tribunals do not provide *locus standi* for NGOs before the Courts, since the criminal proceedings are initiated and conducted by the Prosecutor against those who appear to have committed crimes of war or against humanity. In the ICC, the Prosecutor can initiate an investigation based on information referred by a State party to the Statute or by the UNSC, and also by *proprio motu*, relying, in the latter situation, on the seriousness of the evidence provided. The Statutes of both the ICTR and the ICTY have similar provisions, although expressly defining that the Prosecutor shall initiate investigations ex-officio based on information obtained, among other sources, from NGOs.[29] The proceedings of the current cases before the tribunals have revealed the importance of the information gathered and provided by humanitarian NGOs, which perform an essential, yet unofficial, ancillary investigative role to the Prosecutors' office that might make us doubt the effectiveness of the tribunals if the NGOs did not exist.[30]

Another noteworthy aspect is the participation of NGOs as victims in ICC proceedings. While such a right has been enjoyed in some civil law countries for several decades, it is also true that the participation of victims in ICC proceedings represents an innovative experience in the history of international criminal justice,[31] moreover if we take into account that legal entities, not only individuals, can be regarded as victims of those crimes.

The ICC Rules of Procedure and Evidence have a general provision for victim participation in the Court's proceedings, considering as such those 'organizations or institutions that have sustained direct harm to any of their property which is dedicated to religion, education, art or science or charitable purposes and to their historic monuments, hospitals and other places and objects for humanitarian purposes'.[32] This participation does not represent, however, the admission of NGO victims as parties to the case, neither impose to those organizations the duty to present evidence of the direct harm they suffered, a burden of proof that remains in the hands of the Prosecutor,[33] yet the 'victims participating in the trial proceedings may, in principle, lead to evidence pertaining to the guilt or innocence of the accused and challenge the admissibility or relevance of the evidence'.[34]

As of January 2012, the ICC Prosecutor has been conducting investigations in Uganda, the Democratic Republic of the Congo, the Central African Republic, Sudan (Darfur), Kenya, Libya and Cote d'Ivoire. Despite charges of unnecessary destruction of property, none of the cases evidence NGOs as victims of the accused.

3.1.4. The Court of Justice of the European Union

The Court of Justice of the European Union, the current name of the European Court of Justice (ECJ) is the judicial body of the European Union and of the European Atomic Energy Community. It is made up of three courts: the Court of Justice, the General Court and the Civil Service Tribunal. Their primary task is to examine the legality of European Union measures and ensure the uniform interpretation and application of European Union law. [35] The Court evolved together with the institutions of the European communities and most of its jurisprudence was produced before the Treaty of Lisbon. For this reason, this section will often make reference to community law, instead of European law.

NGOs are authorized to seek judicial protection against illegal acts inflicted on them by EU institutions. Acting as such, they do not do so within the customary scope of activities of an NGO – the defense of public interests – but rather do so in their own private interests. This does not mean, however, that cases brought to the Court on those grounds will not affect international law.

The 9/11 attacks had several consequences at the international level. One of those was the freezing of funds and economic resources belonging to, or owned or held by, a natural or legal person, group or entity supposedly associated with Usama bin Laden, Al'Qaeda or the Taliban, included in the lists released by the UN Security Council, which were reproduced, at the European level, in Council Regulations. A private foundation established in Sweden – the Al Barakaat International Foundation – was listed in Council Regulation 881/2002 and, claiming violation of its fundamental rights of due process and respect of property, challenged the inclusion of its name on the list and the freezing of its assets pursuant to article 230(4) TEC,[36] bringing the case to the CFI, which eventually ended in a judgment of the Grand Chamber of the ECJ.[37] The Chamber understood that the TEC provided the legal basis for financial sanctions against non-state actors but, in a remarkable decision, concluded that *all Community acts, including those that implement the UN Security Council resolution, were reviewable if they violated the fundamental rights of an NGO.* The Court understood that the respect of those rights constituted a condition for the lawfulness of the Community acts and that, in the specific case, 'the rights of the defense, in particular the right to be heard and the right to effective judicial review of those rights were patently not respected'.[38] Moreover, the Court found that the procedure before the UN Security Council's Sanction Committee, in charge of 'de-listing' names, was essentially diplomatic and intergovernmental, and that the persons or entities concerned had no real opportunity of asserting their rights before that body, especially considering that its decisions were made by consensus, each of its members having the right of veto. As a result, the ECJ annulled Council Resolution (EC) 881/2002 insofar as it concerned the Al Barakaat International Foundation and determined the release of its assets after three months starting from the date of delivery of the judgment.

In a further case, the CFI appreciated the same issue, stating that the Council was 'not entitled to base its funds-freezing decision on information or material in the file communicated by a member-state, if the said member-state is not willing to authorize its communication to the Community judicature whose task is to review the lawfulness of that decision', to conclude that the Court must ensure that the right to a fair hearing is observed and that it is even more essential because it constituted the only safeguard to counterweight the need to combat international terrorism and the protection of fundamental rights.[39]

These cases are emblematic because they aimed to ensure that a fair balance is struck between two kinds of obligations assumed by UN member-states, putting on one side the obligation, laid down in article 25 of the UN Charter, to carry out the decisions of the Security Council, making them prevail over any other obligation they may have entered into under an international agreement, and, on the other side, the obligations, laid down in the Universal Declaration of Human Rights, to allow effective judicial remedies against acts violating fundamental rights (art 8) and also to respect the right of property, protecting anyone against arbitrary deprivation of his property (art 17). In other words, the Court compared the 'state-centric' system of international law, where only States are subjects, with a 'civil society-centric' system, where individuals and their organizations are also subjects, and chose the latter, putting fundamental human rights and freedoms above the State covenants, which represents a remarkable achievement in cases brought to court by private nonprofit institutions and clear evidence of the centrality of civil society issues in contemporary international law.

If it is clear that NGOs can freely defend their personal rights before the CFI and the ECJ, it is not that freely, nor clear, that they can defend common and shared rights of the society at large, or even the collective rights of their members before those bodies. In general terms, the *locus standi* of NGOs in relation to measures of general application has been construed very narrowly in the Court case-law.

Taking as an example the *Stichting Greenpeace Council (Greenpeace International) and Others v. Commission* case,[40] we notice that the applicants challenged financial assistance granted by the Commission to Spain for the building of two power stations, on the grounds that the project failed to fulfill environmental regulations. The ECJ, upholding a CFI previous decision, understood that the command of Article 173(4) (now, 230 (4)) of the TEC did not provide *locus standi* to the applicants in the considered situation because, consonant with the settled case-law of the Court, the challenged act had not taken into consideration the specific situation of the entity or its members when it had been adopted, thus concerning the entity in a general and abstract fashion, as well as its members. Additionally, in appraising the applicants' arguments, aiming to demonstrate that the case-law took no account of the nature and specific characteristics of the environmental interests underpinning the case, the Court found that, since they were challenging a Community decision to finance the building of two power stations, it would affect those rights only indirectly, a situation that was not comprised within the scope of the treaty. Thus, the Court established that persons, or associations of persons, other than those to whom a decision is addressed, may claim to be individually concerned only if the decision affects them by reason of certain attributes peculiar to them or by reason of circumstances in which they are differentiated from all other persons and if, by virtue of those factors, it distinguishes them individually in the same way as the person addressed.

In another case addressing environmental affairs, *European Environmental Bureau and Stichting Natuur en Milieu v. Commission*,[41] the applicants supported that it followed from Article 12(1) of Directive 2004/35 that, as NGOs promoting environmental protection and meeting the requirements under Dutch national law, they were entitled to submit observations to the competent authority and to request that authority to take action under that directive. Therefore, they claimed that they had standing to bring an action for annulment of the decisions that authorized the use of certain chemical substances (atrazine and simazine) in farming for the purposes of Article 230(4) of the TEC. However, the Court sustained that the fact that the applicants participated, in one way or another, in the process leading to the adoption of a Community act did not distinguish them individually in relation to the act in question unless the relevant Community legislation had laid down specific procedural guarantees for them. The Court went further to declare that the standing conferred upon the applicants in some of the legal systems of the member-states, accepting that environmental protection associations are directly and individually concerned by acts which adversely affect the interests which they defend, is irrelevant for the purposes of determining whether they have standing to bring an action for annulment of a Community act pursuant to Article 230(4) of the TEC. The Court also stressed that even the special consultative status that the applicants had with the Commission or other European or national institutions, inter alia under Directive 92/43, did not support the finding that they were individually concerned by the challenged decisions, following that 'Community law, as it now stands, does not provide for a right to bring a class action before the Community courts, as envisaged by the applicants in the case' (Para 63).

In another case, the *Association Greenpeace France and Others v. Ministère de l'Agriculture et de la Pêche and Others*,[42] the applicants, to the contrary, were successful in annulling a French decree that authorized release into the environment of genetically modified organisms on the grounds that 'the opinion of the Committee for the Study of the Release of Products of Biomolecular Engineering had been delivered on the basis of a dossier that was incomplete inasmuch as it did not include information that would allow an assessment of the impact on public health of the ampicillin-resistant gene contained in the varieties of transgenic maize that were the subject of the application for authorization'. As observed, the case had not challenged a Community decision, rather attacked the inadequacy of a member-state's administrative procedure before a dossier was forwarded to the Commission.

A third variant of the same theme is observed in the cases *Van der Kooy and Others v. Commission* and *CIRFS and Others v. Commission,* where the Court recognized that the applicant association had specific *locus standi* because of its status as negotiator of the provisions challenged by the Commission and as Commission interlocutor in discussions concerning the establishment, extension and adaptation of a State aid scheme in the sector concerned.[43]

In conclusion, it has been demonstrated that the narrowly construed interpretation of the 'direct and individual concern' *locus standi* under Article 230(4) TEC has created an unbalanced situation in which NGOs, defending their private rights, are more powerful in overruling Community rules than when they defend common and shared rights of the society at large. Furthermore, although not recognizing the NGOs' right to bring class actions before it,[44] the Court recognized that they can challenge those rules with procedural errors, to finally conclude that NGOs with advisory or consultative status before the Community body that enacted the rule cannot challenge it, unless if they can present evidence that they have directly and individually negotiated it.

Lindblom suggested that 'an expansion of *locus standi* cannot take place without a treaty amendment',[45] pointing out that some authors suggest that such broadening depends on the expansion of the CFI, with an increase in the number of judges, the creation of specialized chambers and other measures.[46] It is true that treaty amendment can expand the *locus standi,* just as the admission of new judges leads to faster judicial remedies and specialized chambers provide improved decisions, but all these measures are taken on one side of the 'table' and do not consider the extreme and proven creative capability of civil society. If we move the solution into the realm of civil society we can foresee, for example, that the more specialized the NGOs become, the more keen they are on being considered 'directly and individually' concerned.

For example, one of the first movements of civil society to deal with the restriction was that of creating specialized associations. Settled case-law understood that such associations formed for the protection of the collective interests of a category of persons could not be considered to be individually concerned, for the purposes of Article 230(4) TEC, by a measure affecting the general interests of that category, and, therefore, were not entitled to bring an action for annulment on behalf of its members where the latter could not do so individually.[47] However, in another case addressing a shipping sector aid scheme, albeit confirming the settled case-law, the Court understood that one applicant was in a different position, not by virtue of being an undertaking of the sector affected by the challenged Commission's Decision, which was a class of persons envisaged in a general and abstract manner, but by virtue of being an actual beneficiary of individual aid granted under the scheme.[48]

It seems, then, that there exists some room for improvement of the *locus standi* of NGOs before the ECJ *proprio motu,* as long as they focus their scope and practice in such a way as to become individually concerned, with the Community decision affecting them by reason of certain attributes peculiar to them or by reason of circumstances in which they are differentiated from all other persons. By doing so, they will create the conditions to challenge Community law from an individual standpoint, while aiming at an improved legal framework for the protection of the entire civil society.

3.1.5. The European Court of Human Rights

In 1949, when the Council of Europe was established by ten founding member-states aiming to achieve a greater unity between them for the purpose of safeguarding and realizing ideals and principals of common heritage, it was defined that the maintenance and further realization of human

rights and fundamental freedoms would take a central place, whose violations could lead to the expulsion of the breaching State.[49] According to
Lawson and Schermers, the European Movement, an alliance of NGOs fa-
voring European integration, developed, in 1949, a draft treaty on human
rights in order to supersede the legal weakness of the Universal
Declaration of Human Rights approved by the UN in the previous year.[50]
The proposal was discussed within the Council of Europe and eventually
led to the adoption of the European Convention on Human Rights in 1950,
which established two bodies to ensure the observance of the engagements
undertaken by the contracting States: the European Commission on Human
Rights (EComHR), designated to establish the facts of each case, and the
European Court of Human Rights (ECHR), responsible for delivering binding decisions and giving authoritative interpretation of the Convention,
either in judgments or in advisory opinions.[51] This supervisory system operated until the adoption of the 11th Protocol in 1994, which became effective in 1998.[52]

The Convention originally adopted a criteria, later reproduced in the
American Convention on Human Rights, which consisted of a two phase
protection, where all cases had to be brought firstly to the Commission
and, then, to the Court. The original wording of Article 25 established that
the EComHR might receive petitions from any NGOs or groups of individuals claiming to be victims of a violation by one of the contracting States
of the rights set forth in the Convention, provided that the considered State
had declared that it recognized the competence of the Commission to receive such petitions. Stepping in the same pitfalls that the UN Charter had
entered into when granting consultative status with the ECOSOC, the
Convention neither defined an NGO nor even signaled its main characteristics, a task which the members of the Council of Europe would accomplish
only in 1996, with the adoption of the Strasbourg Convention (ETS
124).[53] The Convention established that although NGOs had *locus standi*
to bring a case before the Commission, they could not act in the same case
before the Court, because Article 44 of the Convention reserved such attributes only to the contracting States and the Commission. Fortunately, with
the adoption of the 9th Protocol, in 1990, the procedure before the Court
was adjusted to be coherent with the right granted before the Commission
and, then, not only the contracting States and the Commission, but also
any persons, NGOs or groups of individuals that had submitted a petition
to the Commission under article 25, were entitled to bring a case before
the ECHR. Despite this adjustment, the entire system was eventually replaced four years later, with the adoption of the 11th Protocol, which introduced a single court of Human Rights, which became operational in late
1998.

Therefore, since 1990, the European Convention on Human Rights has proportioned a clear *locus standi* to NGOs, a situation which is unique in the international sphere.

The ECHR case-law provided a broad understanding of an 'NGO' for the purposes of the application of the Convention. There are cases brought to court by plaintiffs that are commonly regarded as 'NGOs', but also by trade unions, companies, religious entities, newspapers and political parties,[54] therefore, the understanding was assumed that 'NGOs' were all those entities that were not created by the State or a governmental body.'[55] Since the jurisdiction of the Court also comprises individuals and group of individuals, nobody was left aside. This demonstrates the understanding of the complexity of civil society and, once more, the centrality of human rights in contemporary life, which cannot be hindered by any legal requirements or divisions that may be introduced by governments or municipal law.

The Convention ensured to everyone several valued rights such as the freedom of thought, conscience and expression, and the freedom of assembly and association. Article 9(1) of the Convention, for example, ensured to 'everyone, either alone or in community with others and in public or in private, the freedom to manifest his religion or belief, in worship, teaching, practice and observance'. Could this guarantee to joint manifestation of beliefs be protected through a legal entity, if their members decided to express it through one? If Article 25 of the original Convention (article 34 in the current wording) established that NGOs could claim to be victims of a violation of protected rights, could we infer that they are entitled to represent their members if their rights are violated? Addressing these situations, the ECHR understood that a claim brought by an NGO could protect individual interests of its members expressed collectively, such as freedom of expression and assembly.[56] However, regarding the other protected rights, since the Convention requires the submission of the claim by the victim, and, since there is no provision for the representation of third parties by NGOs, these entities can stand before the ECHR only if they have directly suffered a violation of those protected rights, lacking legitimacy when representing other parties, even their members.[57] Juxtaposing those decisions, we can assume that since freedom of expression and assembly are at the core of the way NGOs act, the ECHR understood that they were also an organization's rights, a situation that is not observed in the other protected rights.

This poses an awkward situation: In Europe, everyone can complain, even NGOs, but no one can be represented. Definitively, there is some room for improvement from the 'victims' perspective, because it is often common for victims of human rights abuses to be afraid to present claims due to menaces of reprisals. That is why the representation of the victim is ensured, for example, in the Inter-American system for Human Rights and that in international criminal tribunals, they are represented by the Prosecutor, although they have the right to present evidence pertaining to the guilt or innocence of the accused and challenge the admissibility or relevance of the evidence brought to the Court. Some can argue that the European 'common heritage of political tradition, ideals, freedom and the rule of law', as stated in the Preamble of the Statute of the Council of Europe, ensures that such menaces will never happen in Europe and that, therefore, there is no need to empower NGOs with representativeness of victims. That could be true if the International Criminal Tribunal for the Former Yugoslavia had not existed and if ethnical cleansing on European soil had been just a bad dream.

If NGOs cannot defend collective rights or, better, shared and common rights, they are being denied their very own essence. In such circumstances, they are not NGOs, just private institutions seeking judicial remedies for their own injuries. Therefore, despite the apparent openness of the ECHR to accept submissions of NGOs, they are not allowed to act *as such* before the Court, which authorizes us to affirm that everyone can stand before the ECHR, except NGOs performing their statutory objectives toward public interest.

3.1.6 The Inter-American Court of Human Rights

The Inter-American Court of Human Rights (IACHR) is an autonomous tribunal whose purpose is the application and interpretation of the American Convention on Human Rights (ACHR),[58] exercising both adjudicatory and advisory jurisdictions. Reproducing the model established by the European Convention on Human Rights in 1950, only State parties to the Convention and the Inter-American Commission on Human Rights (IAComHR) can appear as parties before the Court within the adjudicatory jurisdiction, being the advisory one limited to member-states and the Organization of American States (OAS). The direct participation of NGOs within IACHR activities is statutorily limited to cooperation agreements seeking the strengthening and promotion of the juridical and institutional principles of the Convention in general and of the Court in particular.[59]

Neither individuals nor NGOs have *locus standi* before the IACHR, yet they can be heard as witnesses, expert witnesses or act in any other capacity.[60] The alleged victims (individuals, only), their next-of-kin or their representatives may lodge requests, arguments and evidence autonomously.[61] As mentioned above, NGOs cannot stand before the IACHR as victims, a condition guaranteed in the European human rights protection system, but can represent the victims, which gives room for some opportunities to act before the Inter-American human rights protection system on behalf of third parties, a situation not allowed in Europe. The presentation of *amici curiae* is, however, controversial, since it is neither formally admitted nor prohibited. For example, in the *Loayza Tamayo Case,* the Court, upon the request of Peru claiming that two *amici curiae* presented had to be declared inadmissible according to the Court Rules of Procedure, informed that such documents would not be rejected, but rather added to the file 'without being formally incorporated into the record of the proceedings' and that they would be evaluated by the Court in due course.[62] Since the presentation of *amicus* briefs has not been rejected, it has continued to occur, albeit without noticeable improvement in their importance for the judgment of the cases.[63] A different evaluation of NGO reports is, however, observed when they are presented to the Court by the IAComHR. In the *Abella* case, the Court understood that an international organ had recognized authority to freely evaluate probative elements such as reports of NGOs, provided that the conclusions drawn therefrom were consistent with the facts and corroborated the testimony or events alleged by the complainants, since in such cases involving the violation of human rights it is often impossible to obtain evidence without the State's cooperation.[64] These understandings, together with the right to file petitions with the IAComHR granted to NGOs by art 44 of the Convention, have shown that NGOs are likely to be more successful if they start acting at the Commission level, since, according to Lindblom, 'a large part of cases decided upon by the Inter-American Court originated in petition filed by an NGO'.[65]

According to the ACHR, the Commission has the duty to investigate situations brought to its knowledge of human rights violations in the OAS member-states, and any NGOs legally recognized in one of those States are entitled to present such communications regardless of any formal authorization or request of the affected person to do so, yet they need to inform, at least, the name of an effective or potential victim.[66] In spite of the apparent openness, the investigation is not accessible to third parties, since the Commission report is made available only to the States concerned (which shall not be at liberty to publish it), severely reducing the opportunities for the presentation of *amicus* briefs. If the case is not settled between the parties concerned after the Commission's report, then the State party or the Commission can submit it to the Court to seek compensation or remedies, or the Commission can prepare a second report to be made available to the public in general in the Commission's annual reports, then imposing political constraints on the State concerned.

It can be noted, therefore, that NGOs have a wide open door to begin a procedure within the Commission, but, due to confidentiality, a narrow opportunity to join it after its onset, except in the condition of a witness, an expert witness or in any other capacity,[67] and, later on, during the Court procedure, as a non-party, by *amicus curiae*. This particular characteristic of the Inter-American system of protection of human rights has shaped the strategy of NGOs, which focus their efforts on presenting complaints, instead of joining the cases afterwards. Providing evidence of this, nearly half of the cases addressed by the Commission in its annual reports from 1999 to 2007 originated in NGO denunciations and complaints.

As a final remark, recalling the situation of the International Criminal Courts mentioned above, again, no one could think of effective judicial protection of human rights, whether at the international or regional levels, without NGOs.

3.2   Quasi-Judicial Bodies

3.2.1   The European Social Charter and other regional bodies

Apart from the Convention on Human Rights, there are other European instruments protecting human rights that are also relevant. The first one is the European Social Charter, which laid down social and economic rights, adopted in 1961[68] and revised in 1994.[69] The Charter was also amended in 1991[70] and has two Additional Protocols, one from 1988[71] and other from 1995,[72] which introduced a separate supervisory mechanism, the 'System of Collective Complaints'.

The collective aspect of the mechanism implies that only organizations can submit claims on violations of the protected rights before the Committee of Independent Experts (European Committee of Social Rights). Those organizations include the European Trade Union Confederation, the BUSINESSEUROPE (formerly the Union of Industrial and Employers' Confederations of Europe), the International Organization of Employers, INGOs with participatory status before the Council of Europe that have been put on a list for this purpose (currently there are seventy-one),[73] and national employers' organizations and trade unions within the jurisdiction of the State against which they have lodged a complaint.

The Committee of Independent Experts is the body in charge of evaluating the claims, collecting evidence and preparing a report, which is made public and forwarded to the Committee of Ministers, to the complaint organization, to the contracting parties to the Charter and to the Parliamentary Assembly. If the report appoints breach of the obligations set forth in the Charter, the Committee of Ministers shall adopt a recommendation addressed to the State concerned.

Despite having *locus standi* before the Committee to submit collective complaints addressing a State's failure to comply with the Charter, and being capable of doing so without any victim requirement or connection to the alleged violation, the procedure has not attracted the attention of INGOs, for among the fifty-seven complaints presented since 1998, only nineteen have been presented by INGOs and only eleven INGOs have done so.

The second one is the special Committee created by the *European Convention for the Prevention of Torture and Inhuman or Degrading*

Treatment or Punishment adopted in 1987.[74] According to the Convention, a Committee was created to ensure the the compliance with the Convention and was granted unlimited access to information in the places where individuals are deprived of their liberty, including full access to the facilities and the right to move inside such places without restriction and to interview the individuals in custody. The purpose of the Committee is not the condemnation of the State for the identified abuses; rather the body aims to prevent ill-treatment, addressing recommendations to the authorities in order to improve detention conditions or to strengthen safeguards against abuses. The Committee is entitled to assign experts to perform certain attributes within its competence, but, since the reports of the Committee and the experts are confidential, there is no evidence of NGO involvement in their activities, although NGOs usually address the situation of prisons in their reports.[75]

3.2.2   The World Trade Organization

The World Trade Organization (WTO) is a multilateral organization that provides the common institutional framework for the conduct of trade relations among its members in matters related to multilateral trade agreements.[76] It facilitates the implementation, administration and operation of those agreements, as well as providing the forum for negotiations towards improved commercial relations. The organization is not responsible for making commercial decisions based on its own discernment, since the rules applicable to international commerce were negotiated by member-states in the so-called WTO agreements. Due to this particularity, WTO meetings are subject to extensive pressure and monitoring by NGOs.

Acknowledging this, the constitutive act of the WTO established in its Article V(2) that the organization's 'General Council may make appropriate arrangements for consultation and cooperation with non-governmental organizations concerned with matters related to those of the WTO', which was further clarified in the Guidelines for Arrangements on Relations with Non-Governmental Organizations, adopted on 18 July 1996.[77]

The Guidelines recognized the role NGOs can play to increase public awareness with respect to WTO activities and their contribution to the accuracy and richness of public debate, and agreed to improve transparency, making derestricted documents available on the WTO website, and to develop communication with NGOs through various means, 'such as *inter alia* the organization on an *ad hoc* basis of symposia on specific WTO-related issues, informal arrangements to receive the information NGOs may wish to make available for consultation by interested delegations and the continuation of past practice of responding to requests for general information and briefings about the WTO.' An important remark was made in the final paragraph of the Guidelines, in which, while recognizing that the

WTO has the purpose to be a forum for negotiation of commercial agreements, the 'current broadly held view' had the understanding that the consultative arrangements and the commitment to transparency did not imply in the direct involvement of NGOs in the work of the WTO or its meetings, acknowledging that NGOs could play such a role at the national level, which has the 'primary responsibility for taking into account the different elements of public interest which are brought to bear on trade policy-making'.

By doing so, the General Council aimed to re-direct NGO pressure toward the member-states, in an attempt to avoid the assumption of the existence of a global civil society, a marked countersense to the purpose of the WTO and the global scope of a multilateral trading system that aims to protect the environment, foster economic growth and ensure to less developed economies a share commensurate with their needs.[78] Of course, it did not work as planned, as we can observe in the rising NGO pressure, sometimes giving place to turbulence as observed in Seattle, in 1999, and the interference of NGOs in the disputes between the member-states, via *amicus* briefs.

In a bird's-eye view, if a commercial dispute arises as to whether a country has adopted a trade policy measure or has taken some action that one or more WTO member-states considers to be breaking the WTO agreements, or to be a failure to live up to obligations, the case is referred to the Dispute Settlement Body (DSB), which establishes a consultation procedure (in up to 60 days) aiming to reach a settlement between the parties. If one is not reached, then the DSB establishes a Panel of experts to consider the case based on the mentioned WTO agreements. This is the phase in which most NGOs try to interfere, presenting *amicus* briefs.

Once the Panel has been established, the parties present their cases in writing, which are evaluated by the panelists before the first hearing. Then, the countries involved submit written rebuttals, often addressing the *amicus* briefs presented, and present oral arguments at the Panel's second meeting. If one of the parties raises scientific or other technical matters, the Panel may consult experts or appoint an expert review group to prepare an advisory report. Although there is no impediment to NGOs performing such tasks, we have not identified such a precedent within the WTO. After the evidence and arguments have been collected, the Panel submits the descriptive (factual and argumentative) sections of its report to the commentary of the parties, which is followed by an interim report, including its findings and conclusions. A final report is, then, submitted to the parties and, three weeks later, it is circulated to all WTO members. If the Panel decides that the disputed practice does break a WTO agreement or an obligation, it recommends that the practice be made to conform to WTO rules, often suggesting how this could be done. The report becomes the DSB's ruling on recommendation within 60 days, unless a consensus rejects it.

The parties can appeal the Panel's ruling based on points of law, referring the case to the Appellate Body. The appeal can uphold, modify or
reverse the Panel's legal findings or conclusions, but cannot reexamine evidence or appreciate new issues brought by the parties. We have identified
the submission of *amicus* briefs in this phase, but the admissibility of their
arguments suffers the same restriction imposed to the parties to the case,
i.e., they shall be limited to issues of law covered in the Panel report and
legal interpretations developed by the Panel. Again, the decision is submitted to the DSB, which can accept or reject it, being the latter possible
only by consensus.

Neither the *Understanding on Rules and Procedures Governing the
Settlement of Disputes* annex 2 to the WTO Agreement (DSU) nor the
Appellate Review[79] has rules concerning the participation of civil society
before the settlement system. Nonetheless, civil society, mostly through
amicus briefs usually supported in social and environmental concerns, aims
to interfere in the outcome of these disputes. It is beyond any doubt that
the more the States publicly dispute multilateral trade agreements, the more
attention they will attract from the media and civil society, and the more
amicus briefs of self-proclaimed legitimate parties to these multilateral
cases will be presented, leading to more pressure toward governmental officials and more media coverage, retro-feeding the cycle.[80]

A remarkable aspect of this public awareness is observed in the activities
of the dispute settlement panels.[81] These bodies inherited from the sixty
years of practice under the General Agreement on Tariffs and Trade
(GATT) the notion that dispute procedures concerned only the litigating
parties, and therefore were not open to third parties, moreover civil society.
However, in 2005, the European Communities (EC), the United States and
Canada requested that the public could observe their oral hearings, a practice later adopted by the Appellate Body in 2008 under requirement of the
same parties. Although most people had believed this to be impossible
without a modification in the WTO Agreement,[82] currently more than a
quarter of the Panels have public hearings, a practice which appears to be
a consolidated trend to incorporate in the WTO the fundamental feature
– born with the French Revolution – of a fair and public hearing in judicial
proceedings.[83]

If public hearings appear to have had a smooth acceptance, the same is
not observed in the case of *amici curiae,* because the latter do not encompass the passive attitude of observers, rather an active one, and with a concrete potential to interfere in the outcome of the dispute. The DSU and the
WTO Working Procedures provide a place for people acting as 'parties to
the dispute', participants', 'third parties' and 'third participants', but none
of them comprise NGOs, only member-states.

The first WTO case to deal with the issue was the *United States –
Shrimp/Turtles*,[84] which addressed the imposition, by a US law, of certain

measures aiming at the protection of sea turtles during shrimp catching, which received two *amicus* briefs. Having in mind that the briefs had been presented voluntarily by the petitioners, and therefore, that the Panel had not actively 'sought' that information or technical advice under the terms of Article 13 DSU, the panelists understood that the documents could not be accepted by the Panel, observing, however, that any of the parties to the dispute were free to add whatever documents they reputed supportive to their arguments as part of their own submissions.[85] Since the briefs, in general terms, possessed arguments in favor of the contested US law, the US annexed to their second submission part of the briefs prepared by the two US-based NGOs that had prepared them, the Center for Marine Conservation and the Center for International Environmental Law.

When the case was referred to the Appellate Body, it understood that the narrow literal interpretation of the verb 'seek' by the Panel was inaccurate – actually an err – stating that accepting non-requested information from non-governmental sources was not incompatible with the joint interpretation of Articles 11, 12 and 13 of the DSU, therefore, admitting a rather broader interpretation of the verb 'seek', which had not to be understood as a prohibition to accept unsolicited information, but as a discretionary competence to analyze, accept or reject whatever information is submitted to the Panel, required or not. When addressing the suggestion made by the Panel regarding the admission of the briefs with the parties' submissions, the Appellate Body understood that it was within the scope of the Panel's authority pursuant to articles 12 and 13 of the DSU and that even the submission of other briefs as attachments to the arguments of the parties to the Appellate Body had to be understood *prima facie* as within their own submissions, being the submitting party responsible for their content. Since the US informed that the legal arguments of its submission were in the main document and that they accepted the arguments in the briefs to the extent that they were supportive of their arguments, the Appellate Body focused its analysis solely on the main submission.[86]

The second case that dealt with NGOs' *amicus curiae* was the *United States – Carbon Steel*. A first brief was presented to the Panel that, while recognizing its competence to accept it, decided to not consider the document due to its late presentation.[87] In the following phase, another two briefs were presented. The European Community, which had called for the Panel, argued that *amicus* briefs could not be admitted by the Appellate Body, since the previous case had addressed such a possibility at the Panel level under Article 13 of the DSU, an argument that was challenged by the US, which supported that the Appellate Body had the same authority to set its own working procedures under article 17(9) of the DSU. Eventually, the Appellate Body concluded that, although not objectively regulating the admission of those briefs, the DSU and working rules did not hinder the body to accept them. Nonetheless, recalling its understanding on the

previous case, the body stressed that NGOs did not have the right to submit those briefs, since participation in the WTO dispute settlement system
was open only to its member-states.[88]

This second case is interesting because the challenged briefs were submitted by the American Iron and Steel Institute and the Specialty Steel
Industry of North America, two clearly business-oriented NGOs, therefore
aiming to protect the relevant interests of the US-based steel industry,[89] in
a marked shift in the profile of NGOs seeking to interfere in the international judicial and quasi-judicial bodies' decisions. One might say that it
is not totally unexpected - perhaps it could even be regarded as 'natural'-
since the WTO is the intergovernmental organization that represents the
quintessence of business relations in the international sphere.
Notwithstanding, it is beyond any doubt that there is a concrete need to
clearly define what a non-governmental organization is for the purposes of
interaction of international bodies with these entities, in order to separate
those organizations that defend 'the spirit, purposes and principles of the
UN Charter' from those, such as the ones that presented the amicus briefs
in the US – Carbon Steel case, which were working against the substantial
reduction of tariffs and other barriers to trade, the very objective of the
multilateral organization they were addressing.

The most relevant case for the purpose of analyzing the issue of amicus
curiae before the WTO is the European Communities – Asbestos, which
was initiated by Canada challenging French measures determining the ban
of asbestos and products containing asbestos in the country.[90] In the Panel
phase, five amicus briefs were presented, two of them being incorporated
into the EC submission. Two others were not taken into account by the
Panel because they did not bring relevant information to the case and the
last one because it had been submitted too late. The Panel eventually upheld the French prohibition on asbestos. When the case was brought to the
Appellate Body, a new round of brief submissions began. Seeking to establish an organized procedure to deal with such non-party documents, the
Appellate Body, supported by article 16(1) of the working procedures,
adopted Additional Procedures providing, inter alia, that any person,
whether natural or legal, other than a party or a third party to this dispute,
wishing to file a written brief with the Appellate body, had to apply for
leave from the Appellate Body to file such a brief by a determined date.[91]

Although amicus briefs had been received in previous WTO disputes
and in other cases before international tribunals, as we have addressed in
this chapter, never before had such submissions been facilitated by rules
established by a judicial or quasi-judicial body. The outcome was both expected - thirty briefs and applications for leave to file an amicus brief were
received – and unexpected - they were all rejected. The Appellate Body
was successful in attracting the anger of both WTO member-states as well
as NGOs.

From the NGO's side, the criticism was based on the fact that the short deadline (8 days - 16 November 2000 Noon) did not inform that Central European Time had to be considered, leading several submissions to be rejected due to the time difference. Even those eleven requests that were submitted within the conditions imposed by the Additional procedures were denied 'simply' stating that the Body had reviewed and considered each of the applications and had decided to deny their application for leave due to failure to comply sufficiently with all requirements, therefore understanding that none of the applicants had the capacity to 'make a contribution to the resolution of the dispute that was not likely to be repetitive of what had already been submitted by a party or third party to the dispute.' Perhaps the arguments were actually repetitive or, maybe, at that moment, the Appellate Body had made up its mind to confirm the Panel ruling that had upheld the French asbestos ban. However, the introduction of procedural rules for the admission of amicus briefs *politically* implied in the consideration of some of them by the Appellate Body or, at least, a rejection with more *legally* solid reasons.

From the WTO members' side, the criticism was supported by the fact that the WTO agreement had limited the interaction with NGOs to the General Council (Article V.2), which apparently excluded the Appellate Body's capacity to establish rules concerning the participation of NGOs in the disputes, but, mostly, based on the broad interpretation given by the Appellate Body to Article 17(9) DSU, which establishes that 'working procedures shall be drawn up by the Appellate Body in consultation with the Chairman of the DSB and the Director-General, and communicated to the Members for their information'. Upon request of the Informal Groups of Developing Countries, a special meeting of the General Council was convened and occurred on 23 January 2001.[92] During that meeting, the Brazilian representatives argued that the problem at stake was neither the need for transparency in the WTO proceedings nor the participation of NGOs in the WTO; rather it was essentially legal, and relied on the (broad) interpretation of the expressions 'working procedures' and 'seek', and the adoption of additional procedures by the Appellate Body, which might create or subtract rights and obligations for WTO members, with implications in the WTO Dispute Settlement System, since the new rules could be understood as a clear invitation for NGOs to actively participate in the disputes. In summary, Brazil stressed its understanding that, when exercising the authority to draw up their own working procedures, the Appellate Body and Panels should proceed with special circumspection, bearing in mind the distinction between procedural and substantive matters.

The meeting ended with the Chairman concluding, firstly, that there was a need to consider whether it would be possible to put clear rules in place for *amicus* briefs, although there might not be a consensus on the point. Second, in light of the views expressed and in the absence of clear rules, he believed that the Appellate Body should exercise extreme caution in future cases until members-states had considered what rules were needed.

Since the issue is extremely controversial, no rules have been enacted so far, and the acceptance of amicus briefs continues to rely on the discretion of the Panel's and Appellate Body's members.

Notes

1   *Reparation for Injuries Suffered in the Service of the United Nations* (Advisory Opinion) [1949] ICJ Rep 178.
2   In this particular aspect, we would like to point out that States do not usually oppose Court findings on rules of customary international law and when they do so, they attract to themselves a heavy burden of proof that may be quite insurmountable. See, VD Degan, *Sources of International Law* (Brill, Cambridge 1997) 193.
3   The expression 'floodgate' was used by the ICJ Registrar to deny the submission of an amicus curiae before the Court. See letter from the Registrar to Professor Reisman, *Legal Consequences for States of the Continued Presence of South Africa in Namibia (South-West Africa) Notwithstanding Security Council Resolution 276 (1970)*, 1970 ICJ Pleadings, II, 638-639.
4   *Amici curiae* are non-requested briefs presented to the Court by a non-party. NGOs often submit these briefs on the grounds that the case has broad public interest and that, therefore, the perspectives of civil society need to be considered, which entail particular views about legal questions and/or information regarding certain circumstances with the purpose of influencing the court decision. See, in this regard, GC Umbricht, 'An "amicus curiae brief" on amicus curiae briefs at the WTO' (2001) JIEL v 4 n 4, 773-794.
5   H Lauterpacht, 'The Subjects of Law' (1947) LQR n 63, p 453.
6   *Designation of Workers' Delegate for the Netherlands at the Third Session of the International Labor Conference* (Advisory Opinion) PCIJ Series C 1.
7   *Certain German Interests in Polish Upper Silesia (Germany v Poland) PCIJ Rep Series A 7.*
8   *Rights of Minorities in Upper Silesia (Minority Schools) (Germany v Poland)* PCIJ Rep Series A 15.
9   ICJ Rules of Court (adopted 14 April 1978, entered into force 1 July 1978). Article 69 (4).
10 ICJ Practice Direction XII: 1. Where an international nongovernmental organization submits a written statement and/or document in an advisory opinion case on its own initiative, such statement and/or document is not to be considered as part of the case file. 2. Such statements and/or documents shall be treated as publications readily available and may accordingly be referred to by States and intergovernmental organizations presenting written and oral statements in the case in the same manner as publications in the public domain. 3. Written statements and/or documents submitted by international nongovernmental organizations will be placed in a designated location in the Peace Palace. All States as well as intergovernmental organizations presenting written or oral statements under Article 66 of the Statute will be informed as to the location where statements and/or documents submitted by international nongovernmental organizations may be consulted. <www.icj-cij.org/basicdocuments> accessed 20 April 2009.
11 This is particularly true in cases involving environmental issues, such as in the *Gabcikovo-Nagymaros Project* case *(Hungary v Slovakia)*.

12 *Legality on the Threat or Use of Nuclear Weapons* (Advisory Opinion) [1996] ICJ Rep 226.

13 AK Lindblom. *Non-Governmental Organizations in International Law* (CUP, Cambridge, 2005) 221.

14 *Legality on the Threat or Use of Nuclear Weapons* (Judge Oda dissenting opinion) [1996] ICJ Rep 336.

15 The issue was addressed by the Court, which concluded, with one sole dissenting vote (Judge Oda) that 'it is not for the Court itself to purport to decide whether or not an advisory opinion is needed by the Assembly for the performance of its functions. (...) Equally, once the Assembly has asked, by adopting a resolution, for an advisory opinion on a legal question, the Court, in determining whether there are any compelling reasons for it to refuse to give such an opinion, will not have regard to the origins or to the political history of the request, or to the distribution of votes in respect of the adopted resolution'. *Legality on the Threat or Use of Nuclear Weapons* [1996] ICJ Rep 26 para 16.

16 IF Dekker and WG Werner, 'The Completeness of International Law and Hamlet's Dilemma: *non liquet*, the *Nuclear Weapons* case, and Legal Theory', in IF Dekker and HHG Post (eds), *On The Foundations and Sources of International Law* (TMC Asser Press, The Hague 2003) 9.

17 Judge Oda, in his dissenting opinion, realized this purpose when putting the question to the Court, and wrote (para 3) that 'the General Assembly - or those States which took the initiative in drafting the request - clearly *never* expected that it would give an answer in the *affirmative* stating that: "*Yes*, the threat or use of nuclear weapons is permitted under international law in any circumstance [or, in all circumstances]." If this is true, it follows that, in fact, the General Assembly only expected the Court to state that: "*No*, the threat or use of nuclear weapons is not permitted under international law in *any circumstance*." The General Assembly, by asking the question that it did, wished to obtain nothing more than the Court's *endorsement* of the latter conclusion'. He ended his argument supporting that in such a circumstance, the Court should refrain from giving its opinion, which would not be 'advisory' at all, but a mere endorsement to a legal axiom. *Legality on the Threat or Use of Nuclear Weapons* (Judge Oda's dissenting opinion) [1996] ICJ Rep 333 para 3.

18 See, in this regard, H Lauterpacht, 'Some Observations on the Prohibition of "Non Liquet" and the Completeness of the Law', in *Symbolae Verzijl* (Nijhoff, The Hague 1958) 196-221.

19 R Higgins, 'Human Rights in the International Court of Justice', (2007) LJIL, v 20, 746.

20 *South West Africa*, Second Phase, (Merits) [1966] ICJ Rep 6; *Legal Consequences for States of the Continued Presence of South Africa in Namibia (South West Africa) notwithstanding Security Council Resolution 276* (Advisory Opinion) [1971] ICJ Rep 16; *Western Sahara* (Advisory Opinion) [1975] ICJ Rep 12.

21 R Higgins, *Human Rights* (n 19) 747.

22 We can quote, for example, the various NGO reports on disrespect of human rights that provide support for questions during the hearings and for the judgment.

23 Of course, we do not make this reference strictly in the sense of decision enforcement, but rather based on the practical and very effective pressure that NGOs, as watchdogs, put on governments and international organizations to ensure that they will respect the Court decision.

24 LN Sadat, 'Judgment at Nuremberg: Foreword to the Symposium', WUGSLR (2007) v 6, 491.

25 Charter of the International Military Tribunal (adopted 8 August 1945) <http://avalon.law.yale.edu/imt/imtconst.asp> accessed 24 April 2009.

26 Several entities created the NGO Coalition for the International Criminal Court and participated in the work of the UN General Assembly (including its Sixth Committee), which led to the approval of the Statute of Rome and establishment of the Court. See, for example UNGA Res 53/105 (8 December 1998) para 7.

27 The ICTY Rule of Procedure 74 admits the submission of amicus briefs. ICTY-Res 827/93.

28 See UNSC Res 771 and 770. See, also, C Bassiolni, 'The Commission of Experts Established pursuant to Security Council Resolution 780: Investigating Violations of International Humanitarian Law in the Former Yugoslavia' in R Clark and M Sann, *The Prosecution of International Crimes* (Transaction, New Brunswick 1996) 62.

29 Rome Statute of the International Criminal Court (adopted 17 July 1998, entered into force 1 July 2002) UNTS 2187.

30 The importance of NGOs for the ICC can be noticed in the existence of so-called regular 'strategic meetings' of the Court's Registrar and Prosecutor with NGOs involved in the work of the Court. See, also, D Shelton, 'The Participation of NGOs in International Judicial Proceedings' (1994) ASIL n 88, 611, and for an interesting appraisal of NGOs international criminal tribunals, particularly in Chechnya war, see, E Haslam, 'Non-Governmental War Crime Tribunals: A Forgotten Arena of International Criminal Justice', in C Harding and CL Lim, *Renegotiating Westphalia* (Nijhoff, The Hague 1999)153.

31 D Lazic, 'Introductory Note to the International Criminal Court: Prosecutor v. Thomas Lubanga Dyilo (Appeals Chambers, Decision on Victim Participation), ILM (2008) v 47 n 6, 968.

32 ICC Rules of Procedure and Evidence (adopted 9 September 2002, entry into force 9 September 2002) ICC Doc ASP/1/3 (Part.II-A) Rule 85 (b).

33 ICC Statutes, article 66 (2).

34 ICC *Prosecutor v. Lubanga (Appeals Chamber, Decision on Victim Participation)* 47 ILM 972 (2008).

35 See http://curia.europa.eu/jcms/jcms/J02_7024/#jurisprudences accessed in 20 June 2012.

36 Treaty Establishing the European Community (25 March 1957) 298 UNTS 11, amended by Treaty of Amsterdam (2 October 1997) 1997 OJ (C 340) and Treaty of Nice (26 February 2001) 2001 OJ (C 80).

37 ECJ, *Yassin Abdullah Kadi and Al Barakaat International Foundation v. Council of the European Union and Commission of the European Communities.* Joined cases C402/05 P and C414/05 P, Judgment of 3 September 2008. 47 ILM 927 (2008).

38 *Kadi* case (para 334).

39 CFI (7th Chamber), *People's Mojahedin Organization of Iran v. Council of the European Union.* Case T-284/08, Judgment of 4 December 2008.

40 ECJ, *Stichting Greenpeace Council (Greenpeace International) and Others v Commission*, case C-321/95 P, Judgment of 2 April 1998.

41 CFI (2nd Chamber), *European Environmental Bureau and Stichting Natuur en Milieu v Commission.* Joined Cases T-236/04 and T 241/04. Order of 28 November 2005.

42 ECJ, *Association Greenpeace France and Others v Ministère de l'Agriculture et de la Pêche and Others.* Case C-6/99, Judgment 21 March 2000.

43 ECJ, *Van der Kooy and Others v Commission.* Joined Cases 67/85, 68/85 and 70/85 [1988] ECR 219, paragraphs 21 to 24, and *CIRFS and Others v. Commission.* Case C-313/90 [1993] ECR I-1125, paragraphs 29 and 30.

44 *EEB and Natuur in Milieu* case (para 63).

45 AK Lindblom. *Non-Governmental Organizations* (n 13) 268.

46 Lindblom quotes, for that sake, *The Role and Function of the European Court of Justice*, A Report by Members of the EC Section of the British Institute's Advisory

Board chaired by Rt. Hon. The Lord Slynn of Hadley (The British Institute of International and Comparative Law, 1996) 93-94.

47 ECJ, *Fédération Nationale de la Boucherie en Gros et du Commerce en Gros des Viandes and Others v Council*. Joined Cases 19/62 to 22/62 [1962] ECR 491, 499 and 500.

48 ECJ, *Italian Republic and Sardegna Lines v Commission*. Joined cases C-15/98 and C-105/99. Judgment of 19 October 2000.

49 *Statute of the Council of Europe* (adopted 5 May 1949, entered into force 03 August 1949) UNTS 87. Preamble, articles 1 and 3. In fact, this almost came about with Greece, which withdrew from the organization in 1969 to avoid the constraint of being expelled due to recurrent acts of violation of human rights.

50 RA Lawson and HG Schermers (eds) *Leading Cases of the European Court of Human Rights* (Ars Aequi Libri, Nijmegen 1999) xvii.

51 *Convention for the Protection of Human Rights and Fundamental Freedoms* (adopted 4 November 1950, entered into force 3 September 1953). UNTS 213.

52 *Protocol nr. 11 to the Convention for the Protection of Human Rights and Fundamental Freedoms, restructuring the control machinery established thereby* (adopted 11 May 1994, entered into force 1 November 1998). UNTS 2061.

53 It is worth quoting that, to date, neither the Commission's Rules of Procedure nor the Rules of the Court have ever defined an NGO for the purpose of the procedures regulated therein.

54 In this regard, see *Tinnelly & Sons Ltd. and Others and McElduff & Others v The United Kingdom*, 10 July 1998; *Holy Monasteries v Greece*, 9 December 1994; *The Sunday Times v the United Kingdom*, 29 April 1979; *Freedom and Democratic Party (ÖZDEP) v Turkey*, 8 December 1999.

55 The Court rejected the claims of local governmental organizations. See, for example, *Austrian Communes and some of their Councillors v Austria*, 31 May 1974.

56 See, for example, *United Communist Party of Turkey and Others v Turkey*, 30 January 1998; *Socialist Party and Others v Turkey*, 25 May 1998; *Refah Partisi (Prosperity Party) and Others v Turkey*, 31 July 2001 and *Yazar, Karatas, Aksoy and the People's Labor Party (HEP) v Turkey*, 9 April 2002.

57 In the case *Purcell and Others v. Ireland*, 16 April 1991, the Commission understood that two trade unions could not be admitted as complainants because they had not suffered directly the violation of rights protected by the Convention, hence not being considered victims.

58 *American Convention on Human Rights* (adopted 22 November 1969, entered into force 18 July 1978) UNTS 1144

59 *Statute of the Inter-American Court of Human Rights* OAS Res 448 (IX-0/79), articles 1, 2, 28 and 29.

60 This general capacity includes representation of the victim, participation in investigations, preparation of reports, assistance in on-site visits, among other observed activities.

61 *Rules of Procedure of the Inter-American Commission on Human Rights*, rules 23 (1) and 44(1)

62 *Loayza Tamayo v. Peru* (Judgment) (17 September 1997) Series C no 33 [1997] IACHR 6. Para 22.

63 We can quote, for example: *Bámaca Velásques v Guatemala* (Judgment) (25 November 2000) Series C no 70 [2000] IACHR 7, para 64; *Baena Ricardo et al v Panamá* (Judgment) (2 February 2001) Series C no 72 [2001] IACHR 2, para 46; and *The Mayagna (Sumo) Awas Tingni Community v. Nicarágua* (Judgment) (31 August 2001) Series C no 79 [2001] IACHR 9, paras 38, 41, 42, 52 and 61

64 *Juan Carlos Abella v. Argentina* case (Judgment) (18 November 1997) Case 11.137. Paras 407-408.

65 AK Lindblom. *Non-Governmental Organizations* (n 13) 279.

66 *American Convention on Human Rights*, art 44; *Rules of Procedure of the Inter-American Commission on Human Rights*, rules 28.

67 It is, for example, the situation observed in *Maria Eugenia Morales de Sierra v. Guatemala*, case 11.625, Report 28/98 (6 March 1998) para 16, where three NGO officials acted as experts; and in the case of *Desmond Mackenzie v. Jamaica*, case 12.023, Report 41/00 (13 April 2000) para 81, where some NGOs reports were taken as evidence of poor conditions in the country's prisons.

68 *European Social Charter* (adopted 18 October 1961, entry into force 26 February 1962) UNTS 529.

69 *European Social Charter (revised)* (adopted 3 May 1996, entry into force 1 July 1999) UNTS 2151.

70 *Protocol amending the European Social Charter* (adopted 21 October 1991) ETS 142.

71 *Additional Protocol to the European Social Charter* (adopted 5 May 1988, entry into force 4 September 1992) ETS 128.

72 *Additional Protocol to the European Social Charter providing for a System of Collective Complaints* (adopted 9 November 1995, entry into force 1 July 1998) UNTS 2045.

73 < http://www.coe.int/t/dghl/monitoring/socialcharter/OrganisationsEntitled/ OrganisationsIndex_en.asp> accessed 22 April 2009.

74 *European Convention for the Prevention of Torture and Inhuman or Degrading Treatment or Punishment* (adopted 26 November 1987, entered into force 1 February 1989) ETS 126.

75 It is, for example, the case of *Desmond Mackenzie v. Jamaica*, case 12.023, Report 41/ 00 (13 April 2000) para 81, where some NGOs reports were taken as evidence of poor conditions in the country's prisons in a procedure before the Inter-American Committee on Human Rights.

76 *Marrakesh Agreement establishing the World Trade Organization* (adopted 15 April 1994, entered into force 1 January 1995) UNTS 1864.

77 WTO Doc WT/L/162 (23 July 1996). This provision has its origins in 1946, during the negotiations for the establishment of the GATT. According to Charnovitz and Wickman, 'The architects of the post-war trading system saw the appropriateness of providing for NGO participation. It was recognized that NGOs were interested in trade policy and could make a constructive contribution'. See, S Charnovitz and J Wickham, 'Non-Governmental Organizations and the Original International Trade Regime' (1995) Journal of World Trade, v 29, n 5, 122.

78 *Agreement establishing the World Trade Organization*, Preamble.

79 *Understanding on Rules and Procedures Governing the Settlement of Disputes, Agreement Establishing the World Trade Organization, Annex 2*, 1869 (adopted 15 April 1994, entered into force 1 January 1995) UNTS 1869; *Working Procedures for Appellate Review*. WTO Doc WT/AB/WP/5 (4 January 2005).

80 The concern of the WTO with civil society is perceived, for instance, on its web-site, which tries to establish rapport with the common citizen, comparing the WTO with a 'table' and 'superman', an unusual approach on intergovernmental organizations web-sites, even among those in charge of social and environmental affairs. See < http:// www.wto.org/english/thewto_e/whatis_e/tif_e/fact1_e.htm> accessed 22 April 2009.

81 A Reinisch and C Irgel, 'The Participation of Non-Governmental Organizations (NGOs) in the WTO Dispute Settlement System', (2001) Non-State Actors and International Law, n 1 127.

82 That was not the case, since Article 14.1 of the DSU does not prohibit open hearings by stipulating that panel 'deliberations' must be confidential, because 'deliberations'

can be understood to refer to the panel's internal work on the case, including the internal process of decision-making.

83 L Ehring, 'Public Access to Dispute Settlement Hearings in the World Trade Organization', (2008) JIEL v II n 4, 1021-1034.

84 *United States – Import Prohibition of Certain Shrimp and Shrimp Products*. WT/DS58/R (15 May 1998).

85 WT/DS58/R (paras 7.7 -10).

86 *United States – Import Prohibition of Certain Shrimp and Shrimp Products*. WT/DS58/AB/R (12 October 1998) paras 79-110.

87 *United States – Imposition of Countervailing Duties on Certain Hot-Rolled Lead and Bismuth Carbon Steel Products Originating in the United Kingdom*. WT/DS138/R (23 December 1999) para 6.9.

88 *United States – Imposition of Countervailing Duties on Certain Hot-Rolled Lead and Bismuth Carbon Steel Products Originating in the United Kingdom*. WT/DS138/AB/R (10 May 2000) Paras 39-40.

89 The self declared mission of the American Iron and Steel Institute is to influence public policy, educate and shape public opinion in support of a strong, sustainable U.S. and North American steel industry committed to manufacturing products that meet society's needs <www.steel.org> accessed 22 April 2009. The Specialty Steel Industry of North America, on the other hand, is a voluntary trade association representing virtually all the producers of specialty steel in North America. www.ssina.com> accessed 22 April 2009.

90 *European Communities – Measures Affecting Asbestos and Asbestos – Containing Products*. WT/DS135/R (18 September 2000).

91 Communication from the Appellate Body WT/DS/135/9 (8 November 2000).

92 WTO General Council, *Minutes of Meeting*. WT/GC/M/60 (23 January 2001).

CHAPTER 4

NGOS in International Custom

In the early societies, the recurring behavior of individuals defined what was permitted or not in order to meet the needs and protect the values of the group. As communities developed, those rules became more comprehensive and, with the advent of writing, came the first codifications of customary rules, which further received the addition of new written rules enacted by religious leaders, lords, kings and parliaments. If it is clearly noticeable that custom has become cumbersome at the national level, in light of the massive activity of permanent legislative bodies, the same does not occur in the international sphere, where there is no centralized legislative body and custom continues to play a relevant role, being regarded as one of the primary sources of international law, together with the treaties and the general principles of law. It can be observed, for instance, in Article 38(1) of the Statute of the ICJ, which provides that the tribunal will decide applying 'international custom, as evidence of a general practice accepted as law'.

In a nutshell, we can regard international custom as those non-written rules that became obligatory due to the recurrent behavior of States.[1] If customary rules can be deduced from the general behavior of States, how can we affirm that they are 'accepted as law'? In practical terms, only when someone says that it is not. The need to confirm that a certain State practice is 'law' usually arises when a country disrespects it. Not without reason, major evidence of customary law is identified in the decisions of international tribunals or arbitrators.[2] Some authors suggest that by doing so, these decisions not only recognize the existence of custom but also create it, hence making it extremely difficult to delineate where recognition has ended and where creation has begun.[3] Once a custom has been recognized in a court or arbitral decision, this very decision is reflected in the teachings of highly qualified publicists, and both become subsidiary means for the determination of those same rules of law, retro-feeding the existence of the concerned custom.

Traditionally, two different fundaments have been recognized for customary law: the first one (Voluntarism School) is supported in the classical idea of an inter-state society governed by contractual arrangements between their members; the second (Objectivism School), is based on the contemporary idea of a transnational society where custom is created by the spontaneous behavior of States as an answer to the concerns of modern society.[4]

The first theory assumes that international law is created by the voluntary consent of the States, whether in written or tacit agreements. It is observed in the *Lotus* case,[5] when the PCIJ affirmed that 'the rules of law binding upon states therefore emanate from their own free will as expressed in conventions or by usage generally accepted as expressing principles of law and established in order to regulate their relations between the coexisting independent communities or with a view to the achievement of common aims.'

Such a conception is extremely positivist and it is incapable of justifying why new States are bound by customary laws whose creation they have not participated in, and therefore have not expressed their 'free will'.[6] Additionally, it cannot explain why States remain bound even when they express this 'free will' terminating or denouncing a treaty, due to the *jus cogens* established in article 43 of the Vienna Convention on the Law of Treaties,[7] which prescribes that the invalidity, termination or denunciation of a treaty, shall not in any way impair the duty of any State to fulfill any obligation embodied in the treaty to which it would be subject under international law independently of the treaty.

The second theory justifies basing the creation of international customary law on the existence and joint activity of multiple subjects of international law – States and intergovernmental organizations – which, together with other relevant players, such as individuals, multi-national corporations, private financial systems and INGOs,[8] impose a dynamic rhythm on international law, which can create new rules or modify those established, either by custom or treaties, through the adoption of new patterns of behavior.[9] However, as noted by Shaw, 'amidst a wide variety of conflicting behavior, it is not easy to isolate the emergence of a new rule of customary law and there are immense problems involved in collating all necessary information'.[10]

Nonetheless, it seems that a certain agreement prevails that the creation of a new custom neither requires the participation of the (now greatly expanded) entire international community nor demands the repetition of a new pattern of behavior over a large period of time.[11] With regards to the element of time, in the *North Sea Continental Shelf* cases, the ICJ noted that

'it is over ten years since the Convention was signed, but that it is even now less than five since it came into force in June 1964, and that when the present proceedings were brought it was less than three years, while less than one had elapsed at the time when the respective negotiations between the Federal Republic (of Germany)

and the other two Parties for a complete delimitation broke down
on the question of the application of the equidistance principle.
Although the passage of only a short period of time is not necessarily, or of itself, a bar to the formation of a new rule of customary
international law on the basis of what was originally a purely conventional rule, an indispensable requirement would be that within
the period in question, short though it might be, State practice,
including that of States whose interests are specially affected,
should have been both extensive and virtually uniform in the sense
of the provision invoked; and should moreover have occurred in
such a way as to show a general recognition that a rule of law or
legal obligation is involved.'[12]

Since custom constitutes 'evidence of general practice accepted as law',
two basic elements must co-exist: one, objective, represented by the recurrent practice (*consuetudo*) and the other, subjective, which is its acceptance
as law, i.e., the certainty that that behavior is deemed obligatory because it
represents essential values and is required from all members of the international community (*opinio juris vel necessitatis*).[13] Only the co-existence of
both elements can create a custom, which by these circumstances differs
from 'usage' that, albeit being a recurrent behavior, does not represent a
legally binding obligation.[14] Custom can be either international, when it
comprises a widespread behavior of States from all regions and with different economic standings, or regional, usually based within continental limits.[15] In certain very specific situations, Court precedents have recognized
the existence of international custom even at the local level.[16] This conceptual framework poses an inherent circularity to customary international
law, as argued by D'Amato, since States behave accordingly because they
believe that it is law but, by behaving in the same manner, they constitute
it as law.[17] Notwithstanding acknowledging this 'chicken-egg' dilemma
and the traditional criticism to customary international law, it is beyond the
scope of this work to appraise the role of custom *as* a source of international law. For that reason, we will assume that custom *does indeed* create
international law.

4.1   The legal status of NGO consultative arrangements

Providing evidence of a custom comprises an empirical survey on States'
and intergovernmental organizations' behavior and an appraisal on how
those subjects of international law understand that behavior. In this chapter,
we will direct our attention to the duration, consistency, repetition and generality of those practices. We will conduct our appraisal taking up Herman
Meijers' concept of 'stages of growth' for guidance.[18] According to his

understanding, a rule of customary international law is formed in two stages, although often overlapping, in which the first is dedicated to the formation of the concerned rule, and the second, to its transformation into a rule of law. To correctly appraise both stages, it is also necessary to pose sub-questions to each of them, addressing in what way those acts took place, who performed them and when they were performed. Merging his conception with Article 38(1) of the Statutes of the ICJ, Meijers regarded the first stage as comprised within the 'evidence of general practice' - with the practice embodying 'custom', - and the second one as hidden in the requirement that there also has to be 'evidence' that the 'general practice' is 'accepted as law'.

It follows that the identification of the legal status that NGOs have in the international sphere depends upon the evaluation of the practices that States and intergovernmental organizations have toward those private entities. If a conduct is repeated in a consistent and general manner over a certain period of time, then it can be regarded as a 'customary rule' in dealing with NGOs, hence accomplishing the first stage. Once a certain qualified number of subjects have expressed their will to adopt such customary behavior as a rule of law, the second stage is fulfilled and the concerned procedure becomes a rule of customary law.

As we could see in the *North Sea Continental Shelf* cases, the ICJ does not place significant importance on the duration of State practices, rather putting more emphasis on the consistency and repetition of the acts of those States that were specially affected. This is also noticeable, for example, in the previous *Asylum* case, where the Court affirmed that one of the contending parties had to prove that the custom rule invoked was 'in accordance with a constant and uniform usage practiced by the States in question' (the *consuetudo*) and that that usage was the 'expression of a right appertaining to the State granting asylum and a duty incumbent on the territorial State' (the *opinio juris vel necessitatis)*.[19] Thus, if a certain conduct is repeated in a virtually uniform way by a certain number of subjects, even for a short period of time, it can lead to the creation of a custom and, further on, customary law, depending on the obligatory aspect of that custom.

The evaluation of the States' and IGOs' practices toward NGOs must address the status of these private institutions before those public entities. Appraising the major worldwide[20] multilateral international organizations (The UN System, WTO and OECD), we have identified the following patterns of practice regarding the participation of NGOs in the decision-making proceedings, supported either by treaty (items 'a' to 'e') or customary (items 'f' to 'h') provisions:

a. Bodies where NGOs are full members:
    None

b. Bodies where NGOs are affiliate members and participate with voting rights in the decision-making structures:
   None

c. Bodies where NGOs are affiliate members and participate without voting rights in the decision-making structures:
   UNWTO

d. Bodies where NGOs have no membership but participate with voting rights in the decision-making structures:
   ILO

e. Bodies where NGOs have no membership but have consultative status with the decision-making structures granted by the constitutive acts of the considered international body, fund or programme:
   ECOSOC, FAO, ICAO, IMO, ITU, UNCDF, UNCTAD, UNEP, UN-HABITAT, UNESCO, UNICEF, UNIDO, UNRWA, WHO, WIPO, WMO, WTO (except amicus briefs in disputes), ICJ (amicus briefs in advisory proceedings, if requested);

f. Bodies where NGOs have no membership but have some level of interaction with the decision-making structures granted by the governing organ of the considered international body, according to defined formal procedures:
   IFAD, UNDP, UNIFEM, UNODC, UPU, WFP, Secretariat (DPI), World Bank (Inspection Panel), World Bank & IMF (Civil Society Policy Forums in annual meetings), OECD (Advisory Committees); ICJ (amicus briefs in advisory proceedings voluntarily submitted); UN (participation in conferences under ECOSOC Res 1996/31);

g. Bodies where NGOs have no membership but have some level of interaction with the decision-making structures granted by the governing organ of the considered international body, on a case-by-case basis:
   General Assembly (Observer status); WTO (amicus briefs in disputes); ICC, ICTR & ICTY (investigation supportive roles);

h Bodies where NGOs do not have membership, participation in the decision-making bodies or consultative status:
   Security Council

The collected data evidences that disregarding interaction with NGOs cannot be taken as a customary practice in worldwide international organizations, since only one international body does so. At the other extreme, complete peer interaction is indeed not observed. The bulk of the situations evidence a practice of interaction with NGOs heavily concentrated on treaty-based provisions, with a second relevant group of initiatives supported by unilateral written sets of procedures that aim to reproduce the same pattern of relationships established in the treaties. Consultative status is evidently backed by established and substantial practice. Could this widespread practice within worldwide multilateral international organizations be regarded as a rule of custom, accomplishing Meijers' stage 1?

Unequivocally yes, because through a consistent repetition a custom is shaped (the *consuetudo*) and worldwide international organizations, while interacting with NGOs, are repeatedly acting in a virtually uniform fashion, establishing consultative relationship according to similar accreditation criteria and functional objectives. The consistency requirement was stressed by the ICJ in the *Asylum* case – a 'constant and uniform usage' - and also reinforced in the *North Sea Continental Shelf* cases, which demanded a practice 'both extensive and virtually uniform'. The existence of such customary rule cannot be challenged on grounds that the international organizations' behavior in establishing consultative relationship with NGOs has some subtle differences, hence not being rigorously uniform, because it is not expected that in the practice of States the application of the rules must be perfectly aligned, it being unnecessary 'for a rule to be established as customary (that) the corresponding practice must be in absolutely rigorous conformity with the rule', as observed in the ICJ decision in the *Nicaragua v. United States* case.[21]

The problem, in the case of consultative relationship between NGOs and worldwide intergovernmental organizations, relies on the appraisal of whether the mentioned acts just contribute to the creation of a rule of custom (Meijers' stage 1) or are capable of converting this rule of custom into a rule of law (stage 2), since, according to him, 'they are often barely distinguishable', both contributing to the custom and to the law-making.[22]

An aspect that seems relevant to the definition of the nature of the consultative relationship with NGOs is the fact that the original provision for such procedure was introduced in the UN Charter, which determined that the ECOSOC should adopt suitable arrangements for consultation with NGOs which are concerned with matters within its competence. Although leading in an opposite direction, if compared to the situation addressed by the ICJ in the *Nicaragua v United States* case, where the Charter gave expression to principles already present in customary international law, it is true that in the situation of the consultative status granted to NGOs, the Charter established a new pattern of behavior, because 'the law has in the subsequent four decades developed under the influence of the Charter, to such an extent that a number of rules contained in the Charter have acquired a status independent of it'.[23]

If there is no doubt about the acceptance 'as law' of the consultative procedures established by international conventions, there is, however, a relevant dissension as to the other forms of evidence that could be accepted as a demonstration of State practices. On one side, said liberal, stand those who support the notion that State behavior is evidenced by a myriad of active attitudes, either at individual (diplomatic correspondence, public statements by heads of governments and other unilateral acts, including domestic law and court decisions) or collective levels (resolutions of the UN Assembly, recitals in international instruments, drafts of the International Law Commission),[24] as well as passive attitudes represented by the tacit acceptance of some practices, represented by the absence of objections.[25] At the opposite, conservative extreme, others argue that what is important is what States 'do' and not what they 'say', therefore regarding the treaties entered into by the States as relevant, but not the statements made by their diplomats.[26] Between both, there are also those who accept a moderate expansion in evidence but exclude some specific ones.[27]

Evidence shows that eleven out of the fifteen UN specialized agencies have provisions for consultative arrangements with NGOs in their statutes, and the remaining four have established these arrangements under decisions from their governing bodies. Similar patterns of behavior can be observed throughout the entire UN system's programmes, funds and relevant subsidiary bodies, except for one: the Security Council. Given its unique characteristic of being a body entitled to impose the use of force and economic sanctions against any member-state except the five permanent members with veto powers, it could be regarded as the exception that confirms the rule of the comprehensive adoption of the practice of granting consultative status to NGOs by similar intergovernmental bodies within the UN system. Therefore, the extensive adoption of the same pattern of acts expressing the will to engage in structured consultations with NGOs may constitute a 'settled practice' within the UN system that produces a fact of law according to international law, i.e., that creates customary international law (the *opinio juris vel necessitatis*).

Furthermore, if we take into account that some reputed authors support that the UN Charter, being the basic document of contemporary international law, 'would be accepted by international law doctrine as a kind of constitution of the international community',[28] it follows that the consultative rights ensured to NGOs by the UN Charter could be understood as extensive not only to the entire UN system but also to any other intergovernmental organizations. In a certain way this assumption can be regarded as correct and effective, since NGOs' consultative rights have been incorporated on a similar basis in the statutes of regional intergovernmental organizations created after the UN, such as the Organization of the American States, the Council of Europe, the African Union and Mercosur.

Resuming Meijers' concept of 'stages of growth' for the creation of customary international law, we are able to acknowledge that recognizing the consultative rights to NGOs is a 'general practice' established by those same multilateral international organizations 'whose interests are specially affected' by the practice, or, putting the same idea into consultative status wording, 'concerned with matters within the entity's competence'. In this aspect, it is noteworthy that, as well as NGOs, most of the mentioned inter-governmental bodies have been established to work in specific technical areas, attentive to some determined needs of people. Due to this character-istic, the representatives of the member-states are usually experts that, knowing 'the needs and the potential for international cooperation in their particular field',[29] regard NGOs as relevant depositories of knowledge and effective partners in dealing with the issues at stake, not only because they have evidenced experience in dealing with those matters and in aggregat-ing experts in the area, but also due to their capacity for testing and imple-menting pilot projects that, once proven successful, can be extended to the entire world and, most relevantly, their capacity for mustering general sup-port for public policies that they have helped to draft and test. Interaction with NGOs represents a serious concern for worldwide intergovernmental organizations whose interests are specially affected by public opinion and the work of those private institutions. Schermers and Blokker, for example, regarded this interaction as mandatory when they affirmed that 'a public international organization *should* maintain contact with the citizens of their member-states'.[30]

It is beyond any doubt that international organizations have not only in-troduced consultative procedures but actually implemented them, holding several consultative procedures, forums, meetings and symposiums regu-larly, clearly fulfilling the 'evidence' condition of customary practice.[31] The juxtaposition of all the elements indicates that there is evidence of an *intra vires* general practice of worldwide and regional multilateral interna-tional organizations engaging themselves in consultative interaction with NGOs within the scope of their activities that may constitute a customary international law for the purposes of Article 38(1) of the Statute of the International Court of Justice.

Albeit extensive at the international level and highly supported by the practice of States at the municipal level - where interaction sometimes gives NGOs some space in public-policies decision making[32] – it is a fact that the strength of these consultation rights extensively recognized by multilateral bodies has not yet been appreciated by the ICJ. The first reason for that is the proper apparently unanimous acceptance of those rights, since no State has challenged them before the Court.[33] The second one, most relevant yet concealed behind widespread practice, is the fact that it will probably never be confirmed by the ICJ, since NGOs do not have *lo-cus standi* before the Court and States cannot stand before the tribunal to seek judicial protection for the rights of third parties. The apparently un-ique option of having it addressed directly by the Court would seem to be possible through a request of an advisory opinion on the subject by a legitimate international body, such as the UN General Assembly.[34] However, as we have appraised in the previous chapter, it does not imply that international judicial or quasi-judicial bodies have not already discussed the participation of NGOs, often through the presentation of *amicus* briefs, in contentious cases brought by third parties. In those cases, it seems that quasi-judicial bodies are keener to accept the participation of NGOs than the Courts, and that regional bodies are more sympathetic to their initiatives than international bodies. If it is true that NGOs can stand as parties before some international tribunals to defend their personal rights, as is the case in the European Court of Justice and the European Court of Human Rights, it is less probable that those rights could be regarded as encompassing the right to intervene in third parties' contentious cases in those situations where this right has not been confirmed by the rules of procedure of the concerned tribunal.

Taking the submission of *amici curiae* as an example, it can be seen that, although the ICJ is statutorily authorized to notify 'any international organization considered by the Court as likely to be able to furnish information on the question submitted for the advisory opinion, that the Court will be prepared to receive written statements or to hear, at a public sitting to be held for that purpose, oral statements related to the question',[35] this practice neither occurs nor is the voluntary submission of these briefs encouraged, since the Courts Practice Direction XII,[36] despite ensuring acceptance of written statements or documents submitted by NGOs in an advisory opinion case on their own initiative, defined that they will not to be considered as part of the case file, except if brought by a party.

From another perspective, if we consider, as affirmed in the *Nicaragua v. United States* case, that 'as to the facts of the case, in principle the Court is not bound to confine its consideration to the material formally submitted to it by the parties (cf. *Brazilian Loans*, PCIJ Series A, no. 20/21, p. 124; *Nuclear Tests*, ICJ Reports 1974, pp. 263-264, paras. 31, 32)',[37] there could be potentially legitimate participation of NGOs in the Court proceedings, since *amici curiae* usually address factual situations. However, we have not found evidence that those briefs have been effectively accepted by the Court.[38]

The situation of NGOs before other judicial and quasi-judicial bodies is not materially different, since the presentation of *amicus curiae* is highly controversial either at the international or regional levels. If we take, for instance, the case of WTO settlement dispute procedures, we have observed that some Panels have accepted the submission of factual briefs based on their legal capability to 'seek' information to the case pursuant to articles 12 and 13 of the DSU,[39] a procedure that was later adopted by the Appellate Body, although restricted to legal matters.[40] When the Appellate Body, laying down article 16(1) of the Working Procedures, adopted Additional Procedures[41] providing, *inter alia*, that any person, whether natural or legal, other than a party or a third party could file a written brief in the *European Communities – Asbestos* case,[42] the decision was heavily opposed by several member-states.[43]

Therefore, the appraisal of the major worldwide international organizations has shown that even though NGOs enjoy consultative rights in matters falling within the competence of specialized international entities, supported either on treaties or governing bodies' decisions, this right is restricted to the executive-like bodies, with severe restrictions on the adoption of the same pattern of behavior by judicial organs, either by the Courts themselves or by the States. Recalling Meijers' model, evidence suggests that international customary law (originated in treaty law, and further widely reproduced in State practice) has legitimized NGOs, ensuring to them the right to engage in consultative procedures with specialized organizations, agencies, funds and programs within the matters of their competence, fulfilling the requirements of stages 1 and 2 of the model. In this particular aspect, we should recall that the ICJ, in the *North Sea Continental Shelf* cases, affirmed that a conventional rule in its origin can pass into the general *corpus* of international law, becoming accepted as such by the *opinio juris,* binding even those countries that were not part to the original conventional instrument.[44] Regarding the participation in proceedings before judicial and quasi-judicial bodies, despite the existence of some room for interaction, evidence shows that there is no consistency and generality in the practice on the matter, which makes both stages unattended.

Assuming that there is a settled *intra vires* customary practice in international organizations, it is worth appraising to what extent this customary practice is *ultra vires,* affecting the member-states. Should they become personally bound by the decisions made, for instance, as a member of a UN organ?

According to Meijers, the answer is evident: when voting on the adoption of rules concerning the granting of consultative status to NGOs in a given UN organ governing body, they are not acting as a State, but as a part of that UN organ, therefore not configuring in such a act a kind of State practice for the purposes of Article 38(1) of the Statutes of the ICJ.[45] Intergovernmental organizations are independent bodies that act by themselves within the limits of the powers that have been attributed to them by their member-states. They do not have the competence to establish their own competences.[46] Since the States are not keen to be individually bound by the acts of those organizations that they have created and that they cannot personally control, as a rule, the constitutive instruments do not attribute representative powers to the organizations, following that the States are not bound by the customary practices of the international organizations in which they participate.

However, should the same rationale be applied when States gather in conferences to approve the establishment of a new intergovernmental organization whose constitutive acts recognize the NGOs' consultative rights?

There is no disputing the fact that the creation of IGOs in multilateral treaties represents the concerted personal will of the contracting parties, containing 'legal standards specifically agreed between the parties to govern their mutual rights and obligations, and that the conduct of the parties will continue to be governed by these treaties, because of the principle of *pacta sunt servanda*'.[47] Hence, we will dwell any longer on the issue. However, if establishing consultative relationship with NGOs in a specific convention binds the contracting States in that case, it is worth asking if the repetitive recognition of such rights constitutes an *opinion juris* that obliges the States to do so in the future.

In the *North Sea Continental Shelf* cases, the ICJ regarded the consistency and repetition of the acts of the States that were specially affected as a relevant aspect of the creation of customary law. The Court also affirmed that a rule, conventional in its origin, can pass into the general *corpus* of international law, becoming accepted as such by the *opinio juris*.[48] In another case, the *Continental Shelf (Libyan Arab Jarnahiriyu/Malta)*, the Court affirmed that 'it is of course axiomatic that the material of customary international law is to be looked for primarily in the actual practice and *opinio juris* of States, *even though multilateral conventions may have an important role to play in recording and defining rules deriving from custom, or indeed in developing them.*'[49]

Hence, one can acknowledge the consistent repetition of NGO consultative provisions in multilateral conventions either as a recording of customary rules already in existence or as a settled extensive practice of specially affected States leading to their development. As we observed in the first part of this chapter, it is a fact that consultative rights have been continuously and extensively ensured to NGOs in a virtually uniform manner in several multilateral agreements since 1945. It is also a truism that this procedure has not received the opposition of the States, rather their effective support, not only expressed through the negotiation and signature of the conventions but also through the subsequent deposit of their ratifications. It is also unchallenged that the rules have been adopted by a qualified majority of those States specially affected by the provision, since all the surveyed organizations, with the exception of the OECD, concentrate the quasi-totality of independent States. All of this evidence suggests the existence of customary international law adopted by States.

Furthermore, in order to support our analysis, we may draw our attention to the judgment of the *Nicaragua v. United States* case. In that situation, the Court understood that 'where two States agree to incorporate a particular rule in a treaty, their agreement suffices to make that rule a legal one, binding upon them.' This is undisputed, since it relies on the principle of *pacta sunt servanda.* However, the Court went further to add that 'in the field of customary international law, the shared view of the parties as to the content of what they regard as the rule is not enough. The Court must satisfy itself that the existence of the rule in the *opinio juris* of States is confirmed by practice' which includes, *inter alia,* 'the attitude of States toward certain General Assembly resolutions'.[50]

The ICJ ruling suggests that not only multilateral conventions, but also General Assembly resolutions, can have a role in the definition of a State practice for the purpose of establishing customary law.

In another case, the *Nuclear Weapons* Advisory Opinion, the Court maintained the same line of thought. In that situation, the Court appraised the successive resolutions passed by the General Assembly, starting with Resolution 1653 (XVI) of 24 November 1961, and found that the existence of a substantial number of negative votes and abstentions, made them 'still fall short of establishing the existence of an *opinio juris* on the illegality of the use of such weapons' to conclude that 'the emergence, as *lex lata,* of a customary rule specifically prohibiting the use of nuclear weapons as such is hampered by the continuing tensions between the nascent *opinio juris,* on the one hand, and the still strong adherence to the practice of deterrence on the other.'[51]

Despite confirming the lack of *opinio juris* on the subject, the Court affirmed, implicitly, that it could be created if the opposition against the nascent *opinio juris* vanished. A central element in this case appears to be the role of General Assembly resolutions in the formation of customary rule. Since the Court was assessing a sequence of UNGA resolutions that declared the illegality of nuclear weapons, it had to appraise the legal strength of these documents. When the Court declared that they '*still* fall short of *establishing* the existence of an *opinio juris*' *(emphasis added)* it understood that they, at least in thesis, can contribute to the creation of customary law.

Judge Schwebel, however, understood in his dissenting opinion that the General Assembly 'has no authority to enact international law' and that it 'can adopt resolutions declaratory of international law only if those resolutions truly reflect what international law is', i.e., if they are 'adopted unanimously (or virtually so, qualitatively as well as quantitatively) or by consensus' and if they 'correspond to State practice'. Since in the considered case, the resolutions 'have been adopted by varying majorities, in the teeth of strong, sustained and qualitatively important opposition' of States that 'bring together much of the world's military and economic power and a significant percentage of its population', it more than sufficed to 'deprive the resolutions in question of legal authority' to give birth to a 'nascent *opinio juris*'.[52]

Judge Schwebel's opinion raises some interesting points: firstly, it asserts that General Assembly resolutions cannot create international customary law, but only declare it, and secondly, it affirms, implicitly, that the two-third majority of member-states that passed the resolution, according to article 18(2) of the UN Charter, could not constitute a qualified majority since the resolution had not obtained the support of those countries that represent, in his own words, 'much of the world's military and economic power and a significant percentage of its population'.

In his first point, he assumes implicitly that State declarations, as is the case of UNGA resolutions, do not have the legal strength to bind the declaring States, because they cannot constitute law. This understanding, however, is not supported by Court precedents, which in the *Nuclear Tests* cases[53] affirmed that:

'It is well recognized that declarations made by way of unilateral acts, concerning legal or factual situations, may have the effect of creating legal obligations. Declarations of this kind may be, and often are, very specific. When it is the intention of the State making the declaration that it should become bound according to its terms, that intention confers on the declaration the character of a legal undertaking, the State being thenceforth legally required to follow a course of conduct consistent with the declaration. An undertaking of this kind, if given publicly, and with an intent to be bound, even though not made within the context of international negotiations, is binding.'

If States are bound by their declarations, it is relevant to evaluate to what extent form affects content. Also in this aspect, the Court understood that 'the question of form is not decisive' and that 'this is not a domain in which international law imposes any special or strict requirement' to conclude that 'the sole relevant question is whether the language employed in any given declaration does reveal a clear intention'.[54]

Hence, having in mind that there is no essential difference if a statement is made orally or in writing, as long as it clearly demonstrates the intention of the parties, it would be senseless to understand that statements made collectively in writing would not be able to create legal obligations to their signatories. As affirmed by the Court, the principle of good faith is a basic principle governing the creation and performance of legal obligations and it is also at the root of the binding character of unilateral declarations.[55] Therefore, one can assume that UNGA resolutions, depending on their wording, can play a relevant role in the establishment of customary international law if they represent collective undertakings of the member-states that have approved them. In doing so, they are material evidence to determine actual State practice.[56] The binding character of UN resolutions is highly influenced by several factors, namely their addressees (member-states, UN bodies), their terminology (shall as opposed to should; demand as opposed to recommend, etc), their purpose (decision on something, declaration of intent, recommendation for doing something), their compatibility with the Charter and other treaty provisions or customary law; and forms of adoption (who is in favor, who is against).[57]

Judge Schwebel, in his second point, trails the path laid down by De Visscher, where some States make heavier footprints than others due to their greater weight.[58] As noted by Shaw, even though custom should to some extent reflect the perceptions of the majority of the States – as is the case of the UNGA Nuclear Weapons resolutions – it is 'inescapable that some States are more influential and powerful than others and that their activities should be regarded as of greater significance'.[59]

If the assumption of a 'heavy footprint' is correct, then we could argue that the recognition of NGO's consultative rights should be regarded as a binding obligation imposed to States by the behavior of a qualified majority[60] of them, which have ensured such rights to NGOs in major international conventions in a consistent, repetitive and general manner, since 1945. Furthermore, we could also argue that all General Assembly resolutions addressing such consultative arrangements are notorious evidence of subsequent practice of this *opinio juris* for the sake of Article 31(3)(b) of the Vienna Convention on the Law of Treaties, while interpreting a treaty,[61] and, borrowing the expression coined by Judge Schwebel in his dissenting opinion, 'authentic interpretations of principles or provisions of the United Nations Charter'.

Hence, evidence suggests that the consultative rights ensured to NGOs, firstly by the UN Charter, and, subsequently, by the statutes of several other multilateral organizations, represent the expression of an *opinio juris* that has migrated from the realm of treaty law to international customary law, therefore legitimating the adoption of consultative procedures by the governing bodies of several other organizations. Additionally, this customary international law binds not only the intergovernmental organizations but also their member-states that have extensively expressed in a virtually uniform manner their free will to be bound by such rule, abdicating from the exclusive representation of the interests of the nations in the international sphere to give space, in consultative procedures, to the opinion of civil society organizations in matters within the competences of the international bodies concerned. Finally, not only multilateral treaties, but also statements individually or collectively made by States regarding rights granted or ensured to NGOs bind the declaring States, indeed having the capacity to constitute general practice and bind the entire international community if made by a qualified majority of States specially affected by their content. Since objects of law cannot bear rights, only subjects, it is worth appraising the impact that these customary practices have made on the legal personality of NGOs.

4.2 The legal status of NGOs in general

When States gather at conferences and adopt multilateral conventions, whether creating new intergovernmental organizations or addressing a concern of contemporary society, they evidence their free will to assume obligations toward the international community. In 1945, the States understood that NGOs were legitimate interlocutors that had to be heard in social and economic matters and agreed to include in the UN Charter a provision establishing a consultative procedure. This decision acknowledged that the public sphere was no longer equal to the governmental sphere, rather larger, in comprising other organizations created by social contracts entered into and between individuals: NGOs.

At that precise moment the State's delegates were not able to conceptualize a 'non-governmental organization', although one can infer that they understood that the term referred to government-like bodies on grounds that they operated in the public sphere, but that, being private, had to be differentiated from the governments, hence leading to the expression 'non-governmental'. Once it had been acknowledged that the public sphere comprehended not only States and State-created organizations, and that other bodies had legitimacy to be heard on matters affecting civil society at large, borrowing the De Visscher expression, the UN founding States took the first step to form a road through a vacant land.[62] With the further adoption of consultative relationship in newly created international organizations, new footprints were added to the initial path. As the empirical survey demonstrates, several organizations, both with universal or regional characters, have recognized such consultative rights and have operated maintaining close ties with NGOs, transforming the initial uncertain direction taken in 1945 into a secure road regarded as the only regular way to deal with the contemporary challenges of the society.

The rule of law established by the custom of the States and the intergovernmental organizations does not rely solely on the formal consultative procedures, rather on the effective partnership with NGOs in dealing with contemporary developmental challenges. In this part of this chapter, we will address the effectiveness of consultative rights, as well as other State practices in dealing with NGOs, and their contribution to the definition of the legal status of NGOs in the international sphere.

As acknowledged by the UN Secretary General, the importance of NGOs can be seen in their influence in the debate regarding development, 'in particular through the adoption of policies and strategies that emphasize the need to place people at the centre of the development processes, the importance of participatory approaches, and the priorities that need to be given to poverty alleviation, social equity, environmental protection and regeneration, and cultural identity', which have, in the last decades, become essential components of development strategies.[63] The recognition of the important role played by NGOs was laid down in the UN Charter and it is currently evidenced at all levels of the UN System: policy making, research, information, education and advocacy, and operational activities. The innumerable contractual arrangements regulating international cooperation, according to a UN agency report, have made UN-NGO relations evolve into a 'symbiotic relationship'[64] that far exceed the original scope of the provision of the UN Charter, restricted to economic and social matters. Currently, a diversified and pulsing NGO sector is acting in the entire UN system according to its thematic interests and often participates in the decision-making activities through a variety of informal types of collaboration. It has made NGOs legitimated actors in the multilateral system, and 'continuing and indispensable participants with governments and secretariats in support of international cooperation'.[65]

Could this relationship with NGOs be regarded as custom? Moreover, could it constitute a rule of customary law? To what extent do State and intergovernmental practices recognize NGOs as subjects of international law? In order to try to answer these questions, the analysis of the status of NGOs in the international arena must address the practice of the States toward NGOs in relevant manifestations of their will, such as treaties and conventions, and their participation in conferences and on policy agenda setting.

4.2.1   Role in the practice of treaties and conventions

As we have seen in Chapter 2, NGOs have a 'recognized and indispensable participation' in some labor,[66] human rights[67] and environmental[68] conventions, as well as participatory rights in the Council of Europe,[69] together with the consultative rights ensured in the statutes of several UN specialized agencies addressed in the first part of this chapter. The observation of these multiple provisions clearly demonstrates that NGOs currently exercise duties at the: (i) advisory level (Consultative status in general and participatory status, in the Council of Europe); (ii) decision-making level (ILO); and (iii) executive level (Ramsar and Geneva Conventions).

a.   Advisory level

At the Advisory level, as we have observed, several multilateral conventions have given NGOs the right to be heard in consultative procedures in matters falling within the competence of the intergovernmental body. Their situation has been improved at the European level due to several acts adopted by the Council of Europe member-states and governing bodies.

Following the practice established in the UN, in 1952 the Council of Europe introduced consultative arrangements with NGOs.[70] Due to the relevant place that democracy played in Western European countries, the practice evolved in Europe at a faster pace than that observed at the UN, which suffered the restraints of the Cold War regarding the recognition of the role of NGOs and pluralist democracy in the member-states. This democratic background and the acknowledgement of the importance of active participation of citizens in conducting public affairs fostered the creation of a favorable environment for the adoption of the Strasbourg Convention in 1986.[71]

In 2003, recognizing that the system of co-operation introduced by consultative status 'largely permitted the development and strengthening of co-operation between the Council of Europe and the voluntary sector' and that the evolution of the rules 'to reflect the active participation of INGOs in the Council's policy and work programme' was 'indispensable' , the situation improved again, with INGOs achieving important regional advancements by the recognition of *participatory rights at the Council of Europe*, although without membership and voting power.[72]

The difference between 'participation' and 'consultation' is fundamental in international law.[73] With regard to ECOSOC, for instance, the UN Charter established that participation was granted to States not members of the Council and specialized agencies (arts 69 and 71), leaving the consultative arrangements with NGOs to article 71. Hence, at the European level, NGOs have obtained a treatment only reserved to States and IGOs at the international level.

Based on the arguments concerning the creation of international customary law presented in the first part of this chapter, there is evidence of the existence of a regional customary practice of interaction with INGOs at the European level that has determined the evolution of consultative rights into participatory rights aiming, as asserted in the 2003 resolution, to facilitate participation and access of INGOs to the decision making bodies of the CoE with the purpose of allowing them to 'continue to draw the Council's attention to the effects of changes in European societies and the problems facing them'. The Strasbourg Convention, on the other hand, expresses the recognition of the Council of Europe member-states that NGOs operating at the international level deserve the recognition of a specific legal status that can enable them to operate in several countries.

b. Decision-making level

From the decision-making perspective, NGOs have achieved the highest level of participation, even though unique in character, at the ILO, a major intergovernmental organization. Together with member-states they choose the employers' and workers' delegates to the International Labor Conference, the plenary policy-making body. Every three years, the delegates of each category (member-state, workers and employers) organize themselves into electoral colleges to elect their representatives to the ILO Governing Body, a non-plenary policy-making organ.

The situation of NGOs in the ILO provides an interesting starting point for the enhancement of their participation in the decision-making processes of intergovernmental organizations. According to Schermers and Blokker, an international organization exists if three elements are observed: (i) it is created by an international agreement concluded between States or, more rarely, with the participation of other international organizations; (ii) it is a legal person with at least one organ with a will of its own, therefore being able to bear rights and obligations; and (iii) it has been established under international law.[74]

All three elements are fulfilled by the ILO, which still has ensured the participation of NGOs in its decision-making process, by the establishment of a provision that the member-states should nominate their delegates 'in agreement with the industrial organizations ... which are the most representative of employers or work people ... in their respective countries'.[75] Hence, even though not addressing the international legal personality of NGOs, a treaty almost one century old established a way in which civil society organizations could participate in an intergovernmental organization. It cannot be regarded as a rule of custom, since it is effective in one single intergovernmental body, but may be a seed for a future State practice.

c.   Executive level

At the executive level, NGOs perform two different roles. In the four Geneva Conventions (1949) and its additional Protocols (1977), the International Committee of the Red Cross (ICRC) was allowed to enter the conflict areas to exercise its humanitarian functions for the protection of prisoners of war and civilians, therefore helping to ensure respect for the convention by the conflicting parties. The duty attributed to the International Union for Conservation of Nature and Natural Resources (IUCN) by the Ramsar Convention is different, since it was authorized to act as the substantive Secretariat of the Convention,[76] performing the continuing bureau duties under the Convention.

The situation of the ICRC in international law is extremely peculiar. It is a private non-profit association with room for only twenty five members, all Swiss citizens, established according to the Civil Code of Switzerland, a State that only joined the UN on 10 September 2002. Notwithstanding, it is widely recognized that this private entity holds an international legal personality.[77]

The IUCN, on the other hand, is an international association of governmental and non-governmental members established under the Swiss Civil Code that currently has more than 1100 members, being composed of roughly 200 governments (87 States and 120 government agencies, as well as political and/or economic integration organizations) and 900 NGOs.[78] It is also unique in its genre because it merges the participation of NGOs, States and intergovernmental organizations into one single membership organization performing public tasks that include the exercise of the roles of Secretariat to a major environmental treaty. The international character of its work and the presence of several States as members have led to the admission of the IUCN as Observer to the UN General Assembly, as has the ICRC.[79]

Both cases express the flexibility of international law and the failure of the positivist model, in which States, being the only subjects of international law are the only legal entities capable of bearing rights and obligations under it. Schermers and Blokker, addressing the theme of the international legal personality of international organizations, asseverated the existence of three schools of thought: (i) the first supported that the recognition of international personality only existed if it had been explicitly attributed to the organization in its constitutive acts; (ii) the second supported that it was a status achieved *ipso facto*, if the organization had at least one organ with a will of its own; and (iii) the third, currently prevailing, supports that 'organizations are international legal persons not *ipso facto*, but because the status is given to them, either explicitly or, if there is no constitutional attribution to this quality, *implicitly*'.[80]

Nevertheless, could these theories explain the emergence of individuals and some NGOs – as is the case of the ICRC – as subjects with rights in the international sphere? It does not appear probable, because all three have as common ground the presumption that the considered organization has been created by States, disagreeing only as to whether the concerned organization has an original legal personality (defended by the second school) or has derived powers (first and third schools). They do not comprise the hypothesis that individuals can bear rights and obligations under international law, as declared, for instance, by the International Military Tribunal at Nuremberg, which held that 'crimes are committed by men, not by abstract entities,' therefore affirming that individuals, not only States, could be subjects of international law and, as a consequence, acquire duties and rights.[81] They also do not comprise that 'the subjects of law in any legal system are not necessarily identical in their nature or in the extent of their rights and their nature depends upon the needs of the community', as declared by the ICJ in the *Reparation for injuries* case, which, albeit addressing the case of the UN, and therefore, not appraising the situation of individuals and NGOs, has irremediably torn down the State-only theory of international legal personality.[82]

It appears that, as long as one private institution, the ICRC, is widely recognized as having international legal personality[83] and that, together with a second one, the IUCN, can bear rights and obligations under a multilateral treaty, and that several other NGOS can have consultative rights or even participatory rights under the aforementioned arrangements, one cannot argue that it is impossible to recognize their international personality. The practice of a qualified majority of States has shown it to be possible.

Even though the number of situations such as those of the ICRC and
IUCN does not suggest the existence of a settled universal practice in
granting extended rights and obligations to NGOs, it is a truism that the international customary practice of consultative status and the European
practice of participatory rights at the CoE level, have attributed some rights
to NGOs. And, after all, if being an international person means being capable of bearing rights and duties, this does not suffice, as pointed out by
Schermers and Blokker, to answer the question regarding what rights and
duties they will have.[84]

4.2.2   State practice in NGO participation in conferences

Practice has shown that each UN organ convening an international conference is entitled to establish its own rules for participation of NGOs in the
event, directly or based on the recommendation of the preparatory body for
the conference. These rules generally cover the criteria for both accreditation and participation and, as expressed in a UN Secretary General report,
in 1994, 'the rights to attend and participate have varied from one conference to another' but there is a visible trend 'towards greater flexibility in
granting NGOs access to international conferences'.[85] The UNSG report
has surveyed the practice of all twenty-five international conferences convened by the UN between 1976 and 1996, in which the following pattern
of behavior can be observed:
a. Eight conferences defined the ECOSOC consultative status as a general
   criteria for participation;
b. Fifteen conferences defined the ECOSOC consultative status as a preliminary criteria for participation, but only accepted those NGOs which
   were directly concerned with the scope of the conference;
c. Thirteen conferences disregarded the ECOSOC consultative status as a
   necessary criteria for participation, defining that only NGOs which
   were directly concerned with the scope of the conference could
   participate.

The recurrent recognition of ECOSOC consultative status as criteria for
participation in UN convened conferences (23 out of 25) during the surveyed twenty years led to the establishment of the *right of accreditation of
NGOs with consultative status in UN convened conferences* in 1996, when
the ECOSOC defined that those organizations as a rule shall be accredited
for participation.[86]

   The expansion of the scope of consultative rights ensured to the NGOs
by the UN Charter and similar provisions in the constitutive acts of other
UN agencies, funds and programmes has led to the establishment of rules
for the participation of other NGOs, either at local, national or regional levels, in those conferences.[87] Surprisingly, those rules were defined by the

ECOSOC in the same resolution that granted participatory rights to the organizations with consultative status, in a marked widening of the interpretation of both the ECOSOC mandate and the scope of the consultative status under article 71 of the UN Charter.[88] Therefore, since 1996, the up to then large freedom of UN Agencies to establish the procedures for participation in conferences became restricted by the rules defined by the ECOSOC.

The possibility of an enlargement in the interpretation of the content of the UN Charter provision was appraised by the ICJ in the *Certain expenses of the UN* advisory opinion.[89] The situation at stake had its core in a dispute as to whether a UNGA Resolution on the UN operations in the Congo and the operations of the UN Emergency Force in the Middle East could be regarded as a modification of the balance between two internal bodies of the organization (the General Assembly and the Security Council). In that case, the Court, according to the previous occasions when it had had to interpret the UN Charter, regarded it as a multilateral treaty, albeit with certain special characteristics. Following the principles and rules applicable in general to the interpretation of treaties, which included consideration on 'the structure of the Charter' and, moreover, the 'manner in which the organs concerned have consistently interpreted the text in their practice', the Court concluded that the *practice* of the organization throughout its story could bear out the elucidation of the disputed term included in a UN Charter provision.[90] From a certain perspective, the Court implicitly understood that the UN Charter could be modified, if the practice evidenced a wider interpretation of one of its provisions.[91]

Based on the Court ruling, the unopposed adoption and implementation of the ECOSOC Res 1996/31 and the large participation of NGOs in UN convened conferences, the evidence suggests that the consultative status has been expanded to include other opportunities of interaction in matters falling within the scope of the ECOSOC, i.e, that NGOs could be heard *ratione materiae* in other situations.

In a subsequent report on the participation of NGOs in the UN activities prepared by the UN Secretary General in 1998, he affirmed that the involvement of NGOs in the global conferences 'reached unprecedented levels and led to an important breakthrough in the perception by UN officials and member-states alike of the role of NGOs', that are 'no longer seen only as disseminators of information, but as shapers of policy and indispensable bridges between the general public and the intergovernmental processes'.[92] This report was circulated for consideration of NGOs, UN bodies and member-states. Not surprisingly, it received different commentaries that reflect the perception of each of the parties on the placement that each type of entity must have on the international chessboard. The commentaries were consolidated in another UNSC report.[93] Although nearly all member-states that responded recognized the relevant contribution of NGOs to operations of the UN system, several of them stressed (para 16) that their participation in the decision-making process 'could give rise to significant distortions' and could 'undermine the principle of sovereign equality of States and equitable consideration of the interests of all the regions of the world'.[94] Some States also supported that the NGOs should limit their interaction *ratione personae* to the ECOSOC (para 15). The report does not provide information about the number of member-states that responded to it nor is it clear as to the characteristics of those States that are comprised within the 'several' and 'some' supporters of certain ideas and statements contained in the document. Hence, we cannot use the information of the report as evidence of State undertakings towards NGOs.

Nevertheless, it is acknowledgeable that the *accreditation of NGOs with consultative status in UN convened conferences has passed to the realm of international customary law*, because, recalling Meijers' 'stage of growth' model, there is extensive, constant and virtually uniform 'evidence of general practice' in their accreditation as participants to the events, and also 'evidence' that the 'general practice' is 'accepted as law', moreover after the adoption of ECOSOC Res 1996/31.[95]

In regard to the situation of NGOs in general, i.e., those without consultative relationship with the ECOSOC, the settled practice determines that they must be invited to participate, their accreditation remaining a prerogative of member-states, exercised through the respective preparatory committee. Such accreditation should be preceded by an appropriate process to determine their eligibility, according to the requirements set forth in ECOSOC Res 1996/31. In this aspect, generally, the resolution defined a procedure in which the interested NGO must apply to the secretariat of the conference providing information concerning its purpose and activities and its relevance for the conference agenda, as well as its interest in the goals and objectives of the meeting, together with documentary evidence such as statutes, annual reports, and membership and governing body directories. If the evidence satisfies the preliminary secretariat criteria for admission, the applications will be disseminated to member-states for comments, which shall be communicated to the NGO concerned for rebuttal, if deemed necessary. After that, the secretariat will decide upon their accreditation.[96]

The accreditation, however, cannot be regarded as identical to the one ensured to State representatives and intergovernmental organizations' officials. Attendance does not represent the admission of a negotiating role to NGOs, which also cannot vote because this right is ensured only to member-states, there being no dispute as to that. When accredited, they are entitled to attend the sessions of the preparatory committee as well as the conference itself, but this attendance does not mean that they can join all meetings held at the conference because some of them, according to UN tradition, have restricted participation. As a rule, all accredited participants have access to plenary meetings. There are, however, closed meetings, open to certain defined participants of the conference (regional groups, G-77, G-20, etc.) where the admission of NGOs to the venues depend on invitation of a participant and/or authorization from the chairperson of the session. Finally, there are other kind of meetings that definitively are not open to NGOs, such as the 'true' negotiation meetings between diplomats on sensitive issues, the actual Summit of Heads of State and those of the operational structures of the conference (credentials, main committee, etc).[97]

The interference in the conference's agenda, however, is rather unclear. NGOs have proven to be successful in setting the wider agenda even before the conference is convened (as in the case of Landmines and Biodiversity conventions), showing therefore a powerful influence. But, concerning the definition of the conference's agenda itself, they have to rely on lobbying the intergovernmental officials and diplomats and on the presentation of short oral briefs in accordance with established UN practice and at the discretion of the chairperson and the consent of the body concerned. The submission of written presentations is a right widely recognized but they shall not be issued as official documents except if in accordance with United Nations rules of procedure.

Albeit the differentiation between NGOs with consultative status and those without it in the rules for participation in UN convened conferences, it is noteworthy the perception, particularly by the UN officials, and some member-states alike, that the participation of NGOs in those multilateral meetings represents an opportunity in terms of transparency, democracy and efficacy of the decisions eventually taken, since the greater transparency results in stronger agreements between the governments that became accountable for their actions.[98] Probably, this is the reason for their regular admission as observers in the regular Conference of the Parties established by some environmental conventions.[99]

From a substantive perspective of the conferences, it is a truism that the influence of NGOs in the international sphere has gone far beyond that which the traditional 'social-environmental' binomial appears to evidence. For example, the New York Convention on the Recognition and Enforcement of Foreign Arbitral Awards[100] has its origins in a proposal presented to the ECOSOC by the International Chamber of Commerce, an NGO with consultative status before that Council, half a century ago.[101]

In the realm of humanitarian law, the influence is more than a century old, going back to the ICRC efforts to establish the 1864 Geneva Convention for the Amelioration of the Condition of the Wounded in Armies in the Field, to pass through the four 1949 Geneva Conventions and their 1977 Additional Protocols, to finally reach the more recent 1997 Ottawa Convention on the Prohibition of the Use, Stockpiling, Production and Transfer of Anti-Personnel Mines and on their Destruction.[102] In the latter case, the convention is the result of the work of an NGO coalition – the International Campaign to Ban Landmines – which started in 1992 with six NGOs but that managed to draw the attention of the media and raise public society awareness on the use of the most cowardly weapon ever invented, which continues to make victims years after the end of the hostilities.[103] The role of the NGOs was acknowledged in the Preamble to the Convention.[104] The campaign was awarded the Nobel Peace Prize in 1997 for its successful work.

From the international environmental law perspective, the multiplicity of participants in multilateral negotiations can be observed in particular, with an increase in the participation rate of NGOs, not only represented by access to the negotiation venues, but also by their increasing role 'as catalysts to initiate such negotiations and to assist in the implementation of the resulting agreements'.[105] The IUCN, for instance, played an essential role in the drafting of the CITES,[106] as well as of the Biodiversity Convention, which originated from a draft text prepared by the IUCN under request of the UNEP in 1989.[107] The unprecedented procedure in assigning the draft of a multilateral convention to an NGO was, however, severely criticized by some diplomats, who argued that the situation might represent the usurpation of the functions of governments and UN officials. Notwithstanding, the actual convention materially relies on the proposed draft.[108]

NGOs have been extremely successful in mobilizing public opinion and States toward the adoption of environmental and humanitarian questions, a situation evidenced by the international conventions mentioned above,[109] even though other authors suggest that they have had a minimum impact on the negotiations.[110] This may be particularly true if we appraise the negotiations themselves, since, as observed above, NGOs have no negotiation or voting rights, nor are admitted to the closed meetings where the relevant agreement is obtained, only being allowed to attend those plenary meetings, which are often filled with a sequence of speeches with poor practical results or, in the best of circumstances, for the public ratification of what had been agreed upon behind closed doors. However, it we take the entire negotiation procedure, starting with the sowing of the issue by the preparation of technical reports, creation of public awareness, mobilization of diplomats from 'heavy foot-printer' countries and/or senior UN officials to call the conference; passing through the conference itself and the adoption of the convention, to end with the pressure for its ratification, entering into force and effective monitoring, we could regard that they *do* have a relevant impact on the outcome.

In spite of their undisputable achievements, the influence of NGOs on the agenda for the adoption of new multilateral treaties relies on the political sphere, as pressure groups, and cannot be regarded as evidence of customary law. Nevertheless, NGOs have attained some participatory rights in conferences based on international customary law, which can be summarized as follows: (i) the guaranteed accreditation to UN convened conferences if the concerned NGOs have consultative status with the ECOSOC; (ii) the right of any accredited NGO to participate in all open meetings, either preparatory or at the conference itself; and (iii) the right to circulate written statements to the participants of the conference, which shall not be issued as official documents except if in accordance with United Nations rules of procedure.

4.3   NGOs' unchallenged rights under international customary law

A crucial aspect to consider regarding whether a given international customary practice has become an international customary rule of law is the appraisal of the existence of substantive objection by States. As Shaw noted, 'one can conclude by stating that for a custom to be accepted and recognized it must have the concurrence of the major powers in that particular field'.[111] However, one does not need to prove that the concerned rule has been recognized as a rule of customary law by a sufficient number of subjects in international law, because that 'would imply that the recognition as existing customary law is conditional to the formation of customary law'.[112] International custom, therefore, is created by the extensive and constant practice of States in a virtually uniform manner, and does not require a formal announcement of a State declaring that it is bound by it. We could say that it is created by the recurrent silent reproduction of the same pattern of behavior by a major number of specially affected States during a relevant period of time, capable of defining it as a settled practice.

However, States can oppose its creation, but for that purpose, they must evidence their disagreement to the custom in formation, by objecting to it, and must be relevant players in the field. Objections presented by isolated States are too fragile to be considered as capable of avoiding the establishment of a custom.[113] If we take the ICJ decisions on the subject into consideration, we can observe that the silence of nations in a given matter is particularly relevant to the formation of customary international law. In the *Anglo-Norwegian Fisheries* case, for example, the general toleration of the international community to the notorious new fisheries' rules established by Norway imposed those rules even against a 'heavy foot-printer' such as the United Kingdom - 'a coastal State on the North Sea, greatly interested in the fisheries in this area, as a maritime Power traditionally concerned with the law of the sea and concerned particularly to defend the freedom of the seas' - because the UK government remained silent during an extended period of time, therefore granting its tacit consent to the new rules.[114]

Therefore, objection in due time is essential, and must be made public, and on a continuous basis, against the acts which have led to the new rule of law. Under those circumstances, some authors support that the practice will evidence that the establishment of the new rule was made without the participation of the protesting State and, once it has become a rule of law, is not binding to that State.[115]

The problem with the practice of 'persistent objection' is whether the objection of a country that is not among the major relevant ones is capable of avoiding the establishment of a customary rule of law that will bind it in the future. As the ICJ pointed out in the *North Sea Continental Shelf* cases, 'State practice, including that of States whose interests are specially affected, should have been both extensive and virtually uniform'. Due to the use of the word 'extensive', the participation of all States is not necessary to establish a customary rule of law; 'extensive practice' cannot be taken as 'universal practice', rather as 'qualified practice'. Although the legal conception exists that all States are equal at the international level, some of them are more influential and, in certain situations, more representative than others. Hence, the appraisal of whose States' practice must be considered to evidence the existence of a given customary law and whose persistent objection will produce 'libratory rights' depends on the context, subject and territorial scope of the considered practice and States.

In the case of the role and rights of NGOs under customary international law, based on the facts appraised in this chapter, and, moreover, on the non-existence of evidence of objection in due time from a substantive number of States, we can conclude that:

(i) The consultative rights ensured to NGOs, firstly by the UN Charter, and, subsequently, by the statutes of several other multilateral organizations, represent the expression of an *opinio juris* that has migrated from the realm of treaty law to international customary law. These consultative rights comprehend:

    a.   the right to engage in consultative arrangements with UN specialized agencies, funds and programmes within the field of competence of the concerned NGO;

    b.   the right to be accredited in any UN convened conference, if the concerned NGO has previously obtained its consultative status with the ECOSOC, in general, or with the UN body convening the conference, in particular;

    c.   once accredited, the right to submit written statements and reports to the participants of the conference and the right of access to the venues of all open meetings of the preparatory works and during the conference itself;

(ii) The participatory rights ensured to NGOs at the European level have evolved from the previous consultative rights and also represent the expression of an *opinio juris* that has migrated from the realm of treaty law to international customary law at the regional level. These participatory rights are summarized in Council of Europe Committee of Minister Res 2003(8);

(iii)   There are solid evidences that NGOs possess international legal personality because they bear duties and rights under multilateral treaties;

(iv)   There is no worldwide settled practice capable of forming an international customary rule of law regarding the NGOs' right to orally address the participants of UN convened conferences or to perform negotiating roles;

(v)   There is no worldwide settled practice capable of forming an international customary rule of law regarding the NGOs' right to submit *amicus curiae* briefs to judicial and quasi-judicial bodies.

Notes

1   See, D Carreau, *Droit International* (7th edn Pedone, Paris 2001) 262; R Unger, *Law in Modern Society* (Free Press, London 1976) 49; H Meijers, 'On International Customary Law in the Netherlands, in IF Dekker and HHG Post (eds), *On The Foundations and Sources of International Law* (TMC Asser Press, The Hague 2003) 79; J Kammerhofer, 'Uncertainty in the Formal Sources of International Law: customary International Law and Some of Its Problems' (2004) EJIL v 15 n 3, 523.

2   GFS Soares, *Curso de Direito Internacional Público* (1st edn Atlas, São Paulo 2002) 81.

3   D Carreau, *Droit International* (n 1) 265; PM Dupuy, *Droit International Publique* (6th edn, Paris, Dalloz) 320; MN Shaw, *International Law* (5th edn CUP, Cambridge 2003) 67. See, also, *Colombian-Peruvian Asylum case*. Judge Azevedo's dissenting opinion [1950] ICJ Rep 332: 'It should be remembered, on the other hand, that the decision in a particular case has deep repercussions, particularly in international law, because views which have been confirmed by that decision acquire quasi-legislative value, in spite of the legal principle to the effect that the decision has no binding force except between the parties and in respect of that particular case (Statute, Art. 59).'

4   D Carreau, *Droit International* (n 1) 266; PM Dupuy, *Droit International Publique* (n 3) 317.

5   *Lotus (France v Turkey)* PCIJ Rep. Series A 10, 28.

6   The voluntarist approach was at the base of the developing countries' attempt to establish a new economic order in the 1970s, since they had not participated in the world design. However, the view of the majority is that new states are bound by existing custom at the time of their existence. See, in this regard, American Law Institute, (Third) Restatement of the Law: the Foreign Relations Law of the US (1987) Sec. 102, comment d; GFS Soares, *Curso de Direito Internacional Público* (n 2) 81.

7   (Adopted 23 May 1969, entered into force 27 January 1980) UNTS 1155.

8   D Carreau, *Droit International* (n 1) 198, 264.

9   D Carreau, *Droit International* (n 1) 265; GFS Soares, *Curso de Direito Internacional Público* (n 2) 85. See, in this regard, the preamble of the Vienna Convention on Consular Relations (adopted 24 April 1963, entered into force 19 March 1967) UNTS 596 p 261, which affirmed that the rules of customary international law continue to govern matters not expressly regulated by provisions of the convention.

10 MN Shaw, *International Law* (n 3) 69.

11 See, for example, D Carreau, *Droit International* (n 1) 269-270; MN Shaw, *International Law* (n 3) 70, 76; PM Dupuy, *Droit International Publique* (n 3) 317; H Meijers, *On International Customary Law in the Netherlands*, (n 1) 82.

12 *North Sea Continental Shelf* cases (Judgment) [1969] ICJ Rep 3 para 74 (*emphasis added*). Another example of 'quasi-instantaneous' international custom is the creation of the concept of exclusive economic zones in the law of the sea, proposed in 1972 and almost immediately incorporated in the municipal law of almost all countries with access to the sea.

13 MN Shaw, *International Law* (n 3) 71; D Carreau, *Droit International* (n 1) 271-278; GFS Soares, *Curso de Direito Internacional Público* (n 2) 82. H Kelsen, *Principles of International Law* (Lawbook Exchange, Clark, 2003) 307

14 Examples of usage in the international sphere include humanitarian support in catastrophes and the presence of national representatives at heads of state's marriages and funerals. See, *North Sea Continental Shelf* cases (Judgment) [1969] ICJ Rep 3 para 77.

15 *Colombian-Peruvian asylum* case (Judgment) [1950] ICJ Rep 266; *Case concerning rights of nationals of the United States of America in Morocco* (Judgment) [1952] ICJ Rep 176.

16 *Right of Passage over Indian Territory (Portugal v India)* (Judgment) [1960] ICJ Rep 3.

17 A D'Amato, *The Concept of Custom in International Law* (Cornell, New York 1971) 53.

18 H Meijers, *On International Customary Law in the Netherlands*, (n 1) 80.

19 *Colombian-Peruvian asylum* case (Judgment) [1950] ICJ Rep 266

20 For the purpose of our survey in this chapter, we have decided to divide the international organizations into two categories, being 'worldwide' those which accept members from all continents, and 'regional' those that restrict their membership to states of a given territorial area.

21 *Military and Paramilitary Activities in and Against Nicaragua (Nicaragua v United States)* (Judgment) [1986] ICJ Rep 14 para 186

22 H Meijers, *On International Customary Law* (n 1) 85. These situations support the criticism to the artificial division proposed by the theory. See, in this aspect, PM Dupuy, *Droit International Publique* (n 3) 322.

23 *Military and Paramilitary Activities in and Against Nicaragua (Nicaragua v United States)* (Judgment) [1986] ICJ Rep 14 para 181

24 M Akerhurst, *Custom as a Source of International Law* (1974/75) BYIL 3; D Carreau, *Droit International* (n 1) 272; H Meijers, *On International Customary Law* (n 1) 83-84. In 1950, the International Law Commission listed the following sources as forms of evidence of customary international law: treaties, decisions of national and international courts, national legislation, opinions of national legal advisors, diplomatic correspondence, and practice of international organizations. UN Doc. A/CN.4/Ser.A/1950/Add.1. See, also *North Sea Continental Shelf* cases (Judgment) [1969] ICJ Rep 3 para 77.

25 Worthy of note, in this regard, is the understanding of the ICJ on the *Fisheries* case (Judgment) [1951] ICJ Rep 1951 paras 138-139: 'The United Kingdom Government has argued that the Norwegian system of delimitation was not known to it and that the basis of a historic title enforceable against it. The Court is unable to accept this view. *As a coastal State on the North Sea, greatly interested in the fisheries in this area, as a maritime Power traditionally concerned with the law of the sea and concerned particularly to defend the freedom of the seas, the United Kingdom could not have been ignorant* of the Decree of 1869 which had at once provoked a request for explanations by the French Government. *The Court notes that in respect of a situation which could only be strengthened with the passage of time, the United Kingdom Government refrained from*

formulating reservations. The notoriety of the facts, the general toleration of the international community, Great Britain's position in the North Sea, her own interest in the question, and her prolonged abstention would in any case warrant Norway's enforcement of her system against the United Kingdom' (emphasis added).

26 A D'Amato, *The Concept of Custom in International Law* (n 17) 88.

27 The US Department of State, for instance, does not accept resolutions of international bodies as evidence of state practice.

28 G Tunkin, 'Is General International Law Customary Law Only?' (1993) EJIL n 4, 541; B Fassbender, 'The Better Peoples of the United Nations? Europe's Practice and the United Nations' (2004) EJIL v 15 n 5, 879.

29 HG Schermers and NM Blokker, *International Institutional Law* (4th edn Martinus Nijhoff, The Hague 2003) § 63.

30 HG Schermers and NM Blokker, *International Institutional Law* (n 29) § 188 *(emphasis added).*

31 In the *Nicaragua v. United States* case, the ICJ adopted a liberal understanding on the evidence of behavior of states, affirming that 'the provisions of the Statute and Rules of Court concerning the presentation of pleadings and evidence are designed to secure a proper administration of justice, and a fair and equal opportunity for each party to comment on its opponent's contentions. *The treatment to be given by the Court to communications or material emanating from the absent party must be determined by the weight to be given to these different considerations, and is not susceptible of rigid definition in the form of a precise general rule.' (emphasis added). Military and Paramilitary Activities in and Against Nicaragua (Nicaragua v United States)* (Judgment) [1986] ICJ Rep 14 para 30

32 That is the case, for instance, of the Brazilian Constitution, which defined that several public policies should be defined, implemented and monitored by councils with the participation of NGOs. See, in this regard, SLM Alves, 'O papel constitucional da sociedade civil na definição de políticas públicas', in E Szazi (ed), *Terceiro Setor Temas Polêmicos v 2* (Peiropolis, Sao Paulo 2005) 217.

33 This does not mean, however, that the relationship has been smooth. Rather, it has often been tense, with NGOs struggling to acquire more power, while States struggle to resist NGOs efforts. See P Alston (eds) *The UN and Human Rights* (Clarendon Press, Oxford, 1992) 202.

34 A similar procedure was adopted by NGOs in the *Legality on the Threat or Use of Nuclear Weapons* (Advisory Opinion) [1996] ICJ Rep 226.

35 ICJ Statute, article 66(2).

36 ICJ Practice Direction XII: '1. Where an international non governmental organization submits a written statement and/or document in an advisory opinion case on its own initiative, such statement and/or document is not to be considered as part of the case file. 2. Such statements and/or documents shall be treated as publications readily available and may accordingly be referred to by States and intergovernmental organizations presenting written and oral statements in the case in the same manner as publications in the public domain. 3. Written statements and/or documents submitted by international non governmental organizations will be placed in a designated location in the Peace Palace. All States as well as intergovernmental organizations presenting written or oral statements under Article 66 of the Statute will be informed as to the location where statements and/or documents submitted by international non governmental organizations may be consulted.' < www.icj-cij.org/basicdocuments> accessed 20 April 2009.

37 *Military and Paramilitary Activities in and Against Nicaragua (Nicaragua v United States)* (Judgment) [1986] ICJ Rep 14 para 30.

38 Certain NGOs tried to submit briefs in the *Asylum* case and in the *Advisory Opinion on the International Status of South-West Africa* and the *Advisory Opinion on Namibia* but were not successful. See, in this particular aspect, AK Lindblom, *Non-Governmental Organizations in International Law* (CUP, Cambridge, 2005) 303-306.

39 *Understanding on Rules and Procedures Governing the Settlement of Disputes, Agreement Establishing the World Trade Organization, Annex 2,* 1869 (adopted 15 April 1994, entered into force 1 January 1995) UNTS 1869.

40 *Working Procedures for Appellate Review.* (4 January 2005) WTO Doc WT/AB/WP/5.

41 Communication from the Appellate Body (8 November 2000) WTO Doc WT/DS/135/9.

42 *European Communities – Measures Affecting Asbestos and Asbestos – Containing Products.* WT/DS135/R (18 September 2000).

43 WTO General Council, *Minutes of Meeting* (23 January 2001) WTO Doc WT/GC/M/60.

44 *North Sea Continental Shelf* cases (Judgment) [1969] ICJ Rep 3 para 71. See, also, GFS Soares, *Curso de Direito Internacional Público* (n 2) 84.

45 H Meijers, *On International Customary Law* (n 1) 84. This is the same position taken up by the US Department of State. See AW Rovine (ed), *Digest of United States Practice in International Law* (1974); H Hillgenberg, 'A Fresh Look at Soft Law' (1999) EJIL v 10 n 3, 515; B Fassbender, *The Better Peoples* (n 28) 865.

46 HG Schermers and NM Blokker, *International Institutional Law* (n 29) § 209.

47 *Military and Paramilitary Activities in and Against Nicaragua (Nicaragua v United States)* (Judgment) [1986] ICJ Rep 14 para 180.

48 *North Sea Continental Shelf* cases (Judgment) [1969] ICJ Rep 3 para 71. See, also, GFS Soares, *Curso de Direito Internacional Público* (n 419) 84.

49 *Continental Shelf (Libyan Arab Jarnahiriyu/ Malta)* (Judgment) [1985] ICJ Rep 29-30 para 27 *(emphasis added).*

50 *Military and Paramilitary Activities in and Against Nicaragua (Nicaragua v United States)* (Judgment) [1986] ICJ Rep 14 para 184.

51 *Legality on the Threat or Use of Nuclear Weapons* (Advisory Opinion) [1996] ICJ Rep 226 paras 71-73.

52 *Legality on the Threat or Use of Nuclear Weapons* (Advisory Opinion) (Judge Schwebel dissenting opinion) [1996] ICJ Rep 309.

53 *Nuclear Tests (New Zealand v France)* (Judgment) [1974] ICJ Rep 457 para 46; and *Nuclear Tests (Australia v France),* (Judgment) [1974] ICJ Rep 253 para 43 *(emphasis added).*

54 *Nuclear Tests (New Zealand v France)* (Judgment) [1974] ICJ Rep 457 para 48.

55 *Nuclear Tests (New Zealand v France)* (Judgment) [1974] ICJ Rep 457 para 49.

56 D Carreau, *Droit International* (n 1) 575; PM Dupuy, *Droit International Publique* (n 3) 325; MN Shaw, *International Law* (n 3) 78.

57 MD Oberg, 'The legal effects of Resolutions of the UN Security Council and General Assembly in the Jurisprudence of the ICJ' (2005) EJIL v 16, no 5, 880.

58 PE Corbett (tr) C de Visscher, *Theory and Reality in Public International Law* (2nd edn, PUP Princeton 1957) 147.

59 MN Shaw, *International Law* (n 3) 75.

60 On the sufficiency of a majority, see D Carreau, *Droit International* (n 18) 269; H Meijers, '*On International Customary Law in the Netherlands,* (n 1) 86; HHG Post, 'The role of State Practice in the Formation of Customary International Humanitarian Law' in IF Dekker and HHG Post (eds), *On The Foundations and Sources of International Law* (TMC Asser Press, The Hague 2003) 142.

61 H Hillgenberg, *A Fresh Look at Soft Law* (n 45) 514.

62 C de Visscher, *Theory and Reality in Public International Law* (n 58) 147.

63 UNGA 'Report of the Secretary General on General Review of Arrangements for Consultations with non-governmental organizations' (26 May 1994) UN Doc E/AC.70/1994/5. para 13.

64 UN ECOSOC NGO Committee, *The NGO Committee: a ten year review* (New York 2008) 5.

65 UNGA 'Report of the Secretary General on General Review of Arrangements for Consultations with non-governmental organizations' (26 May 1994) UN Doc E/AC.70/1994/5. paras 42-43.

66 *Constitution of the International Labor Organization* (adopted 19 November 1946, entered into force 14 December 1946) UNTS 1.

67 *The Geneva Convention relative to the Treatment of Prisoners of War* (adopted 12 August 1949, entered into force 21 October 1950) UNTS 75.

68 *Convention on Wetlands of International Importance especially as Waterfowl Habitat* (adopted 2 February 1971, entered into force 21 December 1975) UNTS 14583. Further amended by the Paris Protocol, 3 December 1982, and Regina Amendments, 28 May 1987.

69 CoE Res (2003)8 (19 November 2003).

70 CoE Res. (51) 30F (3 May 1951) para 4.

71 *European Convention on the Recognition of the Legal Personality of International Non-Governmental Organizations* (adopted 24 April 1986, entered into force 1 January 1991) ETS 124.

72 The participatory rights were granted by Resolution Res(2003)8 (19 November 2003) of the Committee of Ministers of the Council of Europe. The role of NGOs in the Council of Europe member-states was extensively addressed in the document *Fundamental Principles on the Status of Non-Governmental Organizations in Europe and explanatory memorandum.* CoE Doc RAP-ONG(2003)4 (24 March 2003).

73 P Sands and P Klein, *Bowett's Law of International Institutions* (Thompson, London, 2001) 61.

74 HG Schermers and NM Blokker, *International Institutional Law* (n 29) § 32.

75 ILO Constitution, article 3(5).

76 In this particular case, it is worth quoting that the Ramsar Convention did not create a new intergovernmental organization, but rather a treaty organ. See, e.g. HG Schermers and NM Blokker, *International Institutional Law* (n 29) § 386-387.

77 HG Schermers and NM Blokker, *International Institutional Law* (n 29) § 47. See, also, J Pictet, *Une institution unique en son genre : Le Comite International de la Croix-Rouge* (Pedone, Paris 1985) 99.

78 According to IUCN statutes (articles 1 and 4). See <www.iucn.org/about/> accessed 4 May 2009.

79 ICRC, UNGA Res. 45/6 (16 October 1990); IUCN, UNGA Res 54/195 (17 December 1999).

80 HG Schermers and NM Blokker, *International Institutional Law* (n 29) § 1566.

81 LN Sadat, 'Judgment at Nuremberg: Foreword to the Symposium', WUGSLR (2007) v 6, 491.

82 *Reparation for Injuries Suffered in the Service of the United Nations* (Advisory Opinion) [1949] ICJ Rep 178.

83 The ICRC signed a Headquarter Agreement with Switzerland on 19 March 1993, which recognized the international juridical personality of the ICRC and ensured inviolability of premises and archives, immunity from Swiss taxation, legal process and execution and secure communication privileges at the same level as foreign embassies, among other matters. The full text of the agreement is available at <http://icrc.org/Web/eng/siteengo.nsf/html/57JNX7> accessed 4 May 2009.

84 HG Schermers and NM Blokker, *International Institutional Law* (n 29) § 1570.

85 UNGA Report of the Secretary General on 'General Review of Arrangements for Consultations with non-governmental organizations' (26 May 1994) UN Doc E/AC.70/1994/5 para 1003.

86 ECOSOC Res. 1996/31 (25 July 1996) para 42.

87 G Breton-Le Goff, *L'Influence des Organisations non Gouvernamentales (ONG) sur la negotiation de quelques instruments internationaux* (Bruylant, Brussels 2001) 59.

88 See, e.g.. S Ahmed and D Potter, *NGOs in international politics* (Kumarian Press, Bloomfield 2006) 79. Alston points out that there has always been a major disparity between the *de facto* rule permitted to NGOs and the *de facto* role played. P Alston (eds) *The UN and Human Rights* (Clarendon Press, Oxford, 1992) 202.

89 *Certain expenses of the United Nations (article 17, paragraph 2, of the Charter)* (Advisory Opinion) [1962] ICJ Rep 151.

90 In that specific case, the term 'action' in the last sentence of article 11(2), which addressing the issue of maintenance of international peace, worded that 'Any such question on which action is necessary shall be referred to the Security Council by the General Assembly either before or after discussion'.

91 D Carreau, *Droit International* (n 1) 284. The dispute on the interpretation of terms in treaties is neither new nor does it seem that it will be solved in the future. In this aspect, see the case of the interpretation of the word 'seek' on the duties of the panels in WTO dispute settlement procedures, addressed in Chapter 3.

92 UNGA Report of the Secretary General on 'Arrangements and practices for the interaction of non-governmental organizations in all activities of the United Nations system' (10 July 1998) UN Doc A/53/170 paras 57-59.

93 UNGA Report of the Secretary General on 'Views of Member States, members of the specialized agencies, observers, intergovernmental and non-governmental organizations from all regions, on the report of the Secretary General on Arrangements and practices for the interaction of non-governmental organizations in all activities of the United Nations system' (8 September 1999) UN Doc A/54/329 para 16.

94 Needless to say, the 'heavy footprint' theory also acts against such equality and equitable consideration of interests, as observed, for instance, in the *Threat of Nuclear Weapons* case.

95 This assertion is not, however, undisputed. Dailler and Pellet, for instance, support that it is premature to view NGO participation at international conferences as a true legal obligation for the organizers of these diplomatic meetings. P Daillier and A Pellet, *Droit international public* (7th ed LGDJ, Paris 2002) 653.

96 ECOSOC Res. 1996/31 (25 July 1996) paras 41-54.

97 We witnessed this practice during the 2002 Johannesburg World Summit on Sustainable Development, as a participant of the Brazilian contingent to the conference. See, also, G Breton-Le Goff, *L'Influence des Organisations non Gouvernamentales* (n 87) 104.

98 PS Chasek, *Earth Negotiations: Analyzing thirty years of Environmental Diplomacy* (UN University Press, Tokyo 2001) 231; G Breton-Le Goff, *L'Influence des Organisations non Gouvernamentales* (n 87) 59; A Alkoby, 'Non-State Actors and the legitimacy of international environmental law' (2003) Non-State Actors and International Law v 3 n 1, 23.

99 JM Lavieille, *Droit International de l'Environment,* (Ellipses, Paris 1998) 83.

100 (adopted 10 June 1958, entered into force 7 June 1959) UNTS 330.

101 GFS Soares, *Curso de Direito Internacional Público* (n 2) 88.

102 (adopted 3 December 1997, entered into force 1 March 1999) UNTS 2056.

103 For an appraisal of the campaign, see, e.g. S Ahmed and D Potter, *NGOs in international politics* (Kumarian Press, Bloomfield 2006) 153; and K Anderson, 'The Ottawa

Convention banning Landmines, the role of International Non-Governmental Organizations and the Idea of International Civil Society' (2000) EJIL, v 11, n 1, 91.

104 The 8th paragraph is worded as following: 'Stressing the role of public conscience in furthering the principles of humanity as evidenced by the call for a total ban of anti-personnel mines and recognizing the efforts to that end undertaken by the International Red Cross and Red Crescent Movement, the International Campaign to Ban Landmines and numerous other non-governmental organizations around the world.'

105 PS Chasek, *Earth Negotiations* (n 98) 28.

106 *Convention on International Trade in Endangered Species of Wild Fauna and Flora* (Adopted 3 March 1973, entered into force 1 July 1975) UNTS 993. Further amended at Bonn, on 22 June 1979.

107 A Kiss and JP Beurir, *Droit International de l'Environment,* (2nd edn Pedone, Paris 2000) 91.

108 G Breton-Le Goff, *L'Influence des Organisations non Gouvernamentales* (n 87) 34.

109 G Breton-Le Goff, *L'Influence des Organisations non Gouvernamentales* (n 87) 124 ; MM Betsil and E Corell (eds) *NGO Diplomacy : The influence of NGOs in International Environmental Negotiations* (MIT Press, Cambridge, 2008) 186.

110 PS Chasek, *Earth Negotiations* (n 98) 231.

111 MN Shaw, *International Law* (n 3) 76. See, also, D Carreau, *Droit International* (n 1) 269.

112 H Meijers, *On International Customary Law in the Netherlands* (n 1) 79.

113 PM Dupuy, *Droit International Publique* (n 3) 323.

114 *Fisheries* case (Judgment) [1951] ICJ Rep 1951 paras 138-139

115 H Meijers, *On International Customary Law in the Netherlands* (n 1) 88.

CHAPTER 5

NGOs in General Principles of Law

5.1 A civilized world built on the seeds of Natural Law

Article 38(1)(c) of the Statutes of the ICJ established that the Court will adopt 'the general principles of law recognized by civilized nations' as a source of law. The purpose of this provision is to close the gap that may exist in those situations where the non-existence of treaty provisions or international customary law on a subject is identified, therefore authorizing the Court to reach its decision supported on the general principles that guide the legal systems, hindering the Court's capability to create Law *ex nihilo* and also avoiding, at least in theory, the possibility of a *non liquet*.[1]

In 1919, when the Advisory Committee of Jurists of the League of Nations[2] was drafting the statute of the PCIJ, a dispute arose between the positivists and the jusnaturalists, the latter represented by Baron Descamps, himself an active supporter of the 'civilizing' efforts of the European nations, particularly in Africa,[3] which proposed that the Court had to decide based upon the '*conscience juridique des peuples civilisés*'. The final result is the product of a compromise between both schools. The text of Article 38(1)(c) is an exact word-for-word reproduction of the one observed in the Statute of the PCIJ. For that reason, a trace of the Eurocentric spirit of those times can still be noticed, as expressed in the reference to 'civilized nations', which indirectly assumes that uncivilized nations exist(ed).[4]

Such a kind of Eurocentric understanding was not particularly new, since it can be observed, for example, in the 1856 Treaty of Paris, which admitted Turkey '*aux avantages du droit public et du concert européens*'.[5] If the expression might be regarded as contemporary at a time when European nations were struggling to dominate Africa, the Middle East and most of Asia under colonial regimen, it was definitively unacceptable in 1945, when the Statute of the ICJ was approved. This aspect was addressed by Judge Ammoun in his Separate Opinion on the *North Sea Continental Shelf* case, when he supported that the Court could omit the adjective 'civilized', because:

'The discrimination between civilized nations and uncivilized nations, which was unknown to the founding fathers of international law, the protagonists of a universal law of nations, Vitoria, Suarez,

Gentilis, Pufendorf, Vattel, is the legacy of the period, now passed
away, of colonialism, and of the time long-past when a limited number of Power established the rules, of custom or of treaty-law, of a
European law applied in relation to the whole community of
nations.'[6]

Despite any debate on the appropriateness of the reproduction of such adjective in a new treaty provision, there has been a noticeable shift from the
end of World War I to the end of World War II with respect to the content
of the expression 'civilized nations'.

   If it was Eurocentric in the 1920s, less than three decades later, when
the UN Charter was adopted, the idea was abandoned by the founding nations, which reaffirmed their faith in 'fundamental human rights' and in
'equal rights of men and women and of nations large and small' to establish, among the purposes of the newborn organization, the 'development of
friendly relations among nations based on respect of the principle of equal
rights and self-determination of peoples'. It certainly delivered a deadly
blow to colonialism and to any differentiation between nations on grounds
of 'civility'. Therefore, for the purpose of the interpretation of the Statute
of the ICJ, the adjective became senseless, seeing as all nations had (and
have) to be regarded civilized, an assumption that we strongly support.

   Additionally, for the sake of our appraisal, we will assume that the reference to 'nations' must be understood as 'States', since they are the traditional subjects of international law. As we have mentioned elsewhere, in
the beginning of the 20th century there were few independent States and a
large part of the world's territory and population were under the colonial
domination of a couple of European nations, which imposed upon them
their legal system and 'superior' condition.[7] Finally, we also assume that
the mainstream doctrine understands that the General Principles of Law
have their roots laid down in Natural Law.[8]

   If the general principles of law constitute a concrete manifestation of the
idea of Natural Law in contemporary international law – a fact acknowledged by Judge Ammoun's reference to Vitoria, Suarez, Gentilis,
Pufendorf and Vattel - then, it is arguably possible to establish an evolutionary chain of international law, starting with Natural Law, passing
through the General Principles of Law, reaching International Custom, and
finally, ending in Treaty Law. This chain is, for instance, identifiable, in
both the cases of prohibition of individual submission of one person to another (slavery) and the collective submission of one people to another (colonialism), now regulated in treaty law.

   Given that Natural Law is the base of the juridical conscience of humankind, it is the seed of the evolutionary process of the general principles of
law that will further constitute the basis of *jus cogens,* whose commands
cannot be derogated by the States, as declared in article 43 of the Vienna

Convention on the Law of Treaties.[9] One cannot assume that the general principles of law are static, for they experience a slow but steady development. Of course, the more complex the legal system, the less they appear, though this discretion does not mean that they do not have 'great normative potential and dynamic force'.[10] Not without reason, the ICJ has never released a decision exclusively supported in those principles, even though they have been mentioned *en passant* in some decisions and can be perceived, hidden in the rationale, in several other cases. What appears to be beyond any doubt is that they are necessarily the offspring of Natural Law, the first step in the transformation of those abstract notions into more objective rules of law. In the continuous sophistication of the legal system, they will be, themselves, the source of customary and even written rules of law, validating the mentioned evolutionary chain.[11]

Daillier and Pellet affirmed that, even though they are transitory and recessive sources of traditional international law because their repetitive application transforms them into customary rules of law, general principles of law are expanding in new dominions.[12] The shift in the very concept of 'civilized' and the recognition of the principle of self-determination of peoples portray the latter perspective. Hence, even considering that Natural Law is an old tree, dating back, at least, to the early Greeks, it is still capable of sowing seeds, as we will evidence hereinafter.

5.2   Offspring in Municipal Legal Systems

Since the establishment of the PCIJ, there has been some doctrinaire debate on the correct sense of the expression 'general principles of law', which, according to Carreau, has led to five distinct theories, according to which they could be regarded as: (i) general international law; (ii) a fundamental norm of international law; (iii) a general norm; (iv) political-juridical principles; and, finally, as (v) principles common to the major contemporary legal systems applicable to the international order.[13]

Given the apparent existence of a converging understanding that the general principles of law are evidenced in municipal legal concepts of the major contemporary legal systems,[14] we will assume so for the appraisal of the impact that they have on civil society at large, and NGOs in particular, and to what extent they are capable of being transposed to international law. This assumption, however, imposes a practical problem: bearing in mind the existence of 193 States that are members of the UN, how could one identify them?

The Statute of the ICJ provides the answer, when it states in Article 9 that at every election, the electors (the UNGA and UNSC) shall bear in mind not only that the persons to be elected should individually possess the qualifications required in their respective countries for appointment to the highest judicial offices, or are jurisconsults of recognized competence in international law, but also that *in the body as a whole the representation of the main forms of civilization and of the principal legal systems of the world should be assured*. This principle has found its expression in the practice of dividing the seats at the Court among the several regions of the globe.[15]

Given the geographical mix in the composition of the Court and considering that the elected individuals are qualified to occupy the highest judicial offices in their own countries or are recognized jurisconsults in international law, one could argue that all major contemporary legal systems are represented in the Court, which is also composed of individuals who have profound knowledge of their own legal systems and their general principles. Hence, the Court is capable of delivering in its judgments and advisory opinions, an understanding supported on the general principles of law recognized by the civilized nations if its members collectively agree on the matter.[16] For that reason, it seems appropriate to appraise the Court decisions on the matter.

5.3   Blooming in ICJ decisions

The ICJ has never justified its ruling upon the application of article 38(1) (c) of its Statute, because it has always found sufficient support in customary or written international law. It has also neither addressed an issue directly involving international NGOs, nor appraised a case concerning the rights of civil society at large in any of its judgments or advisory opinions. But in some cases brought before it, it has appreciated specific situations where it has recognized that some rights had their roots in general principles of law. These cases will drive our analysis on the extent of individuals and NGOs' rights in international law. For such a purpose, we will add some decisions of the PCIJ, whose statutes were materially the same.

In the *Minority Schools* case,[17] the PCIJ appraised the question as to whether a person belonged or not to a racial, linguistic or religious minority under the Treaty with regard to the Protection of Minorities adopted on 28 June 1919. In the case, Germany supported that it was a matter of 'subjective expression of the intention of the persons concerned' and that such an intention had to be respected by the authorities even where it appeared to be contrary to the actual state of facts. Poland, on the contrary, supported that it was a 'question of fact and not one of intention' and that any person that declared to belong to a minority contrary to the facts was committing an abuse which could not be tolerated. During the judgment, the Court understood that there were a multitude of cases in which the question of whether a person belonged to a minority did not appear clearly from the facts, notably in those circumstances, with regards to the language, of people who spoke the two languages or none of them in a 'correct literary' manner and, with regards to the race, of people born from mixed marriages. In those situations, it would be possible that people who did not belong to the minority could be treated as though they belonged thereto, but it would be better to over-extend the minority rights than limit them. Hence, the Court's final decision understood that concerning the rules applicable to Upper Silesia, 'every national had the right freely to declare according to his conscience and on his personal responsibility that he did or did not belong to a racial, linguistic or religious minority' and to declare what was the language of a pupil or child for whose education he was legally responsible, even though such declarations could comprise, when necessary, the exercise of some discretion in the appreciation of the circumstances by the authorities, and did not constitute an unrestricted right to choose the language in which instruction had to be imparted or the corresponding school.

The PCIJ decision addressed a key element of pluralist democracy, i.e., the respect to the rights of minorities and the illegality of the imposition of bureaucratic restraints on the exercise of such rights. Even though not clearly mentioning a specific general principle of law on the matter, because the question was regulated by a treaty provision, it undoubtedly went through the entire line of thought and, moreover, imposed to the States the duty to assume the good faith of the individuals while applying for the exercise of the ensured rights.

The germane question of non-discrimination and non-separation based on race was later addressed by the ICJ in the *South West Africa* case, where it was understood that the condition of 'general principles' could be ascertained as fulfilled by the 'presence of laws against racial discrimination and segregation in the municipal systems of virtually every State'.[18]

In another judgment, in the *Corfu Channel* case,[19] the ICJ ruled that Albania was obliged to notify, for the benefit of shipping in general, the existence of a minefield in its territorial waters, warning the approaching ships of the imminent danger to which the minefield exposed them, on grounds that such obligations were based on well-recognized principles, such as 'elementary considerations of humanity'. Again, even though not clearly mentioning that the obligation was laid down in general principles of law, the decision affirmed the existence of certain rules applying to the common life of men in society arisen out of Natural Law, subsumed on the 'elementary' considerations of humanity, which, however, the Court did not detail.

In the *Reservation to the Convention on Genocide* advisory opinion,[20] the ICJ addressed the legal implications of certain States' reservations to the Convention on the Prevention and Punishment of the Crime of Genocide,[21] which had been objected to by some other States. The Court concluded that the convention had special origins and a unique character.

In regard to its origins, the Court acknowledged that 'it was the intention of the United Nations to condemn and punish genocide as "a crime under international law" involving a denial of the right of existence of entire human groups, a denial which shocks the conscience of mankind and results in great losses to humanity, and which is contrary to moral law and to the spirit and aims of the United Nations.' In regard to its character, the Court asserted that the *principles underlying the Convention are principles which are recognized by civilized nations as binding on States, even without any conventional obligation*, therefore recognizing their *jus cogens* nature.

Unfortunately, in a subsequent case, *South West Africa*,[22] the ICJ backed away from its understanding in the *Corfu Channel* and in the *Reservation to the Convention on Genocide* cases to regrettably affirm that humanitarian considerations were not sufficient in themselves to generate legal or right obligations if they were not sufficiently expressed in legal form. Notwithstanding, the interpretation of the concept laid down in Article 38 (1)(c) of the Statute of the ICJ was extensively addressed in Judge Tanaka's remarkable dissenting opinion.[23]

At the very beginning of his analysis, he supported that as long as the general principles of law are not qualified, the 'law' had to be understood 'to embrace all branches of law, including municipal law, public law, constitutional and administrative law, private law, commercial law, substantive and procedural law, etc.', even though it did not imply in their mechanical transference to international law. Rather, the interpreter had to search for the 'fundamental concepts of each branch of law as well as to law in general' in order to reach the understanding that they are recognized by civilized nations as the 'juridical truth'.[24]

With regards to human rights law, he remarkably ascertained that what was involved was not the 'application by analogy of a principle or a norm of private law to a matter of international character, but the recognition of the juridical validity of a similar legal fact without any distinction as between the municipal and the international legal sphere,' because human rights are based on Natural Law, the 'only and the same law that exists and is valid through all kinds of human societies' either in domestic or international spheres.

Judge Tanaka also affirmed that the 'principle of protection of human rights is derived from their concept of man as a *person* and his relationship with society which cannot be separated from universal human nature', to further conclude that their existence does not depend on the will of the State, because States 'are not capable of creating human rights by law or by convention; they can only confirm their existence and give them protection', adding that they have always existed together with the human being, 'independently of, and before, the State'. The recognition of the inalienable and inviolate character of certain rights 'deeply rooted in the conscience of mankind and of any reasonable man,' that exist independently of the will of the State and, accordingly, cannot be abolished or modified even by their constitutions, will be resumed in item 4.4 below.

In the *Nicaragua v. United States* case,[25] the ICJ addressed the content of a UN General Assembly resolution entitled 'Declaration on Principles of International Law concerning Friendly Relations and Co-operations among States in accordance to the Charter of the United Nations'.[26] It understood that the consent to the text of such a resolution had to be considered as the acceptance of the validity of the rule or set of rules declared by the resolution by the parties. Moreover, it considered that there was 'an obligation on the United States Government, in the terms of Article 1 of the Geneva Conventions, to "respect" the Conventions and even "to ensure respect" for them "in all circumstances", since such an obligation does not derive only from the Conventions themselves, but from the general principles of humanitarian law to which the Conventions merely give specific expression.' Similarly to the *Corfu Channel* and the *Reservation to the Convention on Genocide* cases , the Court understood that certain general principles of law, chiefly principles of humanitarian law, had to be respected even if they were not protected by treaty provisions, therefore acknowledging the imperative character (*jus cogens*) of those principles, which cannot be changed by way of agreement between States.

In the *LaGrand* case,[27] the Court recognized that individuals possess the personal right to have consular assistance under Article 36(1) of the Vienna Convention on Consular Relations[28] and that the US had failed in its obligation of consular notification to the detriment of German nationals, therefore deciding that it committed the US to effectively allow the review and consideration of the conviction and sentences of the fifty-two individuals by taking into account the violation of the rights set forth in the Convention. This case is interesting because it evidenced the existence of fundamental rights of individuals in a treaty apparently aimed at regulating the relationship between States. Even if we consider that consular relations were conceived to protect the individuals of one State when they are in another State, it is noteworthy that the Court interpretation led to the establishment of higher standards of State practice in a sensitive matter in an era where there are hundreds of millions of international travelers per year.[29]

In the *Avena* case,[30] the Court, supported on the previous ruling in the *LaGrand* case, reaffirmed that individuals possess the personal right to have consular assistance under Article 36(1) of the Vienna Convention on Consular Relations and, since the US had failed in its obligation to inform the Mexican nationals upon their detention of their rights under the convention; to notify the appropriate Mexican consular post without delay about the detention of Mexican nationals; and to ensure to Mexico the right to communicate with and visit its nationals in prison and to arrange for their legal representation, it had the obligation to make reparations in an adequate form. However, in response to the Mexican claim that the consular notification and consular communication under the Convention were fundamental human rights whose infringement *ipso facto* vitiated the entire process, the Court, acknowledging the sensitiveness of the issue, sensibly understood that this was not a matter that it had to appreciate in the case (para 124).

In the *Wall* advisory opinion,[31] the UN General Assembly asked the Court about the legal consequences arising out of the construction of a wall surrounding East Jerusalem and the occupied Palestinian territories in the West Bank, therefore encompassing the assessment of whether the construction was in accordance with certain rules and principles of international law. In its opinion, the Court understood that such rules and principles could be found in the UN Charter and certain other treaties, in customary international law and in the relevant resolutions adopted pursuant to the Charter by the General Assembly and the Security Council.

As regards international humanitarian law, the Court, refuting the Israeli argument that the State was not bound by the Fourth Hague Convention of 1907, because it was not part of it, raised the particularly sensitive precedent of the International Military Tribunal of Nuremberg, which had found that the 'rules laid down in the Convention were recognised by all civilized nations, and were regarded as being declaratory of the laws and customs of war' (para 89). Despite the clear reference to the recognition of the rules by civilized nations, an apparent reference to the source defined in article 38(1)(c) of its Statute, the Court concluded that 'the provisions of the Hague Regulations have become part of customary law', as acknowledged by all the participants in the proceedings before the Court.

5.4   New seeds in contemporary international law

As mentioned above, once the general principles of law are evidenced by customary practices or treaty provisions, they seem to disappear, in a fashion similar to the seed, which, upon giving birth to a new plant, can no longer be observed. However, in both circumstances, it would be impossible to have the plant if the seed had not been sown there. Like the seeds of an oak, the general principles of law do not have to germinate at the same time at the international level.

Apart from those traditionally recognized specific principles of international law,[32] as well as those that could be regarded as procedural,[33] some others are flourishing. The general principles of law must be understood as truly 'general', i.e., as covering all branches of law and not only the mentioned ones, shaped on a faraway pure inter-state understanding of international law. If it is a truism that international law has evolved to aggregate new fields directly related to the *human being* – the human rights law and humanitarian law – it is also true that it has evolved to embrace the

common concerns of humankind, as expressed by international environmental law, and also *political participation in public affairs.* For that reason, the principles themselves are very extensive and 'can be interpreted to
include not only the general theory of law, but the general theories of each
branch of municipal law, so far as recognized by civilized nations. They
may be conceived, furthermore, as including not only legal principles but
the fundamental legal concepts of which the legal norms are composed
such as person, right, duty, property, juristic act, contract, tort, succession,
etc.' [34]

International law is no longer concerned only with the relations between
States; it now regulates domains formerly reserved to State regulation and,
for that reason, it is fed by them. Recent decades have shown the offspring,
mostly from municipal law, of several other general principles of law related to civil society at large, which have been transposed to international
law, as we will see hereinafter.

5.4.1 Environmental Protection

The Rio Declaration made reference to some Principles on Environment
and Development that included, among others, the States' responsibility to
ensure that activities within their jurisdiction or control do not cause damage to the environment of other States or of areas beyond the limits of
national   jurisdiction   (Principle   of   Prevention   of   Transboundary
Environmental Damage). [35]

A corollary of this obligation is the enforcement of two other germane
principles. The first is the 'Polluter Pays Principle', making the party responsible for pollution responsible for bearing the costs for the damage
done to the environment, firstly mentioned in Principle Twenty-One of the
Stockholm Declaration [36] and further reproduced in the sixteenth principle
of the Rio Declaration. The second is the Compensation for Victims of
Pollution and other Environmental Damage Principle, recognized as the
thirteenth principle of the Rio Declaration, by which 'States shall develop
national law regarding liability and compensation for the victims of pollution and other environmental damage and shall also cooperate in an expe-
ditious and more determined manner to develop further international law
regarding liability and compensation for adverse effects of environmental
damage caused by activities within their jurisdiction or control to areas beyond their jurisdiction.'

The legal doctrine attributes the birth of these principles to the Trail
Smelter case, which dealt with claims of trans-frontier air pollution and de-
rived damages caused to privately owned agricultural and forest lands in
the state of Washington by the fumes discharged from the smelter of the
Consolidated Mining and Smelting Co. located at Trail, British Columbia. [37]
This case gave birth to the Convention for Settlement of difficulties arising

from operation of Smelter at Trail signed between the United States and Canada,[38] which provided that Canada would pay the sum of USD 350,000 as a compensation for 'all damage which occurred in the United States prior to 1 January 1932, as a result of the operation of the Trail Smelter' (Article I). The convention also agreed to the establishment of an arbitral tribunal to access the damages caused before the date thereof, with the power to define the possible remedies, indemnities or compensations.

Together with these principles, originated in municipal legal systems and further transposed to international law, some others were incorporated directly in the realm of international law.[39] They are:

- The State Cooperation Principle, recognized as the Rio Declaration's seventh principle, by which it is defined that 'States shall cooperate in a spirit of global partnership to conserve, protect and restore the health and integrity of the Earth's ecosystem. In view of the different contributions to global environmental degradation, States have common but differentiated responsibilities. The developed countries acknowledge the responsibility that they bear in the international pursuit of sustainable development in view of the pressures their societies place on the global environment and of the technologies and financial resources they command';

- The Precautionary Principle, firstly mentioned at the international level in the UN World Charter for Nature,[40] and later formally recognized as the fifteenth principle of the Rio Declaration, which is worded as follows: 'In order to protect the environment, the precautionary approach shall be widely applied by States according to their capabilities. Where there are threats of serious or irreversible damage, lack of full scientific certainty shall not be used as a reason for postponing cost-effective measures to prevent environmental degradation'.

- The Sustainability Principle, i.e., the balanced exercise of economic exploitation of natural resources with respect for human developmental and environmental needs of present and future generations, which is enshrined in several principles of the Rio Declaration, notably from the first to the ninth;

- The Public Participation Principle, which was declared in the tenth principle of the Rio Declaration and later recognized by the Aarhus Convention;[41]

- The Environmental Impact Assessment Principle, covering the proper appraisal of proposed activities that are likely to have a significant adverse impact on the environment, recognized in the seventeenth principle of the Rio Declaration.

As can be observed, these general principles of law concern environmental issues. Some of them have been incorporated into effective international *hard law* (treaty) provisions, such as the State Cooperation principle, defined in the Convention on the Law of the Seas;[42] the rights for public access to information, public participation and access to justice, in governmental decision-making processes on matters concerning the local, national and trans-boundary environment, defined in the Aarhus Convention, and the precautionary principle adopted, for instance, in the Biological Diversity Convention[43] and the Stockholm Convention on Persistent Organic Pollutants.[44] Other principles took a different direction and, as prescribed in the Rio Declaration, were transposed to regional or municipal law from international law, namely the precautionary principle[45] and the Environmental Impact Assessment principle.[46]

Recalling Judge Takada's opinion in the *South West Africa* case, if the 'general principles of law' are to be interpreted as including 'the general theories of each branch of municipal law', they necessarily comprehend environmental law, since it is indisputable that the environment is a common concern of people and that it embraces areas considered as common heritage of Humankind,[47] and that the current rhythm of the planet's degradation may impose severe harm to the long-run life of our civilization. One cannot leave unnoticed that Grotius, in *Mare Liberum* wrote, back in 1609, 'that all surely might use common things without the damage of all and, for the rest, every man contented with his portion shall abstain from another's'.[48] If we assume that environmental protection is a general principle of law applicable to international law, it follows that, while completely disregarding the abstract States' boundaries, it actually poses a severe challenge to the concept of State sovereignty, construed upon the idea that the State would have absolute and exclusive control over its territory and peoples and things therein. As facts have shown, no theory could be more fallacious from an environmental perspective. Therefore, the traditional function of international law, conceived of as a 'tool' to mediate the relationship between States in a *ex*-territorial environment (given that it would not regulate the activities within State boundaries), had to be adjusted to cover the entire territory of the planet, proposing that each State would have 'common but differentiated responsibilities to conserve, protect and restore the health and integrity of the Earth's ecosystem', i.e., assuming that their active and passive attitudes would affect the territories and peoples of all other States. The general principles of law applicable to environmental protection have brought about a shift in the perception of international law, which has definitively moved to a neo-Grotian approach, founded on the idea of an international society supported in a community of interests and responsibilities. But, as practice has demonstrated, it definitively must involve people, the ultimate actor of the degradation and beneficiary of a healthier environment. Hence, civil (and, consequently, political) participation is fundamentally necessary.

5.4.2 Civil and Political Participation

Since the Bill of Rights, adopted by the parliament of England in 1689, men and women have sought the freedom to govern their own lives without the interference of self-proclaimed sovereigns. Not without reason, the Bill of Rights established that suspending the laws or the execution of laws by real authority was illegal and that the election of members of Parliament ought to be free, as well as freedom of speech and debates or proceedings in Parliament ought not to be impeached or questioned in any court or place out of Parliament.[49]

In 1776, the United States Declaration of Independence recognized that people had the inherent right of political independence, 'to which the Laws of Nature and of Nature's God entitle them', being these same laws the source of the self-evidence that all men are created equal and endowed with certain unalienable rights, for whose guarantee governments are instituted, 'deriving their just powers from the consent of the governed.' When the US Constitution was approved, in 1787, it established a republican democratic regime by which citizens would elect their representatives to the legislative bodies and their representatives for the election of the President.

When the Declaration of the Rights of Man and the Citizen was adopted in 1789, in France, it recognized that the *sovereignty resided essentially in the Nation, i.e., in the people*, and that no body or individual can exert authority which is not emanated expressly from it (article III). The Declaration also stated that law is the expression of the general will and that all citizens have the right to contribute personally, or through their representatives, to its formation (Article VI). The French Revolution, as pointed out by Cassese, introduced the concepts of *individual, nation, people* and *equal sovereignty,* which started to circulate among States, leading to a new perspective in which State became to see themselves no longer as supreme potentates but as 'simple managers of human communities'.[50]

These three documents are supported in general principles of law that ensured people the right to govern themselves, being construed upon them. Jointly, they can be regarded as the most important legal foundations of the civil and political participation of people in the conduct of State's affairs.

One fact that cannot go unnoticed is the current incapacity of States to control the development of the right that people have to govern their lives. In this particular aspect, it is noteworthy to mention that reputed scholars, not long ago, could affirm that

> 'The right of self determination has never been recognized as a genuine positive right of 'peoples' of universal and impartial application, and it will never will, nor can be recognized in the future.'[51]

As one can observe in the *East Timor* case, less than thirty years after this peremptory (yet, fortunately, wrong) anticipation of the future, the ICJ recognized self determination as a right with an *erga omnes* character. If a relevant part of legal scholars is capable of writing accurately about the past, it is also a fact, aptly pointed out by Sir Robert Jennings, that the 'isolation of academic international lawyers is especially worrying ... if they remain studying the international law that was devised for yesterdays problems'.[52]

Hence, the study of international law cannot remain self-restricted by theories conceived of in a period in which individuals were regarded as mere objects of law and people were either under colonial domination or under oppressive governments. The world has changed dramatically. The centrality of the human being in international law is undisputed. As we have seen in Chapter 3, an individual and an NGO were capable of obtaining from an international tribunal a ruling against an intergovernmental body decision supported in a UN Security Council resolution. This would have been considered a heresy by positivists a couple of decades ago, but now it is a reality and fully supported by international law. As affirmed by Michael Reisman,

> 'International law still protects sovereignty, but – not surprisingly – it is the people's sovereignty rather than the sovereign's sovereignty'.[53]

The general principles of law strongly embedded in natural law could survive the positivist tide that swept international law in the 19th century, which, fortunately, is gone, albeit some scholars insist on affirming that it is still ruling. As noted by Brierly, any criticism to the abstract character of Natural Law 'do not affect the permanent truths in the conception of a law of nature, and though today we generally use a different terminology, we recognize the validity of these truths as fully as ever'.[54] The principles have been largely recognized and adopted by all other nations since then, albeit with some periods of suspension due to dictatorships and tyrannies, either laic or religious. Some evidence of this is presented as follows.

a.   The International Covenant of Civil and Political Rights

In 1966, the UN General Assembly adopted the International Covenant of Civil and Political Rights (CCPR),[55] which was ratified by 167 States, from all regions of the world, covering nearly 90% of the entire world's population.[56] The comprehensiveness of the States' ratifications and the very nature of the document – a covenant – make it clear that the rights set forth in the agreement have been recognized by all contemporary legal systems and, therefore, could be regarded as rooted in general principles of law recognized by all civilized nations.

The CCPR acknowledged that men and women have equal and inalienable rights, being the States obliged to promote universal respect for, and observance of, those human rights and freedoms, derived from the *inherent* dignity of the human being, hence, from the Natural Law, the 'only and the same law that exists and is valid through all kinds of human societies'. As noted by Cançado Trindade, 'all initiatives in strengthening of the international protection of Human Rights are ultimately part of the process of construction of a universal culture of observance of Human Rights'.[57]

The first right is the 'right of self-determination'. If it is arguable that it is not properly new in the international realm, since it was recognized within the purposes of the UN in the organization's Charter (article 1(2)), one must notice that the right of self-determination has been extensively qualified in the CCPR, which, in addressing civil and political rights, expanded it beyond the narrowly interpreted boundaries of the 'right of people to be independent' that had been imposed by the context of colonialism. In the covenant, self-determination is more than being independent from foreign control, moreover because very small parts of the world were under that regime in 1966, when it was adopted.

From an individual perspective, the CCPR recognizes self-determination in the voluntary participation in medical or scientific experiments (Article 7); in the freedom from slavery, servitude and forced labor (Article 8); in the freedom of movement and residence settlement (Article 12); in the freedom to defend himself in person or through legal assistance of his own choosing in any trials (Article 14); in the prohibition of arbitrary or unlawful interference in his privacy, family, home or correspondence (article 17); in the freedom of thought, conscience and religion, as well as the freedom, either individually or in community with others and in public or private, to manifest his religion or belief in worship, observance, practice and teaching (article 18);[58] in the freedom of expression and the right to hold opinions without interference and to seek, receive and impart information (Article 19) and in the freedom to freely marry (Article 23).

From a more collective perspective, the CCPR recognized:
- that everyone shall be entitled to a fair trial by a competent, independent and impartial tribunal established by law, which will be public, except when the interest of the private lives of the parties so requires and in some situations where reasons of morals, public order or national security in a *democratic society* deem it necessary (Article 14);
- the right of peaceful assembly without restrictions, except those imposed in conformity with the law and which are necessary in a *democratic society* in the interests of national security or public safety, public order, the protection of public health or morals or the protection of the rights and freedoms of others (Article 21);
- that everyone has the right to freedom of association with others, including the right to form and join trade unions for the protection of his

interests, and that no restrictions may be placed on the exercise of this right other than those which are prescribed by law and which are necessary in a *democratic society* in the interests of national security or public safety, public order, the protection of public health or morals or the protection of the rights and freedoms of others (Article 22);

– that (Article 25) every citizen shall have the right and the opportunity, without distinction of any kind, such as race, color, sex, language, religion, political or other opinion, national or social origin, property, birth or other status and without unreasonable restrictions:

- To *take part in the conduct of public affairs*, directly or through freely chosen representatives;
- To *vote and to be elected* at genuine periodic elections which shall be by universal and equal suffrage and shall be held by secret ballot, guaranteeing the free expression of the will of the electors;
- To have access, on general terms of equality, to public service in his country.

As can be observed, the CCPR only accepted restrictions to the collective exercise of individual political rights – the right of peaceful assembly and the freedom of association - under the guidance of parameters commonly deemed necessary in democratic societies. The right to live in a democracy can also be perceived in the references to voting and candidacy in periodic universal elections and in the right to take part in the conduct of public affairs, directly or through representatives.

Democracy is the ultimate expression of the general principle of law that recognizes a people's right to self-determination. This right is laid down in Natural Law. Vitoria has argued, back in the 1500s, that people had the immanent power to rule themselves. As we have said, its existence does not depend on the 'will' of the State, moreover if we take into consideration that the creation of a new State itself results from this very right to self-determination exercised by people against the controlling power of another State.[59]

According to Cassese, the ideological and political origins gave to self-determination a multifaceted and ambiguous concept that is

> 'at the one and same time, both boldly radical (in that it promotes democratic self-government, and free access of peoples to the role of international actors) and deeply subversive and disruptive (in that it undermines territorial integrity and may lead to the fragmentation of international community into a myriad of national and ethnic entities, all poised to fight one another)'.[60]

What appears to be beyond any doubt is that self-determination has two dimensions: an external, related to colonial or foreign oppression, and an internal, related to participation of people of all racial, religious and social background in public affairs, through a pluralist democratic government.[61] This latter dimension has been ensured, as observed, on article 25 of the CCPR and has been proclaimed by the UN General Assembly on the 'Declaration on Friendly Relations'[62] and on the 'Declaration on the granting of independence to colonial countries and peoples'.[63] At European level, the Charter of Paris for a New Europe[64] provided a clear link between democracy, political pluralism, human rights and the rule of law.[65]

Democracy is also deeply imbedded in the UN, its specialized agencies, funds and programs, and any other international or regional bodies. These intergovernmental bodies are, in regard to States, democratic par excellence, at least formally. The freedom of association is widely recognized, even in those organizations that, having a territorial scope, are logically open to only certain potential candidates. Within the organizations, election to the governing bodies is a rule, and all members who have fulfilled their obligations can vote and submit their candidacy. All assemblies and governing bodies' meetings are public and open to members. Votes are counted by head and the decisions are taken by majority (simple or qualified),[66] the casting vote being adopted only in situations of deadlock. All states have equal rights, whether large or small, rich or poor, new or old.

Hence, undoubtedly, while operating at the international level, States have accepted *democracy as a rule*.

The CCPR also ensured another peculiar civil and political right: everyone shall have the right to recognition everywhere as a person before the law. The purpose of this provision was to ensure that no one could be deemed not protected by the CCPR on grounds of non-recognition of legal personality, i.e., of his condition of subject of law. History is full of evidence of this tortuous practice: slaves were not regarded as persons, but things; children could be sold by their parents because they 'belonged' to them; indigenous people had no soul, hence were not regarded as persons by the Christian conquerors, and so on. Fortunately, these outrageous practices have been buried once and for all by a multi-lateral covenant ratified by the wide majority of States that, recognizing the undisputable physical existence of human beings, assumed the undertaking to respect and ensure respect of their legal existence, as subjects of law, *everywhere*. Everywhere?

Not exactly, because the CCPR regarded 'everywhere' as within the territorial boundaries of the State-parties and within their municipal legal systems (Article 2). Notwithstanding it, although not declaring the legal personality of individuals at the international level, there is no rule that an individual cannot be a subject of international law,[67] and for that reason, the CCPR has sown a seed of great potential growth.

b.   The Aarhus Convention

The democratic axioms of the CCPR have flourished in another realm: environmental protection, through the Aarhus Convention, which has linked international environmental law to international human rights.[68] A relevant aspect of the Aarhus Convention is the recognition of *access to information, public participation in decision-making, and access to justice in environmental matters as rights.* This treaty provision was construed upon several binding precedents, either at the international and regional levels, such as the 1985 EEC Directive on the assessment of the effects of certain public and private projects on the environment,[69] the 1990 EEC Directive on the freedom of access to information on the environment,[70] the 1991 UN/ECE Espoo Convention on Environmental Impact Assessment,[71] the 1991 UN/ECE Helsinki Convention on the Transboundary Effect of Industrial Accidents,[72] the 2003 CoE Lugano Convention on Civil Liability for Damage Resulting from Activities Dangerous to the Environment,[73] and the 1993 North-American Agreement on Environmental Cooperation.[74]

Ideally, public participation has been conceived as involving the participation of civil society in partnership with governmental officials to reach an optimal result in decision-making and policy-making in environmental affairs. Though the convention does not prescribe a full recipe for this participation, it requires, at minimum, 'effective notice, adequate information, proper procedures, and appropriate taking account of the outcome of public participation'.[75]

A remarkable aspect of this convention relies on its capability to put together, in a treaty provision, general principles of law regulating distinct aspects of life in society. In Chapter 1, we recalled Grotius' ideas concerning peoples' rights over common things, having quoted his assertion that 'all surely might use common things without the damage of all and, for the rest, every man contented with his portion shall abstain from another's'.[76] A corollary of his axiom is the necessary civil society participation in any decision-making and monitoring procedures that may materially impact the environment in order to avoid the 'damage of all', because public scrutiny appears to be the best and legitimate strategy to avoid abusive use of the 'common thing'. For this reason, democratic participation is fundamental to ensure that the protection of the environment is duly fulfilled.

The global dimension of the environmental challenges of our times and their definitive linkage with human rights, a fact made clear in the Rio[77] and Johannesburg[78] Declarations, demand a cooperative approach at the international level, a conclusion largely evidenced by the several bilateral and multilateral agreements, international conferences and intergovernmental organizations and funds dealing with the subject.

The Aarhus Convention recognized this linkage in its first article, in which it declared that the convention had the objective to 'contribute to the protection of *the right of every person* of present and future generations to live in an environment adequate to his or her health and well-being'. To ensure that substantive right, the convention established procedural rights to be guaranteed by the States, being these rights the above mentioned access to information, public participation in decision-making, and access to justice.

One aspect that may go unnoticed is the very substantive right to a healthy environment. The convention did not provide this right; rather it implicitly assumed that it existed and that it had been construed upon other sources of law, albeit some countries have declared that it constitutes only an aspiration.[79] If the convention did not ensure the right to a healthy environment, what did it guarantee?

Given that the right was recognized as pertaining to the realm of every person, existing or to be born, it ensured the right to participate in the decision-making procedures that affect the life of civil society at large. It recognized the right of self-determination, either on an individual or collective perspective. By doing so, the convention set a valuable precedent, because it established - in a document regulated by international law - that individuals have the democratic right to participate in the decision-making processes that affect matters not only comprised in the realm of one single State.

If the worldwide adoption of democratic practices has ensured people the right to participate at the municipal level, according to the rules established in each State, the convention established a participatory practice that went beyond the generic right set down in article 25 of the CCPR when it considered, as 'public authority', the institutions of any regional economic integration organization constituted of sovereign State members of the Economic Commission of Europe if these States have transferred to them their competence over matters governed by the convention (article 2(2)(d)). One example is the European Community, which signed and ratified the convention, whose institutions – the European Commission, the Council of the European Union, the Economic and Social Committee, the Committee of the Regions and the European Environmental Agency – are to be considered 'public authorities'. By doing so, it legitimated the participation of individuals in decision-making at the regional level, a condition reinforced by the provision in article 3(7) that the States parties to the convention shall promote the application of the principles in international environmental decision-making processes and within the framework of international organizations in matters relating to the environment.

Furthermore, when it considered that NGOs promoting environmental protection had to be regarded as 'public concerned', i.e., as the public affected or likely to be affected by, or having an interest in, the environmental decision-making, it gave them legitimacy to have access to information and to participate in the decision-making and also, most importantly, *locus standi,* i.e, the right to seek judicial protection if those rights were not respected by the public authorities. The convention regulated this right in article 9, establishing that any person could seek judicial measures before a court of law or another impartial body established by law, but defined that each party to the convention should do so 'within its national legislation'. Considering that the European Union is party to the convention, we understand that any conflicts involving its institutions must be referred to the Court of Justice of the European Union that, according to its statutes, is the judicial organ of the EU.

To guarantee that the participation in the decision-making process is not only formal, but also substantial and equitable, the convention ensured access to comprehensive information. To confirm that these rights are effective, it provided judicial protection. By doing so, the States and intergovernmental organizations parties to the convention relied on the general principle of law that ensures the right of self-determination of the peoples, which is experiencing a steady development, notably at the European level.

5.5   Democracy: a general principle of law?

In the previous chapters we have addressed on some occasions the participatory rights ensured to NGOs within the Council of Europe. As we have stated, the relationship of the Council with NGOs had begun in 1951, following the adoption of consultative arrangements by the UN Charter. In 2003, consultative rights were expanded to become participatory rights, even if these did not mean either the admission of NGOs as members of the Council nor voting rights.[80] As we saw in Chapter 3, NGOs have *locus standi* before the European Court of Justice and can seek judicial protection against illegal acts inflicted to them by Community institutions, including the restrictions to participate in the decision-making processes in environmental matters, covered by the Aarhus Convention. Even if we consider the apparent stumble of the Strasbourg Convention, which has been ratified by few States since its adoption in 1986, why do NGOs experience such a remarkable legitimacy in Europe?

While it is undisputed that the richest NGOs are in the US, the space conquered by NGOs in Europe does not seem to have been 'bought' by multi-million dollar programs or luxurious headquarters at noble addresses. Rather, the legitimacy of NGOs in Europe appears to have stronger, deeper roots, laid down in human beings, on their right to be regarded as *persons* that are capable of deciding their own destiny and of sharing the results for the benefit of the community. Of course, one could argue that the pacific and cooperative society that we observe today in Europe is recent and that its people have shed much blood and have fought many wars throughout centuries to reach such a stage. This fact was acknowledged in the preamble of the Charter of Paris, which declared that Europe was 'liberating itself from the legacy of the past'. It is true, but it must be understood as liberation from the legacy of tyranny and 'over-mighty' States, because the seeds of international law as it is conceived and practiced today have its origins in European thought and, more precisely, in some general principles of law forged on the continent.

In this chapter, we have studied the general principles of law as a source of international law. As we have sustained, they are often hidden behind customary rules of law and treaty provisions that are frequently invoked as the main sources of international law. Disregarding the general principles as a relevant source of law only because they are not quoted in judicial decisions does not seem to be adequate. Relegating them to a secondary role only because they are often mentioned in the preamble of the conventions rather than in the articles, is also incorrect. It is inappropriate to assume that because they are imbedded in the *rationale* of the legislator and the judge, orienting them as to what is right and what is not. And, given their contribution towards the formation of Law, they have played an important role, albeit discreet and sometimes unperceived. After all, as pointed out by Lauterpacht, the general principles of law, being the expression of natural law, have the role to correct and supplement positive international law and, thus, prevent its disconnection from justice.[81]

One of the principles that we have appraised is the principle of self determination. We have seen that it cannot be taken as a principle that will vanish when every part of the world has become independent, because it cannot be taken as a synonym for 'freedom from colonialism'. It is more. It is the right that the peoples have to determine, by themselves, their future, as affirmed by Vitoria five centuries ago. It is the right to participate in public affairs, as stated in the CCPR. It is the right to have access to information and to participate in the decision-making processes, as ensured by the Aarhus convention. Moreover, it is the right to be heard, to discuss, to propose, to share views, opinions and concerns, as ensured by the CoE participatory rights. It is the right to pursue judicial remedies from the State against unlawful acts practiced by the very same State. Finally, as noted by Thornberry, the principle possesses a 'sense in which people is entitled to exercise a continuing democratic control over governments', it is, he adds, a 'continuing right that is not exhausted by the achievement of independence'.[82]

Hence, self-determination, in the contemporary world, is the right to have a democracy, to participate in the conduct of public affairs.[83] It was acknowledged in the UN Charter, which, albeit not mentioning 'democracy', invoked in its very first words – We the Peoples of the United Nations – a fundamental principle of democratic doctrine, i.e., that the sovereignty of the member-states, and consequently, the legitimacy of the Organization, had its origins in 'the people'.

Beyond a shadow of a doubt, the CCPR clearly embodies an ideological commitment toward Western liberal political thought. The right to participate in public affairs, directly or through freely chosen representatives is, par excellence, an expression of pluralist democracy. Actually, Western ideology is not only a source of interpretation of the covenant, it is also its dominant factor.[84] Given the CCPR liberal accent, one cannot expect democracy to be restricted to national boundaries. In the 21st century, citizenship goes beyond the traditional borders of the nation-state.[85] As argued by Dominicé,

'Le principe de légitimité démocratique fait-il aujourd'hui irruption in droit des gens. Le droit des peoples à vivre dans les régimes démocratiques fait son chemin en droit international en liaison tout d'abord avec le recherché de la paix.'[86]

If democracy has been adopted as a rule while the States are interacting among themselves in the realm of international law and if democracy is also a right that citizens have in the realm of their countries, ensured by international law provisions, it appears that there are general principles of law, State practices and treaty provisions that permit the integration of these two realms in order to legitimize the right of people to participate in the determination of the future of humankind, not only through the State, but also through other actors, the IGOs and NGOs. But, firstly, it seems appropriate to address the conceptual framework of legal personality in international law, a task that we will bear in the next chapter.

Notes

1   However, this situation occurred in the *Legality on the Threat or Use of Nuclear Weapons* (Advisory Opinion) [1996] ICJ Rep 226, as we have pointed out in Chapters 3 and 4.
2   The Eurocentric flavor of the Committee is noticeable. It was composed of ten people, seven being from Europe (UK, France, Italy, Belgium, the Netherlands, Spain and Norway), two from America (US and Brazil) and one from Asia (Japan).
3   E Descamps, *New Africa: an essay on Government Civilization in New Countries and on the foundation, organization and administration of the Congo Free State* (Sampson Low, London 1903).
4   For a criticism of the theory of civilized nations, see, G Abi-Saab, 'Humanité et Communauté Internationale dans la Dialectique du Droit International' in *Humanité et Droit International: Mélanges René-Jean Dupuy* (Pedone, Pais, 1991) 1.
5   General Treaty for the Re-Establishment of Peace between Austria, France, Great Britain, Prussia, Sardinia and Turkey, and Russia, signed at Paris on 30 March 1856 [1969] 114 *The Consolidated Treaty Series* 409, at 410. Addressing the issue, PM Dupuy wrote that for the assembled nations at the Berlin Conference of 1885, universal international law meant 'European Public Law'. PM Dupuy, 'Some Reflections on

Contemporary International Law and the Appeal to Universal Values: A Response to Martii Koskenniemi' (2005) EJIL v 16 n 1, 131.

6   *North Sea Continental Shelf* cases (Judge Ammoun Separate Opinion) [1969] ICJ Rep 3, 133-136.

7   In this particular aspect, albeit not contemporary, we can quote a letter sent by Lord Dorchester to Lord Sydney on 8 November 1788 addressing the adoption of an Assembly in the province of Quebec, which reproduces the overall state of mind of the colonizers, where he affirmed that the local English gentlemen objected to the introduction of a new body of laws, to the extent that they are 'strangers' and expressed apprehension regarding the introduction of an assembly in a country of 'farmers' since the 'low state of learning and knowledge in the country would lay them open to the pursuit and adoption of wrong measures, and to dangers, which a more enlightened people would not be exposed to'. Certainly, one could interpret 'wrong measures' as 'measures towards independence'. AB Keith, *Selected Speeches and Documents on British Colonial Policy 1763-1917* (OUP London, 1948) Part I, 82.

8   See, JL Brierly, *The Law of Nations* (6th edn, Clarendon Press, Oxford 1963) 23; H Lauterpacht, *International Law: Collected Papers* (CUP, Cambridge 1975) 307; MN Shaw, *International Law* (5th edn CUP, Cambridge 2003) 93; D Carreau, *Droit International* (7th edn Pedone, Paris 2001) 287; PM Dupuy, *Droit International Publique* (6th edn Dalloz, Paris) 326; GFS Soares, *Curso de Direito Internacional Público* (1st edn Atlas, São Paulo 2002) 91; CD Albuquerque Mello, *Curso de Direito Internacional Público* (8th edn, Freitas Bastos, Rio de Janeiro 1986) 230; B Cheng, *General Principles of Law as Applied by International Courts and Tribunals* (CUP, London 1953) 24-26.

9   (Adopted 23 May 1969, entered into force 27 January 1980) UNTS 1155.

10   A Cassese, 'The international Court of Justice and the right of peoples to self-determination' in R Jennings, V Lowe and M Fitzmaurice (eds) *Fifty years of the International Court of Justice* (CUP, Cambridge 2007) 351.

11   In this aspect, see Judge Quintana's dissenting opinion on the *Right of Passage* case, which stated, while appraising the claimed right of passage, that a treaty provision, if non-existent, could be replaced by a customary rule of law, which, if one did not exist, could also be replaced by a general principle of law. *Right of Passage over Indian Territory (Portugal v India)* [1960] ICJ Rep 90.

12   P Daillier and A Pellet, *Droit international public* (7th ed LGDJ, Paris 2002) 353.

13   D Carreau, *Droit International* (n 8) 290-291.

14   See, MN Shaw, *International Law* (n 8) 94; D Carreau, *Droit International* (n 8) 291; PM Dupuy, *Droit International Publique* (n 8) 327; GFS Soares, *Curso de Direito Internacional Público* (n 8) 92; CD Albuquerque Mello, *Curso de Direito Internacional Público* (n 8) 230; F Raimondo, *General Principles of Law in the Decisions of International Criminal Courts and Tribunals* (Nijhoff, The Hague 2008) 2.7.

15   The current practice reserves three seats for Africa, two places for Latin America and the Caribbean, three for Asia, five for Western Europe and other States and two for Eastern European states.

16   M Virally, 'Fuentes del Derecho Internacional' in M Sorensen (ed) *Manual del Derecho Internacional* (Fondo de Cultura Económica, México 1985) 184; D Carreau, *Droit International* (n 8) 299.

17   *Rights of Minorities in Upper Silesia (Minority Schools) (Germany v. Poland)* PCIJ Rep. Series A 15.

18   *South West Africa* Second Phase (Judge Tanaka's Dissenting Opinion) [1966] ICJ Rep 6, 295

19   *Corfu Channel case (UK v Albania)* (Judgment) [1949] ICJ Rep 4.

20   *Reservation to the Convention on Genocide* (Advisory Opinion) [1951] ICJ Rep 15.

21 (Adopted 9 December 1948, entered into force 12 January 1951) UNTS 78.

22 *South West Africa* Second Phase [1966] ICJ Rep 6, 34.

23 *South West Africa* Second Phase (Judge Tanaka's Dissenting Opinion) [1966] ICJ Rep 6, 294-299.

24 B Cheng, *General Principles of Law* (n 8) 24.

25 *Military and Paramilitary Activities in and Against Nicaragua (Nicaragua v United States)* (Judgment) [1986] ICJ Rep 14.

26 UNGA Res 2625(XXV) (24 October 1970).

27 *LaGrand (Germany v. United States of America)* (Judgment) [2001] ICJ Rep 466.

28 (adopted 24 April 1963, entered into force 19 March 1967) UNTS 596.

29 According to data provided by the Airport Council International < www.airport.org> accessed 6 May 2009, there are more than 1,35 billion international flights per year.

30 *Avena and Other Mexican Nationals (Mexico v. United States of America)* (Judgment) [2004] ICJ Rep 12.

31 *Legal Consequences of the Construction of a Wall in the Occupied Palestinian Territory* (Advisory Opinion) [2004] ICJ Rep 136.

32 *E.g.*, Non-interference in internal affairs of another State, limitations of State sovereignty and limitation of the right of self-defence.

33 *E.g.*, *Pacta sunt servanda, res judicata,* estoppel, respect for acquired rights, good faith and liability for unlawful harm to third parties and extinctive prescription.

34 *South West Africa* Second Phase (Judge Tanaka's Dissenting Opinion) [1966] ICJ Rep 6, 295.

35 Rio Declaration on Environment and Development (1992) Principle 2.

36 Declaration of the United Nations Conference on the Human Environment, or Stockholm Declaration, adopted 16 June 1972.

37 GFS Soares, *Curso de Direito Internacional Público* (n 8) 92.

38 (Adopted 15 April 1935) US Treaty Series 893.

39 JJ Ruiz, 'Los principios fundamentales del derecho internacional ambiental' in PB Casella (ed) *Dimensão Internacional do Direito* (LTr, São Paulo 2000) 243-264.

40 UN Doc A/RES/37/7 (28 October 1982). See item II, 11 (b).

41 *Convention on Access to Information, Public Participation in Decision-making and Access to Justice in Environmental Matters* (adopted 25 June 1998, entered into force 30 October 2001) UNTS 2161.

42 *UN Convention on the Law of the Sea* (adopted 10 December 1982, entered into force 16 November 1994) UNTS 1833, Article 118.

43 *Convention on Biological Diversity* (adopted 5 June 1992, entered into force 29 December 1993) UNTS 1760, Preamble.

44 (Adopted 22 May 2001, entered into force 17 May 2004). UNTS 2256.

45 See, in this particular, at the European Level, the Communication from the Commission on the precautionary principle (EC Doc COM (200) final (2 February 2000); in Brazil, National Environmental Policy (Law 6938, 31 August 1981).

46 See, in this particular, at the European Level, the *Convention on Environmental Impact Assessment in a Transboundary Context* (adopted 25 February 1991, entered into force 10 September 1997) UNTS 1989 and the *Convention on Civil Liability for Damage Resulting from Activities Dangerous to the Environment* (adopted 21 June 2003, not entered into force yet) ETS 150. In Brazil, see Constitution, article 225.

47 The concept of common heritage of mankind was first mentioned in a speech made by the Maltese representative at the UN General Assembly in 1967, in a reference to the seabed. Later on, it evolved to encompass areas of Antarctica and outer space that, together with the seabed, should not be monopolized for the benefit of one state or group of states alone, but should be treated as if they are to be used to the benefit of all. See, in this aspect, the UN Convention on the Law of the Sea (adopted 10

December 1982, entered into force 16 November 1994) UNTS 1833, Article 136. See, also K Baslar, *The concept of the Common Heritage of Humankind* (Nijhoff, The Hague 1998).

48 H Grotius, *The Free Sea* (Natural Law and Enlightenment Classics, Liberty Fund, Indianapolis 2004) 6.

49 An Act Declaring the Rights and Liberties of the Subject and Settling the Succession of the Crown < http://avalon.law.yale.edu/17th_century/england.asp> accessed 14 May 2009.

50 A Cassese, *The Human Dimension of International Law: Selected Papers* (OUP, Oxford, 2008) 91.

51 JHW Verzijl, *International Law in Historical Perspective* (Sijhoff, Leiden 1968) v 1, 324.

52 R Jennings, 'Broader Perspectives in International Law' in A Anghie and G Sturgess, *Legal Visions of the 21st Century: Essays in Honor of Judge Christopher Weeramantry* (Kluwer, The Hague, 1998) 497-507.

53 WM Reisman, 'Sovereignty and Human Rights in Contemporary International Law' (1990) AJIL n 84, 866.

54 JL Brierly, *The Law of Nations* (n 8) 23.

55 (adopted 16 December 1966, entered into force 23 March 1976) UNTS 999.

56 See   < http://treaties.un.org/Pages/ViewDetails.aspx?src=TREATY&mtdsg_no=IV-4&chapter=4&lang=en > accessed 20 June 2012

57 AA Cançado Trindade, 'International Protection of Human Rights' in *Boutros Boutros-Ghali Amicorum Discipulorumque Liber* (Bruylant, Bruxelles, 1998) 986.

58 See, in this particular aspect, T Franck, 'Is Personal Freedom a Western Value? (1997) AJIL n 91, 593.

59 The ICJ recognized that self-determination is a right with *erga omnes* character. See, in this particular aspect, *Case Concerning East Timor (Portugal v Australia)* [1995] ICJ Rep 89, para 29.

60 A Cassese, *The International Court of Justice* (n 10) 351.

61 A Cassese, *The International Court of Justice* (n 10) 353; T Franck, 'The Emerging Right to Democratic Governance' (1992) AJIL, v 86, 46; AM Slaughter, 'International Law in a World of Liberal States' (1995) EJIL v 6, 503; MJ Glennon, 'Self-determination and Cultural Diversity' (2003) FFWA v 27 n 2, 75; H Fan, 'The Missing link between Self-determination and Democracy: the Case of East Timor' (2007) NJIHR v 6 n 1, 176; D Archibugi, 'A Critical Analysis of the Self-determination of Peoples: A Cosmopolitan Perspective', (2003) Constellations v 10 n 4, 488.

62 UNGA Res 2625(XXV) (24 November 1970).

63 UNGA Res 1514(XV) (14 December 1960) para 5: 'immediate steps shall be taken ... to transfer all powers to the peoples of those territories ... in accordance to their freely expressed will and desire, without any distinction as to race, creed or colour, in order to enable them to enjoy complete independence and freedom'. See, also, UNGA Res 1541 (XV) (15 December 1960), principles VII and IX.

64 Charter of Paris for a New Europe (21 November 1990).

65 A Cassese, *Self-determination of Peoples: A legal reappraisal* (CUP, Cambridge 1995) 294.

66 Even in those organizations, such as the International Monetary Fund, that have defined different voting weights par states, they are proportional to the contributions of each of them.

67 I Brownlie, *Principles of Public International Law* (7th edn OUP, Oxford 2008) 65.

68 *Convention on Access to Information, Public Participation in Decision-making and Access to Justice in Environmental Matters* (adopted 25 June 1998, entered into force 30 October 2001) UNTS 2161.

69 Directive 85/337/EEC (27 June 1985).

70 Directive 90/313/EEC (7 June 1990).

71 *Convention on Environmental Impact Assessment in a Transboundary Context* (adopted 25 February 1991, entered into force 10 September 1997) UNTS 1989.

72 *Convention on the Transboundary Effect of Industrial Accidents* (adopted 17 March 1992, entered into force 19 April 2000) UNTS 2105.

73 (adopted 21 June 1993, not entered into force yet) ETS 150.

74 *North American Agreement on Environmental Cooperation* (adopted August 1993, entered into force 1 January 1994).

75 United Nations, *The Aarhus Convention: an implementation guide* (UN, New York and Geneva 2000) 85.

76 H Grotius, *The Free Sea* (Natural Law and Enlightenment Classics, Liberty Fund, Indianapolis 2004) 6.

77 Rio Declaration on Environment and Development (14 June 1992).

78 Johannesburg Declaration on Sustainable Development (4 September 2002).

79 The UK stated that it understood the reference to express an aspiration which motivated the negotiation of the convention and that each party undertook to guarantee only the rights to access to information, public participation in decision-making, and access to justice. <http://treaties.un.org/Pages/ViewDetails.aspx?src=TREATY& mtdsg_no=XXVII-13&chapter=27&lang=en#EndDec> accessed 14 May 2009.

80 CoE Res. (2003)8 (19 November 2003).

81 H Lauterpacht, *International Law: Collected Papers* (CUP, Cambridge 1975) v 2, 307.

82 P Thornberry, 'The Principle of Self-Determination', in C Warbrick and V Lowe, *The United Nations and the Principles of International Law* (Routledge, London, 1994) 175.

83 R. Higgins, *Problems and Process: International Law and How We Use It*, (OUP, Oxford 1994) 120; S van Bijsterveld, *The Empty Throne: Democracy and the Rule of Law in Transition* (Lemma Publishers, Utrecht 2002) 353.

84 OM Garibaldi, 'On the Ideological Content of Human Rights Instruments: the Clause "in a Democratic Society"', in T Buergenthal, *Contemporary Issues in International Law: Essays in Honor of Louis B. Sohn* (NP Engels Publisher, Kehl, 1984) 23.

85 K Rubenstein, 'Citizenship in a Borderless World', in A Anghie and G Sturgess, *Legal Visions of the 21st Century: Essays in Honor of Judge Christopher Weeramantry* (Kluwer, The Hague, 1998) 183-205.

86 C Dominicé, 'Organisations Internationales et Démocratie' in LB de Chazournes and V Gowland-Debbas, *The International Legal System in Quest of Equity and Universality* (Martinus Nijhoff, The Hague 2001) 731.

CHAPTER 6

NGOS in International Public Law Doctrine

6.1   International legal theory and non-state actors

In the previous chapters, we have addressed the legitimacy of NGOs under several sources of international law. Generally speaking, NGOs are comprised within the comprehensive category of non-state actors, which, in turn, can easily be defined as those actors that are not States. Of course, this double negativity may be considered worthless, since nothing can truly be defined as 'not-something'. Classical international legal theory has proven, however, to be an exception.

It is well-known that classical international legal theory has been construed to privilege the States to the detriment of anything else. Hence, once the theoretical conception of State was defined and its attributes and characteristics became well understood, everything that did not fulfill all of the statehood requirements could be regarded as a 'non-state' and discarded as something irrelevant to international law. If the rather straightforward binomial division of State/Subjects – Non-State/Objects had worked well during a certain period of history, it is definitely incapable of maintaining its performance today.[1] Appraising its contemporary shortcomings requires understanding first what a State is in classical international legal theory, a task that we will start with the help of a legal dictionary. According to Black's Law Dictionary, a State is 'a people permanently occupying a fixed territory bound together by common law habits and custom into one body politically exercising, through the medium of an organized government, independent sovereignty and control over all persons and things within its boundaries, capable of making war and peace and of entering into international relations with other communities of the globe'.[2]

This succinct definition provides the two physical elements classically required for the existence of a State: People and Territory; in the absence of either one of them, no State is deemed possible. The dictionary entry also puts forward other intangible aspects of statehood: the organization of people into a political body, independent control over the territory and all people and things therein according to its own set of rules, and capability to interact with other similar entities. While the first aspect may be understood as the fictional figure of the State itself, the latter two are attributes of its sovereignty. With them, one reaches the third element required to achieve statehood: the existence of a sovereign political body capable of controlling the two aforementioned physical elements.

These three elements gave form to a legal order established in Europe in the 17th century and reflect the motivations and presuppositions in the history of the continent, which led to the creation of the concept of the (European) Modern State, later extended to the entire world.[3] When the Peace of Westphalia consecrated the rule *cujus regio, ejus religio,* putting an end to the Thirty Years' War, it also blessed the statehood trinity: people, territory and sovereignty. Moreover, it laid down the basis to justify the claim that only States could possess international legal personality, because no territory in the world could be governed by more than one sovereign, who would concentrate in his hands full power over the territory and the people therein. Once the sovereign States were juxtaposed on the world map, a puzzle was formed and any other territory still not under the control of one of those European States became subject to conquest, speeding up the process of colonialism.[4] If every inch of land and every human being was under the sovereign power of a State, then only States would be capable of representing them, following that only States could interact between each other. Furthermore, given that no State could regulate, according to its own rules, its relationship with another State, a new set of rules above and beyond any specific national legal system[5] – international law – had to be established.

In this chapter we will not address the foundations of international law - as was done in Chapter 1 – nor will we address the role of States as representatives of their peoples in the realm of international law – a task to be performed in the next chapter. We will, however, appraise one specific and fundamental concept in international law: international legal personality.

In any legal system, there are subjects of law, i.e., those natural persons and legal entities recognized by law as capable of possessing rights and bearing duties under that system. By doing so, the concerned legal system regard those individuals and entities a 'legal person' (the expressions 'legal person' and 'subject of law' are, thus, interchangeable).[6] Another relevant characteristic of Law is the uniform treatment that objects receive in any legal system: they have neither rights nor duties.[7]

None of the existing legal systems gives the same rights or imposes the same duties indiscriminately on all its subjects of law. It goes without questioning that differentiation is necessary and also desirable. For example, in the parent-child relationship, domestic law often imposes a heavier burden of duties on parents when their children are very young, but the balance shifts when children have reached adulthood and their parents have become elderly and dependent. In both cases, we have exactly the same individuals, in the same familiar relationship, and with the same duties and rights: material and emotional support. But, *once the context has changed, the same happens with the balance of duties and rights.*

Some authors support that the dichotomy subject/object is a positivist trap that hinders the full comprehension of the views of participants of international law, sustaining that the meaningful inquiry concerns 'not what persons are technically subjects but who actually participates in the global process of decision-making and who perform what functions'.[8] Despite the quality of the argument, given that the dichotomy is traditionally observed in municipal legal systems, we consider appropriate its use in international law.

When international legal theory flourished in the 17th century, it proposed a shift from the universal political organization that existed in Western Europe in the Middle Ages (in which all rulers had to share authority with vassals beneath them, and with the Pope and, in certain territories, with the Holy Roman Emperor above) towards a state-centric model, in which each territory would be governed by a single sovereign. The situation at that time contributed towards the perspective encountered nowadays. At the international level, intergovernmental organizations did not exist, individuals did not possess rights and duties under international law, and no one had ever dreamed of NGOs; at the domestic level, the right to self-determination was not even an embryonic theory, slaves and servants abounded everywhere and democracy definitively was not a rule; it was, rather, a revolutionary exception proposed by Spinoza in his *Theological-Political Treatise*. Therefore, a new set of practices, aimed at regulating this relationship, was established and, for that purpose, assumed that only sovereign kingdoms and principalities – the States – possessed legal personality. In other words, the theory assumed that international legal personality was a corollary of State sovereignty, a situation that drives us back to the necessary appraisal of the statehood trinity. This circular movement can be observed, for instance, in the Montevideo Convention on Rights and Duties of States, which established that the existence of a permanent population, living in a defined territory under the command of a government, capable of entering into relations with other States would lead to the qualification of a State, considered, *as such,* a person of international law.[9] Despite having a regional scope - the Americas - the convention addressed substantive aspects of statehood.[10] Hence, it is arguable that a State obtains international legal personality once it evidences that it has sovereignty over a given territory and people. But, at this point some problems arise.

Let us begin with the territory, the immovable physical element. How could one declare that one has sovereignty over a given territory? This is a factual situation that leads to a legal one. Would this claim require defined and settled boundaries? No, since history has shown that a State can be recognized even with border disputes and, according to the ICJ, 'there is for instance no rule that the land frontiers of a State must be fully delimited and defined, and often in various places and for long periods they are not, as is shown by the case of the entry of Albania into the League of Nations (Monastery of Saint Naoum, Advisory Opinion, 1924, P.C.I.J., Series B, No. 9, at p. 10)'.[11]

Moving on to the second physical element, how many people are deemed necessary to live in a territory to allow the recognition of a State? As Shaw has pointed out, 'there is no specification of a minimum number of inhabitants'.[12] Additionally, the ICJ, while addressing the Declaration on Principles of International Law concerning Friendly Relations and Co-operation among States in accordance with the Charter of the United Nations[13] in the *Western Sahara* case, pointed out that certain populations did not constitute a 'people' entitled to self-determination, thus supporting that the analysis had to focus not only on quantity, but also on quality.[14] In that case, the Court understood that 'territories inhabited by tribes or peoples having a social and political organization were not regarded as *terrae nullius*',[15] to later conclude that to pass the essential test 'where a group, whether composed of States, of tribes or of individuals, is claimed to be a legal entity distinct from its members' it is necessary to appraise the 'many ties of a racial, linguistic, religious, cultural and economic nature' and the existence of 'common institutions or organs, even of quite minimal character'.[16] Thus, it is not a people, rather a Nation that is required to form the legal entity, i.e., the State.[17] This is a truism since, after the fall of the Berlin Wall in 1989, we have seen the dismemberment of existing solid States (USSR and Czechoslovakia) and the fusion of others (Germany) based on nationhood.

The permanent habitation of a certain nation in a given territory is not enough if both are ruled by a third party. In those circumstances, they are not a State, rather a colony or an occupied territory. Thus, we reach the third element of the trinity: sovereignty. When a nation settles in a territory on a permanent basis and is capable of living therein according to its own rules under the command of its own independent government, one could argue that the territory is self-governed and, apparently, has fulfilled all conditions for statehood.

However, to become a State and, thereafter, acquire legal personality under international law, a self-governed people and territory must be recognized as a State by other States.[18] This is an awkward aspect of international law: despite, for instance, the clear provision in the Montevideo Convention that 'the political existence of the State is independent of recognition by the other States' (article 3), only the other States' recognition will entitle the newborn State to interact with them. Up until this moment, the effectiveness of its independence had been limited to own its territorial boundaries.

Hence, the existence of a State's international legal personality is, in a certain way, conditioned not only to the fulfillment of specific objective criteria – a people, a territory and an independent government – but also to the *subjective* attitude of the other States, which, having international legal personality, will entail, or not, relations with the newcomer.[19] Some authors have suggested that widespread international recognition makes the appraisal of statehood criteria more flexible, while little recognition imposes a more rigorous analysis of them.[20] This is true, moreover if we take into consideration that some States remain recognized as such even after the debacle of their governmental structure amidst civil war. In this particular aspect, Rosalyn Higgins went straight to the point when she affirmed that 'once in the *club*, the rules by which admission is tested – and that always with a degree of flexibility – become less important'.[21] Should international legal personality, then, be regarded as membership to a *club*?

This is an aspect of substantive importance that puts positivists and naturalists in opposition. According to the former, only States could be regarded as subjects of international law.[22] The latter, on the contrary, relying on Natural Law, have recognized that other actors possess rights and duties under international law.[23]

Since the *Reparation for injuries* case,[24] it has become clear that States are not the only entities bearing international legal personality, and, therefore, that such condition does not depend upon sovereignty over a given people and territory. In that case, the ICJ clearly set out broad principles that could be applied to any non-state actor on the international plane.[25] Similarly, a private association, the ICRC, is widely recognized as bearing international legal personality[26] and, together with a second one, the IUCN, bear rights and obligations under a multilateral treaty.[27] Furthermore, since the International Military Tribunal at Nuremberg, it has been stated that individuals could be subjects of international law with *locus standi* before Criminal Tribunals and, as a consequence, acquire duties and rights, a condition fully acknowledged in the statutes of the subsequent International Criminal Tribunals.[28]

If one bears in mind the 'Club' perspective, it is possible to argue that the recognition of the international legal personality of the ICRC was laid down by the States' free will, since they were not obliged to assign any specific humanitarian attributions to a private institution at the international level. The same could be argued in regard to the substantive secretariat attributions assigned to the IUCN in an environmental convention. Additionally, all intergovernmental organizations, having been created by States, could be regarded as specific collective bodies established to coordinately perform certain attributions that were in the realm of the States, therefore, acting as States' delegates on the matters concerned. In sum, the States, the members of the Club, would decide who would join them at the bridge table, and under which terms and conditions.

The Club concept is supported on the doctrine of the 'derived' legal personality of intergovernmental organizations, through which the legal personality of a relevant entity has not arisen out of the general principles of international law, but rather from the desire of the States, which have delegated certain limited functional capacities to them.[29] The idea was observed, implicitly, in the *Reparation for injuries* case, when the ICJ affirmed that the UN Charter equipped the organization with organs and had given it special tasks, with the intention to allow the enjoyment of 'functions and rights which can only be explained on the basis of the possession of a large measure of international personality and the capacity to operate upon an international plane'.[30] Daillier and Pellet support the same understanding in regard to private entities, such as the aforementioned ICRC and IUCN, which would have a derived, functional and relative international legal personality granted by the States.[31]

If the theory, at first glance, seems to suffice to explain the rights and duties of legal entities, it is not capable of justifying the rights and duties of individuals in international law. It lacks coherence. As clearly affirmed by Cançado Trindade,

> 'The doctrinal trend which still insists in denying to individuals the condition of subjects of international law is ... unsustainable [and] apparently trying to make believe that the intermediary of the State, between the individuals and the international order, would be something inevitable and permanent. Nothing could be more fallacious.'[32]

In this particular aspect, if we assume that the State itself is the product of the self-determination of people, both in its internal and external dimensions – an idea that nowadays appear to be unchallenged - *then* the State would necessarily have *derived* powers, since it was created to act on behalf of the individuals that compose the represented nation.[33] George Scelle, for instance, considered '*non le gouvernement, mais le peuple, comme élément capital de l'Etat et même comme élément unique*'.[34]

At this moment, it is appropriate to pose a question: why were States created? We know that scholars are debating it since immemorial times and that several theories have been conceived to answer this question. However, it is beyond the scope of this essay appraise them in detail. For that reason, we beg the pardon of the reader to straightforwardly answer the question affirming that States were created by people to protect their lives, liberties and estates. It were real people, not the abstract State, who were actually living, occupying space, planting, hunting, fighting, disputing things and moving across the territories that would be used to conform the States. Independent of any legal theory, States were created to protect the lives, liberties and estates of those people. And for that purpose, they had to have a monopoly over the legitimate use of physical force to ensure it.[35]

If the sovereign State failed in protecting its own people or enacted laws that were against Natural Law, then, according to Aquinas, Vitoria and Grotius, just to quote some of the founders of international law, people could disobey the sovereign or even rebel. The naturalist understanding of the role of the State is fundamental for the protection of the human condition of individuals. The positivist doctrine that regarded the State as an organism to whom everyone had to profess his unconditional allegiance allowed authoritarian practices that led to massive killings in Nazi Germany, perpetrated by the government against the German people. Fortunately, this kind of omnipotent State was also burnt in the crematoriums of Auschwitz, and gave birth to a new understanding of the place of the individual within the State in which participation was essential, because men are free as long as it acts in the public realm. As Arendt puts it:

'Action, the only activity that goes on directly between men...corresponds to the human condition of plurality, to the fact that men, not Man, live on the earth and inhabit the world. While all aspects of the human condition are somehow related to politics, this plurality is specifically the condition - not only the conditio sine qua non, but the conditio per quam - of all political life'[36]

On another perspective, some authors support that the Modern State flourished together with the establishment of bureaucracy.[37] If this assertion is true, then one could argue that, under the peoples' perspective, the State has a *functional* purpose of satisfying the needs of the nation it governs. In the colonial context, for example, Brownlie argued that it was very probable that the populations of non-self-governing territories within the meaning of Chapter XI of the UN Charter possessed legal personality, albeit a special one.'[38] The immanent international legal personality of the individuals, then, legitimized them to declare independence. Hence, if a Nation is unsatisfied, it is capable of reforming the State, or even rejecting it, creating a new one. The former situation can be observed, for instance, in the changes of regimens (Capitalism v. Socialism; Republic v. Monarchy; Unitary v. Federative governments), the latter being the case in particular of Yugoslavia, whose statehood has been in a legal limbo since the creation of the States of Slovenia, Croatia and Bosnia-Herzegovina.[39] Modern history has evidenced that even powerful States and bureaucracies are incapable of continuing to protect people's lives, liberties and estates through the use of force if these same people decide to live under different arrangements and exercise their right to self-determination.

We will resume the appraisal of the legal condition of the State in the next chapter, but assuming that the nations have the right of self-determination if they permanently occupy a territory and are capable of creating an independent government, then, *they* possess the inherent right to interact with other nations, doing so *through* the States. As noted by McDougal and Reisman,

> 'Traditional international law is a legacy of conceptualizations in which collective entities, often endowed with mystical characteristics, all but supplanted the individual human being. Let's emphasize that the ultimate actor in every interaction is the individual.'[40]

Of course, the States continue to be the main participants in the international legal system, although, as recognized by Weeramantry, 'international law is moving inexorably out of the idea that its subjects are only sovereign States [and] individuals are moving closer to center stage in public international law'.[41] Definitively, we are not defending the idea that every individual or nation should interact directly with others at the international level. This would cause the collapse of the relations. If it (interaction) does not work at the town level, it certainly will not be functional at the global level. Direct democracy may be feasible among a handful of people, but does not prove to be so at a greater range. NGOs are evidence of this.

When a small group of individuals decides to 'do something for the planet', they start working and deciding everything together. According to the growth of their activities and the admission of new members to the group, they begin to divide up tasks and assign responsibilities. Further on, written rules are enacted by the group and a permanent staff is hired, capable of passing other rules, fundraising, lobbying the authorities, drawing the attention of the media, interacting with peer organizations, attracting more donors and members, until they have reached a situation where the NGO has become rich, powerful and managed by a competent professional staff capable of 'doing something for the planet'. An NGO is hence, in sum, a quintessential representative of Weberian civil service.

We have made this anecdotal parallel with the State to show that the same social machinery that gave birth to States is capable of giving birth to other representatives. If individuals possess international legal personality and the right to self-determination, which encompasses the right to participate in public affairs, directly or through representatives, then they can determine the way they will be represented in the international realm.

But, if States and NGOs consider themselves legitimate representatives of their constituencies, they must necessarily assume that those constituencies are the original bearers of the rights that they are defending, from which it follows that States and NGOs really do have a *derived* and *functional* legal capacity, which is, also, *relative*, since none of them are entitled to act against the fundamental rights of their constituencies. For this reason, for example, no one can argue that States have created human rights or support that States are not obliged, by *jus cogens,* to respect certain rules strictly connected with them. It was acknowledged by D'Amato, who affirmed that 'human rights brought two things: first, that the individual has legal standing to make claims and second, that a State cannot defend itself against such claims by the notion of sovereignty.'[42] If the sovereignty of the individual is stronger than that of the State, and States were created by individuals under their right to self-determination, it necessarily follows that, de facto, States possess a relative legal capacity toward their constituencies. Likewise, NGO – and also IGO - officials are obliged to act in strict conformity with the objectives of the organizations established in their statutes and can be overthrown by the members if they do not behave accordingly.

Hence, supported in qualified worldwide legal doctrine, we can affirm that individuals possess international legal personality[43] and, consequently, are capable of creating legal entities to represent them in the realm of international law.

This assertion will most certainly be criticized based on certain long-established positivist legal doctrine. But the strength of the criticism is also its weakness. When such theories of international legal personality were laid down, several factors were not yet interacting in the international sphere. International Human Rights Law, for example, did not exist. Would it be possible to conceive of a theory in which States would only be bound when they chose to be, as supported by positivist scholars, if International Human Rights Law were before their eyes? We do not believe so. Moreover, could legal doctrine construe a theory of sovereignty in which the State would be empowered to do whatever it wanted within its boundaries if International Environmental Law existed? We can hardly agree. Presenting a concluding remark: would it make sense to submit for trial or appreciate claims brought by an object of law in an International Court?

If not, then why do some contemporary authors insist in the positivist theory in which only States have original legal personality and any other non-state actors are objects, or, slightly better, have a derived, functional and relative legal personality?

In our opinion, it is because the theory was construed upon some *functions* performed by the States on behalf of the represented nations, but that were regarded as States' fundamental rights. As pointed out by Shaw, 'the fundamental rights of States exist by virtue of the international legal order, which is able, as in the case of other legal orders, to define the characteristics of its subjects'.[44] He further summarizes these rights as being independence, legal equality and peaceful co-existence. To those rights, we can add the right to engage in relationships with other States, to declare war and make peace, and to submit claims before international tribunals.

If the fundamental rights of States exist by virtue of the international legal order, the fundamental rights of human beings are positioned *above* and *beyond* any legal order and, once they are inserted into positive law, all legal order tends to be rebuilt accordingly to the their exigencies.[45]

Therefore, considering that human rights are naturally inherent to people and are at the core of the Social Contract theories that legitimate the power granted to the State, their expansion into the realm of international law necessarily drives adjustments in international law theory, especially in the aspects concerning the recognition of international legal personality.[46]

This shift is noticeable and has been addressed in the previous chapters. Firstly, through the recognition that the public sphere is no longer equal to, but wider than, the governmental sphere and that peoples have the right to be heard at the UN – 'We, the peoples of the United Nations...' To allow the exercise of this right in an organized manner, other legal entities representing those peoples were legitimized for consultancy: the NGOs. As we have seen, these consultative rights expanded throughout the entire UN system and now permeate all its bureaucratic bodies and decision-making structures, whether permanent or not, as is the case of the conferences. Human rights – hence, people - have been placed at the center of judicial decisions,[47] and individuals have become capable of being prosecuted by international criminal courts, as well as entitled to bring claims against States at the regional level if their fundamental rights have been impaired or threatened by States, a postulating capacity extended also to NGOs, which, in turn, are continuously interacting with tribunals through *amicus* briefs. Court decisions, despite not mentioning it explicitly, are often ruling in strict accordance to general principles of law laid down in Natural Law, which are inherently linked to the rights of the people. Finally, civil society organizations are performing executive tasks in humanitarian and environmental affairs, together with States and IGOs, a fact that cannot be regarded as a mere coincidence, because all three of these legal structures represent, in different manners and scopes, the interests of people, which, in humanitarian and environmental issues, are not restricted to the territorial boundaries of the States.

The evidence addressed in the previous chapters has led us to conclude that individuals have international legal personality, although the effectiveness of the inherent rights of such a legal personality depends on the collective representation of individuals through legal structures defined under international law, which exercise, on their behalf, several activities defined therein. Hence, the fundamental rights of the States have to be reinterpreted as the fundamental rights of the nations they represent. This can be noted, for instance, in the parallelism between the State's rights under the Draft Declaration on Rights and Duties of States[48] prepared by the International Law Commission and those peoples' rights enshrined in the International Covenant of Civil and Political Rights,[49] which are compared below.

Declaration on Rights and Duties of States	*Covenant of Civil and Political Rights*
Every State has the right to independence and hence to exercise freely, without dictation by any other State, all its legal powers, including the choice of its own form of government. Every State has the right to exercise jurisdiction over its territory and over all persons and things therein, subject to the immunities recognized by international law.	All peoples have the right of self-determination. By virtue of that right they freely determine their political status and freely pursue their economic, social and cultural development. All peoples may, for their own ends, freely dispose of their natural wealth and resources without prejudice to any obligations arising out of international economic co-operation, based upon the principle of mutual benefit, and international law. Every citizen shall have the right and the opportunity, without any distinctions and without unreasonable restrictions to take part in the conduct of public affairs, directly or through freely chosen representatives.
Every State has the duty to refrain from intervention in the internal or external affairs of any other State.	All peoples have the right of self-determination. By virtue of that right they freely determine their political status and freely pursue their economic, social and cultural development.
Every State has the duty to refrain from fomenting civil strife in the territory of another State, and to prevent the organization within its territory of activities calculated to foment such civil strife.	Any propaganda for war shall be prohibited by law. Any advocacy of national, racial or religious hatred that constitutes incitement to discrimination, hostility or violence shall be prohibited by law.
Every State has the right to equality in law with every other State.	All persons shall be equal before the courts and tribunals. Everyone shall have the right to recognition everywhere as a person before the law.
Every State has the duty to treat all persons under its jurisdiction with respect for human rights and fundamental freedoms, without distinction as to race, sex, language, or religion.	All persons are equal before the law and are entitled without any discrimination to the equal protection of the law. In this respect, the law shall prohibit any discrimination and guarantee to all persons equal and effective protection against discrimination on any ground such as race, colour, sex, language, religion, political or other opinion, national or social origin, property, birth or other status.

Declaration on Rights and Duties of States	Covenant of Civil and Political Rights
Every State has the duty to ensure that conditions prevailing in its territory do not menace international peace and order. Every State has the duty to refrain from resorting to war as an instrument of national policy, and to refrain from the threat or use of force against the territorial integrity or political independence of another State, or in any other manner inconsistent with international law and order. Every State has the duty to refrain from giving assistance to any State which is acting in violation of article 9, or against which the United Nations is taking preventive or enforcement action.	Any propaganda for war shall be prohibited by law. Any advocacy of national, racial or religious hatred that constitutes incitement to discrimination, hostility or violence shall be prohibited by law. Everyone shall have the right to freedom of association with others, including the right to form and join trade unions for the protection of his interests. No restrictions may be placed on the exercise of this right other than those which are prescribed by law and which are necessary in a democratic society in the interests of national security or public safety, public order (ordre public), the protection of public health or morals or the protection of the rights and freedoms of others.
Every State has the duty to settle its disputes with other States by peaceful means in such a manner that international peace and security, and justice, are not endangered.	Everyone has the right to liberty and security of person. No one shall be subjected to arbitrary arrest or detention. No one shall be deprived of his liberty except on such grounds and in accordance with such procedure as are established by law. All persons shall be equal before the courts and tribunals. In the determination of any criminal charge against him, or of his rights and obligations in a suit at law, everyone shall be entitled to a fair and public hearing by a competent, independent and impartial tribunal established by law. No one shall be imprisoned merely on the ground of inability to fulfil a contractual obligation.
Every State has the duty to refrain from recognizing any territorial acquisition by another State acting in violation of article 9.	All peoples have the right of self-determination. By virtue of that right they freely determine their political status and freely pursue their economic, social and cultural development.
Every State has the right of individual or collective self-defence against armed attack.	Every human being has the inherent right to life. This right shall be protected by law. No one shall be arbitrarily deprived of his life.

Declaration on Rights and Duties of States	Covenant of Civil and Political Rights
Every State has the duty to carry out in good faith its obligations arising from treaties and other sources of international law, and it may not invoke provisions in its constitution or its laws as an excuse for failure to perform this duty.	Where not already provided for by existing legislative or other measures, each State Party to the present Covenant undertakes to take the necessary steps, in accordance with its constitutional processes and with the provisions of the present Covenant, to adopt such laws or other measures as may be necessary to give effect to the rights recognized in the present Covenant.

Therefore, if States continue to play the role of main *Actors* in international relations and also the main subjects of international law – and we are not disputing that – they do so as representatives of the *Authors*, the individuals, men and women of the several nations. This Hobbesian-like conception, for instance, was acknowledged by Nijman that supported that individuals possessed a primary international legal personality and that States possessed a secondary one.[50]

But individuals, having retained those rights granted by Natural Law that cannot be derogated by their representatives, the States, also regard, as legitimate, the expression of their opinions, concerns and needs through another kind of organization, the NGOs, which do not limit themselves to the puzzle-like physical division of the planet, seeing any fictional territorial boundaries established by States as irrelevant. NGOs and States cannot be regarded as representatives of individuals in the same dimension because States exercise their representative role circumscribed to a physical dimension, while NGOs perform it based on a thematic one. It follows that, if States are legitimated to represent *all* concerns of people *within* a territorial boundary, NGOs can be legitimate representatives of *specific* concerns of people *without* territorial limitations.

The path that leads to the recognition of the international legal personality of NGOs has been solidly paved by the States' acknowledgement that thematic organizations could better address common concerns of the several nations of the world, which could not be satisfactorily managed on a national basis. When States assumed that they could not deal alone with those issues, and for that purpose, established hundreds of thematic intergovernmental organizations, either at the regional or international levels, they implicitly recognized that territorial boundaries could hinder, perhaps even threaten, the satisfaction of their peoples' rights and aspirations and that they *had to* cooperate. But, how could States cooperate in a world where international legal theory is based on the axiom *cujus regio, ejus religio?*

Once the context changes, the balance of duties and rights has to follow suit. Again, we are not postulating that the State is not the most important subject of international law. It is and will continue to be. Rather, we postulate that individuals possess a primary international legal personality, which is primordially exercised by the States as representatives of their nations, the States therefore having, in regard to the nations they represent, a *derived* and *functional* legal capacity under international law. Accordingly, in order to make the system work properly to pursue the satisfaction of the aspirations of the peoples and the protection of their rights, the States are entitled to exercise, on behalf of the nations they represent, some rights at the international level, which are counterbalanced by duties before other peoples, represented by other States, and their own people. For that reason, States are bound in a twofold manner to people: to their own, through mechanisms of accountability and transparency democratically established, and to other States' people, through the respect of the covenants established with their representatives, the other States, and of *jus cogens*, in a kind of direct relationship with every human being.

Given that States are the main representatives of people at the international level, they can engage themselves in agreements with other States to address some issues coordinately, through intergovernmental organizations. But, once States assumed that territorial boundaries were limitations that had to be discarded, that the interests at stake were uniformly affecting all nations in the globe, or, at least, at the regional level, and that to satisfy those interests they had to cooperate, the sacrosanct statehood trinity, which according to the positivists was the source of the State's international legal personality, suffered an impact.

As we have mentioned, just a couple of years after the creation of the UN, the ICJ recognized that the newborn entity possessed international legal personality, though noting that 'the subjects of law in any legal system are not necessarily identical in their nature or in the extent of their rights, and their nature depends upon the needs of the community.' [51] In this case, the UN General Assembly had requested the Court's advisory opinion on whether the UN possessed the capacity to bring claims against States under international law. The Court understood that, given the fact that the expression 'international legal personality' sometimes gave rise to controversy, the Court would adopt it to refer to an entity with the capacity to maintain its rights by bringing international claims.

This very aspect, the capacity to present claims before international courts, has been considered by some scholars as a justification for denying international legal personality to individuals and, consequently, to NGOs, on the grounds that they lacked such power.[52] We must regard this aspect with caution. Verzijl, one of the supporters of the theory, argued that the 'true test' of legal personality would seem to be not whether an individual or legal entity possessed rights under a given legal order, but whether they were in position to pursue or enforce them within that order.[53] Hence, according to him, if an individual was not entitled to pursue a right, it would not be a subject of law. Lauterpacht, on the contrary, sustained that one could not exaggerate the importance of such a procedural rule, because a person may be in possession of a plenitude of rights without at the same time being able to enforce them in his own name.[54] Rosenne adopts the same rationale, considering misleading the traditional international law inclination to classify the individual as anything but a subject of international law because it confused the ability of the individual to act on international plane.[55] Cançado Trindade also asserts that 'justiciability' of a right cannot be erected as a *conditio sine qua non* of its existence and recognition.[56]

As the ICJ ruled in the *Reparation for injuries* case, in any legal system, the subjects of law do not necessarily have the same rights. It is often common to have an unbalance between the capacity of being a defendant and a plaintiff in national legal systems. This can also be verified in international law. As we have seen in Chapter 3, individuals can stand as defendants in international criminal tribunals, but they are not allowed to bring a claim against States in the same Courts, a task that is performed solely by the Prosecutor. However, they are entitled to bring claims against States to the European Court of Justice and to the European Court of Human Rights, and also to quasi-judicial bodies such as the Inter-American Commission on Human Rights. Likewise, NGOs have identical rights before the same *fora*. Thus, arguably the procedural convention precluding individuals and NGOs to bring a claim in international courts was somewhat tempered,[57] being such movement one of the most remarkable developments in contemporary international law.[58] We understand that the lack of capacity to stand before the International Court of Justice, either as a defendant or a plaintiff, does not impair the recognition of the international legal personality of individuals.[59] On the *Avena* and *LaGrand* cases, for instance, the ICJ understood that individuals possessed rights – thus, were subjects of law - which, in those particular cases, were pursued with the intervention of the States.[60] One cannot challenge the position of the individual as a subject of international law by supporting the claim on the failure to distinguish between the entitlement to rights and the capacity to enforce them. The fact that the beneficiary is incapable of taking independent steps in his own name to enforce his rights does not mean that he is not a subject of law.[61] In any case, given that individuals and NGOs have access to certain international tribunals to challenge the States, then, we could also support that they have passed Verzijl's 'true test'.

Some authors also argue that international legal personality cannot be recognized to individuals or NGOs on grounds that they cannot enter into international agreements with States. We have not found evidence that this has ever happened between individuals and States, but we will not make the same mistake incurred by Verzijl in regard to self-determination, by affirming that it is substantively impossible for it to happen in the future, specially bearing in mind the wealth of some individuals and the small dimensions of some States. However, as we have pointed out in Chapter 2, there are several types of *soft law* agreements entered into by States and NGOs, and also some *hard law* ones such as the Headquarter Agreement signed between the ICRC and Switzerland in 1993, which extended to this private organization the same treatment, including immunity of correspondence and personnel, which is granted to intergovernmental organizations.[62]

The appraisal of the situation of individuals and NGOs in treaties, customary practices, Court decisions and general principles of law vehemently suggests that it is not possible to continue supporting the theory that States are the only subjects of international law. So, borrowing from a lapidary statement coined by Rosalyn Higgins, we may ask: Why have we erected an intellectual prison of our own choosing and then declared it to be an unalterable constraint? [63]

To which we can respond: Because we have forgotten that international law is deeply imbedded in Natural Law. This amnesia can be attributed to the efficient work carried out by positivist scholars in divulging their theory that States were only bound by their covenants, which has gained apparent strength due to the exponential growth of written international law, i.e., treaties and conventions, since then.[64]

The theory began to collapse when the major multilateral treaty – the UN Charter – accepted the admittance of civil society organizations at some of the Club's events, recognizing, also, that an immense group of objects, individuals, possessed the right (!!) to self-determination, and moreover, that the organization and its members had to 'achieve international co-operation in solving international problems of an economic, social, cultural, or humanitarian character, and in promoting and encouraging respect for human rights and for fundamental freedoms for all without distinction as to race, sex, language, or religion'.[65] Later on, each treaty ensuring respect to human rights, civil society participation in decision-making processes or *locus standi* before tribunals, as well as each Court decision accepting *amicus* briefs, by the same token helped to define a way out of that prison, removing another brick in the wall.[66]

Given that both International Law and Human Rights Law share the same roots in Natural Law, one can expect that they are capable of producing similar offspring .i.e., the recognition that the human being is at the core of the legal system and that every theoretical construction thereafter considers the individual as its original source of legitimacy. It follows that the definition of the role of States, Intergovernmental Organizations and NGOs at the international level necessarily requires the appraisal of their legitimacy, a task that we will perform in the forthcoming chapters.

However, before concluding this chapter, we deem it appropriate to appraise the situation of individuals and international NGOs before the last subsidiary source of international law, the teachings of the most highly qualified publicists of the various nations. For that purpose, we have decided to focus on the work of major organized law doctrine bodies, having selected three of them - the International Law Commission, the Institut de Droit International and the International Law Association - whose seriousness, membership, and reputation unequivocally fulfill the scope of Article 38(1)(d) of the Statute of the ICJ.[67]

6.2   Organized Law doctrine bodies

6.2.1   The International Law Commission

The International Law Commission (ILC) was established by the UN in 1948, therefore being a public international body, which differentiates it from the two other organized law doctrine bodies, incorporated under private law. Its members have originated from various segments of the international legal community, such as academia, the diplomatic corps, government ministries and international organizations, in order to reflect a broad spectrum of expertise and practical experience within the field of international law.

According to Article 1(1) of its Statute, the ILC 'shall have for its object the promotion of the progressive development of international law and its codification'. Article 15 makes a distinction between progressive development, defined as meaning 'the preparation of draft conventions on subjects which have not yet been regulated by international law or in regard to which the law has not yet been sufficiently developed in the practice of States' and codification, defined as meaning 'the more precise formulation and systematization of rules of international law in fields where there already has been extensive State practice, precedent and doctrine'.[68]

The ILC has concerned itself primarily with public international law, but it is not precluded from entering the fields of private international law and international criminal law. In the latter case, the ILC appraised the formulation of the Nuremberg principles and the consideration of the question of international criminal jurisdiction back in 1949, a work that culminated in the completion of the draft Statute for an International Criminal Court in 1994, and the draft Code of Crimes against the Peace and Security of Mankind in 1996. For that reason, we can regard that the ILC has worked towards the international legal personality of individuals, by defining that they would have *locus standi*, as defendants, in international criminal tribunals.

Apart from the appraisal of individuals as subjects of international criminal law, we have not identified further studies of the ILC on the international legal personality of civil society organizations or any other non-state actors.

6.2.2 The International Law Association

The International Law Association (ILA) is a private institution founded in 1873 in Belgium, and currently headquartered in London. The objectives of the ILA are the study, clarification and development of international law, both public and private, and the furtherance of international understanding and respect for international law.[69] Currently the organization congregates nearly 3,700 practitioners of international law in 45 countries covering the major legal systems of the world.[70]   The ILA operates through International Committees, established to undertake research and to prepare reports on areas of international law (public, private or commercial), which are discussed and considered by the membership and other interested parties at the biennial conferences. The reports take various forms: a re-statement of the law; a draft treaty or convention; an elaboration of a code or rules or principles of international law; or a review of recent developments of law or practice.

In September 2007, the ILA established a Committee for the study of the rights and obligations of non-state actors under international law with the purpose to 'contribute to the larger academic debate on non-state actors under international law as well as the identification of the legal problems in the relationship between states and non-state actors as well as international governmental organizations and non-state actors at the international level'.[71] At the ILA Conference, held in The Hague in 2010, the Committee presented a 24 page report of its activities, in which it set the methodology, scope, aims and working definitions of the study, as well as three themes considered more relevant for mapping rights and obligations related to non-state actors activities: (1) norm creation (treaty, customary, general principles and 'soft'), (2) monitoring compliance (administration), and (3) enforcement (dispute settlement, accountability/responsibility and immunity).

The report is not conclusive, but has shown some evidences that non-state actors, including NGOs, have limited formal roles in international norm-creation, being also involved in international law-monitoring in specific international regimes (human rights and environmental in particular). It found that, although having some participatory rights in international dispute settlement mechanisms, non-state actors generally do not incur direct responsibility for transgressions of international law, and are not entitled to immunity. More important, the research found that 'there is a need for clarity to improve understanding of the appropriate roles of all actors, State and non-State, active in the international legal plane and to improve their responsibility/accountability to the international community as a whole. Arguably, clarifying the legal status of diverse NSAs and giving a voice to new participants should enrich and increase the legitimacy of international legal processes and improve the chances of wider compliance with international norms.'[72]

6.2.3   The Institut de Droit International

The Institute de Droit International (IDI) is a private institution with scientific aims founded on 8 September 1873 in Belgium, whose purpose is to 'promote the progress of international law',[73] which congregates prominent jurisconsults in international laws from the major legal systems of the world.[74] According to its practices, the associates and members of the IDI meet every two years, when they can adopt Resolutions of a 'normative character', which are brought to the attention of governmental authorities, international organizations as well as the scientific community, aiming to highlight the characteristics of the *lex lata* in order to promote its respect. Sometimes the IDI makes determinations *de lege ferenda* in order to contribute to the development of international law.[75]

In 1923, the IDI prepared a draft convention regarding the legal status of international associations. It did not declare the legal personality of those entities under public international laws, even though it referred to them as 'international'. Rather, it defined such entities as those associations established under private law that, while accepting membership from several countries, had the purpose to pursue non-profit aims with an international interest.[76] According to the draft convention, the statutes of the organizations had to be submitted to a Commission created by the convention and headquartered in Brussels, composed of diplomatic representatives of the States parties to the convention, which would have the support of a Secretariat. Once the statute was duly fulfilled, the entity would be granted the condition of having the same rights as those ensured to national associations by the State parties where it had operations, which included, at least, the right to have assets, to engage into contracts, standing before tribunals and similar fiscal benefits. The entities would also have the obligation to annually submit their financial statements to the Secretariat.

Since the first attempt did not produce any echo under the auspices of the League of Nations, in 1950, the IDI returned to the subject, having prepared a draft convention with a content very similar to the previous one, this time attributing the status not only to associations but also to private foundations. Again, the convention did not provide international legal personality to the concerned bodies and, in a certain way, proposed a step backwards in the truly international scope of its proposal, by abandoning the idea of the Commission composed of representatives of the States' parties, which was replaced by a registration procedure defined by each State party.

One can observe some similarities between the proposals of these two drafts and the Strasbourg Convention, adopted by the Council of Europe in

1996, formerly addressed in this work. However, all these documents have missed the exact same point: they refrain from clearly recognizing the international legal personality of NGOs, despite naming them international. Despite the aspects analyzed in the first part of this chapter, there is strong evidence that NGOs possess international legal personality, an issue that we will address in the conclusion of this work. But first, we shall focus our analysis on the legitimacy of other legal structures that have been conceived to represent the individuals in the realm of public international law.

Notes

1　Rosenau, for instance, rejects the expression 'non-state actor' as it 'creates a residual category for all collectivities other than States, implying that they occupy subordinate statuses in the rankings of post-international politics'. See JN Rosenau, *Turbulence in World Politics: a Theory of Change and Continuity* (Princeton University Press, Princeton 1990) 36.

2　Black's Law Dictionary (6th edn West Publishing, St Paul's 1990) 1407.

3　N Bobbio, N Matteucci and G Pasquino, *Dicionário de Política* (UnB, Brasilia 2004) 425.

4　This was observed, for instance, in the Berlin Congress (1885) that divided the territory of Africa between the European powers regardless of their occupation or even exploration!

5　See the *Serbian Loans* case PCIJ Rep Series A No 14.

6　JHW Verzijl, *International Law in Historical Perspective* (Sijhoff, Leiden 1968) v 2, 1.

7　See, in this regard, J Combacau and S Sur, *Droit International Public* (7th edn Montchristien, Paris 2006) 313; and P Malanczuk, *Akerhurst's Modern Introduction to International Law* (7th edn, Routledge, New York, 1997) 91.

8　LC Chen, *An Introduction to Contemporary International Law* (2nd edn, Yale University Press, New Haven 2000) 79. Rosalyn Higgins also supports the shift of subjects/objects to participants. See R Higgins, *Problems and Process: International Law and How We Use It*, (OUP, Oxford 1994) 40.

9　*Montevideo Convention on Rights and Duties of States* (adopted 26 December 1933, entered into force 26 December 1934).

10　For an appraisal of the Brazilian State practice in international law addressing, among other subjects, the conditions for statehood, see AA Cançado Trindade, *Repertorio da Prática Brasileira do Direito Internacional Publico* (Fundação Alexandre de Gusmão, Brasilia, 1988).

11　*North Sea Continental Shelf* cases [1969] ICJ Rep 32.

12　MN Shaw, *International Law* (5th edn CUP, Cambridge 2003) 178.

13　UNGA Res 2625(XXV).

14　*Western Sahara* (Advisory Opinion) [1975] ICJ Rep 25.

15　*Western Sahara* (Advisory Opinion) [1975] ICJ Rep 39.

16　*Western Sahara* (Advisory Opinion) [1975] ICJ Rep 63.

17　There have been attempts to define a 'nation' by establishing objectives criterion such as common language, cultural heritage, race, religion, interests and territory, or the presence of a historical association of destiny. However, we could not find a widely accepted definition. See, in this particular aspect, 'International Meeting of Experts on Further Study of the Concept of the Right of People' (UNESCO, Paris 27-30 November 1989) UNESCO Doc SHS-89/CONF.602/7, and HJ Roethoff, 'The

Republic of South Moluccas: an existing state', in *Symbolae Verzijl* (Nijhoff, The Hague 1958) 295-313.

18 R Jennings and A Watts (eds), *Oppenheim's International Law* v 1 (9th edn Longman, London, 1996) 16; I Brownlie, *Principles of Public International Law* (7th edn OUP, Oxford 2008) 57; J Crawford, *The Creation of States in International Law* (Clarendon Press, Oxford 1979) 25.

19 Although the apparent consensus on the conditions for statehood, the Dayton Agreements, a set of international treaties that ended the Balkan's war in 1995, made references not only to recognized States (Yugoslavia, Croatia and Bosnia and Herzegovina) but also to the Republic of Srpska, constituted by the Bosnian-Serb insurgents that were controlling part of the territory and population of Bosnia and Herzegovina, which were represented by the President of Serbia. The recognition of international legal personality to insurgents to allow them to conclude a treaty renouncing to their claim of secession certainly poses different challenges to the concept of statehood. See, in this aspect, P Gaeta, 'The Dayton Agreements and International Law' (1996) EJIL v 7, 147.

20 MN Shaw, *International Law* (n 12) 178.

21 R. Higgins, *Problems and Process* (n 8) 41 *(emphasis added)*.

22 D Anzilotti, *Cours de Droit International* (Recueil Sirey, Paris 1929) 134; G Schwarzenberger, *International Law: as applied by International Courts and Tribunals* (3rd edn London 1957) v 1 140-155; C Rousseau, *Droit International Public* (Sirey, Paris, 1974) v II, 696.

23 H Lauterpacht, *International Law: Collected Papers* (CUP, Cambridge 1975) 489; R Higgins, *Problems and Process* (n 8) 49. See also F Vitoria, *De Indis et de Jure Belli* and Chapter 2 of this essay.

24 *Reparation for Injuries Suffered in the Service of the United Nations* (Advisory Opinion) [1949] ICJ Rep 174.

25 R McCorquodale, 'The individual and the International Legal System', in MD Evans, *International Law* (2nd edn, OUP, Oxford 2006) 309.

26 MN Shaw, *International Law* (n 12) 243.

27 *Convention on Wetlands of International Importance especially as Waterfowl Habitat* (adopted 2 February 1971, entered into force 21 December 1975) UNTS 14583. Further amended by the Paris Protocol, 3 December 1982, and Regina Amendments, 28 May 1987.

28 *Rome Statute of the International Criminal Court* - for responsibilities, article 25; for rights, articles 22, 23, 24, as well as procedural rules. *Statute of the International Criminal Tribunal for the Former Yugoslavia* - for responsibilities, articles 6 and 7; for rights, article 10, as well as procedural rules. *Statute of the International Criminal Tribunal for Rwanda* - for responsibilities, articles 5 and 6; for rights, article 9, as well as procedural rules.

29 Encyclopedie Juridique – Repertóire de Droit International (Dalloz, Paris 1968) 499.

30 *Reparation for Injuries Suffered in the Service of the United Nations* (Advisory Opinion) [1949] ICJ Rep 179.

31 P Daillier and A Pellet, *Droit international public* (7th ed LGDJ, Paris 2002) 646.

32 *Advisory Opinion on the Legal Status of Human Rights of the Child* (Advisory Opinion) (2004) International Human Rights Reports n 11, 510 (Concurring Opinion of Judge Cançado Trindade) para 26-27.

33 PM Dupuy support that international law is non longer defined by reference to States but also through consideration of the content of the international norm that, as acknowledged by Lauterpacht, are 'in the final instance structured towards the realization of respect for the rights and interests of human beings'. PM Dupuy, 'Some

Reflections on Contemporary International Law and the Appeal to Universal Values: A Response to Martii Koskenniemi' (2005) EJIL v 16 n 1, 131.

34 G Scelle 'Obsession du Territoire', in *Symbolae Verzijl* (Nijhoff, The Hague 1958) 347-361.

35 M Weber, *Politics as a Vocation* (1919). See, also, B Spinoza, *Theological-Political Treatise* (CUP, Cambridge 2007) Chapter 20 [6].

36 H Arendt, *The Human Condition* (2nd edn, UCP, Chicago 1998)

37 See, e.g, O Hintze, 'The State in Historical Perspective' in R Bendix (ed) *State and Society: a Reader in Comparative Political Sociology* (2nd ed UC Press, Berkeley 1973); M Weber, 'Bureaucracy and Political Leadership', in R Bendix (ed) *State and Society: a Reader in Comparative Political Sociology* (2nd ed UC Press, Berkeley 1973); M Weber, *Economy and Society* (UC Press, Berkeley, 1978); M Garcia-Pelayo, *Burocracia y tecnocracia y otros escritos.* (Alianza, Madrid 1984).

38 I Brownlie, *Principles of Public International Law* (n 18) 62.

39 R. Higgins, *Problems and Process* (n 8) 40.

40 MS McDougal and WM Reisman, *International Law Essays: a Supplement to International Law in Contemporary Perspective* (Foundation Press, New York 1981) 201.

41 CC Weeramantry, *Universalizing International Law* (Nijhoff, Leiden 2004) 171.

42 A D'Amato, *International Law: Process and Prospect* (Transnational, Irvington 1995) 204.

43 George Scelle, for instance, regarded international law as the legal order of the community of peoples or the universal society of men, in which the individual was the primary subject of law. G Scelle, *Précis de Droit de Gents* (Recueil Sirey, Paris 1932). See, in addition to the already mentioned authors supporting our claim, H Lauterpacht, *International Law and Human Rights* (Steven & Sons, London 1950) 72; DP O'Connell *International Law* (2nd edn, Stevens and Sons, London 1970) v 1 116; A Cassese, *International Law* (2nd edn OUP, Oxford 2005) 217; IA Shearer, *Starke's International Law* (11th edn, Butterworths, London 1994) 61; DK Anton, P Mathew and W Morean, *International Law* (OUP, Oxford, 2005) 131; CA Norgaard, *The Position of the Individual in International Law* (Munksgaard, Copenhagen 1962); G von Glahn, *Law among Nations* (4th edn, MacMillan, New York, 1981) 185; S Oda, 'The Individual in International Law', in M Sorensen, *Manual of Public International Law* (MacMillan, New York 1968) 47; N Mugerwa, 'Subjects of International Law', in M Sorensen, *Manual of Public International Law* (MacMillan, New York 1968) 266; GFS Soares, *Curso de Direito Internacional Público* (1st edn Atlas, São Paulo 2002) 158; CD Albuquerque Mello, *Curso de Direito Internacional Publico* (8th edn, Freitas Bastos, Rio de Janeiro 1986) 569.

44 MN Shaw, *International Law* (n 12) 178. In the same sense, Combacau affirmed that 'le statut legal d'une catégorie d'être est la qualité que leur est attribuée ou reconnue par le droit objectif avant qu'il ne définisse leur condition, c'ést-à-dire le 'regime legal (droits, obligations et puvoirs) que les caractérise'. J Combacau and S Sur, *Droit International Public* (n 7) 309.

45 O de Frouville, *L'intangibilité des droits de l'homme en droit international* (Pedone, Paris, 2004).

46 T Meron, *The Humanization of International Law* (Nijhoff, The Hague 2006); A Pronto 'Human-Rightism' and the development of General International Law (2007) LJIL 20, 753; PM Dupuy, *Droit International Publique* (6th edn Dalloz, Paris) 26; G von Glahn, *Law among Nations* (4th edn MacMillan, New York 1981) 185.

47 R Higgins, 'Human Rights in the International Court of Justice', (2007) LJIL, v 20, 746.

48 ILC, *Draft Declaration on Rights and Duties of States* [1949] Yearbook of the International Law Commission. UNGA Res 375 (IV) (6 December 1949).

49 (adopted 16 December 1966, entered into force 23 March 1976) UNTS 999.

50 JA Nijman, *The Concept of International Legal Personality* (TCM Asser Press, The Hague 2004) 473.

51 *Reparation for Injuries Suffered in the Service of the United Nations* (Advisory Opinion) [1949] ICJ Rep 178.

52 JW Verzijl, *International Law in Historical Perspective* (Sijhoff, Leiden 1968) v 1, 3; P Daillier and A Pellet, *Droit international public* (n 31) 651.

53 JHW Verzijl, *International Law* (n 6) v 1, 5.

54 H Lauterpacht, *International Law: Collected Papers* (CUP, Cambridge 1975) v 1, 286.

55 S Rosenne, *The perplexities of modern international law* (Nijhoff, Leiden 2004) 267.

56 AA Cançado Trindade, paper for the Global Consultation on the Right of Development as a Human Right (United Nations, New York, 1991) UN Doc HR/RD/1990/CONF.36, 8.

57 IA Shearer, *Starke's International Law* (11th edn, Butterworths, London 1994) 61.

58 S Oda, 'The Individual in International Law', in M Sorensen, *Manual of Public International Law* (MacMillan, New York 1968) 471.

59 See, in this aspect, H Lauterpacht, *International Law and Human Rights* (n 43) 27; J Combacau and S Sur, *Droit International Public* (n 7) 319.

60 In the same line, the PCIJ stated that 'the capacity to possess civil rights does not necessarily imply the capacity to exercise those rights oneself'. The rather obvious conclusion is that the capacity to enforce rights is different than the capacity to bear them. Appeal from a Judgment of the Hungaro/Czecoslovak Mixed Arbitral Tribunal (The Peter Pázmány University) PCIJ Rep Series A/B nr 61, 231.

61 N Mugerwa, 'Subjects of International Law', in M Sorensen, *Manual of Public International Law* (MacMillan, New York 1968) 266.

62 The full text of the agreement is available at <http://icrc.org/Web/eng/siteengo.nsf/html/57JNX7> accessed 4 May 2009.

63 R. Higgins, *Problems and Process* (n 8) 49.

64 For a recognition of Natural Law as a formal source of international Law and for a criticism to positivist emphasis on treaty Law, see, GG Fitzmaurice, 'Some Problems Regarding the Formal Surces of International Law', in *Symbolae Verzijl* (Nijhoff, The Hague, 1958) 153-176.

65 *UN Charter*, article 1

66 Even today, confronted with so many evidences, some authors support contorting arguments to deny the obvious situation that objects cannot posses rights and, hence, that the purportedly objects are, in fact, subjects of law. See, for example, Cassese, that wrote that 'in sum, in contemporary international law, individual possess *international legal status*, [although] it implies in a *lopsided position in international community*. As far as their obligations are concerned, they are associated with all members of that community, in contrast, they do not possess rights in relation to all members, they have a *limited legal capacity.*' A Cassese, *International Law* (2nd edn OUP, Oxford 2005) 150.

67 For an interesting appraisal of the contribution of state's legal advisers, see UN, *Collection of Essays by Legal Advisers of States, Legal Advisers of Intergovernmental Organizations and Practitioners in the field of International Law* (UN, New York 1999).

68 *Statute of the International Law Commission.* UN GA Res 174(II) (21 November 1947).

69 Constitution of the Association (adopted August 2004) Article 3.1.

70 For membership, see <http://www.ila-hq.org/en/branches/index.cfm> accessed 18 May 2009.

71 ILA document named Preliminary Work Plan September 2007, available at <http://www.ila-hq.org/en/committees/index.cfm/cid/1023> accessed 21 May 2009.

72 ILA document named 'First Report of the Committee Non-State Actors in International Law: aims, approach and scope of project and legal issues' available at <http://www.ila-hq.org/en/committees/index.cfm/cid/1023> accessed 20 June 2012.

73 According to its Statute, the Institute will do so: a) by striving to formulate the general principles of the subject, in such a way as to correspond to the legal conscience of the civilized world; b) by lending its co-operation in any serious endeavour for the gradual and progressive codification of international law; c) by seeking official endorsement of the principles recognized as in harmony with the needs of modern societies; d) by contributing, within the limits of its competence, either to the maintenance of peace, or to the observance of the laws of war; e) by studying the difficulties which may arise in the interpretation or application of the law, and where necessary issuing reasoned legal opinions in doubtful or controversial cases; and f) by affording its co-operation, through publications, public teaching and all other means, in ensuring that those principles of justice and humanity which should govern the mutual relations of peoples shall prevail.

74 For an appraisal of the membership, see <http://www.idi-iil.org/idiE/navig_members.html> accessed 18 May 2009.

75 According to the entity's website <http://www.idi-iil.org/idiE/navig_history.html> accessed 18 May 2009.

76 *Projet de convention relative à la condition juridique des associations internationales* [1923] Brussels' Session.

CHAPTER 7

Legitimacy of States

7.1 The concept of Modern State; a contractual arrangement in evolution?

For international law, States are subjects of law. And, for that reason, they are entitled with several rights and possess some legal capacities. The Montevideo Convention on Rights and Duties of States defined a sovereign State as 'something' that has: (i) a permanent population, (ii) a defined territory, (iii) a government, and (iv) the authoritative power to enter into relations with other States.[1] The treaty, however, was not capable of defining *why* States exist, *how* they had been formed, *who* had formed them and *what* their purposes were.

In Chapter 1, we succinctly presented the ideas of some classic scholars about the nature of the State and the origins of international law that have tried to answer those questions. Their theories, in short, supported that men had inherent non-derogable rights arisen out of Natural Law and that, having an innate inclination to live peacefully and acknowledging their incapacity to protect their lives, liberties and estates in a state of nature, they established a covenant – the so-called Social Contract – for the creation of the State, which, possessing the arbitrary control over men and the monopoly of use of force, ensured those threatened rights. A State's legitimacy, thus, relied on a contract entered into by free individuals. As pointed out by Thomas Franck,

> 'The social contract and its canon embody the secular community's response to commonly perceived dangers of chaos, disorder, or other overweening threats to its security and material progress.'[2]

The Social Contract theory, which dominated legal thought during the 17th and 18th centuries, was further criticized by several authors, including Hegel. According to him, legitimacy relied on the reciprocal recognition of one human being with a stranger. At a macro level, this reciprocal recognition was manifested in shared state-centric institutions and law, i.e., on 'ethicality' or 'ethical life'. For Hegel, men were thinking individuals that could not be regarded as free if a State, external to human consciousness, had the power to control all men within a territory and possessed the monopoly of use of force. For him, any legal order based upon the idea of a social contract lacked legitimacy because it would neither be the sum of the wills of the people nor would it give birth to an organic legal order of a public character, rather to the institutionalization of the arbitrary wills of some individuals, as the Reign of Terror that followed the French Revolution had demonstrated. To avoid this, he argued, the objectiveness of the institutions and their laws had to be incorporated into the conscious-ness of the individual, thereby making the private realm public. [3]

Notwithstanding the sophistication of the legal reasoning of Hegel, his thought failed – in contemporary terms - to associate States with civiliza-tion by assuming that 'peoples of low level of culture' (*vulgas*) lived in a 'pre-legal age' and could not achieve statehood. For him, international law 'entitled civilized nations to treat as barbarians other nations which are less advanced', to conclude that 'the rights of these other nations are not equal to theirs and that their independence is merely formal.'[4] Such reasoning provided philosophical legitimacy for colonialist initiatives and for the con-formation of Eurocentric international law, which, even today, can be ob-served in article 38(1)(c) of the Statute of the ICJ, addressed in Chapter 5. Fortunately, such a differentiation between people is now outlawed in the international sphere.

Another aspect of his thought that deserves attention is the State. He considered the State 'an end in itself', which would have overwhelming power, as observed, for instance, in the arguments that individuals had to sacrifice their lives for the State and that nations do not deserve recognition and that history only begins when a nation is recognized as a State. His conception is hardly acceptable today, with, for instance, the emergence of fundamental human rights and the recognized *erga omnes* character of self-determination. In another dimension, the characteristics of a Hegelian State, as noticed throughout *The Philosophy of Right,* fit perfectly the cri-teria of the Montevideo Convention and, for that reason, we will not ex-pend more time on them. However, two other aspects of Hegel' State de-serve attention: firstly, his understanding that States were bound only by the agreements they entered into with other States, hence affiliating himself to the Positivist School; and, secondly, his particular appreciation for bu-reaucracy – the universal class, a structure that we will appraise in ensuing section of this essay.

It follows that, even though his appreciated bureaucracy flourished, rele-vant aspects of his theory have become outdated with the strengthening of the principles of self-determination and *jus cogens* and the emergence of human rights, which, in our understanding, represent a late rebirth of some aspects of Natural Law. By saying so, we are not supporting that Natural Law, as conceived centuries ago, is strictly applicable to the complex con-temporary world. This is not the case. However, it cannot go unnoticed that the development of international human rights law and international humanitarian law has, as precisely acknowledged by Rosalyn Higgins and discussed in Chapter 3, put the human being in the centre of the decisions made in the international legal system,[5] even justifying – albeit seriously disputed - foreign intervention in the internal affairs of sovereign States if gross violations to those rights are occurring. This represents notorious evidence of the superposition of the sovereignty of men over the sovereignty of States, of naturalism over positivism.

If men and women possess non-derogable rights under international law, they are necessarily subjects of international law, a condition that we appraised in the previous chapter. Objects of law cannot possess rights, even more non-derogable ones. It is illogical. But it would also be unreasonable to imagine that men and women, while having those rights, could exercise them directly at the international level. As we have said, and it is quite obvious, it would not work. Even worse, it would lead to the very negation of those same rights, because rights that cannot be protected under a legal framework may even exist but, in practice, can be regarded as non-existent. For that purpose, States, these abstract persons, were created, according to the natural law tradition that underpins the creation of international law. States, thus, are not an end in themselves, rather they are structures created by people to protect their lives, liberties and estates.[6]

Some of the criticism of the Enlightenment theories relied on the apparent naivety of the notion of 'men in the state of nature' whose existence could not be precisely defined in time and space. Of course, it was just a hypothetical situation to justify an actual proposal of legitimacy of statehood. In spite of this, it provided a good starting point, which, regrettably, can be noted today, in the so-called failed States. Let's take Somalia as an example. The overthrowing of the central government in 1991 and the subsequent humanitarian crisis motivated the envoy of twenty-five thousand US soldiers to the country at the end of 1992 with the purpose of supplying the hungry population with food and medicine. At that time, Somali territory was being disputed by at least fourteen different groups and food had become a valuable item for payment of loyalty and guns. The unexpected difficulties faced by the Americans led to the deployment of an UN-led force composed of troops from twenty-one countries to supply food and rebuild the Somali State. However, things did not work well even then and after an outstanding failure of US elite troops to capture a warlord, which culminated in the loss of two helicopters, the death of eighteen US soldiers and injuries in eighty more, the US and the UN abandoned the country in 1993. Today, almost two decades later, Somalia makes world news, due to the threat it poses to international navigation, caused by pirates acting in its territorial waters. Those individuals are subjects of international law under the Convention on the Law of the Seas.[7] However, could Somalia be regarded as a State for the sake of the Montevideo Convention and the mainstream understanding of statehood if it does not have a central government capable of controlling its territory and population? We hardly would say yes. In our understanding, the term 'failed State' is a euphemism for a 'non-existing State' and was coined because the community of States cannot accept the 'death' of one of its members and the consequent statehood lacunae in a given territory. But if no State exists in that territory and its people are struggling to live in a lawless environment amidst everyday disputes for food, water, lodging and security, they are experiencing a situation that substantially resembles the Enlightenment' state of nature.

States, hence, are necessary; but they are necessary to ensure that men and women can live their lives and enjoy their liberties and estates according to their innate inclination for peaceful co-existence in a society governed by rational rules. The so-called founders of international law – Vitoria, Grotius, Pufendorf, Wolf and Vattel – just to mention a few, conceived their theories with deep roots in natural law. If their theories were somewhat overshadowed by the teachings of Hegel and other positivists during the late 19th and in the first half of the 20th century, the latter have also been undermined by the emergence of human rights and the consolidation of liberal democracy as the generally pursued form of government. As noticed by Brierly, the positivist political philosophers failed to see that with the coming of democracy, a new theory of the nature of governing power was called for.[8]

States exist to ensure the well-being of people and, by performing this task, allow them to live their lives and pursue their happiness with their rights protected within a rational legal structure. To ensure that all rights are protected, as well as peaceful co-existence, the individuals have *delegated* to the State the monopoly of the use of physical violence, which is only legitimated if exercised in accordance to those rights. Once the State uses violence against those who it was supposed to protect without a pre-established rational reason, such use becomes illegitimate. The sovereignty of the human being – expressed by Human Rights – limits the sovereignty of States.

Given that men, in the words of Aristotle, are 'political animals', they necessarily live in society and, for that reason, have settled in determined territories where they could interact with one another. The development of different languages and patterns of behavior during immemorial generations of shared experiences has led to the formation of what would be known as nations. If the individuals created the States to protect them against themselves, the same abstract structure was legitimized to protect them against threats from other nations, following that the States became the representatives of their nations toward other nations in the realm that would be later called inter-*national*.

At the domestic level, States are, among other attributions, responsible for ensuring respect to private property, which, even in communist regimes, encompassed the right to possess determined properties for living or working. This micro-level occupation of territories, when exercised collectively by the individuals of a given nation, gave birth to one of the fundamental aspects of State sovereignty: the exclusive control of a determined territory and everything therein. If one individual leaves a territory to settle in another one and that move implies in a change of State, then, he will be submitted to another set of rules. Men are thinking beings and the pursuit of self-consciousness and the innate desire for freedom drives men toward self-governing. But, once self-governing may be restrained by others' self-governing initiatives, the State appeared as a solution to regulate it. Again, roughly speaking, the extrapolation of the individual micro-level towards the macro level, leads the State to the position of being the (self) government of the nation within that territory.

There is, hence, a marked parallelism between the way men behave at the micro-level and the attributions of the State at the international level. Men occupy space, interact with others, exercise self-defense and are self-conscious, with an innate desire for freedom; Statehood relies on people occupying a territory under a government capable of entering into relations with others, within a broad concept of sovereignty.[9] After all, as clearly stated by Lauterpacht, States are not *like* individuals, they are actually *composed of* individual human beings. Consequently, it was human beings who created international society.[10]

If men possess this innate individual behavior and it is exercised collectively through an abstract person, it occurs because this person, the State, has obtained such powers by delegation of those whom it represents - through a contractual arrangement, the decanted Social Contract - following that it is not actually the ultimate bearer of any rights, rather the one that exercises them on behalf of others. Fundamental rights of States are, actually, fundamental rights of people which are, for practical reasons, exercised by the latter under generally acceptable circumstances. As appointed by Freeman

'Rather than being a particular kind of ethical view, the general notion of agreement functions as a framework for justification in ethics. This framework is based on the liberal idea that the legitimacy of social rules and institutions depends on their being freely and publicly acceptable to all individuals bound by them. If rational individuals in appropriately defined circumstances could or would agree to certain rules and institutions, then insofar as we identify with these individuals and their interests, what they accept should also be acceptable to us now as a basis for our cooperation. Seeing in this way, the justificatory force of social contract views depends only in part on the idea of agreement; even more essential is the

conception of the person and the conception of practical reason that
are built into particular views.'[11]

The Social Contract theory had a later rebirth in 1971, when Rawls published *A Theory of Justice*, in which he aimed to develop a theory of justice from the idea of social contract found in Locke, Rousseau and Kant[12]
that could be compatible with freedom and equality, the core values of justice in a democratic society. He departs from an *Original position*, a hypothetical situation that resembles the state of nature, to determine the principles that will govern the people's lives thereafter.[13] According to him,
these principles are the 'liberty principle' and the 'difference principle'.
Concerning the first, he states that 'each person is to have an equal right to
the most extensive scheme of equal basic liberties compatible with a similar scheme of liberties for others'.[14] The second principle claims that social
and economic inequalities are to be arranged so that they are to be of the
greatest benefit to the least-advantaged members of society and that offices
and positions must be open to everyone under conditions of fair equality
of opportunity.

The basic liberties mentioned in the first principle comprehend several
freedoms already enshrined in the International Covenant of Civil and
Political Rights (CCPR) such as the freedom from arbitrary arrest (art 9),
freedom of thought and conscience (art 18), freedom of expression (art
19), freedom of association and assembly (art 21 and 22) and political liberty to participate in public affairs (art 25). Hence, these basic liberties are
already protected by a covenant, which is not a philosophical construction,
but rather a tangible written agreement enforceable under international law.
Regarding equality and fairness, the underlying elements of the second
principle, legal protection is neither very clear nor widely assured. Despite
some arguments that the CCPR and several other conventions and binding
international documents (such as the Universal Declaration on Human
Rights) have addressed equality and fairness to some extent, none of the
documents has made it clear as to whether those rights could be opposable
to third parties or States in an international legal system with solid liberal
roots. If, for instance, equality of States is a basic norm in international
law, fairness in their relations does not have the same legal standing or protection, even if we consider WTO dispute settlement procedures.

Notwithstanding, Rawls' theory on the 'original position' has contributed towards putting the idea of the Social Contract once again into the debate of international legal theory, which, in our opinion, has proven to be
helpful, especially if one bears in mind that the concept has been resumed
in a far friendlier context than the one that existed during the
Enlightenment: Now, men do not have rights arisen out of the abstract
Natural Law, rather they are guaranteed by *hard law* international agreements and States' constitutions supported in the concepts of the former;

human rights have also moved from the periphery to the centre of international law decisions, replacing States' rights and, finally, States have established organic bodies – rational-legal bureaucracies - to deal with specific aspects of the whole pack of covenants comprised within the Social Contract, both at the municipal and international levels. The social contract, now, is in front of our eyes and we can read it and sue the State, if it fails to fulfill its obligation thereunder.

In 1999, Rawls published a second work, called *The Law of Peoples*, in which he returned to the concept of original position to support a 'particular political conception of right and justice that applies to the principles and norms of international law and practice'.[15] In this work, by 'peoples' he meant 'the actors in the Society of Peoples, just as citizens are the actors in domestic society', making, therefore, a distinction between the law of peoples and the law of nations, or international law. While the latter is an existing legal order, however incomplete it may be in some ways, the former, by contrast, is 'a family of political concepts with principles of right, justice, and the common good, that specify the content of a liberal conception of justice worked up to extend to and to apply to international law.'[16] The principles and corresponding support in international *hard law* are the following:

The Law of Peoples' principles	Corresponding international law
Peoples (as organized by their government) are free and independent, and their freedom and independence is to be respected by other peoples.	UN Charter, Art 1(2) and art 2(1)
Peoples are equal and parties to their own agreements.	UN Charter, Art 2(1)
Peoples have the right of self-defense but no right to war.	UN Charter, Art 2(1), art 33, art 51
Peoples are to observe a duty of non-intervention.	UN Charter, Art 2(4)
Peoples are to observe treaties and undertakings.	Pacta sunt servanda
Peoples are to observe certain specified restrictions on the conduct of war (assumed to be in self-defense).	Geneva Conventions
Peoples are to honor human rights.	Mainly, the Universal Declaration of Human Rights and International Covenant of Civil and Political Rights
Peoples have a duty to assist other peoples living under unfavorable conditions that prevent their having a just or decent political and social regime.	

The above comparative chart shows that even though a major part of Rawls' principles is actually part of international law, one of them – solidarity among peoples – still does not have a counterpart. Not coincidentally, the latter is the subject of intense struggles in international relations, usually divided up into economic/social and political matters, which often place the contending groups in reciprocally opposing sides: when the developed States intend to intervene in other States on grounds of improving justice or decency in their political regimes (i.e., introducing democracy) the target States raise the argument of sovereignty and non-intervention in internal affairs; when the latter seeks more justice in the North/South social and economic relations, the richer States argue the same sovereignty and the equality among States.

Given that international law is a liberal system, there appears to be an insoluble dispute between freedom and justice, a fact recognized by Rawls, who regarded his *Law of Peoples* as a realistic utopia: *realistic* because it is possible and may be achieved; *utopia*, because States will most probably never reach it.

7.2   The concept of Democracy: the contractual arrangement framework

Under the Social Contract theory that established the States, people agreed to *delegate* – not to transfer – to the State some of their powers in order to have a 'comfortable, safe, and peaceable living one amongst another, in a secure enjoyment of their properties, and a greater security against any that are not of it'.[17] According to Locke, it implied in making collective decisions and in the submission of each individual to the decision of the majority. Since direct participation was not feasible, such decision would be reached through the parliament, which would occupy the center of his account of political legitimacy.[18]

Parliaments adopt either a unicameral or bi-cameral format and are classically composed of representatives of people chosen with the purpose to enact the laws that will govern the State and the lives of people therein. The parliament represents empirical evidence that the people has the original power to control their lives, which was partially delegated to people's representatives that form the State. The further development of liberalism with its emphasis on fundamental freedoms and the enforcement of human rights both at the municipal and international levels, adds renewed arguments to contractualism.

The nature of parliament traditionally expresses the idea of self-determination - people approving the rules that will govern their lives – and democracy – achieving that goal through debates among representatives of diverse segments of the society by majority vote. Self-determination can be enjoyed either individually or collectively. While the first is customarily expressed by fundamental freedoms, the latter is often associated with democracy. But, democracy can be analyzed under two different approaches. The first one looks at systems of government and the relations between institutions. The second looks at the attributes of a democratic process and the qualities it should incarnate. Therefore, as affirmed by Schumpeter, *democracy is a political method*, i.e., an institutional arrangement executed under the two mentioned approaches to reach a decision, following that it cannot be an end in itself.[19] Democracy, as a system of government, is expressed by parliament and periodical free elections of its members; as a democratic process, it is observed in the debates involving several constituencies potentially affected by the decision to be made, its lawful approval by a qualified majority according to established rules of procedure, and the publicity and enforceability of the outcome.

In his seminal article on Democratic Governance, Thomas Franck pointed out that the quality of a rule, or a system of rules, or a process of making or interpreting rules had legitimacy only to the extent that they could pull both the rule-makers and those addressed by the rules toward voluntary compliance. For that purpose, one had to appraise four indicators: *pedigree,* referring to the depth of the rule's roots in a historical process; *determinacy,* in regard to the rule's ability to communicate content; *coherence,* regarding the rule's internal consistency and lateral connectedness to the principles underlying other rules and; *adherence,* referring to the rule's vertical connectedness to a normative hierarchy.[20] According to him, self-determination provided the pedigree of a democratic entitlement. As we appraised in Chapter 4, self-determination has solid roots in Natural Law and it has been experiencing continuous development in the realm of international law, widely acknowledged by decisions of the international tribunals and State practices. Self-determination is also in the origin of the theory of Social Contract, which has been empirically and repeatedly observed in the formation of dozens of new States during the last forty years, and in the growth of fundamental freedoms and human rights, recognized by several declarations and multilateral treaties. It is not our purpose to appraise in this essay the evolution of the principle of self-determination at length, but one aspect that deserves attention is the fact that its expansion has not taken place without repeated complaints from those same countries that composed the classic *droit public et concert européens*, which invoked the principle of non-intervention in domestic affairs to retain their colonial empires throughout Africa, the Middle East and Asia. The emergence of the right of self-determination of people under colonial domination ultimately worked against the interests of 'heavy foot-printer' countries, hence, proving its strength in international law.[21]

Democratic entitlement has also had its determinacy expressed in several rules, which, according to Franck, can be regarded as composing three different generations or 'building blocks': self-determination, as the first; freedom of expression as the second; and finally, the right to free and open elections, as the third. If self-determination was enshrined in the UN Charter (art 73), the other building blocks were clearly determined in a binding treaty only in 1966, with the International Covenant on Civil and Political Rights, addressed in Chapter 4, which comprehended the right to self-determination, freedom of expression and electoral rights, the latter inferred from the rights of association and participation in public affairs. The remaining two indicators, coherence and adherence, are also clearly observable, with the three blocks making up the 'closely interwoven strands of a single fabric'[22] aiming to create the opportunity for all persons to assume responsibility for shaping the world where they live and work, which, in turn, adhere to a 'higher' principle that defines the social contract theory and even international law: the right to peace.

Franck affirms that democratic governance is an emerging right and that that right has reached its latest, third generation, with rules concerning free elections. We are inclined to agree with him to the extent in that the several arguments presented in his essay and just briefly summarized above, have focused on parliament. His analysis was written in 1992 and was certainly influenced by the dismantling of the Soviet Union in the previous years, but lacked the necessary widening to cover democracy beyond the parliament.

The traditional division of the State in three branches established its outer governance framework: the Legislative establishes the rules; the Executive delivers the services and the Judiciary decides the disputes within civil society and between civil society and the State. In this simple trinity, civil society was represented in the parliament, thus hypothetically controlling the bureaucracy, nested in the Executive, with the enactment of the rules that had to be followed and would be enforced by the Judiciary. However, the complexity of State affairs has distorted the model and such a fact has gone unnoticed in Franck's essay. In 1992, a major part of the rules had already been enacted by the Executive, i.e., by the bureaucracy, and it has experienced a steady growth since then. The economic strength of the Executive, that often gathers no less than ninety percent of the State's budget, impairs the equilibrium between the powers, also threatened by the nomination of members of the Supreme Courts by the Executive. With political parties having little (if any) real programmatic differentiation, parliament's power to shape the State was impaired, even in parliamentary democracies.

What appears to be unquestionable in current days is that the right to participate, directly or not, in public affairs has gone beyond the participation in free elections. The expansion of the conceptual understanding of the legal principle of self-determination, together with the political rights ensured by the CCPR, have given men and women a prominent role, from either a collective or an individual perspective, which cannot be confused with the role of the State (the parliament) as their representatives. For example, when van Kersbergen interpreted the chain of over two million people that united the capitals of Latvia, Estonia and Lithuania in the 50th anniversary of the Molotov-Ribbentrop pact as an 'impressive demonstration of national sovereignty',[23] he did it in a context that seemed to refer to States. It was a 'people' who were exercising their rights to create a State, not a State that was emerging *proprio motu*. Definitively, it tended more towards Kant than Hegel.

The right to intervene in public affairs, however, has experienced an internal change. In the late 19th and in the beginning of the 20th century, political parties and labour unions catalyzed the opportunity to change. Anarchism, communism, socialism, social democracy, fascism and all their variances represented a rich menu for avid consumers of political participation. Strikes, parades of public protest and political gatherings in public venues attracted hundreds of thousands of people. Unions and political parties *really* presented different options for civil society and in that period, nonprofit institutions were only focused on providing direct services to people in need. Parliament, however, is susceptible to degenerating into factions representing special interests gathered in a forum for inter-party compromises, creating conditions for the strengthening of the executive as the 'democratic representative' of people, a fact acknowledged by Carl Schmitt in regard to the Weimar Republic.[24] Since World War II, a slow but steady pasteurization-like process took over in politics: the unions and political parties continuously lost their capacity to offer real alternatives to *status quo*. In the late 1960s, change no longer was promoted by them: students in Paris, Vietnam war protesters in Washington, civil rights and feminist movements, none of the Western countries' major political demonstrations of the decade had been convened by unions or political parties, but rather by citizens at large. After the fall of the Berlin Wall, with the definitive death of the remote hypothesis of communism in the West, the alternatives narrowed even more.

While parties and unions were fading out, other players, the NGOs, began to take their place as *fora* for engagement of people in public affairs. But this was not just a matter of replacing one political actor by another, because there was one substantive difference: if political parties seek to operate within the State, NGOs operate *beyond* it; if unions work within corporative boundaries, NGOs operate beyond them, at the *universal* level. With NGOs, politics has crossed the borders of parliament.[25] Presently, no political parties are capable of attracting multitudes; they all look alike. Unions, in turn, have become working dogs. Actually, both have an undeniably bureaucratic flavor.

The apparent tranquility brought by neo-liberalism and the widespread adoption of market economies in the 1990s conceals a threat to the core of democracy: pluralism. This concept corresponds in the political sphere to competition on the economic market. If all political parties look alike and if the State is governed by a self-oriented bureaucracy, even with free elections, we may be living under a monopoly or an oligopoly. This condition impairs democracy in a way similar to how it impairs the market. When we discuss democracy, we necessarily have to discuss tolerance, diversity and openness. When we talk about State governance, we have to appraise the manner in which power is exercised in the management of the State, thus necessarily passing through the legitimacy of authority and accountability. Democratic governance tries to deal with all of these aspects, having in mind the purposes of the State, i.e., the fulfillment of the Social Contract.

The Social Contract must be enforced in some other manner. Civil society must control the State. Liberalism has adopted rationalism to ensure fundamental freedoms, hence, the latter commands the former, and not the contrary. The primacy of individual rights over State rights was acknowledged by international law when it accepted restrictions to the States' sovereignty if this proved necessary to ensure human rights. The prohibition of foreign intervention in the internal affairs of States, for instance, is no longer a dogma in international law, yet fiercely defended against neo-colonization initiatives hidden under the veil of the establishment of (permanently tutored and/or militarily enforced) democratic regimens.

At the domestic level, NGOs are energizing the public sphere and improving the pluralist debate within the States in order to ensure a better accomplishment of the Social Contract. In several States, public policies are now discussed between State officials and civil society representatives in official *fora*, such as thematic councils and cyclical conferences.[26] NGOs can encourage local political processes that support democracy with the purpose to strengthen civil society in general, without becoming partisan in a political party's sense.[27] Fostering such civil participation in the public arena is essential for the health of democracy: it ensures the rights of freedom of thought and participation in public affairs in harmony with the rational-legal structure of the State. It preserves the structure while it improves it. Moreover, it allows an effective counterbalance against self-oriented bureaucracies that may undermine democracy. Such measures have proven their efficiency by destroying the most powerful *bureaucracy* of the 20th century: the Soviet Union.

As is well-known, the connection between socialism and democracy seemed quite obvious in the years before the Russian Revolution. Marxist thought regarded private control over the means of production as the reason underpinning not only the capitalistic economic exploitation of the proletariat but also its (capitalistic) ability to impose its interests upon politics. Once the means of production changed to the hands of people, the same would happen with political power, which would be the 'rule of people'.[28]

That would have been 'fantastic' for the proletariat if the Communist Party, after assuming power, had not regarded governing a 'science' that should be put in the hands of a skilled group of professionals capable of implementing the required policies. After all, government being a complex task, the sum of individual ignorance would not produce collective wisdom through free elections, and the 'dictatorship of the proletariat' began. However, one must note that the dictators were not proletarians, but skilled people that composed a *bureaucracy*

Of course, appraising the reasons for the collapse of the Soviet Union can demand a book in itself, but it is arguable that the Soviet empire was undermined by the incapacity of its bureaucracy to comply with the covenant established in 1917, especially in a context of liberalization and democratization. When Gorbachev became General Secretary, in 1988, he convinced the Communist Party to hold elections for a new legislature to be called the Congress of People's Deputies. The elections eventually replaced important party officials with some critics of the Communist Party leadership, hence allowing some fresh air in the political thought of the country. In the following year, *glasnost* (openness) was introduced, together with freedom of speech and publication. The path to democracy was paved. With the breakdown of the centralized command economy, liberal winds began to blow and at the end of the year the Berlin Wall fell together with the Iron Curtain. How could such a bureaucratic stronghold fall without a single shot having been fired? The answer is not simple, but democracy surely has played a key role.

Since then, democracy has become the political orthodoxy, and some are tempted to say, the political religion of the West.[29] But, as we have seen, democracy is a method and if it is the only existing remedy to protect the abstract States and respective covenants with their nations against the illnesses caused by self-oriented bureaucracies, then it is important to appraise what instruments are at our disposal. The parliament is the classical antibiotic, but it is loosing effectiveness. For that reason, it is important to enhance the performance of the immunological system with a new, fourth generation of 'participatory rights'. McDougal and Reisman argued that

'The core demand for the availability of genuine individual participation [in public affairs] may be made comprehensively explicit in an overriding policy of inclusivity.'[30]

NGOs have evidenced that are structures capable to increase political density in societies, fostering the plurality of ideas and debate, exercising oversight and monitoring the bureaucracy. As affirmed by Lindahl, 'who is affected and what is the problem to be solved are matters of substance that require deliberation, yet deliberation cannot kick off without a prior determination of the members and the problem of the deliberative body.'[31] If democratic governance requires continuous improvement, then it is necessary to appraise who is taking the decisions, a task that necessarily drives us to the bureaucracy.

7.3   The concept of Bureaucracy: the contractual arrangement operator

States, as abstract bodies, cannot operate by themselves. They need to be structured, and for that purpose, together with the creation of the modern State, bureaucracy flourished. Hegel's aforementioned admiration of the Napoleonic restructuring of France was not senseless. His homeland Prussia was living under a feudal regimen of several principalities, and for that reason, in his *Philosophy of Right*, he dedicated considerable efforts to justifying the desirability of a 'universal' class of civil servants to provide the organic character of a legal order, the State, in Germany, sowing the seed that would later grow in Weber's work and definitively blossom in the intergovernmental organizations, a quintessential (however stateless) bureaucracy. Weber once wrote that

> 'Experience tends universally to show that the purely bureaucratic type of administrative organization is, from a purely technical point of view, capable of attaining the highest degree of efficiency and is in this sense formally the most rational known means of carrying out imperative control over human beings.'[32]

When Weber wrote his seminal book on the economic and social order, he was impacted by the transformations that were occurring in Russia and, particularly, in Germany at the beginning of the 20th century. He was unable to foresee that the rational-legal machinery that he had so precisely conceptualized would develop in his homeland to such an extent that it would be able to bureaucratically control the murder of millions of people, including German citizens, as described by Hannah Arendt.[33]

However, his perception of the power of bureaucracies is noteworthy: when asked how those subjected to bureaucratic control could seek to escape from its apparatus, he answered that this would happen 'normally' by their establishing an organization of their own, which would be equally subjected to the process of bureaucratization! Although apparently outrageous, hir assertion has found an echo in reality: when a large group of people decide to challenge the apparatus of one State, they create another State; when a small group decides to do so, they create an NGO. In spite of this, there is an aspect of Weber's theory that cannot go unnoticed: the undeniable purpose of bureaucracy is control, which is exercised on the basis of knowledge. He makes no reference to any other relevant purpose.

Contemporarily, the rational-legal organicity of bureaucracy is defined in the Constitutions of the States, which confer the necessary legitimacy to put it in authority to operate the State. Considering, also, that the Constitutions express the contractarian nature of the States, it follows that bureaucracy is necessary to implement the Social Contract *within* the States. However, giving life to an 'organic body' is always risky. Straightforwardly, you know how you created it, but you often do not know how to – or worse, cannot – control it. Hegel's *Philosophy of Right* postulated that the State (government) would have a pyramidal structure whose components – the several offices - would be linked both vertically and horizontally to form a unity or 'singleness' (§ 321) that would have 'absolutely universal ends' (§ 256). This would not be particularly a problem if he had not postulated that 'the sphere of civil society passed over into the State' (§ 256) and had not discredited the self-determination of people.[34] By doing so, Hegel's philosophy allowed, though it did not encourage, bureaucracy, a self-determining organism-like institution, to pursue its own self-interests under the loose justification of the universal will *within* the States. This could be observed, for instance, in the aforementioned reference to the Soviet Union.

In the next chapter we will see that bureaucracy managed to spread widely throughout the international system, summing up more bodies (intergovernmental organizations) than States, and living *beyond* them. One cannot overlook some notable similarities with a famous fictional novel written by one of Hegel's contemporaries, the daughter of William Godwin, the leading English theorist of the French Revolution, whose main character trades domestic happiness for the chimaeras of scientific power: *Frankenstein, or the Modern Prometheus.*[35] Bureaucracy, thus, must be controlled and this can be done only to the extent that people possess the power to enforce the fulfillment of the Social Contract entered into with the States. It is only possible in democracy and, moreover, in those democratic regimes that have adopted mechanisms of civil participation. If civil society cannot hold States' bureaucracies accountable for their decisions, relying on loose controls established by the State itself,[36] that control will be just a formal, fictional and ineffective one.

Schumpeter said that

'Revolution need not mean an attempt by a minority to impose its will upon a recalcitrant people; it may mean no more than the removal of obstructions opposed to the will of the people by outworn institutions controlled by groups interested in their preservation'.[37]

7.4   Adding a fourth building block to the emerging right to democratic governance

If one talks about change, one may be thinking either of something becoming something else (A => B) or of something changing internally (A *version* 1.0 => A *version* 2.0). Lock noted that in the present-day debate on political change, a widespread tendency has been occurring due to the unfolding of the liberal-democratic ideology and some of its elements, individualism, rationalism and anti-dogmatism.[38]

Individualism is a key element in liberal thought. The more individual freedoms a given regimen has, the more liberal it is; the more *sovereign* the people, the more liberal the State. It follows that liberal individualism is expressed in the realm of law in the form of fundamental freedoms and rights and democratic participation in the decision-making processes of public affairs. In the international law, it is also possible, because, as we have observed, individuals possess primary international legal personality.

The other element, rationalism, finds an echo in the pursuit of constant progress and efficient use of resources. The more organized the State, the keener it will be to progress. Therefore, a rational-legal structure that respects individual rights and contributes to the achievement of their final ends is liberal *par excellence*. But, as we have noted, being rational is not enough, it is necessary to be democratic. Economic progress requires independent-minded technical workforces and it is incompatible with the political censorship encountered in oppressive regimens. The more a certain economy is developed, the more it requires a skilled middle class to run its businesses and (the more) this middle class demands its political rights.

The third element invokes the negation of dogmas, a concept with origins in religious thought and that can be defined as an irrevocable doctrine revealed by God that, once and for all, settles a question or a problem that concerns faith or morals.[39] The transposition of this concept to political thought implies necessarily in adjustments. When one argues that liberalism is anti-dogmatic, it is not with the intention of considering it 'heretic', but rather it means to say that it does not accept unquestionable truths. Is this true? We can hardly say so, because liberal ideology regards the idea of fundamental freedoms as something that it is not negotiable, because it is innate to human beings. When Franck affirmed that 'self-determination postulates the right of a people organized in an established territory to determine its collective political destiny in a democratic fashion',[40] he did so supported in a right arisen out of Natural Law, which, according to Aquinas, 'is nothing else than the rational creature's participation in the eternal law'.[41] Liberal thought, hence, is anti-dogmatic only to the extent that it is capable of criticizing, transforming and replacing any structure or theory that does not challenge the fundamental freedoms of individuals, the core dogma of liberal thought.

NGOs, for instance, are individualistic initiatives that often swing to-and-fro between rationalism and dogmatism while dealing with States. They are rational bodies, because they are organizations established by individuals under contractual arrangements to pursue a public interest objective and are always questioning models, theories and structures. But they are also dogmatic when they justify the innate right of civil society to intervene in public affairs.[42]

To add a fourth building block to the right to democratic governance, it is necessary to remove 'obstructions opposed to the will of the people by outworn institutions', which necessarily passes through the acceptance that individuals possess legal personality in international law.

As pointed out by Grahame Lock,

> 'Contractualism is of course a very old idea. But much newer – dating from the end of the Cold War – is the situation in which the contractualist metaphor, posited as a generally valid picture of human society, hardly meets with any resistance.[43]

International law is a legal system arguably born from Natural Law and liberalism that has recognized States as the representatives of people. Why should it continue rejecting the idea that its 'parents' could give birth to sibling liberal structures capable of fostering the fundamental freedoms of men and of ensuring their lives, liberties and estates? Competition for power and 'parental' preference?

Given that legal entities are commanded by people with feelings and aspirations, and that State's official can, indeed, feel threatened by the close NGOs' scrutiny on their work, answering these questions would lead our analysis away from the field of Law, which is not the purpose of this essay. Nevertheless, it appears that change is needed. Evidence presented in the previous chapters has shown that individuals do possess rights and obligations under international law, as are NGOs, private bodies created by those same individuals to pursue their interests, supposedly protected and defended by the contractualist metaphor.

We do not see NGOs, nor IGOs, competing with States. States are and will remain the major actors in international law. If States possess the global means and IGOs possess the knowledge to, jointly, ensure the Social Contract, NGOs possess the capacity to make them accountable for their acts and decisions and ensure plurality during their decision-making processes. We are inclined to affirm that States represent their people only in those situations in which the representation is carried out by freely elected representatives. Considering that diplomatic corpses are members of bureaucracy, hence not elected, the argument that they democratically represent their countrymen lacks empirical evidence. When Franck presented his building-block theory on the right to democratic governance, he focused on democratic elections, which imply in choosing hundreds of thousands of peoples' representatives to the parliaments around the world and, comparably, a handful of Heads of State in presidential republics. But, as is well-known, national parliaments do not act at the international level - a domain reserved to the Head of Government - neither does there exist a world parliament. Even Heads of Government have a limited role in international affairs, mostly concentrated in the hands of diplomats and other bureaucrats, following that the major *condotieri* of international affairs does not have, themselves, a democratic pedigree.

If one compares NGOs to international bureaucracy, remarkable differences will be observed. International NGOs, for instance, have strong supporters around the world. The few examples mentioned in the Preliminary Chapter evidence that they can reach millions of supporters in dozens of countries. These civil society roots imply in transparency and accountability, mostly because NGOs traditionally depend on private funding. If individuals are not satisfied with the performance of a given NGO, they will not contribute to it nor volunteer to participate in its activities, and the entity will suffer. Of course, one can argue that NGOs' transparency and accountability is not that good and that it demands improvement. Yes, it is right, and, fortunately, such criticism evidences the strength of NGOs: the more an organization represents and is relevant for civil society, the more it is scrutinized. No one would care about accountability if representativeness were not at stake. These are the two sides of the same coin. This duality is the very reason for NGO criticism to State's and IGO's lack of transparency and accountability, or, in more common words, 'democratic deficit'. If they are in charge of delivering 'services' to people, they have to be held accountable. We shall resume this issue in the conclusion of our study.

One could say that the conception of a 'good government' is somewhat 'consumer-led': customers and voters are sovereign. If companies should live and die by market competition, governments should likewise rise and fall by popular judgment of their performance.[44] This often happens when people go to the polls, but, as we have mentioned formerly, the programs of political parties are almost the same and the change of the Head of State does not represent a huge variation in the State's route in an apparently universal liberal environment. Moreover, the State is in the hands of bureaucracy, a permanent staff that is barely affected by the polls.

Bureaucracy often claims that NGOs were not elected by the people. In a narrow interpretation of an 'election' as a cyclical democratic process where people go to the polls to choose representatives within a set of candidates, this is unequivocally true. But, if one interprets elected as supported by a large group of people, the result will be different.

The CCPR (article 25), for instance, ensured to every citizen, without distinctions of any kind and without unreasonable restrictions, the right and opportunity to take part in the conduct of public affairs, directly or through freely chosen representatives. If the CCPR ensured the right to direct participation in public affairs, which can be performed by freely chosen representatives, without unreasonable restrictions, then, *international law does not impose any limitations whatsoever that such participation be carried out through NGOs*. Hence, it appears to be beyond a doubt that there is legal space to add a fourth block in the emerging right to public governance: the participation of NGOs, as subjects of law, in international organizations.[45]

Some aspects of the international legal personality of NGOs have been addressed in the previous chapters: they have consultative rights ensured by treaties; they can participate in international conferences under customary law and have legal standing, as claimants, before certain international courts and can participate, through *amicus* briefs, in some other situations. Some of them, such as the IUCN, have achieved more rights than others and one of them, the ICRC, has a widely recognized international legal condition. Similarly, we have demonstrated that individuals possess international legal personality according to the understanding of representative contemporary legal doctrine, which acknowledged the remarkable changes in international law since World War II. Moreover, we saw that the CCPR ensured to individuals the right to participate in public affairs as well as the widespread democracy provided the adequate environment for the exercise of that right. Therefore, individuals in general, and NGOs in particular, cannot continue to be regarded as objects dispossessed of international legal personality. States, IGOs and NGOs perform different, but complementary roles, in international law and for that purpose they all must have an international personality, although with different legal capacities, a theme that, in regard to NGOs, we will return to in the ensuing chapters. All of them have been created to help people to live their lives and enjoy their liberties and estates in a peaceful and democratic environment. It is, as usual, always important to remember the thoughts of Lauterpacht, who regarded the individuals as the real subjects of international duties and rights.

Democracy necessarily requires the engagement of several constituencies presenting their opinions and debating the issue at stake, and for that purpose, parliaments were created, but they are not the only form of doing this. Plurality is essential. Furthermore, States are not just a matter of debate; they have to act and deliver services to the nation. That is the role of the Executive, and, in particular, of bureaucracy. So, there are times when debate has to be replaced by action. But action depends on decisions, which, in turn, depend upon legitimate authority and comprehensive debate over the options, means and consequences at stake. This reminds us of an anecdote about a president who had called a cabinet meeting to discuss a relevant issue. During the long meeting he listened quietly to the opinions of all his ministers to finally say: 'Thank you ladies and gentlemen. The meeting is over. Now I will decide.'

We think that democratic governance is all about that: the State has to listen, but it has to decide alone. It can share the debate, but not the decision, because the State will always be ultimately accountable for the outcome. Hence, the participation of NGOs in the international realm, together with States and IGOs, does not imply in giving them decision-making power, but rather, in safeguarding their participatory power and plurality. The traditional doctrine regarded the States as the only subject of law, but there has always been a wide discrepancy between this verbal doctrine and practice in the international arenas: while the organized ones tended to set up rigid requirements for participation, the unorganized – and sometimes most effective - ones have not. However, since 1945, the trend has clearly moved toward broader participation.[46]

The NGOs' role is to enhance the debate with different points of view, concerns and alternative models, qualifying the decision that will be made by the States and IGOs bureaucracy. However, participatory rights are not enough, because NGOs are closer to the people than any of the States and IGOs. The improvement of the right to democratic governance requires access to information with the purpose of holding those who have made the decision or executed them, accountable for their performance.

Accountability may be defined as the scrutiny of actions and performance of those who hold power. It can be carried out by the public in general or by specialist institutions, such as NGOs with direct or indirect mandate granted by the public. We consider direct mandate those situations where a close contractual-like relationship between principals and an agent exists, such as the IUCN toward its own members and the contracting-states in regard to the compliance of the substantive Secretariat of the Ramsar Convention. The indirect mandate, in the same case, is toward the people at large.

States, IGOs and NGOs are somehow representatives of the primary subjects of international law, the individuals, in the international sphere and, for that reason, to understand the possible development of the role of NGOs under international law, it seems appropriate to appraise the role of their more recent next-of-kin, IGOs.

Notes

1   *The Montevideo Convention on Rights and Duties of States* (adopted 26 December 1933, entered into force 26 December 1934).

2   T Franck, 'The Relation of Justice to Legitimacy in the International System', in *Humanité et Droit International: Mélanges René-Jean Dupuy* (Pedone, Paris, 1991) 159.

3   GWF Hegel, *Elements of the Philosophy of Right* (CUP, Cambridge 1991).

4   GWF Hegel, *Philosophy of Right* (n 3) § 351.

5   R Higgins, 'Human Rights in the International Court of Justice', (2007) LJIL, v 20, 746.

6   J Locke, *Two Treatises of Government*, 2nd Treatise, Chapter IX (Rethinking the Western Tradition series, Yale University Press, New Haven, 2003) 155.

7   *UN Convention on the Law of the Sea* (adopted 10 December 1982, entered into force 16 November 1994) UNTS 1833.

8   JL Brierly, *The Law of Nations* (6th edn, Clarendon Press, Oxford 1963) 14.

9   In this aspect, Lauterpacht affirmed that 'the analogy – say, the essential identity – of rules governing the conduct of States and of individuals is not asserted for the reason that States *are like* individuals; it is due to the fact that States *are composed of* individual human beings; it results from the fact that behind the mystical, impersonal, and therefore necessarily irresponsible personality of the metaphysical State there are the actual subjects of rights and duties, namely individual human beings. This is the true meaning of the Grotian analogy of States and Individuals'. H Lauterpacht, *International Law: Collected Papers* (CUP, Cambridge 1975) v 2 336.

10 P Allott, 'Reconstituting Humanity – New International Law' (1992) EJIL n 3, 219.

11 S Freeman, *Justice and the Social Contract: Essays on Rawlsian Political Philosophy* (OUP, Oxford 2007) 17.

12 J Rawls, *Collected Papers* (Harvard University Press, Cambridge 1999) 614.

13 J Rawls, *A Theory of Justice* (19th edn, OUP, Oxford, 1992).

14 J Rawls, *A Theory of Justice* (n 13) 53.

15 J Rawls, *The Law of Peoples: with "The Idea of Public Reason Revisited"* (Harvard University Press, Cambridge 1999) 3.

16 J Rawls, lecture on the Law of Peoples, < http://usm.maine.edu/~bcj/issues/three/ rawles.html> accessed 28 May 2009.

17 J Locke, *Two Treatises of Government*, 2nd Treatise, Chapter VIII (Rethinking the Western Tradition series, Yale University Press, New Haven, 2003) 142.

18 I Shapiro, 'John Locke's Democratic Theory', in J Locke, *Two Treatises of Government*, 2nd Treatise, Chapter VIII (Rethinking the Western Tradition series, Yale University Press, New Haven, 2003) 309.

19 J A Schumpeter, *Capitalism, Socialism and Democracy* (Harper, New York, 1975) 242.

20 T Franck, *The Emerging Right to Democratic Governance* (1992) AJIL v 86, 50.

21 Sovereignty of people supersedes the sovereign' sovereignty. WM Reisman, 'Sovereignty and Human Rights in Contemporary International Law' (1990) AJIL n 84, 866.

22 T Franck, *The Emerging Right* (n 20) 77.

23 K van Kersbergen, 'National Political Systems: the Changing Boundaries of Politics', in K van Kersbergen, RH Lieshout and G Lock (eds), *Expansion and Fragmentation: Internationalization, Political Change and the Transformation of the Nation State* (AUP, Amsterdam 1999) 77.

24 C Schmitt, *The Crisis of Parliamentary Democracy* (MIT Press, Cambridge 1988).

25 K van Kersbergen, *'National Political Systems* (n 23) 72.

26 In Brazil, for example, several covenant issues such as Health, Education, Environmental Protection, Social Security, Childhood and Elderly protection, and Tourism have their decision-making, monitoring and implementation process executed through thematic councils with equal representation of State and civil society.

27 A Clayton (ed) *Governance, Democracy & Conditionality: What role for NGOs?* (Intrac, Oxford 1994) 117.

28 J A Schumpeter, *Capitalism, Socialism and Democracy* (n 19) 235. See, also, T von Puschen (tr) K Marx and F Engels, *O Manifesto Comunista* (Centauro, São Paulo 2005) 68

29 R Jackson, *The Global Covenant: Human Conduct in a World of States* (OUP, Oxford 2000) 340.

30 MS McDougal and WM Reisman, *International Law Essays: a Supplement to International Law in Contemporary Perspective* (Foundation Press, New York, 1981) 201.

31 H Lindahl, 'Sovereignty and Representation in the European Union' in N Walker (ed) *Sovereignty in Transition* (Hart, Oxford 2003) 93.

32 M Weber, *The Theory of Social and Economic Organization* (The Free Press, New York 1964) 337. One may say that bureaucracy has biblical origins, as observed, for instance, in Chapter 17 [11] of Spinoza's *Theological-Political Treatise:* 'First the people were commanded to construct a building to be as it were the palace of God, i.e, the palace of the supreme authority of this state. This was to be built at the expense of all the people, not of one man, so that the house where God was to be consulted should belong to all. The Levites were chosen as the officials and administrators of this divine palace (...) Moses ordained rather that this tribe should be maintained by the rest of the tribes, so that it would always be held in the greatest honor by the common people since it alone was dedicated to God.'

33 H Arendt, *Eichmann in Jerusalem: a Report on the Banality of Evil* (Penguin, New York, 1992).

34 *Philosophy of Right* (remark to § 322): 'Those who talk of the 'wishes' of a collection of people constituting a more or less autonomous state with its own centre, of its 'wishes' to renounce this centre and its autonomy in order to unite with others to form a new whole, have very little knowledge of the nature of a collection or of the feeling of selfhood which a nation possesses in its independence. Thus the dominion which a state has at its first entry into history is this bare autonomy, even if it be quite abstract and without further inner development. For this reason, to have an individual at its head - a patriarch, a chieftain, &c. - is appropriate to this original appearance of the state'.

35 M Shelley, *Frankenstein, or the Modern Prometheus: the 1818 text* (University of Chicago Press, Chicago 1982).

36 These practices vary from State to State and comprise, for instance, the Executive budget's control by the Parliament, External Oversight governmental bodies, the publication of budget and execution reports in official gazettes or their posting on the internet, just to quote a few. The problem with all these mechanisms is their emphasis on cash (which definitively is important) and their frequent incapacity to ensure that, albeit expended according to the norms, they have been carried out in order to effectively fulfill the covenant.

37 J A Schumpeter, *Capitalism, Socialism and Democracy* (n 19) 236.

38 G Lock, 'Ringing the Changes: Mutations in the Idea of Political Change', in K van Kersbergen, RH Lieshout and G Lock (eds), *Expansion and Fragmentation: Internationalization, Political Change and the Transformation of the Nation State* (AUP, Amsterdam 1999) 25-27.

39 JC Fenton, 'The Definition of a Dogma', The Catholic Mind, (1950) January, 11.

40 T Franck, *The Emerging Right* (n 20) 52.

41 *Summa Theologica*, I-II, q. 91 a. 2

42 J Boli and GM Thomas, 'INGOS and the Organization of World Culture' in J Bolli and GM Thomas, *Constructing World Culture: International Nongovernmental Organizations since 1875* (Stanford University Press, Stanford 1999) 13.

43 G Lock, *Ringing the Changes* (n 38) 31.

44 A Clayton, *Governance, Democracy & Conditionality* (n 27) 14.

45 In the same line of our claim, see J Crawford, 'Democracy and the Body of International Law, in GH Fox and BR Roth, *Democratic Governance and International Law* (CUP, Cambridge 2000) 91.

46 MS McDougal, HD Laswell and WM Reisman, 'The World Constitutive Process of Authoritative Decision', in R Falk, *The Future of International Legal Order* (PUP, Princeton 1969) v 1, 94.

CHAPTER 8

Legitimacy of Intergovernmental Organizations

8.1 IGOs' rising number and importance

In the opening phrase of his book, Bowett affirmed that the development of intergovernmental organizations is, primarily, a response to practical needs, rather than to the philosophical or ideological appeal of the notion of global development.[1] Schermers and Blokker support the same rationale, stating that the interdependence of States has led to international solutions,[2] being followed by Amerasinghe, who affirmed that the birth of such organizations was a response to the imperative need to regulate the relations between the peoples of different countries.[3] The baseline of their assertions appears to be a State's perceived need to find solutions to growing common problems of their populations that could not be solved on an individual basis. To achieve the desired outcome, States understood that they had to delegate certain attributions comprised within their national self-regulatory powers to a new kind of body that had until then not existed: intergovernmental organizations (IGOs).

It cannot go unnoticed that this situation resembles the decanted 'state of nature' hypothesis, which supports some theories on the creation of the State. Of course, despite some striking similarities – a prior state of confusion in which everyone acts individually to access common concerns and further delegation of power to an established 'collective' legal entity – there is one marked and undisputed difference: States have not created a Super-State, even if we do have the UN in mind. Rather, they have created IGOs to organize their lives and, consequently, the lives of the nations they represent. Could this inference be considered reasonable? Would it be possible for us to unravel our appraisal from any philosophical or ideological aspects to concentrate on the operational effectiveness of these organizations?

Before answering these questions, it seems appropriate to identify how many organizations have been created to face up to the challenges imposed to the nations of our so-called 'global village'. But, at this point, a problem arises. The scholars aforementioned adopt different figures. Bowett and Amerasinghe rely on the same source of information, the *Yearbook of International Organizations,* but reach different final figures, with the former affirming that there are 1,839 IGOs[4] while the latter supports that it is unlikely that 5,131 IGOs exist, but that there could be more than 232, to conclude, through conjecturing, that the final quantity is probably between 500 and 700,[5] a number that is taken up by Blokker and Schermers as the best estimate available.[6] Barnett and Finnemore, also relying on the same source, have found 'at least' 238 IGOs.[7]

The difficulty to reach an accurate record of the number of organizations created by the fewer than 200 States unveils the challenges imposed to international law when it abandons the rather parochial physical boundaries of single-headed States to enter into the realm of the global intangible issues of a multi-faceted society and anticipates the enormous challenge in dealing with NGOs and other non-state actors.

When the first IGOs were created in the 19th century, they aimed to provide the States with a permanent body capable of dealing with recurrent pluri-national practical needs which were being dealt with by *ad hoc* international conferences, such as rivers (the Rhine, Elbe, Douro, Po and Pruth), railway transportation, and telegraphy and postal communications. The advent of such a type of organization demonstrates its rather pragmatic purpose of facilitating commercial interaction between the various States. A Grotian conception of a community of nations was, hence, not at sight; practical needs demanded the creation of IGOs, which were capable of imposing uniform rules and standards on several matters such as metrics and railway gauges. Due to their 'private' orientation, they were not regarded as capable of threatening the core of the States' sovereignty, even if we consider that the International Office of Public Health, established in 1907 with the purpose of implementing sanitary protection in shipping, could impose quarantines and fines for breach of its rules.

However, the proliferation of these disarticulated solution-oriented organizations has created a 'gear' problem. The first attempt to solve it involved concentrating their co-ordination in the League of Nations,[8] which proved unsuccessful due to the overall failure of the organization and its incapability to effectively coordinate the organizations amidst its political concerns. Nevertheless, this unfruitful experience illustrates the difficulties that can arise when technical issues are submitted to political and diplomatic bodies. Furthermore, these difficulties can be considerably greater if the coordinating body is entrusted to overview multiple organizations with several adjacent or, even more troublesome, overlapping agendas. The aforementioned proliferation of IGOs evidences that. In Chapter 2, we appraised the multiplicity of the so-called focal points of the UN in dealing with NGOs: seven, in the 'mother-IGO' alone!

When the UN was created, some of the former 'technical' organizations already in existence were transferred to the coordination of the newly-born universal entity, being later joined by some other specialized agencies, programmes and funds, summing up nearly forty different bodies today.[9] Considering that the States are not obliged to deposit the texts of the treaties that they have entered into before the UN or any other centralizing body to make them legally binding and effective, and that States are free to create bilateral or multilateral entities for whatever purpose they deem convenient or necessary, giving them international legal personality, surprisingly no one really knows how many IGOs exist today.[10] In spite of this, one can identify one of them due to the common features that they share: they are subjects of international law created by treaty and with a governing body capable of expressing an autonomous will distinct from that of its members, States and other IGOs, and of adopting norms addressed to them.[11] Another relevant and virtually unanimous characteristic of IGOs is the existence of a Secretariat, a bureaucratic staff created to fulfill the tasks assigned to the organization.

If the creation of IGOs resembles some characteristics of the hypothesis of the creation of States, the features mentioned have marked similarities with NGOs too, to which we can add others: they are not unique in their field and they are voluntarily created by several constituencies to address a specific matter without territorial limitations. IGOs, similarly to NGOs, also have a substantive liberal character, not only because they have been created mostly by Western States under a voluntary and contractual manner, but especially because they promote liberal values, either in the field of political ideas - such as human rights and democracy – or in economics, supporting the virtues of the market and capitalism. Hence, despite the apparent operational aim of the IGOs, they actually express a liberal ideology. Their marked voluntarism and contractarianism also evidence their embedment in the classical theory of the formation of the State.

Given these aspects, our research suggests that IGOs necessarily play a twofold role: they provide an efficient bureaucracy to cope with contemporary challenges (either by executing programs or developing new regulations in matters of their concern and also offer a *locus* for dialogue between the leading actors of international relations - the States - and new actors of increasing economic and social importance, such as multinational enterprises and NGOs. By doing so, the IGOs congregate some characteristics of both the Executive and Legislative branches of domestic governing structures. As a bureaucracy, they plan and implement; as a *locus* open to dialogue under diverse schemes, such as conferences, consultative status, seminars and assemblies, they may allow a pluralistic debate, thus exercising part of the tasks of the parliament missing at the international level.

If the authority of the States is underpinned by the successful monopoly of the legitimate use of physical force within their territories and, for that purpose, they seek that legitimacy by virtue of legality, i.e., 'by virtue of the belief in the validity of legal statute and functional competence based on rationally created rules',[12] the authority of an IGO, which lacks the use of force as well as a territory to control, relies, firstly, on the specialized knowledge and administrative competence of its bureaucracy. This aspect

is relevant: if, at the national level, bureaucracy depended on the theoretical construction of the State to flourish within its limits, at the international
level, bureaucracy can prescind from the classical attributes of statehood –
territory, people and sovereignty - and gain life beyond them to make
authoritative decisions affecting all territories, all people and all sovereign
states, without the monopoly of force. Additionally, if we bear in mind that
the direct (member states) and the indirect (civil society at large) constituencies have little influence on the daily activities of the organizations,
which were left in the hands of the bureaucracy, their strength is even more
acknowledgeable. However, despite the effective support in international
law, the authority of IGOs also depends upon an effective transparency of
activities and plurality in their decision-making process. As pointed out by
Klabber, contemporary legal research on IGOs does not assume that they
are 'inherently good', often assuming a critical approach.[13] These aspects
impose to IGOs some rising challenges, which will be addressed hereafter.

8.2   IGOs' rising challenges

8.2.1   The first challenge: Social Contract compliance

The widespread adoption of a Weberian civil service by a prolific number
of international organizations has led to a subtle shift in the perception of
State sovereignty in the wording of multilateral treaties. If at the end of the
19th century, States were referred to as 'Powers' represented by 'plenipo-
tentiaries', now they are 'Parties' or 'Members' with 'representatives'.
Although it did not represented a State's *capitis diminutio* being, hence, apparently irrelevant *per se*, this shift evidences a rising tension between the
formal independence of States and their actual interdependence in a world
where multilateral organizations are occupying a growing political and normative space and where States have had to co-operate to cope with issues
that were commonly administered satisfactorily at the national level.

   History has shown that States always engage in major adjustments of international law when they realize their gross failure to comply with the
'Social Contract' they have entered into with the Nations they represent: in
1648, after the carnage of the Thirty Years' War, which involved practi-
cally all of Western Europe, the Peace of Westphalia brought to light the
concept of State sovereignty; in 1919, after the massacre of World War I,
the Treaty of Versailles established the League of Nations and, finally, in
1945, the UN was created, after a death toll of nearly forty million people
in the six years of a global war. The adoption of a worldwide network of
bureaucracies appears to be the last attempt to comply with the established
Social Contract. When the UN was established, the member-states agreed
on the necessity of securing the highest standards of efficiency, competence, and integrity in the employment of the staff and in the determination

of the conditions of service of the organization.[14] By doing so, the States, which had always had their internal bureaucracies, created a supra-national bureaucracy to 'maintain international peace and security' and to 'develop friendly relations among nations'. Not coincidentally, these purposes have always been at the core of the Natural Law tradition that regarded men as having an innate inclination to live peacefully according to certain rational rules[15] and, moreover, in the justification of the classical Social Contract theory.[16]

Legally speaking, the UN and all other IGOs have the duty to comply with that Social Contract, enshrined in different manners in their statutes. For example, while the UN has the purpose to 'maintain peace and security', the WHO follows principles 'basic to the happiness, harmonious relations and security of all peoples', the ILO promotes 'decent work throughout the world' and the IMF works to 'foster global monetary cooperation' and 'to reduce the poverty in the world', just to quote a few of them. To achieve these goals globally, IGOs were put 'in authority', i.e., were empowered by international law to cope with the issues needed to comply with the Social Contract. By providing them with a qualified staff, the States aimed to turn each of them into 'an authority' in their respective fields of competence. This dual role provided IGOs with powerful tools and allowed them to make authoritative decisions in virtually any matter affecting the lives of people.

Bureaucracy is usually seen as something aseptic. It is expected to act rationally, impartially and technically. These characteristics fit perfectly in international law, a normative system expected to bring order to the society to maximize its common good.[17] However, as affirmed by Rosalyn Higgins, this system is not a static set of rules, rather 'a continuing process of authoritative decisions'[18] – hence, paralleling the continuous process of self-determination - that considers accumulated past decisions and their original context, as well as their application in the current context where a decision has to be made. *Once the context has changed*, those who make decisions must make choices between claims that have varying degrees of merit.[19] This is substantively observed in international bureaucracy. Given their liberal roots, IGOs often choose the most liberal option in sight, such as the IMF and World Bank recommendations of liberal economic measures to Latin American countries after the 1980s foreign debts crisis – the so-called Washington Consensus - and the UNHCHR working to increase knowledge and raise awareness about fundamental freedoms. Hence, the establishment of a rational-legal structure with liberal ideals in a wide array of intergovernmental bodies ensured the consolidation of capitalism and *democracy* as the *central components of world culture*,[20] moreover after the collapse of the Soviet Union, which leads us to the conclusion that one must expect an IGO's rational, impartial and technical decision-making to be *within* the boundaries of liberal thought. As pointed out by Barnett and

Finnemore, 'rationalization has given IGOs their basic form (as bureaucracies), and liberalism has provided the social content that all IGOs now pursue'.[21] Human rights and democracy are Western's core goals and values
and are 'generously' being made available to the people of the world by
IGOs that act as missionaries for democracy. However, they cannot be soldiers of democracy to impose, by force, democracy to other nations, because a greater international good than democracy, is pluralism and
freedom.[22]

While IGOs share a common root with States, they also do so with
NGOs. In the former case, the identity relies on the exercise of delegated
attributes of State sovereignty; in the latter, they share contractual and voluntary origins to address themes beyond territorial boundaries. And all
three types of organizations share the same purpose to fulfill the Social
Contract with the original constituencies, the individuals. It follows that
the symbiotic relationship between IGOs and NGOs, addressed in Chapter
2, has come to stay, for IGOs and NGOs are peers that share the same
ideals, social roots and operating structures. Not without reason, the settled
practice of interaction between the two types of bodies through consultative arrangements has evolved into customary international law, as pointed
out in Chapter 4.

Notwithstanding, complying with the Social Contract is no easy task.
IGOs have to deal with multiple pressures from NGOs, multinational enterprises and other forces of civil society at large. They are also pressured by
States, which are bound by the Social Contract, too. If IGOs are amidst the
so-called 'North-South' dispute, they also have to offer 'social value' for
the resources received from the States, seek that same value when they
sponsor NGO activities, and be accountable for what they have done, not
only procedurally but specially substantively. This situation leads to another kind of challenge: transparency.

8.2.2   The second challenge: effective transparency

IGOs and NGOs share several common features and both suffer growing
pressure to reach greater accountability toward their stakeholders, which,
given their global agenda, comprise not only their inner circle of members,
financial supporters and staff, but also a wide outer circle, which includes
the communities where they are actually operating and, in the background,
civil society at large. But if a glass were to be so transparent to the point
that, while existing, no one could see it, the same occurs with information.
More important than the act of disclosure, information must be easily accessible and capable of providing useful data, not only about actual results,
but also about plans, strategies and goals, and decision-making procedures,
organized in such a way as to permit comparability.

Transparency is intimately related to democracy, which, in turn, is embodied in the principle of self-determination of the peoples. If the nations, according to the International Covenant of Civil and Political Rights (CCPR), are free to pursue their economic, social and cultural development and can dispose of their resources based upon the principle of mutual benefit, having also the right to take part in the conduct of public affairs, directly or through freely chosen representatives, they are also legally entitled to pursue a higher level of transparency from those who represent them and manage resources on their behalf.

The necessary responsiveness to the needs, interests and expectative of the citizens, as well, as the liberal accent of the CCPR suggest a right to transparency. This would necessarily comprise access to the *procedures* adopted during the decision-making process, i.e., the capacity to appraise their compliance with the substantive rules on the matter; access to the *content* of the decision; and the appraisal of its *effectiveness* in pursuing goals consistent with the Social Contract. However, despite the pursued co-existence of the aforementioned dimensions, evidence has shown that the decision-making procedures are often opaque, the content of the decisions are rather vague and succinct, and effectiveness is sometimes hindered by procedural rules wisely established to protect those who decide.[23]

Bijsterveld has argued that the principle of transparency is an emerging counterpart of the classical principle of legality.[24] Legality, on one hand, is at the core of liberal thought and represents a barrier of the individuals against abusive acts of State. It classically encompassed the right to participate, often through parliaments, in the adoption of new rules, which were expected to have generality and to be formulated in advance to any action taken by the State. From an institutional dimension, the principle of legality is expressed in the definition of the formal structure of a legal entity, its purposes and competences, its governing bodies, and its relationship with its constituencies. One could say that it is embodied in the Statute of the organization concerned. Straightforwardly, if, in a democratic regimen, legality is having the decision made correctly by the correct body aiming at the correct purpose and the correct beneficiaries, transparency is allowing anyone to see all this correctness at any time.

The UN Charter provided basic mechanisms of transparency, determining that the Secretary General, the Security Council and other organs shall present annual reports to the General Assembly, which will also consider and approve the budget of the organization and any financial and budgetary arrangements with specialized agencies, as well as examine the administrative budgets of such specialized agencies.[25] Nevertheless, these mechanisms are markedly bureaucratic and limited. For example, the Charter does not impose clear guidance on the content of the reports nor does it determine that it must inform the rationale of the decision-making process or even an appraisal of the context. Moreover, it does not impose any guideline for measuring the capacity of the staff to fulfill the aims of the organization. Hence, the UN's current transparency mechanisms could be compared to the image observed in the rearview mirror of a car which is being driven by a hopefully qualified *chauffeur* who purportedly knows where the passengers want to go: They show the past, cannot help in foreseeing the future and do not provide any information about the rationale of the decisions made by the driver.

Even if we consider that the General Assembly bears the capacity to demand enhancement of the quality of the reports and the budgetary considerations, it appears to be beyond any doubt that enhanced transparency is not only desirable, but necessary, not only in the UN, but also in all of its specialized agencies, funds and programmes, as well as in other intergovernmental bodies with an international or regional scope.

From a financial perspective, in recent years the UN General Assembly has adopted some resolutions to ensure better quality of information. Worth quoting are the independence of internal oversight bodies,[26] the availability of internal audits to the General Assembly,[27] and the adoption of international accounting standards.[28] Unfortunately, all these initiatives have focused on a 'business-like' approach of financial expenditures and have placed little importance on the quality of the information, with regards to the goals of the organization. After all, if in a company the 'end' is money and the services are 'means', in an IGO, money is a 'mean' to render services to achieve the statutory 'ends'. Therefore, considering that reports must access the achievement of the ends, the current ones possess a gross misconception. A similar approach can be observed in other initiatives addressing whistleblower protection, the establishment of an Ethics Office to appraise the conduct of the staff, and employees' financial disclosure policies.[29] They are important, but are just instruments of control of 'means'. Of course one cannot accept transparency as the simple publication of decisions in official gazettes and websites, auditing financial statements and employment policies.[30] It is far more than this.[31]

At the European level, a first noteworthy movement toward qualified transparency can be observed in the Treaty of Amsterdam, which, in amending the Treaty of the European Union, stated that the decisions would be made 'as openly as possible and as closely as possible to the citizen'.[32] By doing so, the treaty recognized that transparency possessed a two-fold dimension: access to information (openness) and civil participation (closeness). In a subsequent important movement toward enhanced transparency in international organizations, the EC Commission released in 2001 a white paper on Governance proposing the adoption of five principles combined to form the basis of good governance: **openness**: the European institutions should attach more importance to transparency and communication in their decision-making; **participation**: citizens must be more systematically involved in the drafting and implementation of policies; **accountability**: the role of each party in the decision-making process needs to be clarified - each actor involved should then assume responsibility for the role given to them; **effectiveness**: decisions need to be made at the appropriate level and time, and deliver what is needed; and **coherence**: the EU conducts extremely diverse policies which need to be pursued coherently. [33] At the international level, major evidence of the introduction of this perception of transparency into the realm of international law is observed in the Aarhus Convention,[34] addressed in Chapter 5.

When the aforementioned treaties established the right of access to information, they understood that it was a necessary requirement for an effective democracy. It was linked to another expression of effective democracy: access to the decision-making policy. One cannot be regarded as a true participant if one has not had access to the same information as the other participants. This participation does not represent, of course, the negation of the State and the IGOs, or the replacement of representative democracy, and much less their diminution. Rather, it represents enhanced accountability of the States' and IGOs' acts toward their final constituencies, the nations.

We can regard the increase in transparency as a natural outcome of the democratic wave that has swept the world after the fall of the Berlin Wall. It can also be acknowledged as skepticism toward the prolific (how many?) international bureaucracies that often influence outcomes by manipulating information, i.e., by releasing selected 'processed' information in order to foster a given behavior, hindering other ones and, by doing so, shaping another social model for the world. This is rather obvious if we consider their liberal background and their capacity to adopt authoritative decisions and recommendations because they are legally 'in authority' of the concerned matter and possess a bureaucratic staff that could be regarded as 'an authority' on the issue. The less they share, the more they shape.

Thus, the openness of information and the closeness of civil society in the decision-making process may be regarded as a counterbalancing initiative to those powers and an effective contribution to the reduction of the democratic deficit of IGOs, which, albeit liberal, are, in regard to citizens, undemocratic par excellence. The importance of transparency in the decision-making process for the strength of public confidence in the international institutions and their democratic nature was acknowledged by several decisions made by the Court of First Instance.[35] Transparency may also add another feature to democracy: peace, the ultimate aim of the UN. According to the former UN Secretary General, Boutros Boutros-Ghali,

'la transparence des gouvernements démocratiques et l'obligation qui leur est faire de render compte aux citoyens, généralement d'autant moin désireux de fair la guerre qu'ils ont à en supporter les risques et le fardeau, peuvent aider à prévenir les conflits armés avec dáutres Etats'.[36]

If transparency is important, one cannot lose sight of the fact that it is not an end in itself, but just a means to appraise if the considered body or organization is on the correct path. Therefore, it has an instrumental role in allowing individuals to monitor the performance of the States and IGOs. Notwithstanding its importance, transparency cannot preclude a far more relevant challenge imposed to IGOs: accountability.

8.2.3   The third challenge: Ends-oriented Accountability

In the previous chapter, we have appraised the power of bureaucracies and their undeniable purpose to control civil society on the basis of knowledge. So, how can people control the controllers? By making them widely accountable for the decisions made and the results obtained. Holding bureaucracies accountable enables two relevant outcomes: it curbs bureaucracy's inherent centripetal tendency, i.e., its inclination to work for its own maintenance; and it permits the appraisal of its legally established purposes and obligations. The strategy for democratic promotion necessarily must address two complementary goals: strengthening change actors, and weakening veto players.[37] The more individuals participate, the less the bureaucracy governs alone.

Theoretically, intergovernmental organizations possess derived international legal personality, which they have been granted for the purpose of achieving some ends clearly defined in their statutes. So, differently from the classical Weberian civil service, which, comprised within the apparatus of the State, had the purpose of controlling a people in a territory, the bureaucracies of IGOs have been established as rational bodies with economic considerations: they must deliver a service to the States and to the Nations that they represent. For that reason, it can be argued that they were established as a special kind of principal-agent relationship under international law where the States (the principals) hire the IGOs (the agents) to pursue the interests (in terms of health, financial stability, human rights protection, etc.) of the former.

It follows that the relationship is based necessarily on a contractual arrangement, in this case represented by the constitution or statutes of the IGOs and underpinning treaties or conventions, which, in turn, demand necessary evaluation of their performance. If one can say that the existence of a Social Contract between peoples and their States is doubtful, it appears undoubtedly certain that a covenant aiming to pursue the same ends as those of the Social Contract exists between the States and the IGOs. Given that a principal-agent agreement exists, it shall be potentially submitted to the problem traditionally encountered in this kind of relationship, i.e., that the principal often does not know enough about whether or to what extent the covenant has been satisfied. For that purpose, the establishment of legal procedures capable of making IGOs accountable for their acts is essential. In this particular aspect, the interests of States and civil society converge: both desire to make IGOs accountable for their past and future actions and decisions, for their planning, and for the verified outcome. The measurement of their performance has two defined parameters: the statutory objective of the concerned organization or the purposes of the convention, and the budgetary considerations. The more information that is shared, the less the world is shaped by bureaucrats.

In the first section of this chapter we addressed the twofold role of IGOs: they are organizations endowed with specific tasks to be performed by bureaucrats; and they are a locus for dialogue between actors of international relations with regard to common concerns to mankind, i.e., particular aspects of the Social Contract. In both cases, transparency is deemed necessary and this tool was appraised in the previous section. However, one can be transparent evidencing a tremendous success, displaying nothing relevant, or, even worse, presenting a gross failure. Thus, transparency at large is not enough: it is necessary to qualify the information and the procedure of access in order to hold IGOs accountable for their performance in fulfilling both roles.

The appraisal of the performance of IGOs according to the aforementioned parameters comports roughly two lines of work: (i) the fulfillment of the objectives, plans and budgetary considerations of the organization (the substantive dimension) and (ii) the fulfillment of the legal requirements (the legal dimension). Straightforwardly, it is important to evaluate if they have done the right thing, in the right way. Holding IGOs accountable in their first role – as a task-oriented bureaucracy – appears to be an easier task. After all, they have been established to pursue a specific goal and have been equipped with staff, money and legal capacity to do so, or, in the words of the ICJ, 'its members, by entrusting certain functions to it, with the attendant duties and responsibilities, have clothed it with the competence required to *enable those functions to be effectively discharged*'.[38] However, this may prove to not be so easy.

From the substantive dimension, the appraisal of their performance occurs mainly at formal events, when the reports of the Secretariat are submitted to the member-states gathered in formal assemblies of short duration and a long list of matters to cover, the topic usually being one of the last items on the Agenda, falling under the depreciated generic heading of 'organizational, administrative and other matters.'[39] The reports, though large documents, do not clearly define the actual achievements (ends), rather focusing on the activities (means).[40] From the legal dimension, the Articles on Responsibility of States for International Wrongful Acts[41] prepared by the International Law Commission (ILC) focused only on States' responsibility, although making a general reference to IGOs in article 57, when it stated that the 'articles are without prejudice to any question of the responsibility under international law of an international organization, or of any state for the conduct of an international organization'. While the UNGA Sixth Committee is currently working on the issue of ensuring the accountability of UN staff and experts on mission with respect to criminal acts committed in mission,[42] there is no clear resolution, treaty or convention regulating, in general terms, the responsibility of IGOs and their staff.[43] Nevertheless, it is beyond any doubt that this *lacunae* does not entitle IGOs to 'violate the principles they were established to serve'.[44]

It follows that there is great room for improvement. Not coincidentally, such enhancements are occurring through the interference of non-state actors, such as NGOs. In Chapter 2, for example, we briefly mentioned the World Bank Inspection Panel. This (then) cutting-edge structure was established in 1993 with the purpose to allow third parties to file complaints regarding the bank's failure to follow its own policies and procedural requirements of its projects.[45] A similar structure, albeit focused on States' failure to comply with environmental legislation, has been introduced by the North American Agreement on Environmental Cooperation (NAAEC).[46] In Chapter 3, we studied that NGOs can lodge complaints before the European Court of Justice to seek judicial protection against illegal acts inflicted on them by Community institutions. However, apart from this narrow opportunity, none of the existing international courts enjoys jurisdiction to hear complaints brought directly against international organizations.

As we have mentioned, holding an entity accountable encompasses its past and future actions and decisions. If inspection panels and claims before tribunals are valid instruments to appraise the past, they are not keen, except from a 'lessons-learned' point of view, to (accurately) envision the future. For this latter perspective, the reliance on the principal-agent relationship appears to provide the best channel for better IGO accountability, albeit this channel is, in principle, open only to member-states. Notwithstanding, if we take into consideration the second role of IGOs - a locus for dialogue - new opportunities are visible.

From a general viewpoint, considering that IGOs operate worldwide and are capable of affecting the lives of the entire society, consultative arrangements with NGOs may play a relevant role. As we have seen, INGOs with consultative status before the ECOSOC can submit written statements, as well as participate in UN convened conferences. Similar opportunities are ensured by the statutes, written rules and customary practices of several other organizations. In Europe, IGOs have achieved improved rights, with the recognition, in 2003, of their participatory status; in South America, they participate in the MERCOSUR Social Economic Consultative Forum;

in Africa, they have a seat in the ECOSOCC and in Asia, they are associates to the ASEAN.[47]

Considering that NGOs have access to the aforementioned IGO structures with a possibility to address the member-states that participate in the collegiate and also interact with the bureaucracy of the mentioned organizations, the existing channels can be used for compliance review and for submission of proposals, interfering in the decision-making process and, in addition, appraising the principal-agent relationship. In this aspect, it is important to take into consideration that, similarly to States, IGOs, as subjects of international law, are bound by *jus cogens* and customary international law,[48] which recognize the inalienable right of people to several economic and human rights and fundamental freedoms, including political liberty to participate in public affairs, the utmost purpose of the Social Contract. For that reason, better governance is desirable.

8.3   A pressing requirement: Democratic Governance

The word 'democracy' is not mentioned in the UN Charter nor is it formally required as one of the criteria for admission of new member-states. In 1948, in its very first advisory opinion, the ICJ concluded that the admission of new member-states could not depend on conditions not expressly provided by the Charter.[49] Hence, despite the liberal roots of international law, democracy was not regarded as a necessary condition to join the UN. Interestingly, several NGOs which were active at the San Francisco conference supported the idea, basing their argument on *realpolitik,* by stating that 'a union of democratic states might find itself confronted by a union of non-democratic states; and recent history has shown that a union of like-minded states of a certain mind may lead to union of like-minded states of another mind'.[50]

The UN is a universalistic organization whose history has evidenced that it has made room for liberal and non-liberal states, treating them equally, regardless of their political or social ideology, size or population. By doing so, it was capable of congregating opposite sides during the Cold War and several real wars. But as time goes by, seeds flourish and walls fall. *Things have to change once the context has changed.* Currently, the UN is effectively engaged in building democratic governance throughout the world, supporting several initiatives in parliamentary development, the electoral system and processes, e-governance and access to information to promote citizens' participation in public affairs, public administration reform and anti-corruption, mostly through the UNDP, supported by budgetary resources and also additional ones, gathered through the Democratic Governance Thematic Trust Fund, established in 2001.

If there is a 'global acceptance of democracy as a universal value'[51] and the Universal Declaration of Human Rights has enunciated the essentials of democracy, the International Covenant of Civil and Political Rights (CCPR) has ensured to any citizen the *right to take part in the conduct of public affairs* directly or through freely chosen representatives. IGOs are engaged in public affairs, but their bureaucrats were not freely chosen. The CCPR must be applied in the realm of IGOs.

At the international level, the consultative rights ensured to NGOs, their participation in conferences, *locus standi* before certain Tribunals and quasi-judicial bodies and authorization to submit *amicus* briefs in third parties cases and the participation in decision-making processes under certain treaties represent unequivocal evidence that democratic participation is largely recognized by international law. Similarly, several ICJ decisions, studied in Chapter 3, evidence a wide array of recognition that individuals possess rights under international law, which, it is worth stating, were not granted by the States or the IGOs, but deeply embedded in Natural Law.

As demonstrated in Chapter 6, peoples have the right of self-determination, hence it follows that *they* possess the inherent right to interact with other peoples, doing so *through* the States. Considering that the States have created the IGOs with the purpose to comply with several attributions that were comprised in their own responsibilities toward their citizens, it necessarily appears that citizens have an inherent right to have some kind of participation in the governance of IGOs. We may say so because the ultimate purpose of the IGOs is to satisfy the peoples' needs and, therefore, they are held accountable not only to the direct constituencies – member-states – but also to their (States) own constituencies, the people. Furthermore, as we pointed out in the previous section, States and people have converging interests in the matter: both want to appraise the effectiveness of the activities performed by the IGOs: the States, because they are the financial supporters and will be held ultimately responsible for any failure, not only covering any financial costs related to that failure, but moreover, the inherent political costs; the people at large, because they are the ultimate beneficiaries of those actions. If both States and people have motives and means to enhance the governance of IGOs, this suffices to promote changes.

Strengthening the governance of IGOs will not imply in any weakening of State sovereignty. Recent studies have shown that States are still strong and adapted to new world circumstances.[52] Statehood remains a top priority for those peoples struggling for their self-determination. IGOs will not replace States nor resuscitate, as rulers, the empires buried in history. Not even the 'multi-level governance' which establishes direct contact between the European and the infra-national levels of government, thus bypassing the monopoly of central governments in the international arena, has been capable of removing their prominence in defining EU spending.[53]

However, that is not to say that States and IGOs cannot be more open to civil society. The almost unanimous conversion of States' economies into capitalist practices and the growing adoption of liberal democracy throughout the world claim a higher level of citizen participation in the policy decision-making of IGOs and this can be done with the help of NGOs. Pluralism is critical. As pointed out by Schermers and Blokker, interest groups, such as NGOs, have some right of initiative in decision-making in those organizations in which they possess a consultative status. The procedure ensures that matters of particular concern to NGOs will receive at least some attention from the considered organization.[54]

It is beyond any doubt that the end of the Cold War and the movement of States towards liberal democracies have changed the context in which international law and IGOs, in particular, have been conceived. As stated by Rosalyn Higgins, if law, as rules, requires the application of outdated and inappropriate norms, then law as a process, encourages interpretation and choice, which is more compatible with the values one seeks to promote and the objectives one seeks to achieve.[55] If contemporary society values pluralist democracy, then greater involvement of civil society in IGOs is not only desirable, but necessary to achieve the ultimate ends of the Social Contract established with the States.

We do not see such an integration as outrageous, because the IGO profile parallels, to some extent, the same legal regimen observed by NGOs:

Intergovernmental Organization	Non-Governmental Organization
Created by written agreement (Treaty)	Created by written agreement (type varies according to the country)
Entity governed by a statute and with public interest aims, focusing on a group of constituencies broader than its creators	Entity governed by a statute with public interest aims, focusing on a group of constituencies broader than its creators
Creators become members. New members can be admitted, if accepted by the current ones	Creators become members. New members can be admitted, if accepted by the current ones.
The IGO has a legal personality distinct from its members and both are generally governed by the same legal system (international law)	The NGO has a legal personality distinct from its members and both are generally governed by the same legal system (municipal law)
Members make decisions in assemblies, by vote (often by majority)	Members make decisions in assemblies, by vote (often by majority)
The IGO has a governing body capable of making distinct decisions from that of its members, thus not being capable of binding them.	The NGO has a governing body capable of making distinct decisions from that of its members, thus not being capable of binding them.

These features make it clear that IGOs and NGOs have similar structures and are governed by the same rationale: they are legal bodies voluntarily created by their members to pursue public interest goals for the benefit of a wider array of constituencies. However, in some other aspects, they are materially different:

Intergovernmental Organization	Non-Governmental Organization
Generally, 'self governed' by its own constitutive acts. Customary international law and general principles of law also apply	Extensively regulated by written municipal law
Entity with privileges and immunities at the national level	No similar privileges and immunities at the national level (except some tax benefits)

We believe that the widely acceptance of pluralist democracy as the best form of government throughout the world authorizes adding a fourth building block to the right to democratic governance. The similarities between IGOs and NGOs provide a good opportunity for that. However, in order to make such arrangements effective, it is necessary to re-arrange the form by which the IGOs recognize relevant international NGOs. If NGOs can bear rights and obligations under international law, it is necessary to acknowledge their international legal personality. If they represent an expression of the right of people to participate directly or indirectly in public affairs, then new forms of interaction must be established. If the social contract is to be fulfilled, then democratic governance and transparency, as means to hold States and IGOs accountable, are essential. These challenges will be addressed in the next, conclusive, chapter.

Notes

1   P Sands and P Klein, *Bowett's Law of International Institutions* (Thompson, London 2001) 1.
2   HG Schermers and NM Blokker, *International Institutional Law* (4th edn Martinus Nijhoff, The Hague 2003) § 1.
3   CF Amerasinghe, *Principles of the Institutional Law of International Organizations* (2nd edn CUP, Cambridge 2005) 2. See, also, CA Coliard and L Dubois, *Institutions Internationales* (10th edn Dalloz, Paris 1995) 167.
4   P Sands and P Klein, *Bowett's Law* (n 1) 5.
5   CF Amerasinghe, *Principles* (n 3) 16.
6   NM Blokker and HG Schermers (eds), *Proliferation of International Organizations* (Kluwer, The Hague 2001) 2-4.
7   M Barnett and M Finnemore, *Rules for the World: International Organizations and World Politics* (Cornell UP, Ithaca, 2004) 1.
8   *Covenant of the League of Nations*, article 24.
9   This is, for instance, the case of the ILO, UPU and ICAO.

10 Even considering that article 102(1) of the UN Charter provided that all states 'shall as soon as possible' register any treaties entered into before the UN, there is no definitive survey on the effective number of IGOs operational in the world nowadays.

11 P Sands and P Klein, *Bowett's Law* (n 1) 16; CF Amerasinghe, *Principles* (n 3) 9; HG Schermers and NM Blokker, *International Institutional Law* (n 2) § 44.

12 M Weber, *Politics as a Vocation* (1919).

13 J Klabbers, 'The Life and Times of the Law of International Organizations' (2001) NJIL 70, 287-317.

14 UN Charter, Article 101(3).

15 H Grotius, *The Rights of War and Peace*, Prolegomena VI, 79-81.

16 T Hobbes, *Leviathan*, (1651), S Pufendorf, *On the Duty of Man and Citizen* (1675); J Locke, *Two Treatises of Government and a Letter Concerning Toleration* (1689); JJ Rousseau, *The Social Contract* (1762).

17 R Higgins, *Problems and Process: International Law and How We Use It*, (OUP, Oxford 1994) 1.

18 R Higgins, 'Policy Considerations and the International Judicial Process' [1968] 17 ICLQ 58.

19 H Lauterpacht, *The Development of International Law by the International Court* (London 1958) 399.

20 T Franck, *The Emerging Right to Democratic Governance* (1992) AJIL v 86, 50; AM Slaughter, 'International Law in a World of Liberal States' (1995) EJIL v 6, 503.

21 M Barnett and M Finnemore, *Rules for the World* (n 7) 166.

22 R Jackson, *The Global Covenant: Human Conduct in a World of States* (OUP, Oxford, 2000) 365.

23 One example of this is the overwhelming silence of the UN at the beginning of the 1994 events in Rwanda, which were regarded as civil war, and therefore, as an internal affair of a State, a situation that was actually a genocide that killed eight hundred thousand people in just one hundred days, perpetrated with the acquiescence of the Rwandan government and the bureaucratic silence of the UN. As affirmed by Barnett and Finnemore, 'a Secretariat that professed humanitarian goals used peacekeeping rules to conclude that humanitarian intervention was not warranted to stop crimes against humanity.' See M Barnett and M Finnemore, *Rules for the World* (n 7) 122.

24 S van Bijsterveld, *The Empty Throne: Democracy and the Rule of Law in Transition* (Lemma Publishers, Utrecht 2002) 42.

25 *UN Charter*, Articles 15, 17 and 98.

26 A/Res/48/218B para 5(a).

27 A/Res/59/272 paras 1(c) and 2.

28 A/Res/60/283, section IV para 1

29 Respectively, documents ST/SGB/2005/21, ST/SGB/2005/22 and ST/SGB/2006/6.

30 For a comprehensive survey of the financial statements' disclosure practices of the UN system, see document CEB/2005/HLCM9/INF.1/Rev.2 (19 April 2005).

31 In light of revelations that the government of North Korea had misused humanitarian UN funds, in 2007 the US crafted an initiative, called 'UN Transparency and Accountability Initiative', which identified eight areas for enhancement of transparency, having included, among them, public access to all relevant documentation related to operations and activities, also involving budget information and procurement activities. However, no evidence has been found that this proposal has been implemented.

32 *Treaty of Amsterdam* (adopted 2 October 1997) Article 1(4)

33 Commission (EC) 'European governance' (White Paper) COM(2001) 428 final, 25 July 2001.

34 *Convention on Access to Information, Public Participation in Decision-making and Access to Justice in Environmental Matters* (adopted 25 June 1998, entered into force 30 October 2001) UNTS 2161.

35 CFI, *Hautal v. Council*, case T-14/98, Judgment of 19 July 1999; *The Bavarian Lager Co. v. Commission*, case T-309/97, Judgment of 14 October 1999; *Interporc Import und Export v. Commission*, case T-92/98, Judgment of 7 December 1999.

36 B Boutros-Ghali, *Paix, Developpement Democratie: trois agendas pour gerer le planete* (Pedone, Paris 2002) 152.

37 A Magen and L Morlino, *International Actors, Democratization and the Rule of Law* (Routledge, New York 2009) 256.

38 *Reparation for Injuries Suffered in the Service of the United Nations* (Advisory Opinion) [1949] ICJ Rep 179 *(emphasis added)*

39 This was the case, for instance, of the UNGA 63rd Session, where the report was placed as the 100th and the financial statements as the 106th items on the Agenda.

40 The 2006/2007 Secretary General Report, for instance, dedicated only 37 of its 275 pages to 'key results achieved by the UN', 1 ½ pages being dedicated to human rights and humanitarian affairs. In these pages, it informed that the OHCHR had increased its staff in 45%, enhanced its communications, and operated in a significantly changed environment, but could not inform how many refugees had received the support of the UN. Actually, it did not inform anything that really mattered.

41 UNGA Res. 56/83 (12 December 2001). Since 2002, the ILC has been working on the responsibility of international organizations but no document has been released for consideration yet.

42 UNGA Res 62/63 (6 December 2007), 6th Committee draft resolution A/C.6/63/L.10 (14 November 2008).

43 It has, however, been recognized by the ICJ that it exists. See *WHO Regional Office* case [1980] ICJ Rep 73.

44 MH Arsanjani, 'Claims Against International Organizations: *Quis Custodiet Ipsos Custodes*' (1981) YJWPO n 7, 133.

45 For an appraisal of the mechanism, see E Suzuki and S Nanwani, 'Responsibility of International Organizations: the Accountability Mechanisms of Multilateral Development Banks' (2006) MJIL v 27, 177 and ER Carrasco and AK Guernsey, 'The World Bank's Inspection Panel: Promoting True Accountability through Arbitration' (2008) CILJ v 41, 577.

46 *North American Agreement on Environmental Cooperation* (adopted August 1993, entered into force 1 January 1994)

47 For an appraisal of the ASEAN, see, D McGoldrick, 'The Asean Charter', ICLQ v 58 n 1, 197.

48 HG Schermers and NM Blokker, *International Institutional Law* (n 2) § 1339; CF Amerasinghe, *Principles of the Institutional Law of International Organizations* (n 3) 399.

49 *Admission of a State to the United Nations (Charter, art 4)* (advisory opinion) [1948] ICJ Rep 57.

50 UNCIO III 'American-Canadian Technical Plan', United Nations Technical Plan (23 April 1945) UNCIO Doc 2 6/7, 79.

51 UNGA Secretary General Report 'In Larger Freedom' (2005) para 148.

52 W Hout and RH Lieshout, 'The Limits of Theory: Detecting Contemporary Global Change and Predicting the Future of State System, in K van Kersbergen, RH Lieshout and G Lock (eds), *Expansion and Fragmentation: Internationalization, Political Change and the Transformation of the Nation State* (AUP, Amsterdam 1999) 68.

53   H Wallace and W Wallace, *Policy Making in the European Union* (4th edn, OUP, Oxford 2000) 31.
54   HG Schermers and NM Blokker, *International Institutional Law* (n 2) § 720.
55   R Higgins, *Problems and Process* (n 17) 10.

CONCLUSION

NGOs, Legitimate Subjects of International Law

McDougal, Laswell and Reisman wrote, back in 1969, that

> 'It is correctly common to characterize the 19th century as the era of the nation-state and the 20th century as the era of the intergovernmental organization. Posterity may characterize our period as the renascent of the individual.'[1]

At the beginning of this 21st century, the individual appears to occupy the central stage of international law. Never before, in the history of Humankind, have people possessed so many rights and freedoms opposable to sovereign States. If democracy is currently the major political regimen of the world, it is a fact that parliament is no longer the only legitimate channel available for the expression of the views, claims and opinions of individuals. Bernard Manin, for instance, has argued that the media has replaced parliament as the *locus* for public debate, an affirmation apparently confirmed by the special attention that politicians currently devote to media training and opinion surveys. Of course, the widespread use of instruments of communication with the masses necessarily drives our attention to the ideas of Ortega y Gasset and the risks to democracy and individual liberty portrayed in his *Rebelión de las Massas* (1930) if the society were to end up dominated by masses of mediocre and indistinguishable individuals. But, if national parliaments are no longer capable of dealing with the complexities of contemporary globalized life and, in turn, the international sphere does not possess a parliament-like institution, how will society be able to cope with the challenges of ensuring pluralist democracy in the 21st century, with 193 interdependent nation-states and 6 billion people?

Some authors have argued that in a world with fragile national borders and rising interdependence, the sovereign nation-states, as we know of them nowadays, would come to an end. Ali Khan, for example, supports their replacement by a 'Free State', a kind of transposition, at the global level, of the administrative model that is observed within unitary countries (such as France), where internal divisions would be established for administrative purposes.[2] Others, such as Hedley Bull, support that States will disappear and will be replaced by a neo-medieval world governmental system of overlapping authority and multiple loyalty, similar to the one that existed in Western Christendom during the Middle Ages.[3] The fragility of the State may be appraised from another perspective: pluralism. Michael Reisman, for example, supports that undemocratic governments lack the legitimacy to participate fully in the international community, hence, authorizing foreign intervention to restore democracy.[4] Following along the same line of thought, Anne Marie Slaughter rejects the long-established equality among States to declare that 'the most distinctive aspect of liberal international relations theory is that it permits, indeed mandates, a distinction among different types of states based on their domestic political structure and ideology'.[5] Both authors, in their vehement defense of liberalism, ended up rejecting its own essence, i.e., the respect to fundamental freedoms of expression and self-government.

Is the world moving toward a situation in which the very pillars of international law will be destroyed? If we assume it, what will emerge from the rubble? A world controlled by the masses? What will prevail: Khan's global government, Bull's neo-medievalism or Reisman's and Slaughter's illiberal liberalism? Could international law, which so bravely resisted several 'hot' wars and a cold war, be destroyed by the so sought-after and dreamt-of widespread democracy and cooperation between States?

During our research, we have demonstrated that international law has indeed been changing to accommodate new legitimated actors that were not conceivable under positivism. The first, classical one is the individual; the second, contemporary ones are the NGOs. The individual is the origin and also the final addressee of law. He is at the origin, because laws are made by individuals acting on behalf of other individuals in abstract structures; he is at the end, since all laws aim at regulating the individual or collective behavior of every human being, endeavoring to ensure a peaceful existence. This rather obvious circularity had not been acknowledged by international law, which, left in the hands of positivists, had conceived of a model in which individuals and private persons were matters falling within the control of the States, which possessed absolute competence to regulate their lives without the interference of other States. Considering that the world was divided into several States, international law acted as the 'grease' used to reduce the friction between the world's 'tectonic plates'. In this model, only diplomats and soldiers were visible.

However, as we have already mentioned, the positivists failed to acknowledge the emergence of democracy in the West and, arguably, the impact that industrialization and the massive movement of people to urban settings had on their access to information and, also, the expansion of their cognitive capacities, proportional to their increasingly universal access to education. Once men acquire self-consciousness, they tend to reject oppression. One cannot forget that the more educated an individual is, the more claims he makes and the more things he demands. This situation was acknowledged, in a certain way, by Ortega y Gasset when he affirmed that 'minorities are individual or groups of individuals especially qualified [and] the masses are the collection of people not specially qualified.'[6] During the 20th century, the States' concerns steadily shifted from deterrence to cooperation, moreover after the end of the Cold War. Paralleling this cooperative tendency, the individual emerged as a subject of law possessing rights and duties under international law. In a certain way, the positivist theory, which had always denied such a possibility, led to its emergence when, having pushed to one extreme by totalitarian States, it collapsed under the heavy toll of the massacres of human beings. Certainly, if the 20th century had experienced a less severe form of positivism, the current situation would be different. Hence we must be careful, when defending the ideas of liberalism and democracy, to act more like missionaries than like soldiers.

Nonetheless, the individual was at the center of the political theories that conceived the State before Hegel and positivism. Under the contractarianism of Hobbes, Locke, Rousseau and Kant, the individuals were the original bearers of the power to govern themselves, which was passed on to the sovereign, either under a purely interest-base –as ascertained by Hobbes – or under moral and right concerns, as supported by Locke, Rousseau and Kant. As also affirmed by Grotius, people wanted to live peacefully and possessed the right to enjoy the common things. After the interlude of the 19th century, the individual re-emerged, but now in a different condition: the social contract was no longer a complete metaphor: it could be read hidden in laws ensuring fundamental rights and freedoms as well as obligations of the States toward their citizens; it could be understood as embodied in the States' democratic constitutions. Idealism had somehow found its way into the legal system.

Lauterpacht, for instance, was the forerunner in acknowledging the emergence of international human rights and freedoms, and, particularly, of the international legal personality of individuals when, joining the preparatory works for the Nuremberg Tribunal, he contributed to the recognition that individuals possessed duties (and rights) under international law. As a neo-Grotian, his conception of international law was deeply embedded in natural law and in the conviction that men desired to live peacefully in society. But, as a Jew who had fled from the Nazis and had seen the atrocities of the War, his idealism had to cope with the hard realism of the period. Therefore, while recognizing that the individual was the original subject of law, he rationally supported the conception that States had to act, hence joining mainstream international law, though *representing* their citizens because the international norm had to be regarded 'in the final instance [as] structured towards the realization of respect for the rights and interests of human beings.'[7] States, then, were not Authors, bodies with their own souls, but Actors.

The atrocities of totalitarianism also affected the understanding of the place of the individual in political science. Hannah Arendt, for example, dedicated considerable efforts towards demystifying the mighty-State. In her first major work, *On Totalitarianism* (1951), she insisted that Nazism and Stalinism, which were built on an ideological appeal to the masses, indeed denied the 'humanity' of individuals and destroyed the public realm as a space of liberty and freedom. With individuality lost indistinguishably in a mass of mediocrity, terror could be implanted with the massive killings of degenerated races or opponents of bourgeoisie. She supported that totalitarianism was the outcome of a series of social pathologies that had de-legitimated political institutions and atrophied the principles of citizenship and pluralist participation in deliberative consensus, which constituted the core of democracy. It is a timeless truth that once bureaucracies, even lawfully, deny the participation of individuals in the public realm, they weaken their legitimacy and put democracy in jeopardy.

In her following major work, *The Human Condition* (1958), Hannah Arendt continued her journey in reasserting politics as a valuable and effective realm of human action, hence capable of distinguishing it from any other forms of animal life. While Labor, performed by 'unfree' *animal laborans*, was related to the relentless activities required to supply the needs of the natural and biological dimensions of life, Work, performed by the *Homo Faber*, possessed an inherent distinctly humane character, because it was connected to the construction of both physical (buildings, for instance) and cultural (law) walls separating the human realm from that of nature and providing a 'common world' of public institutions and spaces for the unfolding of human life in a political community. It follows that even in a society said (considered) liberal and capitalist, where individuals seek affluence (as apparently occurs in the one we live in today), the *animal laborans* may threaten the *homo faber*, because the focus shifts from the latter's view of a permanent common world to the former's need of consumption of perishable 'must-have' goods, which cannot ensure an enduring public and shared environment for our existence. So liberalism may conceal a trap to men in drawing their attention and efforts only towards the fulfillment of their basic, though rising consumer needs. By doing so, men tend to alienate themselves from political life and end up losing their freedom. To avoid this, men must depart from the Work done by the *homo faber* and Act in a political community, being such Action necessary to achieve plurality, which is 'specifically *the* condition - not only the *conditio sine qua non*, but moreover the *conditio per quam* - of all political life'. Straightforwardly, for Hannah Arendt, participation in public affairs is an intrinsically humane condition and a secure barrier against totalitarianism, whatever the form or the mermaid's chant that it performs. But, how will men be able to exercise their pluralist humane condition in the international realm?

As seen in Chapter 5, the general principles of law constitute a concrete manifestation of the idea of Natural Law in contemporary international law, which, in turn, embeds an innate humane condition of self-governing. The right of individuals' participation in the political sphere was recognized by the UN Charter (1945), which established the principle of self-determination of people and put an end to colonialism, and in the International Covenant of Civil and Political Rights (1966). These two *hard law* commandments did not actually create the right, since 'States are not capable of creating human rights by law or by convention; they can only confirm their existence and give them protection', because those rights had always existed together with the human being, 'independently of, and before, the State'.[8] If, for Hannah Arendt, as well as Grotius, men are political animals in an Aristotelian sense, international law has also acknowledged this condition in the aforementioned major conventions. The philosophical construction, hence, acquired a material body in the international system.

But, in any legal system, possessing rights necessarily implies in assuming that the bearer of those rights is a subject of law, i.e., that he or she possesses a legal personality. If the legal system rejects the subjectivity of the bearer of the rights, it actually denies the existence of any right at all, and, hence, such a system could be regarded as totalitarian in relation to that individual, who no longer stands as a human being, but rather passes into the realm of things. Since immemorial times, law has used the subject/object dichotomy to legitimate the master/servant relation or that of owner/possessed and deny fundamental rights.[9] If individuals possess innate rights to participate in the public sphere and such rights are recognized by highly supported treaty law, then those rights must be raised to State practices at the international level. Such a claim is necessarily a truism if we consider the inherent and always proclaimed characteristic of international law, which, historically, does not look vertically, downward at the States, but horizontally, between the States. Hence, denying the horizontal interstate character of any rights ensured by international law is denying the own coherence of the system.

Considering that, as discussed in Chapter 6, individuals possess an original international legal personality and that, according to the above mentioned treaties they are entitled to fundamental rights under international law, it is important to appraise to what extent those rights can be exercised in a legitimate, rational and effective manner in a system originally conceived to have few interacting parties.

The emergence of intergovernmental organizations, notably in the second half of the last century, has demonstrated that international law is capable of accommodating new actors and procedures in a productive manner. As we have studied and is widely acknowledged, States shifted their emphasis from bilateral contractual arrangements towards bureaucracy-like structures, exporting to the international level the same model that they had successfully implemented within their domestic spheres, which, in democratic regimes, comprehends a wide array of channels of dialogue with individuals and civil society at large that goes far beyond the narrow limits of parliament, neither jeopardizing (in fact, enhancing) the effectiveness and legitimacy of the States nor transferring the decision-making power. These broad dialogue arrangements have the purpose of increasing the State's responsiveness to the needs, interests and expectations of the citizens, ensuring the necessary pluralism in democracy. Given that some studies suggest that democratic States tend not to make war against other democratic States, it appears that some connection can be established between pluralism and peace.

Pluralism is present in the international system supported in various long-established legal doctrines. From a State-centric perspective, the first one is equality between States - whether giants or dwarfs, as Kant said. If all States are equal under international law, then they possess legal conditions to stand at the same level to formulate the destinies of the international community, even though realists, such as De Visscher, relying on the foot-print theory, support that some are more equal than others, and passionate idealists, such as Reisman and Anne-Maria Slaughter, support that they are equal only if they have a democratic pedigree. The second one is the decision by vote in the intergovernmental organization's bodies and the customary quest for consensus in multilateral treaty making. Thirdly, one could argue that pluralism is ensured by the criteria adopted by the UN Charter for admission of its members, which do not impose any restrictions whatsoever on grounds of political or social ideology or form of government. Finally, given that resorting to war was outlawed by the Charter, except in situations of legitimate self-defense, arguably pluralism would not be threatened by the overwhelming military power of one or more States.

However, pluralism is admitted by the Charter from yet another perspective, for it ensured not only pluralism *between* States, but also *beyond* States, when it acknowledged that individuals could interact with the United Nations through non-governmental organizations. By doing so, the Charter, aligned with the respect of human rights of individuals and the right to self-determination of collectivities of individuals (the nations) that constituted the core of its soul, recognized that that right could be exercised, but making concessions to rationality and effectiveness, established that this would be done through a new kind of organization established by the individuals, coining, for the first time in a legal document, the expression 'non-governmental organization'. When individuals were to act in a broader collective perspective, i.e., as a nation, they would do so through governmental organizations (the States); when they were to act in another form, they would do so through *non*-governmental organizations. Pluralism may also be acknowledged from a universal perspective: since nations (and

States) are deeply enrooted in their own cultural background, therefore lacking (*inter*)nationality, the United Nations, having universal aims, had to welcome a different perspective of interaction with individuals from several countries, for which the *inter*national NGOs appeared to be a reasonable solution.

But, as we suggested above, some connection may be established between pluralism and peace. Hence, it is important to bear in mind that peace, as affirmed by Grotius, is respect for rights and, as enshrined in the UN Charter, is the purpose of the organization that congregates peace-loving countries. So, enhancing pluralism is a key element towards fostering the achievement of the main goal of the United Nations and all its specialized agencies, funds and programmes, which, as we have affirmed elsewhere, are in charge of specific elements of the overall idea of peace as respect for rights.

But how could the UN enhance pluralism if virtually all States are already its members and the UN is not inclined to sponsor their dismemberment? The answer appears to be given by the Charter: through interaction with international NGOs. However, such interaction demands an answer to a subjacent question: Should NGOs be regarded as subjects of international law?

NGOs are subjects of law to the same extent that Intergovernmental Organizations are, because they were created by legitimate subjects of international law under a typical principal-agent relationship as rational-legal bodies entrusted with certain functions, which, with the attendant duties and responsibilities, were clothed by its constituencies 'with the competence required to *enable those functions to be effectively discharged*'.[10] It follows that, like intergovernmental organizations, international NGOs do not compete with the States. They are bureaucracies established by formal arrangements to perform a same type of issue-oriented task.

The recognition of the NGOs' legal personality can be observed in several formal sources of law, notably treaties and customary international law, addressed at length in the first chapters of this essay. A noteworthy aspect of the outcome of our research is the overwhelming evidence that this legal personality has been fully acknowledged by acts of States. In Chapter 2, we saw that there are several *hard law* and *soft law* agreements dealing with the relationship between States and international NGOs, which recognized NGOs to have *locus standi* before international courts and quasi-judicial bodies, as appraised in the subsequent chapter. In Chapter 4, we saw that there is strong evidence that NGOs have acquired certain rights under international customary law, supported in constant, extensive and virtually uniform settled practice accepted as law by those parties whose interests are specially affected, without persistent objection. The effectiveness of the enhancement of plurality and the respect of rights with the participation of international NGOs in the UN system is remarkably perceived, for instance, in the recurring struggles in the admission of new NGOs with consultative status before the ECOSOC, as addressed in Chapter 2 (item 2.1.2) and in the submission of *amicus* briefs before judicial and quasi-judicial bodies, studied in Chapter 3. From a less contentious perspective, it is widely acknowledged that the participation of NGOs in UN convened Conferences 'reached unprecedented levels and led to an important breakthrough in the perception by UN officials and member-states alike of the role of NGOs', which are 'no longer seen only as disseminators of information, but as shapers of policy and indispensable bridges between the general public and the intergovernmental processes'.[11] In sum, NGOs constitute a remarkable contribution to pluralism at the international level and, even more importantly, a *fundamental* gust of fresh air in the bureaucracy of the UN system.

As we have stated and is also widely known, bureaucrats are not elected. They do not occupy their chair based on a democratic rotation model; rather, they usually maintain their position until their retirement under generous pension schemes. Hence, they lack what Thomas Franck called a 'democratic pedigree'. Governments come and go and bureaucrats are hardly ever removed, because they have the right to stay there. Sometimes they bend to the wind like stalks of bamboo, but more often they remain as steady as centenary oaks. If bureaucracies are fundamental for the stability of the rational-legal structure of the States and the Intergovernmental Organizations, they also represent a risk of the negation of the public sphere, conceived as such as a locus in which individuals interact.

So, it appears to be important, indeed critical, for the sake of democracy in general, and pluralism in particular, that intergovernmental organizations become more accountable for their achievements and more permeable to the participation of individuals, acting through NGOs. International law has, in Arendtian terms, already Worked. Action is, now, necessary to ensure that the humane condition – the core of the Charter – will be preserved and that in the future, men will not find themselves in the nightmare of global proportions suggested by D'Amato and appraised in the Introduction.

How?

This is no easy task, but it is feasible.

Firstly, the transformation of humankind into a mass of mediocre and indistinguishable individuals in the eyes of international bureaucrats must be avoided. For that purpose, and to enhance their legitimacy, the intergovernmental organizations must establish effective broad *fora* of discussion in which their bureaucrats engage in continuous discussion procedures with international NGOs and State representatives to establish, monitor, appraise, adjust and make public the policies and programs of the organization, under the principles of effective notice, adequate information, proper procedures, and appropriate taking into account of the outcome of public participation, already established by the Aarhus Convention. Similarly, the judicial and quasi judicial bodies, in their search for the truth and relevant facts to deliver a judicious decision, must be prepared to accept information provided by international NGOs relevant to the case in analysis.

Secondly, to ensure the necessary legitimacy, plurality as well as the internationality of the debates, renewed qualified criteria for granting consultative status to international NGOs must be adopted. For such a purpose, we suggest that international non-governmental organizations should be affirmatively defined as *those non-profit legal entities, voluntarily established by citizens or associations of citizens with residence in at least five countries, that are independent from government and political groups that seek political power, whose transnational aims and peaceful operations have international utility and are in conformity with the spirit, purposes and principles of the Charter of the United Nations.*

Acknowledging that NGOs represent the form of participation of individuals in the intergovernmental organizations and that individuals, as well as the international NGOs constituted for such a purpose, are subjects of international law, criteria similar to those adopted by the admission of member-states to the UN must be implemented in regard to NGOs. However, considering that the multiplicity of international NGOs surpasses by far the number of States, the decision regarding admission must shift from approval to rejection, which, in any case has to be justified by the voting State and made widely public.

Assuming that conflicts of interest may arise and that anyone dealing with public concerns must be held accountable for their acts and decisions, necessary checks and balances and appropriate incentives to good governance must be established. We can foresee, for instance, from a 'means' perspective: the prohibition of any NGO receiving funds from the UN or any intergovernmental organization in which it has been accredited; adoption of the same criteria for transparency of reports and financial statements established, from time to time, to the UN; establishment of whistleblower and conflict of interest policies; and adoption of the same accounting standards. From an 'ends' perspective, reports must focus on the achievement of the ends defined in the statutes of the concerned organization according to determined objective criteria, comparing, whenever possible, the goals with the achievements.

Thirdly, given that transparency is not forbidden by international law or the constitutive acts of any of the intergovernmental organizations, some procedures can be established within the decision-making capacities of the governing bodies of the considered organization. Considering the technology available, real-time transmission and interaction should be pursued, as well as on-line user-friendly information sharing.

Fourthly, appraising the effectiveness and coherence of performance is essential. For that purpose, reports must be completely reoriented in order to make the intergovernmental organizations accountable for their past and future actions and decisions, for their planning, and for the verified outcome. The measurement of their performance has two defined parameters: the statutory objective of the concerned organization or the purposes of the convention, and the budgetary considerations.

International NGOs, together with States, can make intergovernmental organizations more pluralist and ends-oriented. NGOs do not represent nations, as do States; they represent individuals exercising their political and participatory rights in the international sphere. When States realized that the world's challenges could not be dealt with on an independent basis and that cooperation was necessary, a new opportunity for development and peace became feasible. Given that States are lasting structures established in a uniform way across the planet, it does not seem probable that neo-medievalism or free states will flourish, because this would necessarily imply in the existence of supra-state structures with a power of their own, which does not appear foreseeable in the future. Sovereignty has proven to be a malleable concept that has managed to keep its strength since the Peace of Westphalia. However, it can be threatened by its very own liberal origins in a world with apparently uniform political regimens. Liberal Democracy cannot be a religion that transforms missionaries into soldiers, or, even worse, into crusaders. Such an approach backfired in the past and it cannot succeed in the future. The West cannot march eastward disseminating its 'religion' because Democracy presupposes plurality; and Freedom and Order are its germane fundamental values in an international system conceived to avoid 'earthquakes' caused by 'tectonic states'. As we have already said, the centrality that 'Common Rights' has in Grotius' work can't go unnoticed. Handling those rights in the 'Common World' of Hannah Arendt requires plurality and this plurality can be achieved in many forms, moreover making international bureaucracy more accountable for its ends-oriented achievements, in which our well-known NGOs can play an important and legitimate role. After all, the 'the ability of citizens to control their own lives, by virtue of their rights as human beings, is the most critical and fundamental human concern at the dawn of the 21st century'.[12]

Notes

1   MS McDougal, HD Laswell and WM Reisman, 'The World Constitutive Process of Authoritative Decision', in R Falk, *The Future of International Legal Order* (PUP, Princeton 1969) v 1, 94.
2   L Ali Khan, *The Extinction of Nation-States: a World Without Borders* (Kluwer, The Hague 1996).

3   H Bull, *The Anarchical Society: a Study of Order in World Politics* (MacMillan, London 1977) 254.

4   WM Reisman, 'Sovereignty and Human Rights in Contemporary International Law' (1990) AJIL n 84, 866.

5   AM Slaughter, 'International Law in a World of Liberal States' (1994) EJIL n 6, 503.

6   Ortega y Gasset, *The Revolt of the Masses* (1930).

7   PM Dupuy, 'Some Reflections on Contemporary International Law and the Appeal to Universal Values: A Response to Martii Koskenniemi' (2005) EJIL v 16 n 1, 131.

8   *South West Africa* Second Phase (Judge Tanaka's Dissenting Opinion) [1966] ICJ Rep 6, 294-299.

9   This reminds us of a situation in which a Brazilian criminal with an arrest order was localized by Interpol in a Southeastern Asian country that did not possess an extradition agreement with Brazil. In order to ensure a quick repatriation, the Brazilian consul, together with immigration officials of the host country, approached the individual in a restaurant and, once the latter asked for his passport, it was handed over to the consular authorities, who, relying on their rights ensured by international norms, cancelled the passport of the individual, instantly making him an illegal immigrant subject to immediate deportation. Since he could only bring a claim against the act of the Brazilian consul before the Brazilian Courts, he had no legal option except to board a plane back to the country that had issued the international order of arrest.

10 *Reparation for Injuries Suffered in the Service of the United Nations* (Advisory Opinion) [1949] ICJ Rep 179 *(emphasis added)*

11 UNGA Report of the Secretary General on 'Arrangements and practices for the interaction of non-governmental organizations in all activities of the United Nations system' (10 July 1998) UN Doc A/53/170 paras 57-59.

12 TE Paupp, *Achieving inclusionary Governance: advancing peace and development in first and third world nations* (Transnational publisher, Ardsey 2000) 464.

SUMMARY IN DUTCH

NGO'S: WETTIGE SUBJECTEN VAN INTERNATIONAAL RECHT

In ons oeuvre verdedigen wij het standpunt dat het pluralisme is toegestaan door het Handvest der Verenigde Naties, niet slechts *tussen* de Staten, maar *verder dan* deze, omdat het Handvest heeft erkend dat individuen in contact zouden kunnen treden met de Verenigde Naties, niet alleen door middel van de gouvernementele organisaties, maar ook door middel van particuliere organisaties.

NGO's zijn kinderen van onze tijd. Als de electorale democratie de overheersende regeringsvorm is in de wereld en de mensen steeds meer deel uitmaken van de publieke sfeer, lijkt het ons ook onbetwistbaar dat het recht van de volkeren op zelfbeschikking zich veel verder heeft uitgebreid dan het recht op onafhankelijkheid van het koloniale systeem, om het recht op democratie te omvatten.

Erkennend dat individuen subjecten zijn van internationaal recht, hierbij uitgaande van de gevestigde hedendaagse doctrine, betogen wij dat, evenals de multilaterale organen juridische internationale persoonlijkheid hebben afgeleid van hun leden, de Staten, de NGO's een soortgelijke wettelijke status hebben verworven, uitgaande van de individuen.

Wij zijn ons bewust dat onze stelling vernieuwend is, en daarom trachten wij onze argumentering te ondersteunen met als uitgangspunt de studie van de NGO's ten opzichte van ieder der bronnen van internationaal recht, zoals opgesomd in artikel 38 van het statuut van het Internationale Hof van Justitie. Bij onze analyse stelden wij vast dat de positivistische theorie dat het internationale recht een wettelijk reguleringssysteem is van de verhouding tussen Staten en dat het aldus nimmer andere rechtssubjecten zou toestaan, niet langer houdbaar is.

Zoals we zullen zien hebben NGO's bepaalde rechten in de sfeer van het Internationale Recht, erkend door verdragen en ook door talloze andere multilaterale handelingen. De constante, extensieve en feitelijk uniforme geconsolideerde praktijk van de Staten en hun relatie met NGO's, als regel aanvaard door allen die daardoor speciaal geraakt worden, zonder enig bestendig bezwaar, bewijst dat het internationaal gewoonterecht ook hun rechten erkent. Op dezelfde wijze hebben NGO's bepaalde rechten bij de internationale hoven, ook al is het niet uniform; zij kunnen bij enkele daarvan *amicus curie* zaken voorleggen, alsook bij andere *locus standi* staande

houden. De situatie van de NGO's vanuit het oogpunt van de algemene beginselen van het internationale recht leidde ons naar het onderzoek van de
ontwikkeling van die beginselen in de beslissingen van het Internationale
Hof van Justitie, waar wij een progressieve uitbreiding aantroffen van de
erkenning van humanitaire beginselen en individuele rechten en ook in een
andere dimensie, de markante verruiming van het beginsel van de zelfbeschikking van de volkeren, die heden ten dage geïnterpreteerd wordt als
recht op deelneming aan publieke aangelegenheden en, waarom het niet te
zeggen, als recht op democratie. De situatie van de NGO's in de oeuvres
van de grote juristen van internationaal recht vereiste nadruk op het onderzoek van de situatie van het individu als subject van internationaal recht.

Het onderzoek van de theorieën over contractualisme betreffende de vor-
ming van de Staat in een hedendaagse zeer democratische ambiance gaf
ons de mogelijkheid te stellen dat het noodzakelijk is een nieuw bestand
toe te voegen aan het model ontworpen door Thomas Franck over
Democratisch Bestuur, door middel van mechanismen van maatschappe-
lijke deelneming in bureaucratische structuren die de multilaterale organen
bewerkstelligen, welke, het dient aangetekend te worden, exponentieel
groeien in aantal en macht, sinds de oprichting van de Verenigde Naties.
Voor deze uitdaging lijken ons de NGO's een redelijke en legitieme
oplossing.

SUMMARY IN FRENCH

ONGs: SUJET LÉGITIME EN DROIT INTERNATIONAL

Dans notre traité, nous soutenons que le pluralisme est admis par la Charte des Nations Unies non seulement *entre* les États, mais *hors* d'eux, puisque la Charte reconnaît que les personnes puissent interagir avec les Nations Unies non seulement au moyen d'organismes gouvernamentaux, mais aussi au moyen d'organisations *non*-gouvernementales.

Les ONGs sont les enfants de notre époque. Si la démocratie électorale est bien la forme prédominante de gouvernement dans le monde et si les citoyens participent toujours plus aux affaires publiques, il nous paraît tout aussi indubitable que le droit des peuples à l'auto-détermination s'est étendu bien au-delà du droit à l'indépendance du régime colonial, afin d'englober le droit à la démocratie.

Reconnaîssant, à partir de la doctrine contemporaine, que les individus sont assujettis au droit international, nous soutenons que de même que les organismes multilatéraux possèdent une personnalité juridique internationale dérivée de leurs associés les États, les ONGs ont, à partir des individus, aquis un statut légal similaire.

Nous avons conscience que notre thèse est novatrice, et pour cette raison recherchons étayer notre argumentaire à partir de l'étude de la situation des ONGs au regard de chacune des sources du droit international, telles qu'énumérées dans l'article 38 des statuts de la Cour Internationale de Justice. Au cours de notre analyse, nous mettons en exergue que la théorie positiviste qui affirme que le droit international est un système légal de régulation des rapports entre États n'est plus valable car elle n'admet jamais d'autres sujets de droit.

Comme nous le verrons, les ONGs détiennent certains droits dans le cadre du Droit International, reconnus par des traités, également par d'innombrables autres actes multilatéraux. La pratique constante, uniforme et répandue des États dans leur rapports aux ONGs accepte comme règle pour quelconque partie qui est spécialement concernée, sans l'ombre d'une objection, l'évidence que le droit coutumier international leur a également reconnu des droits. De la même manière, les ONGs détiennent certains droits par devant les tribunaux internationaux, même de façon non uniforme, pouvant se présenter comme *amicus curie* en certains d'entre eux et jusqu'à jouir de *locus standi* devant d'autres. La situation des ONGs sous l'angle des principes généraux du droit international nous a conduit à l'analyse de l'évolution de ces principes dans les décisions de la Cour Internationale de Justice, où nous avons rencontré une expansion progressive de la reconnaissance de principes humanitaires et de droits individuels ainsi que, dans une autre échelle, l'élargissement marquant du principe de l'auto-détermination des peuples qui est interprété aujourd'hui comme un droit de participation aux sujets publics et, pourquoi ne pas l'affirmer, comme un droit à la démocratie. La situation des ONGs dans les travaux des grands juristes du droit international a demandé à s'attacher à l'analyse de la situation de l'individu en tant que sujet du droit international.

L'analyse des théories de contrats comme formation de l'État dans une ambiance contemporaine amplement démocratique nous a permis d'affirmer qu'il était nécessaire d'ajouter un nouveau bloc au modèle conçu par Thomas Franck sur la Gouvernance Démocratique, par des mécanismes de participation civile au sein des structures bureaucratiques qui régissent les organismes multilatéraux, lesquels, on le voit, croissent de manière exponentielle, en nombre et pouvoir, depuis la création des Nations Unies. Pour répondre à ce défi, les ONGs nous semblent être une solution raisonnable et légitime.

SUMMARY IN GERMAN

NROn: BERECHTIGTES VÖLKERRECHTSSUBJEKTE

In unserer Arbeit stellen wir fest, daß der Pluralismus im Rahmen der VN Karte nicht nur *zwischen* den Staaten erlaubt ist, sondern *darüber hinaus*, weil die Karte anerkannte, daß Personen mit den Vereinten Nationen nicht nur durch staatliche Organisationen interagieren konnte, aber auch von *Nicht*-Regierungs-Organisationen.

NGOs sind Töchter unserer Zeit. Wenn die Wahlkreise Demokratie die vorherrschende Form der Regierung in der Welt ist und die Menschen sich die Öffentlichkeit zunehmen, scheint es uns auch klar, daß das Recht der Völker auf Selbstbestimmung weit über das Recht auf Unabhängigkeit von der Kolonialherrschaftm erweitert hat, um das Recht auf Demokratie zu verstehen.

In dem Erkenntnis, von etablierten zeitgenössischen Lehre, daß die Menschen Subjekte des Völkerrechts sind, argumentieren wir daß, sowie multilateralen Organisationen internationale Rechtspersönlichkeit von ihren Mitgliedern haben, ergibt es sich daß die NROn einen ähnlichen rechtlichen Status von Einzelpersonen erwerben.

Wir sind bewusst, daß unsere Arbeit innovativ ist, und daher versuchen wir unsere Argumente aus den Studien der NROs gegen jede der Quellen des Völkerrechts zu unterstützen, wie im Artikel 38 des Statuts des Internationalen Gerichtshofs. Während unserer Analyse haben wir festgestellt daß die positivistische Theorie, in der das internationelle Völkerrecht ein Rechtssystem des Verhältnis zwischen den Staaten ist, nicht mehr unterstüzbar ist und deswegen würden andere Rechtssubjekte niemals zugegeben.

Wie man sehen wird, NROn haben bestimmte Rechte in dem Völkerrecht, durch Verträge anerkannt und auch von zahlreichen anderen multilateralen Rechtsakten. Die ständige, umfassende und praktisch einheitliche konsolidierte Praxis der Staaten in ihre Beziehungen zu den NROn, in der Regel anerkannt durch alle diejenigen die besonders betroffen sind, ohne anhaltende Einwand, Beweise dafür daß das Völkergewohnheitsrecht auch ihre Rechte anerkannt. Ebenso halten NRO bestimmte Rechte vor internationalen Gerichten, wenn auch in einer uneinheitlicher Weise und kann *amicus curie* in einige von ihnen zu nehmen und *locus standi* vor anderen halten. Die Situation der NROn aus der Perspektive der allgemeinen Grundsätze des Völkerrechts, führte uns auf die Analyse diese Grundsätze in den Entscheidungen des Internationalen Gerichtshofs, Teil einen schrittweiser Ausbau der Anerkennung der humanitären Grundsätze und die Rechte des Einzelnen, aber auch in einer anderer Größe, eine beeindruckende Ausweitung des Prinzips der Selbstbestimmung der Völker, die heute als Recht auf Teilnahme an öffentlichen Angelegenheiten interpretiert ist und für diese Angelegenheit, wie ein Recht auf Demokratie. Die Situation der NROn in den Werken des großen Juristen des Völkerrechts erforderte Schwerpunkt auf der Analyse der einzelnen als Subjekt des Völkerrechts.

Die Analyse der vertragstheoretischen Theorien der Staatsbildung in einer weit demokratische moderne Stimmung lässt uns sagen, daß ein neuer Block um das Modell von Thomas Franck entwickelt über die demokratische Governance hinzufügen muss, durch Beteiligung Mechanismen der Bürger an bürokratischen Strukturen die die multilateralen Organisationen treiben, die exponentiell an Zahl und Kraft wachsen seit der Gründung der Vereinten Nationen. Für diese Aufgabe, scheinen uns NROn eine vernünftige und legitime Lösung zu sein.

SUMMARY IN PORTUGUESE

ONGS: LEGÍTIMOS SUJEITOS DE DIREITO INTERNACIONAL

Em nossa obra, sustentamos que a pluralismo é admitido pela Carta das Nações Unidas não apenas *entre* os Estados, mas *além* deles, porque a Carta reconheceu que indivíduos poderiam interagir com as Nações Unidas não apenas por meio de organizações governamentais, mas também por organizações *não*-governamentais.

ONGs são filhas de nosso tempo. Se a democracia eleitoral é a forma predominante de governo no mundo e as pessoas cada vez mais participam da esfera pública, parece-nos também inquestionável que o direito dos povos à autodeterminação expandiu-se muito além do direito à independência do regime colonial, para compreender o direito à democracia.

Reconhecendo, a partir de estabelecida doutrina contemporânea, que indivíduos são sujeitos de direito internacional, argumentamos que, assim como os organismos multilaterais têm personalidade jurídica internacional derivada de seus associados, os Estados, as ONGs adquiriram semelhante status legal, a partir dos indivíduos.

Estamos conscientes que nossa tese é inovadora, e, por isso, buscamos suportar nosso argumento a partir do estudo da situação das ONGs ante cada uma das fontes do direito internacional, tal como listadas no artigo 38 do estatuto da Corte Internacional de Justiça. Ao longo de nossa análise, identificamos que não mais se sustenta a teoria positivista de que o direito internacional é um sistema legal de regulação do relacionamento entre Estados e que, assim, jamais admitiria outros sujeitos de direito.

Como veremos, ONGs detém certos direitos no âmbito do Direito Internacional, reconhecidos por tratados e, também, por inúmeros outros atos multilaterais. A constante, extensiva e virtualmente uniforme prática consolidada dos Estados em sua relação com ONGs, aceita como regra por todos aqueles que sejam especialmente afetados, sem qualquer persistente objeção, evidencia que o direito costumeiro internacional também lhes reconheceu direitos. Da mesma forma, ONGs detém certos direitos antes tribunais internacionais, embora de uma maneira não uniforme, podendo apresentar *amicus curie* em alguns deles e até deter *locus standi* perante outros. A situação das ONGs sob a ótica dos princípios gerais do direito internacional, nos levou à análise da evolução desses princípios nas decisões da Corte Internacional de Justiça, onde encontramos uma progressiva expansão do reconhecimento de princípios humanitários e direitos individuais e, também, sob outra dimensão, o marcante alargamento do principio da autodeterminação dos povos que hoje vem sendo interpretado como direito à participação em assuntos públicos e, por que não dizer, como direito à democracia. A situação das ONGs nas obras dos grandes juristas de direito internacional requereu ênfase na análise da situação do indivíduo como sujeito de direito internacional.

A análise das teorias contratualistas da formação do Estado em um ambiente contemporâneo amplamente democrático permitiu-nos afirmar que é necessário adicionar um novo bloco ao modelo concebido por Thomas Franck sobre Governança Democrática, através de mecanismos de participação civil nas estruturas burocráticas que operam os organismos multilaterais, os quais, registre-se, crescem exponencialmente, em número e poder, desde a criação das Nações Unidas. Para esse desafio, as ONGs nos parecem uma razoável e legítima solução.

BIBLIOGRAPHY

1) Books, Articles and Periodicals

AHMED, S. and POTTER, D. NGOs in international politics (Kumarian Press, Bloomfield 2006)

AKERHURST, M. Custom as a Source of International Law (1974/75) BYIL 3

ALBUQUERQUE MELLO, C.D. Curso de Direito Internacional Publico (8th edn Freitas Bastos, Rio de Janeiro 1986)

ALI KHAN, L. The Extinction of Nation-States: a World Without Borders (Kluwer, The Hague 1996)

ALKOBY, A. 'Non-State Actors and the legitimacy of international environmental law' (2003) Non-State Actors and International Law, v 3 n 1

ALLOT, P. 'Reconstituting Humanity – New International Law' (1992) EJIL n 3, 219

ALSTON, P. (ed). The UN and Human Rights (Clarendon Press, Oxford 1992)

ALSTON, P. (ed). Non-State Actors and Human Rights (OUP, Oxford 2005)

AMERASINGHE, C.F. Principles of the Institutional Law of International Organizations (2nd edn CUP, Cambridge 2005)

ANDERSON, K. 'The Ottawa Convention Banning Landmines, the role of International Non-governmental Organizations and the Idea of International Civil Society' (2000) EJIL v 11 n 1

ANHEIER, H.; GLASIUS, M. and KALDOR, M (eds). Global Civil Society 2001 (OUP, Oxford 2001)

ANTON, D.K., MATHEW, P. and MOREAN, W. International Law (OUP, Oxford 2005)

ANZILOTTI, D. Cours de Droit International (Recueil Sirey, Paris 1929)

AQUINAS, T. Summa Theologica

ARCHIBUGI, D. 'A Critical Analysis of the Self-determination of Peoples: A Cosmopolitan Perspective', (2003) Constellations v 10 n 4

ARENDT, H. Eichmann in Jerusalem: a Report on the Banality of Evil (Penguin, New York 1992)

ARENDT, H. On Totalitarianism (2nd edn UCP, Chicago 1998)

ARENDT, H. The Human Condition (2nd edn UCP, Chicago 1998)

ARISTOTLE. The Politics.

ARSANJANI, M.H. 'Claims Against International Organizations: Quis Custodiet Ipsos Custodes' (1981) YJWPO n 7

ASIL/NVIR, Contemporary International Law Issues: Conflicts and Convergence, Proceedings of the 3RD Joint Conference. (TMC Asser, The Hague 1996)

ASTON, J.D. 'The United Nations Committee on Non-governmental Organizations: Guarding the Entrance of a Politically Divided House' (2001) EJIL v 12 n 5

AUSTIN, J. The province of jurisprudence determined (1832).

BAHER, P.H. 'Mobilization of the Conscience of Mankind: Conditions of Effectiveness of Human Rights NGOs' in Denters, E; Schrijver, N (eds), Reflections of International Law from the Low Countries (Nijhoff, The Hague 1998)

BARNETT, M. and FINNEMORE, M. Rules for the World: International Organizations and World Politics (Cornell UP, Ithaca 2004)

BARNIDGE JR, R.P. Non-State Actors and Terrorism (TMC Asser, The Hague 2008)

BASLAR, K. The concept of the Common Heritage of Humankind (Nijhoff, The Hague 1998)

BASSIOLNI, C. 'The Commission of Experts Established pursuant to Security Council Resolution 780: Investigating Violations of International Humanitarian Law in the Former Yugoslavia' in R Clark and M Sann, The Prosecution of International Crimes (Transaction, New Brunswick 1996)

BECKER, T. Terrorism and the State: Rethinking the rules of state responsibility (Hart Publishing, Portland 2006)

BENTHAN, J. Introduction to the Principles of Morals and Legislation (London 1780)

BETSIL, M.M. and CORELL, E (eds). NGO Diplomacy: The influence of NGOs in International Environmental Negotiations (MIT Press, Cambridge 2008)

BLACK'S LAW DICTIONARY (6th edn West Publishing, St Paul's 1990)

BLOKKER, N.M. and SCHERMERS, H.G. (eds). Proliferation of International Organizations (Kluwer, The Hague 2001)

BOBBIO, N; MATTEUCCI, N. and PASQUINO, G. Dicionário de Política (UnB, Brasilia 2004)

BODIN, J. De la République (Elibron, Paris 2005)

BOLI, J and THOMAS, G.M. 'INGOS and the Organization of World Culture' in J Bolli and GM Thomas, Constructing World Culture: International Nongovernmental Organizations since 1875 (Stanford University Press, Stanford 1999)

BOUTROS-GHALI, B. Paix, Developpement Democratie: trois agendas pour gerer le planete (Pedone, Paris 2002)

BOYLE, A. and CHINKIN, C. The Making of International Law (OUP, New York 2007)

BRETON-LE GOFF, G. L'Influence des Organisations non Gouvernamentales (ONG) sur la negotiation de quelques instruments internationalux (Bruylant, Brussels 2001).

BRIERLY, J.L. The Law of Nations (6th edn Clarendon Press, Oxford 1963)

BROWNLIE, I. Principles of Public International Law (7th edn OUP, Oxford 2008)

BRUNÉE J. and TOOPE, SJ. Legitimacy and Legality in International Law (CUP, Cambridge, 2010)

BUCHANAN, Justice, Legitimacy and Self-Determination (OUP, Oxford, 2004)

BULL, H. The Anarchical Society: a Study of Order in World Politics (MacMillan, London 1977)

CANÇADO TRINDADE, A.A. O Esgotamento de Recursos Internos no Direito Internacional (Editora UnB, Brasilia 1997)

CANÇADO TRINDADE, A.A. A Proteção Internacional dos Direitos Humanos e o Brasil (2nd edn Editora UnB, Brasilia 2000)

CANÇADO TRINDADE, A.A. (ed). Human Rights, Sustainable Development and the Environment (San Jose, 1992)

CANÇADO TRINDADE, A.A. Repertorio da Prática Brasileira do Direito Internacional Publico (Fundação Alexandre de Gusmão, Brasilia 1988)

CANÇADO TRINDADE, A.A. 'International Protection of Human Rights' in Boutros Boutros-Ghali Amicorum Discipulorumque Liber (Bruylant, Bruxelles 1998)

CARRASCO, E.R. and GUERNSEY, A.K. 'The World Bank's Inspection Panel: Promoting True Accountability through Arbitration' (2008) CILJ v 41

CARREAU, D. Droit International (7th edn Pedone, Paris 2001)

CASSESE, A. International Law (2nd edn OUP, Oxford 2005)

CASSESE, A. Self-determination of Peoples: A legal reappraisal (CUP, Cambridge 1995)

CASSESE, A. 'Terrorism is Also Disrupting Some Crucial Legal Categories of International Law' (2001) EJIL v 12 n 5

CASSESE, A. 'The international Court of Justice and the right of peoples to self-determination' in Jennings, R; Lowe, V and Fitzmaurice, M (eds). Fifty years of the International Court of Justice (CUP, Cambridge 2007)

CASSESE, A. The Human Dimension of International Law: Selected Papers (OUP, Oxford 2008)

CHANDHOKE, C. 'The Limits of Global Civil Society', in Glasius, M; Kaldor, M and Anheier, H (eds). Global Civil Society 2002 (OUP, Oxford 2002)

CHARLESWORTH, H and COICAUD, JM, Fault Lines of International Legitimacy (CUP, Cambridge, 2010)

CHARNOVITZ, S and WICKHAM, J. 'Non-Governmental Organizations and the Original International Trade Regime' (1995) Journal of World Trade v 29 n 5

CHASEK, P.S. Earth Negotiations: Analyzing thirty years of Environmental Diplomacy (UN University Press, Tokyo 2001)

CHEN, L.C. An Introduction to Contemporary International Law (2nd edn Yale University Press, New Haven 2000)

CHENG, B. General Principles of Law as Applied by International Courts and Tribunals (CUP London 1953)

CHINKIN, C. 'The Role of Non-Governmental Organisations in Standard Setting, Monitoring and Implementation of Human Rights', in Norton, J; Andenas, M and Focter,M. The Changing World of International Law in the Twenty-First Century: a tribute to the late Kenneth R. Simmonds, (Kluwer Law, The Hague 1998)

CICCIO, L. 'Patenting drugs from 1st January 2005: implications and problems' in HPDJ 2 (2) 136

CLAPHAM, A. 'Creating the High Commissioner for Human Rights. The Untold History' (1994) EJIL v 5

CLAPHAM, A. Human Rights Obligations of Non State Actors (OUP, Oxford 2006)

CLARK, I Legitimacy in International Society (OUP, Oxford, 2007)

CLAYTON, A. (ed). Governance, Democracy & Conditionality: What role for NGOs? (Intrac, Oxford 1994)

COICAUD, JM and HEISKENEN, V, The Legitimacy of International Organizations (UN University Press, Tokyo, 2001)

COLIARD, C.A. and DUBOIS, L. Institutions Internationales (10th edn Dalloz, Paris 1995)

COMBACAU, J. and SUR, S. Droit International Public (7th edn Montchristien, Paris 2006)

COMMISSION FOR ENVIRONMENTAL COOPERATION, Bringing the Facts to Light: a guide to articles 14 and 15 of the North-American Agreement on Environmental Cooperation (CEC, Montreal 2007)

CRAWFORD, J. The Creation of States in International Law (Clarendon Press, Oxford 1979)

CRAWFORD, J. 'Democracy and the Body of International Law, in GH Fox and BR Roth, Democratic Governance and International Law (CUP, Cambridge 2000)

DAILLIER, P. and PELLET, A. Droit international public (7th ed LGDJ, Paris 2002)

D'AMATO, A. The Concept of Custom in International Law (Cornell, New York 1971)

D'AMATO, A. International Law: Process and Prospect (Transnational, Irvington 1995)

D'AMATO, A. 'On the Legitimacy of International Institutions' in R Wolfrum and V Röben (eds) Legitimacy in International Law (Springer, Berlin 2008)

de FROUVILLE, O. L'intangibilité des droits de l'homme en droit international (Pedone, Paris 2004)

de VISSCHER, C. Theory and Reality in Public International Law (2nd edn PUP Princeton 1957)

DEGAN, V.D. Sources of International Law (Brill, Cambridge1997)

DEKKER, I.F. and WERNER, W.G. Governance and International Legal Theory (Nijhoff, The Hague 2004)

DEKKER, I.F. and WERNER, W.G. 'The Completeness of International Law and Hamlet's Dilemma: non liquet, the Nuclear Weapons case, and Legal Theory', in Dekker, IF and Post HHG (eds). On The Foundations and Sources of International Law (TMC Asser Press, The Hague 2003)

DESCAMPS, E. New Africa: an essay on Government Civilization in New Countries and on the foundation, organization and administration of the Congo Free State (Sampson Low, London 1903)

DICTIONAIRE ENCYCLOPÉDIQUE DE THÉORIE ET DE SOCIOLOGIE DU DROIT (10th edn LGDJ, Paris 1993)

DOMINICÉ, C. 'Organisations Internationales et Démocratie' in LB de Chazournes and V Gowland-Debbas, The International Legal System in Quest of Equity and Universality (Martinus Nijhoff, The Hague 2001)

DUPUY, P.M. Droit International Publique (6th edn Paris, Dalloz)

DUPUY, P.M. 'Some Reflections on Contemporary International Law and the Appeal to Universal Values: A Response to Martii Koskenniemi' (2005) EJIL v 16 n 1

DUPUY, P.M. and VIERUCCI, L. NGOs in International Law: Efficiency in Flexibility? (Edward Elgar, Cheltenham 2008)

EHRING, L. 'Public Access to Dispute Settlement Hearings in the World Trade Organization', (2008) JIEL v 11 n 4

ENCYCLOPEDIE JURIDIQUE – REPERTÓIRE DE DROIT INTERNATIONAL (Dalloz, Paris 1968)

FAN, H. 'The Missing link between Self-determination and Democracy: the Case of East Timor' (2007) NJIHR v 6 n 1

FASSBENDER, B. 'The Better Peoples of the United Nations? Europe's Practice and the United Nations', (2004) EJIL v 15 n 5

FENTON, JC. 'The Definition of a Dogma', The Catholic Mind, (1950) January, 11

FIZMAURICE, G.G. 'Some Problems Regarding the Formal Surces of International Law', in Symbolae Verzijl (Nijhoff, The Hague 1958)

FLETCHER, G.P. Basic Concepts of Legal Thought (OUP, Oxford 1996)

FRANCK, T. 'The Emerging Right to Democratic Governance' (1992) AJIL v 86

FRANCK, T. The Power of Legitimacy Among Nations (OUP, Oxford 1990)

FRANCK T. 'Is Personal Freedom a Western Value? (1997) AJIL v 91

FRANCK, T, 'The Relation of Justice to Legitimacy in the International System', in Humanité et Droit International: Mélanges René-Jean Dupuy (Pedone, Paris 1991)

FRANKLIN, J.H. (ed) On Sovereignty: four chapters from six books of the Commonwealth / Jean Bodin (Cambridge Texts in the History of Political Thought, CUP, Cambridge 1992)

FREEMAN, S. Justice and the Social Contract: Essays on Rawlsian Political Philosophy (OUP, Oxford 2007)

FRIEDRICH, C.J. The Philosophy of Law in Historic Perspective (UCP, Chicago 1958)

FULLER, L The Morality of Law (YUP, New Haven 1969)

GAETA, P. 'The Dayton Agreements and International Law' (1996) EJIL v 7

GARIBALDI, O.M. 'On the Ideological Content of Human Rights Instruments: the Clause "in a Democratic Society"', in T Buergenthal, Contemporary Issues in International Law: Essays in Honor of Louis B Sohn (NP Engels Publisher, Kehl, 1984)

GARCIA-PELAYO, M. Burocracia y tecnocracia y otros escritos. (Alianza, Madrid 1984)

GLENNON, M.J. 'Self-determination and Cultural Diversity' (2003) FFWA v 27 n 2

GROTIUS, H. The Free Sea (Natural Law and Enlightenment Classics, Liberty Fund, Indianapolis 2004)

GROTIUS, H. The Rights of War and Peace (Natural Law and Enlightenment Classics, Liberty Fund, Indianapolis 2005).

HALL, S. 'The Persistent Spectre: Natural Law, International Order and the Limits of Legal Positivism' (2001) EJIL v 12 n 12

HASLAM, E. 'Non-Governmental War Crime Tribunals: A Forgotten Arena of International Criminal Justice', in C Harding and CL Lim, Renegotiating Westphalia (Nijhoff, The Hague 1999)

HEERE, P.W. (ed) from Government to Governance (TMC Asser Press, The Hague 2004)

HEGEL, G.F.W. Elements of the Philosophy of Right (CUP, Cambridge 1991).

HIGGINS, R. 'Human Rights in the International Court of Justice' (2007) LJIL v 20

HIGGINS, R. 'Policy Considerations and the International Judicial Process' [1968] 17 ICLQ 58

HIGGINS, R. Problems and Process: International Law and How We Use It, (OUP, Oxford 1994)

HILLGENBERG, H. 'A Fresh Look at Soft Law' (1999) EJIL v 10 n 3

HINTZE, O. 'The State in Historical Perspective' in Bendix, R (ed). State and Society: a Reader in Comparative Political Sociology (2nd ed UC Press, Berkeley 1973)

HOBBES, T. Leviathan, 1651

HOFFMAN, F. 'Watershed or Phoenix from the Ashes? Speculations on the Future of International Law After the September 11 Attacks' (2001) GLJ n 16

HOUST, W. and LIESHOUT, R.H. 'The Limits of Theory: Detecting Contemporary Global Change and Predicting the Future of State System, in K van Kersbergen, RH Lieshout and G Lock (eds), Expansion and Fragmentation: Internationalization, Political Change and the Transformation of the Nation State (AUP, Amsterdam 1999)

JACKSON, R. The Global Covenant: Human Conduct in a World of States (OUP, Oxford 2000)

JENNINGS, R. 'Broader Perspectives in International Law' in A Anghie and G Sturgess, Legal Visions of the 21st Century: Essays in Honor of Judge Christopher Weeramantry (Kluwer, The Hague 1998)

JENNINGS, R. and WATTS, A (eds). Oppenheim's International Law v 1 9th ed (Longman, London 1996)

JUDT, T. Postwar: A History of Europe since 1945 (Objetiva, Rio de Janeiro 2008)

KAMMERHOFER, J. 'The Armed Activities casa and Non-State Actors in Self-Defense Law' (2007) LJIL 20

KAMMERHOFER, J. 'Uncertainty in the Formal Sources of International Law: customary International Law and Some of Its Problems' (2004) EJIL v 15 n 3

KEANE, J. Global Civil Society? (CUP, Cambridge 2003)

KECK, M.E. and SIKKINK, K. Activist beyond Borders (Cornell University Press, Ithaca 1998)

KEITH, A.B. Selected Speeches and Documents on British Colonial Policy 1763-1917 (OUP, London 1948)

KELSEN, H. Principles of International Law (11th ed. Lawbook Exchange, Clark 2003)

KISS, A. and BEURIR, J.P. Droit International de l'Environment, 2nd edn (Pedone, Paris 2000)

KISS, A.C. Repertóire de la pratique française em matiére de droit international public (Centre National de la Recherche Scientifique, Paris 1962) v 5

KLABBERS, J. 'The Life and Times of the Law of International Organizations' (2001) NJIL 70

KLABBERS, J. '(I can't Get No) Recognition: Subject Doctrine and the Emergence of Non-State Actors' in Petman J and Klabbers, J. Nordic Cosmopolitanism (Nijhoff, Leiden 2003)

KOSKENNIEMI, M. The Gentle Civilizer of Nations: The Rise and Fall of International Las 1870-1960 (CUP, Cambridge 2001)

LAUTERPACHT, H. The Functions of Law in the International Community (Oxford 1933)

LAUTERPACHT, H. 'The Subjects of Law' (1947) LQR n 63, p 453

LAUTERPACHT, H. International Law and Human Rights (Steven & Sons, London 1950)

LAUTERPACHT, H. 'Some Observations on the Prohibition of "Non Liquet" and the Completeness of the Law', in Symbolae Verzijl (Leyden 1958)

LAUTERPACHT, H. The Development of International Law by the International Court (London 1958)

LAUTERPACHT, H. International Law: Collected Papers (CUP, Cambridge 1975)

LAVIEILLE, JM. Droit International de l'Environment, (Ellipses, Paris 1998)

LAWSON, R.A. and SCHERMERS H.G. (eds). Leading Cases of the European Court of Human Rights (Ars Aequi Libri, Nijmegen 1999)

LAZIC, D. 'Introductory Note to the International Criminal Court: Prosecutor v. Thomas Lubanga Dyilo (Appeals Chambers, Decision on Victim Participation), ILM (2008) v 47 n 6

LINDAHL, H. 'Sovereignty and Representation in the European Union' in N Walker (ed) Sovereignty in Transition (Hart, Oxford 2003)

LINDBLOM, A.K. Non-Governmental Organizations in International Law (CUP, Cambridge 2005)

LOCK, G. 'Ringing the Changes: Mutations in the Idea of Political Change', in van Kersbergen, K; Lieshout, RH and Lock, G (eds). Expansion and Fragmentation: Internationalization, Political Change and the Transformation of the Nation State (AUP, Amsterdam 1999)

LOCKE, J. Two Treatises of Government (Rethinking the Western Tradition series, Yale University Press, New Haven 2003)

MAGEN, A. and MORLINO, L. International Actors, Democratization and the Rule of Law (Routledge, New York 2009)

MALANCZUK, P. Akerhurst's Modern Introduction to International Law (7th edn, Routledge, New York, 1997)

MARX, K and ENGELS, F. O Manifesto Comunista (Centauro, São Paulo 2005)

McCORQUODALE, R. 'The individual and the International Legal System', in MD Evans, International Law (2nd edn OUP, Oxford 2006)

McDOUGAL, M.S. and REISMAN, W.M. International Law Essays: a Supplement to International Law in Contemporary Perspective (Foundation Press, New York 1981)

McDOUGAL, M.S., LASWELL, H.D. and REISMAN, W.M, 'The World Constitutive Process of Authoritative Decision', in R Falk, The Future of International Legal Order (PUP, Princeton 1969) v 1, 94

McGOLDRICK, D. 'The Asean Charter', ICLQ v 58 n 1

MEIJERS, H. 'On International Customary Law in the Netherlands, in Dekker, IF and Post, HHG (eds). On The Foundations and Sources of International Law (TMC Asser Press, The Hague 2003)

MERON, T. The Humanization of International Law (Nijhoff, The Hague 2006)

MORAND, C.A. 'La Souveraineté, un concept dépassé', in de Chazournes, LB and Gowland-Debbas, V. The International Legal System in Quest of Equity and Universality (Martinus Nijhoff, The Hague 2001)

MORRIS, D. Charities and the Contract Culture: Partners or Contractors? Law and Practice in Conflict (Charity Law Unit, Liverpool 1999)

MUGERWA, N. 'Subjects of International Law', in M Sorensen, Manual of Public International Law (MacMillan, New York 1968)

MÜLLERSON, R. Ordering Anarchy (Nijhoff, The Hague 2000)

NIJMAN, J.A. The Concept of International Legal Personality (TCM Asser Press, The Hague 2004)

NIJMAN, J.A. Paul Ricoeur and International Law: Beyond the End of Subject (2007) LJIL n 20

NORGAARD, CA. The Position of the Individual in International Law (Munksgaard, Copenhagen 1962)

NORMANDIN, A. Du Statut Juridique des Association Internationales (Librairie Générale de Droit & de Jurisprudence, Paris 1926)

NUSBAUM, A. A concise history of the Law of the Nations (Macmillan, New York 1962)

OBERG, M.D. 'The legal effects of Resolutions of the UN Security Council and General Assembly in the Jurisprudence of the ICJ' (2005) EJIL v 16 n 5

O'CONNELL, DP. International Law (2nd edn, Stevens and Sons, London 1970) v 1

ORTEGA Y GASSET. The Revolt of the Masses (1930)

PAUL, J. The Arria Formula (New York, 2003)

PAUPP, T.E. Achieving inclusionary Governance: advancing peace and development in first and third world nations (Transnational publisher, Ardsey 2000)

POST, H.H.G. 'The role of State Practice in the Formation of Customary International Humanitarian Law' in Dekker, IF and Post, HHG (eds), On The Foundations and Sources of International Law (TMC Asser Press, The Hague 2003)

PRONTO, A. 'Human-Rightism' and the development of General International Law (2007) LJIL 20

PUFENDORF, S. De Jure naturae et gentium libri octo

PUFENDORF, S. On the Duty of Man and Citizen (1675)

RAIMONDO, F. General Principles of Law in the Decisions of International Criminal Courts and Tribunals (Nijhoff, The Hague 2008)

RAWLS, J. A Theory of Justice (19th edn OUP, Oxford 1992)

RAWLS, J. The Law of Peoples: with "The Idea of Public Reason Revisited" (Harvard University Press, Cambridge 1999)

RAWLS, J. Collected Papers (Harvard University Press, Cambridge 1999)

REINISCH, A. and IRGEL, C. 'The Participation of Non-Governmental Organizations (NGOs) in the WTO Dispute Settlement System', (2001) Non-State Actors and International Law, n 1 127

REISMAN, W.M. 'Sovereignty and Human Rights in Contemporary International Law' (1990) AJIL n 84

ROETHOFF, H.J. 'The Republic of South Moluccas: an existing state', in Symbolae Verzijl (Nijhoff, The Hague 1958)

ROSEMAN, N. 'The Privatization of Human Rights Violations – Business Impunity or Corporate Responsibility? The case of Human Rights Abuses and Torture in Iraq' (2007) Non-State Actors and International Law v 7

ROSENAU, J.N. Turbulence in World Politics: a Theory of Change and Continuity (Princeton University Press, Princeton 1990)

ROSENNE, S. The perplexities of modern international law (Nijhoff, Leiden 2004)

ROTH, B. Governmental Illegitimacy in International Law (Clarendon Press, Oxford, 2000)

ROUSSEAU, C. Droit International Public (Sirey, Paris 1974)

ROUSSEAU, J.J. The Social Contract (1762)

RUBENSTEIN, K. 'Citizenship in a Bordless World', in A Anghie and G Sturgess, Legal Visions of the 21st Century: Essays in Honor of Judge Christopher Weeramantry (Kluwer, The Hague 1998)

RUIZ, J.J. 'Los principios fundamentales del derecho internacional ambiental' in Casella, PB (ed). Dimensão Internacional do Direito (LTr, São Paulo 2000)

RYFMAN, P. Non-Governmental Organizations: an indispensable player of humanitarian aid (2007) IRRC v 89 n 865, 21

SADAT, L.N. 'Judgment at Nuremberg: Foreword to the Symposium', WUGSLR (2007) v 6

SALOMON, L and ANHEINER, H.K. The Emerging Sector Revisited: A Summary (John Hopkins Institute for Policy Studies, Baltimore, 1998)

SALOMON, L; SOKOLOWSKI, S.W. and LIST, R. Global Civil Society: an overview. (Center for Social Studies, Baltimore 2003)

SANCHES, M.R. 'Atores não estatais e sua relação com a Organização Mundial do Comércio', in Amaral Junior, A. Direito do Comércio Internacional (Juarez Oliveira, São Paulo 2002)

SANDS, P and KLEIN, P. Bowett's Law of International Institutions (Thompson, London 2001)

SCELLE, G. Précis de Droit de Gents (Recueil Sirey, Paris 1932)

SCELLE, G. 'Obsession du Territoire', in Symbolae Verzijl (Nijhoff, The Hague 1958)

SHEARER, I.A. Starke's International Law (11th edn, Butterworths, London 1994)

SHELTON, D. 'The Participation of NGOs in International Judicial Proceedings' (1994) ASIL n 88

SCHERMERS, H.G. and BLOKKER, N.M. International Institutional Law (4th edn Martinus Nijhoff, The Hague 2003)

SCHIFFER, W. The Legal Community of Mankind (Greenwood, Westport 2004)

SCHMITT, C. The Crisis of Parliamentary Democracy (MIT Press, Cambridge 1988)

SCHUMPETER, J.A. Capitalism, Socialism and Democracy (Harper, New York 1975)

SCHWARZENBERGER, G. International Law: as applied by International Courts and Tribunals (3rd edn London 1957)

SELLARS, K. The Rise and Rise of Human Rights (Sutton Publishing, London 2002)

SHAPIRO, I. 'John Locke's Democratic Theory', in Locke, J. Two Treatises of Government, 2nd Treatise, Chapter VIII (Rethinking the Western Tradition series, Yale University Press, New Haven 2003)

SHAPIRO, P.J. 'New Players on the International Stage', in WM Reisman and others, International Law in Contemporary Perspective (Foundation Press, New York 2004)

SHELLEY, M. Frankenstein, or the Modern Prometheus: the 1818 text (University of Chicago Press, Chicago 1982)

SHAW, MN. International Law (5th edn CUP, Cambridge 2003)

SIMMA, B. and PAULUS, A.L. The 'International Community': facing the Challenge of Globalization (1998) EJIL n 9

SIMMONS, A.J. Justification and Legitimacy (CUP, Cambridge 2001)

SIMPSON, G. 'Two Liberalisms' (2001) EJIL v 12, n 3

SLAUGHTER, A.M. 'International Law in a World of Liberal States' (1995) EJIL v 6

SOARES, G.F.S. 'As ONGs e o direito internacional do meio ambiente' Revista de Direito Ambiental, v 17

SOARES, G.F.S. Curso de Direito Internacional Público (1st edn. Atlas, São Paulo 2002)

SPINOZA, B. Theological-Political Treatise (6th ed. CUP, Cambridge, 2012)

SUZUKI, E and NANWANI, S. 'Responsibility of International Organizations: the Accountability Mechanisms of Multilateral Development Banks' (2006) MJIL v 27

SZAZI, E. (ed). Terceiro Setor Temas Polêmicos v 2 (Peiropolis, Sao Paulo 2005)

SZAZI E. 'Creating a Favorable Environment for Philanthropy and Civil Society: the case of Brazil' in C Sanborn and F Portocarrero, Philanthropy and Social Change in Latin America (Harvard University Press, Cambridge 2005)

THORNBERRY, P. 'The Principle of Self-Determination', in C Warbrick and V Lowe, The United Nations and the Principles of International Law (Routledge, London 1994)

TUNKIN, G. 'Is General International Law Customary Law Only?' (1993) EJIL n 4

UMBRICHT, G.C. 'An "amicus curiae brief" on amicus curiae briefs at the WTO'. (2001) JIEL v 4 n 4

UNGER, R. Law in Modern Society (Free Press, London 1976)

UNITED NATIONS, The Aarhus Convention: an implementation guide (UN, New York 2000).

UNITED NATIONS, Collection of Essays by Legal Advisers of States, Legal Advisers of Intergovernmental Organizations and Practitioners in the field of International Law (UN, New York 1999)

UN ECOSOC NGO Committee, The NGO Committee: a ten year review (UN, New York 2008)

van BIJSTERVELD, S. The Empty Throne: Democracy and the Rule of Law in Transition (Lemma Publishers, Utrecht 2002)

van BOVEN, T. 'The UN High Commissioner for Human rights: The Story of a Contended Project' (2007) LJIL v 20

van KERSBERGEN, K. 'National Political Systems: the Changing Boundaries of Politics', in van Kersbergen, K; Lieshout, RH and Lock, G (eds). Expansion and Fragmentation: Internationalization, Political Change and the Transformation of the Nation State (AUP, Amsterdam 1999)

VEDDER, A. NGO Involvement in International Governance and Policy: Sources of Legitimacy (Nijhoff, Leiden 2007)

VERZIJL, J.W. International Law in Historical Perspective (Leiden 1969)

VINCENT, R.J. 'Grotius, Human Rights and Intervention' in H Bull, B Kingsbury and A Roberts, Hugo Grotius and International Relations (OUP, Oxford 2002)

VIRALLY, M. 'Fuentes del Derecho Internacional' in Sorensen, M (ed). Manual del Derecho Internacional (Fondo de Cultura Económica, México 1985)

VITORIA, F. De Indis et de Jure Belli

VITORIA, F. De Postestate Civili

von GLAHN, G. Law among Nations (4th edn MacMillan, New York 1981)

WALLACE, H and WALLACE, W. Policy Making in the European Union (4th edn OUP, Oxford 2000)

WEBER, M. 'Bureaucracy and Political Leadership' in Bendix, R (ed). State and Society: a Reader in Comparative Political Sociology 2nd ed (UC Press, Berkeley 1973)

WEBER, M. Economy and Society (UC Press, Berkeley 1978)

WEBER, M. Politics as a Vocation (1919)

WEBER, M. The Theory of Social and Economic Organization (The Free Press, New York 1964)

WEIL, P. 'Le judaïsme et le développement du Droit International' (1976) 151 Recueil des Cours de l'Académie de Droit International 253

WEISS, TG and GORDENKER, L (eds). NGOs, the UN, and Global Governance (Lynne Rienner, Boulder/London 1996)

WEERAMANTRY, C.C. Universalizing International Law (Nijhoff, Leiden, 2004)

WISENBERG, LS. 'Protecting Human Rights Activists and NGOs: What Can Be Done? (1991) 13 HRQ n 4

WOLFRUM, R. 'Legitimacy of International Law from a Legal Perspective' in R Wolfrum and V Röben (eds) Legitimacy in International Law (Springer, Berlin 2008)

ZWEIFEL, T.D. International Organizations and Democracy: Accountability, Politics and Power (Lynne Rienner, Boulder 2006)

2) Cases

A. Permanent Court of International Justice

Certain German Interests in Polish Upper Silesia (Germany v Poland) PCIJ Rep Series A 7.

Designation of Workers' Delegate for the Netherlands at the Third Session of the International Labor Conference (Advisory Opinion) PCIJ Rep Series C 1

Lotus (France v Turkey) PCIJ Rep. Series A 10.

Rights of Minorities in Upper Silesia (Minority Schools) (Germany v Poland) PCIJ Rep Series A 15.

Serbian Loans case PCIJ Rep Series A 14

B. International Court of Justice

Admission of a State to the United Nations (Charter, art 4) (advisory opinion) [1948] ICJ Rep 57

Avena and Other Mexican Nationals (Mexico v. United States of America) (Judgment) [2004] ICJ Rep 12

Certain expenses of the United Nations (article 17, paragraph 2, of the Charter) (Advisory Opinion) [1962] ICJ Rep 151

Colombian-Peruvian asylum case (Judgment) [1950] ICJ Rep 266

Continental Shelf (Libyan Arab Jarnahiriyu/ Malta) (Judgment) [1985] ICJ Rep 29

Corfu Channel (UK v Albania) (Judgment) [1949] ICJ Rep 4

Fisheries case (Judgment) [1951] ICJ Rep 1951

Gabcikovo-Nagymaros Project case (Hungary v Slovakia).

LaGrand (Germany v. United States of America) (Judgment) [2001] ICJ Rep 466

Legal Consequences for States of the Continued Presence of South Africa in Namibia (South West Africa) notwithstanding Security Council Resolution 276 (Advisory Opinion) [1971] ICJ Rep 16

Legal Consequences of the Construction of a Wall in the Occupied Palestinian Territory (Advisory Opinion) [2004] ICJ Rep 136

Legality on the Threat or Use of Nuclear Weapons (Advisory Opinion) [2006] ICJ Rep 226

Military and Paramilitary Activities in and Against Nicaragua (Nicaragua v United States) (Judgment) [1986] ICJ Rep 14

North Sea Continental Shelf cases (Judgment) (1969) ICJ Rep 3

Nuclear Tests (Australia v France), (Judgment) [1974] ICJ Rep 253

Nuclear Tests (New Zealand v France) (Judgment) [1974] ICJ Rep 457

Reparation for Injuries Suffered in the Service of the United Nations (Advisory Opinion) [1949] ICJ Rep 174

Reservation to the Convention on Genocide (Advisory Opinion) [1951] ICJ Rep 15

Right of Passage over Indian Territory (Portugal v India) (Judgment) [1960] ICJ Rep 3

South West Africa, Second Phase (Merits) [1966] ICJ Rep 6

Western Sahara (Advisory Opinion) [1975] ICJ Rep 12

WHO Regional Office case [1980] ICJ Rep 73

C. International Criminal Court

Prosecutor v. Lubanga (Appeals Chamber, Decision on Victim Participation) 47 ILM 972 (2008).

D. Inter-American Court of Human Rights

Baena Ricardo et al v Panamá (Judgment) (2 February 2001) Series C no 72 [2001] IACHR 2

Bámaca Velásques v Guatemala (Judgment) (25 November 2000) Series C no 70 [2000] IACHR 7

Desmond Mackenzie v. Jamaica, case 12.023, Report 41/00 (13 April 2000)

Juan Carlos Abella v. Argentina case (Judgment) (18 November 1997) Case 11.137

Loayza Tamayo v. Peru (Judgment) (17 September 1997) Series C no 33 [1997] IACHR 6

Maria Eugenia Morales de Sierra v. Guatemala, case 11.625, Report 28/98 (6 March 1998)

The Mayagna (Sumo) Awas Tingni Community v. Nicarágua (Judgment) (31 August 2001) Series C no 79 [2001] IACHR 9

E. Court of Justice of the European Union

CFI (2nd Chamber), European Environmental Bureau and Stichting Natuur en Milieu v Commission. Joined Cases T-236/04 and T 241/04. Order of 28 November 2005.

CFI (7th Chamber), People's Mojahedin Organization of Iran v. Council of the European Union. Case T-284/08, Judgment of 4 December 2008.

CFI, Hautal v. Council, case T-14/98, Judgment of 19 July 1999.

ECJ, Association Greenpeace France and Others v Ministère de l'Agriculture et de la Pêche and Others. Case C-6/99, Judgment 21 March 2000.

ECJ, CIRFS and Others v. Commission. Case C-313/90 [1993] ECR I-1125.

ECJ, Fédération Nationale de la Boucherie en Gros et du Commerce en Gros des Viandes and Others v Council. Joined Cases 19/62 to 22/62 [1962] ECR 491, 499 and 500.

ECJ, Interporc Import und Export v. Commission, case T-92/98, Judgment of 7 December 1999.

ECJ, Italian Republic and Sardegna Lines v Commission. Joined cases C-15/98 and C-105/99. Judgment of 19 October 2000.

ECJ, Stichting Greenpeace Council (Greenpeace International) and Others v Commission, case C-321/95 P, Judgment of 2 April 1998.

ECJ, The Bavarian Lager Co. v. Commission, case T-309/97, Judgment of 14 October 1999.

ECJ, Van der Kooy and Others v Commission. Joined Cases 67/85, 68/85 and 70/85 [1988] ECR 219.

ECJ, Yassin Abdullah Kadi and Al Barakaat International Foundation v. Council of the European Union and Commission of the European Communities. Joined cases C402/05 P and C414/05 P, Judgment of 3 September 2008. 47 ILM 927 (2008).

F. European Court of Human Rights

Austrian Communes and some of their Councillors v Austria, 31 May 1974.

Freedom and Democratic Party (ÖZDEP) v Turkey, 8 December 1999.

Holy Monasteries v Greece, 9 December 1994.

Purcell and Others v. Ireland, 16 April 1991.

Refah Partisi (Prosperity Party) and Others v Turkey, 31 July 2000.

Socialist Party and Others v Turkey, 25 May 1998.

The Sunday Times v the United Kingdom, 29 April 1979.

Tinnelly & Sons Ltd. and Others and McElduff & Others v The United Kingdom, 10 July 1998.

United Communist Party of Turkey and Others v Turkey, 30 January 1998.

Yazar, Karatas, Aksoy and the People's Labor Party (HEP) v Turkey, 9 April 2002.

G. WTO Appellate Body

European Communities – Measures Affecting Asbestos and Asbestos – Containing Products. WT/DS135/R (18 September 2000).

United States – Import Prohibition of Certain Shrimp and Shrimp Products. WT/DS58/AB/R (12 October 1998).

United States – Import Prohibition of Certain Shrimp and Shrimp Products. WT/DS58/R (15 May 1998).

United States – Imposition of Countervailing Duties on Certain Hot-Rolled Lead and Bismuth Carbon Steel Products Originating in the United Kingdom. WT/DS138/R (23 December 1999).

United States – Imposition of Countervailing Duties on Certain Hot-Rolled Lead and Bismuth Carbon Steel Products Originating in the United Kingdom. WT/DS138/AB/R (10 May 2000).

H. Arbitrations

Texaco Overseas Petroleum Company and California Asiatic Oil Company v. Government of Libyan Republic (Merits) (1979) 53 I.L.R. 389.

3) Treaties

Additional Protocol to the European Social Charter providing for a System of Collective Complaints (adopted 9 November 1995, entry into force 1 July 1998) UNTS 2045.

African Charter on Human and People's Rights (adopted 27 June 1981, entered into force 21 October 1986). OAU Doc. CAB/LEG/67/3 rev. 5, 21.

African Charter on the Rights and Welfare of the Child (adopted July 1990, entered into force 29 November 1990). OAU Doc. CAB/LEG/24.9/49 (1990).

Agreement establishing the International Fund for Agricultural Development (adopted 13 June 1976, entered into force 30 November 1977) UNTS 1059.

American Convention on Human Rights "Pact of San José, Costa Rica" (adopted 22 November 1969, entered into force 18 July 1978) UNTS 1144.

Articles of Agreement of the International Monetary Fund (adopted 27 December 1945, entered into force 27 December 1945) UNTS 2.

Charter of Paris for a New Europe (21 November 1990).

Charter of the International Military Tribunal (adopted 8 August 1945)

Charter of the Organization of American States (adopted 30 April 1948, entered into force date 13 December 1951) UNTS 119.

Constitution of the International Labor Organization (adopted 19 November 1946, entered into force 14 December 1946) UNTS 1-II-9.

Constitution of the United Nations Educational, Scientific and Cultural Organization (adopted 16 November 1945, entered into force 4 November 1946) UNTS 4.

Constitution of the United Nations Industrial Development Organization (adopted 8 April 1979, entered into force 21 June 1985) UNTS 1401.

Constitution of the Universal Postal Union (adopted 10 July 1964, entered into force 1 January 1966) UNTS 611.

Constitution of the World Health Organization (adopted 22 July 1946, entered into force 7 April 1948) UNTS 14.

Convention concerning the Protection of the World Cultural and Natural Heritage (adopted 16 November 1972, entered into force 17 December 1975) UNTS 15511.

Convention establishing the World Intellectual Property Organization (adopted 14 July 1967, entered into force 26 April 1970) UNTS 828.

Convention for Settlement of difficulties arising from operation of Smelter at Trail (BC) signed between the United States and Canada (Adopted 15 April 1935) US Treaty Series 893.

Convention for the Protection of Human Rights and Fundamental Freedoms (adopted 4 November 1950, entered into force 3 September 1953) UNTS 213.

Convention on access to information, public participation in decision-making and access to justice in environmental matters (adopted 25 June 1998, entered into force 30 October 2001) UNTS 2161.

Convention on Biological Diversity (adopted 5 June 1992, entered into force 29 December 1993) UNTS 1760.

Convention on Civil Liability for Damage Resulting from Activities Dangerous to the Environment (adopted 21 June 1993, not entered into force yet) ETS 150.

Convention on Environmental Impact Assessment in a Transboundary Context (adopted 25 February 1991, entered into force 10 September 1997) UNTS 1989.

Convention on International Trade in Endangered Species of Wild Fauna and Flora (Adopted 3 March 1973, entered into force 1 July 1975) UNTS 993.

Convention on Persistent Organic Pollutants (Adopted 22 May 2001, entered into force 17 May 2004). UNTS 2256.

Convention on the International Maritime Organization (adopted 6 March 1948, entered into force 17 March 1958) UNTS 289.

Convention on the Law of the Sea (adopted 10 December 1982, entered into force 16 November 1994) UNTS 1833.

Convention on the Prevention and Punishment of the Crime of Genocide (Adopted 9 December 1948, entered into force 12 January 1951) UNTS 78.

Convention on the Prohibition of the Use, Stockpiling, Production and Transfer of Anti-Personnel Mines and on their Destruction (adopted 3 December 1997, entered into force 1 March 1999) UNTS 2056.

Convention on the Rights of the Child (adopted 20 November 1989, entered into force 02 September 1990) UNTS 1577 3.

Convention on the Transboundary Effect of Industrial Accidents (adopted 17 March 1992, entered into force 19 April 2000) UNTS 2105.

Convention relative to the Treatment of Prisoners of War (adopted 12 August 1949, entered into force 21 October 1950). UNTS 75.

Convention on the World Meteorological Organization (adopted 11 October 1947, entered into force 23 March 1950) UNTS 77.

Convention on Wetlands of International Importance especially as Waterfowl Habitat (adopted 2 February 1971, entered into force 21 December 1975) UNTS 14583.

Declaration of the United Nations Conference on the Human Environment, or Stockholm Declaration, adopted 16 June 1972

European Convention for the Prevention of Torture and Inhuman or Degrading Treatment or Punishment (adopted 26 November 1987, entered into force 1 February 1989) ETS 126.

European Convention on the Recognition of the Legal Personality of International Non-Governmental Organizations (adopted 24 April 1986, entered into force 1 January 1991) ETS 124.

European Social Charter (adopted 18 October 1961, entry into force 26 February 1962) UNTS 529.

European Social Charter (revised) (adopted 3 May 1996, entry into force 1 July 1999) UNTS 2151.

General Treaty for the Re-Establishment of Peace between Austria, France, Great Britain, Prussia, Sardinia and Turkey, and Russia, signed at Paris on 30 March 1856 [1969] 114 The Consolidated Treaty Series 409.

International Covenant of Civil and Political Rights (CCPR) (adopted 16 December 1966, entered into force 23 March 1976) UNTS 999.

Johannesburg Declaration on Sustainable Development (4 September 2002).

Marrakesh Agreement establishing the World Trade Organization (adopted 15 April 1994, entered into force 1 January 1995) UNTS 1864.

Montreal Protocol on Substances that Deplete the Ozone Layer (adopted 16 September 1987, entered into force 1 January 1989) UNTS 1522.

New York Convention on the Recognition and Enforcement of Foreign Arbitral Awards adopted 10 June 1958, entered into force 7 June 1959) UNTS 330

North American Agreement on Environmental Cooperation (adopted August 1993, entered into force 1 January 1994).

Protocol on the Statute of the Court of Justice annexed to the Treaty on European Union, to the Treaty establishing the European Community and to the Treaty establishing the European Atomic Energy Community, in accordance with Article 7 of the Treaty of Nice, amending the Treaty on European Union, the Treaties establishing the European Communities and certain related acts, signed at Nice on 26 February 2001

Protocol nr. 11 to the Convention for the Protection of Human Rights and Fundamental Freedoms, restructuring the control machinery established thereby (adopted 11 May 1994, entered into force 1 November 1998). UNTS 2061.

Rio Declaration on Environment and Development (14 June 1992).

Statute of the Council of Europe (adopted 5 May 1949, entered into force 03 August 1949) UNTS 87.

Statute of the Inter-American Court of Human Rights OAS Res 448 (IX-0/79).

The African Union Constitutive Act (adopted 11 July 2000, entered into force 26.05.2001)

The Montevideo Convention on Rights and Duties of States (adopted 26 December 1933, entered into force 26 December 1934).

Treaty concerning the hydroelectric utilization of the water resources of the Parana River owned in condominium by the two countries, from and including the Salto Grande de Sete Quedas or Salto del Guaira, to the mouth of the Iguassu River (adopted 26 April 1973, entered into force 13 August 1973) UNTS 923.

Treaty Establishing the European Community (25 March 1957) 298 UNTS 11, amended by Treaty of Amsterdam (2 October 1997) 1997 OJ (C 340) and Treaty of Nice (26 February 2001) 2001 OJ (C 80).

Treaty on principles governing the activities of States in the exploration and use of outer space, including the Moon and other celestial bodies (adopted 27 January 1967, entered into force 10 October 1967) UNTS 188.

Treaty on the European Union (adopted 7 February 1992, entered into force 1 November 1993).

UN Framework Convention on Climate Change (adopted 9 May 1992, entered into force 21 March 1994) UNTS 1771.

Vienna Convention for the Protection of the Ozone Layer (adopted 22 March 1985, entered into force 22 September 1988) UNTS 1513.

Vienna Convention on Consular Relations (adopted 24 April 1963, entered into force 19 March 1967) UNTS 596.

Vienna Convention on the Law of Treaties (Adopted 23 May 1969, entered into force 27 January 1980) UNTS 1155.

4) Main Documents

Commission (EC) 'European governance' (White Paper) COM(2001) 428 final, 25 July 2001.

Communication from the Appellate Body (8 November 2000) WTO Doc WT/DS/135/9.

Commission (EC), 'The Commission and non-governmental organizations: building a stronger partnership' (discussion paper) EC Doc CES 811/2000 (18 January 2000)

Fundamental Principles on the Status of Non-Governmental Organizations in Europe and explanatory memorandum. CoE Doc RAP-ONG(2003)4 (24 March 2003).

ILA, 'First Report of the Committee Non-State Actors in International Law: aims, approach and scope of project and legal issues' (2010)

ILC, Draft Declaration on Rights and Duties of States [1949] Yearbook of the International Law Commission. UNGA Res 375 (IV) (6 December 1949).

OASPC 'Report by the Committee on Juridical and Political Affairs on the Status of Non-governmental Organizations (NGOs) in the OAS' (23 May 1997) OAS Doc OEA/Ser.G CP/Doc.2946/97.

OASPC Res. 'Guidelines for the Participation of Civil Society Organizations in OAS Activities' (15 December 1999) OAS Doc OEA/Ser.G CP/RES.759 (1217/99).

OAS Summit of the Americas Secretariat, Manual for Civil Society Participation in the OAS and its Summits of the Americas Process (OAS, Washington 2008)

OECD Financial Action Task Force on Money Laundering, 'Combating the abuse of non-profit organizations, international best practices' (Report) (11 October 2002).

Projet de convention relative à la condition juridique des associations internationales [1923] Brussels' Session.

Proposal for a Regulation of the European Parliament and of the Council on the statute for a European Association. EC Doc 1991/0386/COD.

Statute of the International Law Commission. UN GA Res 174(II) (21 November 1947).

UNGA 'Report of the Secretary General on General Review of Arrangements for Consultations with non-governmental organizations' (26 May 1994) UN Doc E/AC.70/1994/5.

UNGA Report of the Secretary General on 'Arrangements and practices for the interaction of non-governmental organizations in all activities of the United Nations system' (10 July 1998) UN Doc A/53/170.

UNGA Report of the Secretary General on 'Views of Member States, members of the specialized agencies, observers, intergovernmental and non-governmental organizations from all regions, on the report of the Secretary General on Arrangements and practices for the interaction of non-governmental organizations in all activities of the United Nations system' (8 September 1999) UN Doc A/54/329.

UNGA Secretary General Report 'In Larger Freedom' (2005).

US Department of State, 'Guiding Principles on Non-governmental Organizations' (Report) (14 December 2006).

US National Intelligence Council, 'Global Trends 2025 – A Transformed World' (Report)

Working Procedures for Appellate Review. (4 January 2005) WTO Doc WT/AB/WP/5.

INDEX

CURRICULUM VITAE

Eduardo Szazi was born on 14 November 1965 in Sao Paulo, Brazil. In 1985 he began to study law at the University of Sao Paulo and he obtained his bachelor's degree in 1989. He was admitted in the Brazilian Bar Association in 1990. From 1997 to 1999 he studied business administration at Fundacao Getulio Vargas, where he obtained his master's certificate. In 1990, Eduardo worked as lawyer at Companhia Cimento Portland Itau, a leading company of one of the major cement groups in the world. Subsequently, in 1991, he started working at C&A Modas Ltda, a retail company, where he reached the position of manager of the legal dept. in Brazil. In 1997, he joined L.O. Baptista Advogados, a law firm specialized in corporate and international law, becoming an equity partner in 2000. Since 2004, he is a partner at Szazi Bechara Advogados. In 1999, Eduardo started teaching nonprofits law at Fundacao Instituto de Administracao and, in 2002, at Fundacao Getulio Vargas, both leading business schools in Brazil. In 2004, he was admitted as fellow researcher at the London based International Society for Third-Sector Research and, in 2006, as a member of the Advisory Board of the International Center for Not-for-Profit Law, in Washington DC. In 2009, Eduardo joined the American Society of International Law. He has published several books in Brazil on the theme of nonprofit law and often speaks in conferences and seminars on the matter.